SCATTER 2

Scatter 2

Politics in Deconstruction

Geoffrey Bennington

FORDHAM UNIVERSITY PRESS

New York 2021

Library of Congress Cataloging-in-Publication Data
Names: Bennington, Geoffrey, author.
Title: Scatter 2 : politics in deconstruction / Geoffrey Bennington.
Other titles: Scatter two
Description: First edition. | New York : Fordham University Press, 2021. |
    Includes bibliographical references and index.
Identifiers: LCCN 2020041477 | ISBN 9780823289929 (hardback) | ISBN
    9780823289936 (paperback) | ISBN 9780823289936 (epub)
Subjects: LCSH: Political science—Philosophy—History. |
    Democracy—Philosophy. | Sovereignty—Philosophy.
Classification: LCC JA83 .B446 2021 | DDC 320.01—dc23
LC record available at https://lccn.loc.gov/2020041477

Printed in the United States of America
23 22 21   5 4 3 2 1
First edition

for Elissa, again and always

CONTENTS

The *Scatter* project, of which this is the second volume,[1] was originally conceived as calling for a more scattered (Kant would perhaps say "rhapsodic") form of presentation than that of the standard academic monograph. This conception was not supposed to be merely provocative or whimsical, but was called for by the matter at hand, in which I try to demonstrate a persistent and indeed ineradicable plurality and variegation that resists conceptual reduction and that I associate with politics. The working model for that scattered form of presentation was, as had already been the case long ago with my "Derridabase,"[2] an electronic format that would exploit the possibilities of hypertext, and of other subsequent developments—notably the Internet—that had not been available when I wrote that earlier text. I imagined, for example, that direct links to sources could be provided for every footnote and reference, and that primary texts could easily be made available in their entirety, both in their original language and in any number of translations, with the thought that readers might well often choose simply to continue reading those texts for themselves rather than my commentary on them. The inner connections of the work were to be such that, although certain paths of reading would be indicated and perhaps encouraged by a hierarchical ordering of levels of argument and reading (as in the one—unsatisfactory—attempt at a print emulation of a small part of the project),[3] other possibilities and links would remain open, and a system of cross-referencing would enable loops and other more complex patterns to emerge that would disrupt any obvious linear order and induce a certain disorientation in the reader. I imagined, too, that there

1. *Scatter 1: The Politics of Politics in Foucault, Heidegger, and Derrida* (New York: Fordham University Press, 2016).

2. In Geoffrey Bennington and Jacques Derrida, *Jacques Derrida* (Paris: Editions du Seuil, 1991); trans. Geoffrey Bennington (Chicago: University of Chicago Press, 1993).

3. See my "Scatter," *Oxford Literary Review* 30, no. 1 (2008): 1–43.

might be an aleatory element that would make more or less random leaps, or even frustrate apparently attractive pathways through the material. One guiding idea was that the reader would never be able to know for sure that they had read the whole work, as it frayed out into other texts and in principle opened onto the whole universal library, at least as the Internet makes and will increasingly make that available, and as the work would itself be open to ongoing revision, correction, and perhaps wiki-like inputs and other interactive contributions from readers.

In the event, after some unsatisfactory experiments, and some only partially successful forays into electronic publishing,[4] that version of the project has not been (publicly) realized, largely for technical reasons, and both volumes of *Scatter* are in the end more or less recognizable, and relatively self-standing, academic books. The intelligibility of *Scatter 2* does not require the reader to be familiar with *Scatter 1*, although I regularly appeal here to its guiding notion of "the politics of politics," by which I claim that the aspects of politics usually (I believe moralistically) deprecated as sophistry and rhetoric are, like it or not, irreducible, and that there is no politics unaffected by the politics of politics.[5] From the hierarchy of levels of the original design for the *Scatter* project, however, I can rapidly state the "top-level" claims being made here, and although the lower-level organization is no longer conceived in quite the same way (without for all that being entirely linear: there is no really compelling need to read the "chapters" in the order in which they are presented here), the interested reader might nonetheless be able to reconstruct it to some extent. The argument of the book might be presented in a half-dozen propositions:

1. Philosophy has always had the greatest difficulty negotiating the relationship between metaphysics and politics.
2. "Sovereignty" is one traditional name for the—always already failing—metaphysical attempt to deal with that difficulty.
3. That intrinsic failing of sovereignty shows up most acutely around the concept of democracy.

---

4. See http://bennington.zsoft.co.uk for some examples of electronic books, subsequently made available in print-on-demand form.

5. *Scatter 1* attempted to clear some philosophical ground for the readings undertaken here, and notably it attempted to work out some differences between the (fundamentally Derridean) positions I adopt and those of Foucault on the one hand and Heidegger on the other, especially around the concepts of truth and the event. The opening section of Chapter 6 of *Scatter 1* (238–249) offers a summary of Chapters 1–5, and may clarify some of the general issues in play here.

4. Thinking about democracy in this light can help identify problems with teleological thinking more generally.
5. These problems are eminently amenable to deconstructive elaboration.
6. Deconstructive thinking can on those grounds be described as radically political.

Scatter 2 is not primarily concerned with the exposition of what Jacques Derrida wrote about politics (although much of the book begins—and sometimes *departs*—from Derrida's work). While more generally urging the "political" virtues of deconstruction, it does not attempt to advance a politics in any programmatic sense, nor is it concerned to report on my own political opinions or feelings in these generally very dark times for many supposedly democratic institutions, nor to offer concrete analyses of current events.[6] This measure of distance from political actuality does not mean that *Scatter 2* accepts the eminently traditional subordination of politics to philosophy, or of practice to theory (nor indeed the reverse subordination), but that its effort is to deconstruct such oppositions in general or, better, to suggest that they are, from the start, *in deconstruction*.

Most of *Scatter 2* is new and previously unpublished work. Portions of it are, however, based on articles I have published over the past fifteen years or so, listed below. I have also benefited immensely from the repeated experience of teaching much of this material (and more that has, a little to my regret, not made the final cut, especially on Machiavelli and Tocqueville) in graduate seminars at Emory University, New York University, and the European Graduate School, and presenting parts of it to academic conferences. A number of other related essays I had originally hoped to

---

6. At the time of writing this preface (December 3, 2019), the sitting president of the United States of America was facing possible impeachment; the British parliamentary system was in electoral and Brexit-related turmoil; street protests were ongoing in Hong Kong, Santiago de Chile, Beirut, Bogota, and Baghdad, among other cities; and so-called strong men were in power in many supposedly "democratic" countries, according to a pattern of usurpation of sovereignty by executive power we will follow later in the company of Jean-Jacques Rousseau. By the time of copyediting (early March 2020), these concerns had been largely subordinated to the 2020 US presidential campaign, itself overshadowed by the global coronavirus pandemic and the associated stock market turmoil—all events with wildly uncertain outcomes not readily addressed within the temporality of academic publishing.

include in this volume will appear subsequently as a book entitled *Down to Dust: Essays in the Deconstruction of Politics*. My heartfelt thanks to many students and colleagues for their questions, comments, and objections. In all cases, earlier published versions, as listed below, have been (often quite extensively) revised, reorganized, expanded, rewritten, and reintegrated with a view to the relative gathering of this book, however scattered it also remains: "Beastly Sovereignty: Three Unequal Footnotes to Derrida," *Environmental Philosophy* 16, no. 1 (2019): 13–33; "Demo," in *The Politics of Deconstruction*, ed. M. McQuillan (London: Pluto Press, 2007), 17–42; "El Consejo de Hobbes," trans. Matías Bascuñán, *Pléyade* 19 (January–June 2018), 67–89; "The Fall of Sovereignty," *Epoché* 10, no. 2 (2006): 395–406; "For Better and for Worse (There Again . . .)," *Discourse* 30, nos. 1–2 (2008), 191–207, also published in *Diacritics* 38, nos. 1–2 (2009): 1–12; "Political Animals," *theory@buffalo* 15 (2011): 8–26, also published in *Diacritics* 39, no. 2 (2011): 21–35; "Scatter," *Oxford Literary Review* 30, no. 1 (2008): 1–43; "Sovereign Stupidity and Auto-Immunity," in *Derrida and the Time of the Political*, ed. P. Cheah and S. Guerlac (Durham, NC: Duke University Press, 2009), 97–113; "Superanus," *Theory and Event* 8, no 1 (2005).

ABBREVIATIONS OF WORKS
BY JACQUES DERRIDA

Page references are given first to the original French, and then to published translations where these exist. I have very often made slight changes to published translations in the interests of consistency and accuracy.

AEL   *Adieu à Emmanuel Lévinas.* Paris: Galilée, 1997. *Adieu to Emmanuel Levinas.* Trans. Pascale-Anne Brault and Michael Naas. Stanford: Stanford University Press, 1999.

BS I   *Séminaire La bête et le souverain I (2001–2002).* Paris: Galilée, 2008. *The Beast and the Sovereign I.* Trans. Geoffrey Bennington. Chicago: University of Chicago Press, 2009.

BS II   *Séminaire La bête et le souverain II (2002–2003).* Paris: Galilée, 2010. *The Beast and the Sovereign II.* Trans. Geoffrey Bennington. Chicago: University of Chicago Press, 2011.

CFU   *Chaque fois unique, la fin du monde.* Paris: Galilée, 2003. *The Work of Mourning.* Trans. Pascale-Anne Brault and Michael Naas. Chicago: University of Chicago Press, 2001.

DES   *De l'esprit: Heidegger et la question.* Paris: Galilée, 1987. *Of Spirit: Heidegger and the Question.* Trans. Geoffrey Bennington and Rachel Bowlby. Chicago: University of Chicago Press, 1991.

D   *La dissémination.* Paris: Seuil, 1972. *Dissemination.* Trans. Barbara Johnson. Chicago: University of Chicago Press, 1981.

DP   *Du droit à la philosophie.* Paris: Galilée, 1990. *Who's Afraid of Philosophy? Right to Philosophy I,* and *Eyes of the University: Right to Philosophy 2.* Trans. Jan Plug. Stanford: Stanford University Press, 2002, 2004.

EAP   *Etats d'âme de la psychanalyse.* Paris: Galilée, 2000. Trans. Peggy Kamuf as "Psychoanalysis Searches the States of Its Soul," in Jacques Derrida, *Without Alibi.* Stanford: Stanford University Press, 2002.

ED   *L'écriture et la différence.* Paris: Seuil, 1967. *Writing and Difference.* Trans. Alan Bass. Chicago: University of Chicago Press, 1981.

FC   *Feu la cendre.* Paris: Des femmes, 1987. *Cinders.* Trans. Ned Lu-
        kacher. Lincoln: University of Nebraska Press, 1991.

FS   "Foi et savoir: Les deux sources de la 'religion' aux limites de la
        simples raison." In *La religion,* ed. Jacques Derrida and Gianni
        Vattimo, 9–86. Paris: Seuil, 1996. Reprinted in *Foi et savoir, suivi
        de Le siècle et le pardon,* 7–100. Paris: Seuil, 2001. "Faith and
        Knowledge: The Two Sources of 'Religion' at the Limits of
        Reason Alone." In *Religion,* ed. Jacques Derrida and Gianni
        Vattimo, trans. Samuel Weber. Stanford: Stanford University
        Press, 1998.

G   *De la grammatologie.* Paris: Minuit, 1967. *Of Grammatology.* Trans.
        Gayatri Chakravorty Spivak. Baltimore: Johns Hopkins Univer-
        sity Press, 1976.

GIII   *Geschlecht III.* Ed. Geoffrey Bennington, Katie Chenoweth, and
        Rodrigo Therezo. Paris: Seuil, 2018. Trans. Katie Chenoweth
        and Rodrigo Therezo. Chicago: University of Chicago Press,
        2020.

GL   *Glas.* Paris: Galilée, 1974. *Clang.* Trans. Geoffrey Bennington and
        David Wills. Minneapolis: University of Minnesota Press, 2020.

HC   *H.C. pour la vie, c'est-à-dire . . .* Paris: Galilée, 2002. *H.C. for
        Life, That Is to Say . . .* Trans. Laurent Milesi and Stefan Her-
        brechter. Stanford: Stanford University Press, 2006.

HQE   *Heidegger: La question de l'être et l'histoire.* Paris: Galilée, 2013.
        Heidegger: The Question of Being and History. Trans. Geoffrey Ben-
        nington. Chicago: University of Chicago Press, 2016.

LI   *Limited Inc.* [1978]. Paris: Galilée, 1990. *Limited Inc.* Trans. Jef-
        frey Mehlmann and Samuel Weber. Evanston, IL: Northwestern
        University Press, 1988.

M   *Marges—de la philosophie.* Paris: Minuit, 1972. *Margins of Philoso-
        phy.* Trans. Alan Bass. Chicago: University of Chicago Press,
        1982.

MA   *Mal d'archive: Une impression freudienne.* Paris: Galilée, 1995. *Ar-
        chive Fever: A Freudian Impression.* Trans. Eric Prenowitz. Chi-
        cago: University of Chicago Press, 1996.

OTO   *Otobiographies: L'enseignement de Nietzsche et la politique du nom
        propre.* Paris. Galilée, 1984. Partial translation by Tom Keenan
        and Tom Pepper in Jacques Derrida, *Negotiations: Interventions
        and Interviews, 1971–2001.* Ed. Elizabeth Rottenberg. Stanford:
        Stanford University Press, 2002.

PA *Politiques de l'amitié*. Paris: Galilée, 1994. *The Politics of Friendship* (partial translation). Trans. George Collins. London: Verso, 1997.

PAS *Passions: L'offrande oblique*. Paris: Galilée, 1993. "Passions: An Oblique Offering." In *Derrida: A Critical Reader*, ed. and trans. David Wood. Oxford: Blackwell, 1992.

PG *Le problème de la genèse dans la philosophie de Husserl*. Paris: PUF, 1990. *The Problem of Genesis in Husserl's Philosophy*. Trans. Marian Hobson. Chicago: University of Chicago Press, 2003.

PM I *Séminaire la peine de mort, Volume I (1999–2000)*. Paris: Galilée, 2012. *The Death Penalty I*. Trans. Peggy Kamuf. Chicago: University of Chicago Press, 2014.

PM II *Séminaire la peine de mort, Volume II (2000–2001)*. Paris: Galilée, 2015. *The Death Penalty II*. Trans. Elizabeth Rottenberg. Chicago: University of Chicago Press, 2017.

POS *Positions*. Paris: Minuit, 1972. *Positions*. Trans. Alan Bass et al. Chicago: University of Chicago Press, 1981.

PSY *Psyché: Inventions de l'autre*. Paris: Galilée, 1987. *Psyche: Inventions of the Other*. 2 vols. Trans. Peggy Kamuf et al. Stanford: Stanford University Press, 2007.

RES *Résistances de la psychanalyse*. Paris: Galilée, 1996. Trans. Peggy Kamuf, Pascale-Anne Brault, and Michael Naas as *Resistances of Psychoanalysis*. Stanford: Stanford University Press, 1998.

SM *Spectres de Marx: L'état de la dette, le travail du deuil et la nouvelle Internationale*. Paris: Galilée, 1993. *Specters of Marx: The State of the Debt, the Work of Mourning, and the New International*. Trans. Peggy Kamuf. New York: Routledge, 1994.

TR "Qu'est-ce qu'une traduction 'relevante'?" in *Cahier de l'Herne: Derrida* (2004). "What Is a 'Relevant' Translation?" Trans. Lawrence Venuti. *Critical Inquiry* 27, no. 2 (2001): 174–200.

V *Voyous: Deux essais sur la raison*. Paris: Galilée, 2003. *Rogues: Two Essays on Reason*. Trans. Pascale-Anne Brault and Michael Naas. Stanford: Stanford University Press, 2005.

VEP *La verité en peinture*. Paris: Flammarion, 1979. Trans. Geoffrey Bennington and Ian McLeod. Chicago: University of Chicago Press, 1987.

SCATTER 2

Politics in Deconstruction

Et toutefois il n'est point d'héritier si prodigue et nonchalant que
quelquefois ne passe les yeux sur les registres de son père, pour voir
s'il jouit de tous les droits de sa succession, ou si l'on a rien entrepris
sur lui ou son prédécesseur.

—ETIENNE DE LA BOÉTIE, *De la servitude volontaire*

Non seulement il n'y a pas de royaume de la différance mais celle-ci
fomente la subversion de tout royaume.

—JACQUES DERRIDA, "La différance"

"To be . . . means . . . to inherit," writes Jacques Derrida famously in his book
Specters of Marx.[1] At the very least, this means that we can think only to
the extent that we grow up into a language we inherit and do not choose,
and which we are obliged to use, even if our fondest desire were to contest
it and do it down. No one can create *ex nihilo* the language in which they
live and move, nor the concepts they reach for to do their thinking.[2] This

---

1. SM 94/54. Arguably this is itself an affirmative reading of Marx's famous
remark, "Men make their own history, but they do not make it as they please;
they do not make it under self-selected circumstances, but under circumstances
existing already, given and transmitted from the past." A reading that would
somewhat contest whether Marx's next sentence necessarily follows: "The tradition of all dead generations weighs like a nightmare on the brains of the living."
The Eighteenth Brumaire of Louis Bonaparte, (New York: International Publishers,
2017), 15.

2. RES 33/19: "Who, besides God, has ever *created*, literally 'created,' a concept?" The implied difference is perhaps primarily with Deleuze, as suggested in
passing in Derrida's short piece written after the former's death in 1995: "I have

sense of the irreducibility of inheritance means, as Derrida had famously already asserted in *Of Grammatology*, that we have a fundamentally passive relation to the language we speak, that we always find ourselves "in a text already," and that, as he said even earlier, we are always condemned to making a "false start," always already belated and after the beginning. Being has always already begun; language is always already there before us.[3] That text in which we find ourselves is, for us at least, maximally the text, the tradition, that has come to be called "Western metaphysics." Our best efforts to think, and to think something new, contestatory, and even revolutionary, are irreducibly rooted in that tradition.

But, as Derrida also shows in the same passage from his book on Marx, inheritance is not the same as mechanical causality: however much the tradition precedes me and perhaps unconsciously or even nightmarishly weighs on me, I am not exhaustively determined in what I say and think by my inheritance of that tradition. Inheritance is inheritance (rather than fate) to the extent that I can *also* resist, modify, and to some extent refuse what I am inheriting.[4] The possibility of that resistance is built in to the traditionality of the tradition from which I am inheriting, built into what

---

never felt the slightest 'objection' arising in me, not even potentially, against any of his works, even if I happened to grumble a bit about one or another of the propositions found in *Anti-Oedipus* . . . or perhaps about the idea that philosophy consists in 'creating' concepts" (CFU 236/193).

3. "If writing is *inaugural*, it is not so because it creates, but because of a certain absolute freedom of speech to bring forth the already-there in its sign, to take its auspices. A freedom of response that acknowledges as its sole horizon the history-world and the speech that can say only: Being has always already begun" (ED 23/12). And later, interestingly, in view of what awaits us, "Language has begun without us, in us before us. This is what Theology calls God" (PSY 561/2: 166)). On the "false start," see the very early PG, and my discussion in "Write, He Wrote," in *Not Half No End: Militantly Melancholic Essays in Memory of Jacques Derrida* (Edinburgh: Edinburgh University Press, 2010), 120–134.

4. The fuller passage reads: "Inheritance is never a *given*, it is always a task. It remains before us just as unquestionably as, before even wanting or refusing it, we are heirs, and heirs in mourning, like all heirs. In particular of what is called Marxism. *To be*, this word in which earlier we saw the word of spirit, means, for the same reason, *to inherit*. All the questions about being or about what is to be (or not to be) are questions of inheritance. There is no backward-looking fervor in recalling this, no traditionalistic flavor. Reaction, the reactionary or the reactive are simply interpretations of the structure of inheritance. We *are* heirs: that does not mean that we *have* or that we *receive* this or that, that some inheritance en-

makes it a tradition and not a natural law (or law of nature). One name for the place of that possibility of resistance is simply—reading. By *reading* the tradition from which I inherit, I have a chance of not being exhaustively determined and pre-dicted by it. This situation is complicated, certainly, by the fact that the concept of reading, like every other concept, is *itself* inherited from the tradition, so that I also have to read that traditional concept, and perhaps resist its traditional determinations (as, say, interpretation, hermeneutics) if I am to produce a resistant reading more generally. Like *Scatter 1*, *Scatter 2* is not essentially a work of scholarship but a book *of* reading(s) and a book *about* reading.[5]

Thinking (or reading) reading in this way is not a simple matter (we shall see that it engages with difficult questions about, among other things, context, history, and (un)readability), but one of the first features of a reading that resists its traditional determinations might be simply a kind of (willed and therefore not completely naive) "naivety": one thing I will try to do in this volume is to read quite directly a number of texts that are extremely "well known," and to read them, insofar as I am able, as though for the first time. My suspicion is that texts such as Plato's *Republic*, Aristotle's *Politics*, Hobbes's *Leviathan*, or Rousseau's *Social Contract* are "well known" in part just to the extent that they are not, or no longer, being read in the sense advanced here and are generally taken to be the more or less transparent vehicles of now familiar concepts and positions that can henceforth be referred to without extensive engagement with the texts themselves. This claim to "naivety" itself has a political and even militant dimension: it wants to say that these texts, however difficult, however overwritten by the tradition(s) of reading we also inherit, are nonetheless still, at least minimally, freshly readable for us, in principle for anyone, here today: feel free just to read, I say, in the face of all the complex machineries of scholarship and disciplinarity that can certainly inform reading, but that also police it, and sometimes function as an obstacle to it. Not, of course, that we can simply ignore or dismiss those complex machineries and (this time really naively) claim some direct or transparent access to "the texts themselves"—on the contrary; but, as Derrida also said in the *Grammatology*, such machineries can function as a guardrail and help avoid rash

---

riches us one day with this or that, but that the *being* of what we are *is* first of all inheritance, whether we like it or know it or not." (SM 94/54).

5. See too *Scatter 1* (New York: Fordham University Press, 2016), 247, for the claim that deconstructive reading is not hermeneutics.

or unwarranted and arbitrary claims, but they have never of themselves "opened a reading" (227).

This means that, whatever else I am interested in in the attempt to read (with and against the tradition, then), I cannot fail to be interested in what the texts I read have to say about reading, and how they attempt more or less energetically—as all texts do—to guide and control my reading of them in terms of what is sometimes, lazily, called "authorial intention"— lazily and insufficiently, because our best evidence for authorial intention is still and always textual, and therefore that evidence itself always calls for further reading. In the pages that follow, I shall read in some detail the very interesting and often perplexing things that, among others, John of Salisbury and Thomas Hobbes have to say about reading, and attempt to fold the implications of what they wrote into my own ongoing attempt to understand what I am doing as I read. For now, let us simply note the fol- lowing "primal scene," primal—as it happens—both for the question of reading in general, and for the specific parts or strands of the tradition of Western metaphysics I will be attempting to read here:

> Glaucon and the rest entreated me by all means not to let the question drop, but to proceed in the investigation. They wanted to arrive at the truth, first, about the nature of justice and injustice, and secondly, about their relative advantages. I told them, what I really thought, that the enquiry would be of a serious nature, and would require very good eyes. Seeing then, I said, that we are no great wits, I think that we had better adopt a method which I may illustrate thus; suppose that a short-sighted person had been asked by some one to read small letters from a distance; and it occurred to some one else that they might be found in another place which was larger and in which the letters were larger—if they were the same and he could read the larger letters first, and then proceed to the lesser—this would have been thought a rare piece of good fortune.
>
>   Very true, said Adeimantus; but how does the illustration apply to our enquiry?
>
>   I will tell you, I replied; justice, which is the subject of our enquiry, is, as you know, sometimes spoken of as the virtue of an individual, and sometimes as the virtue of a State.
>
>   True, he replied.
>
>   And is not a State larger than an individual?
>
>   It is.
>
>   Then in the larger the quantity of justice is likely to be larger and more easily discernible. I propose therefore that we enquire into the nature of justice and injustice, first as they appear in the State, and

secondly in the individual, proceeding from the greater to the lesser
and comparing them.[6]

In this quite complex and general scene of reading, I have chosen to negotiate the irreducible relation of inheritance to the tradition by reading texts
in "political thought" or "political philosophy." Like all other concepts,
that of "politics" is inherited, and it remains indelibly marked by thinking
around the Ancient Greek polis. But it seems a promising place for the kind
of resistant reading just sketched out, insofar as it has always been a troublesome and unruly concept in the tradition, equaled in its unruliness perhaps only by the concept of poetry, or of literature more generally. From at
least Plato on, the relations not only of philosophy and poetry but also
those of philosophy and politics have been complex, mysterious, and conflictual. As we shall see in some detail with reference to, among others,
Aristotle, Hegel, and Spinoza, as well as Derrida, there is indeed a real and
perhaps irreducible aporia in the way that metaphysics and politics can each
very plausibly claim priority over the other, so that philosophy (metaphysics) can always claim (and often has claimed) to turn away from or rise
above the dirty and dishonest business of politics, but politics can always
laugh right back at philosophy and anything philosophy might say about it,
denouncing philosophy as a pipedream, an ivory tower fantasy, something
that is "all very well in theory but useless in practice,"[7] something that belongs more to the "golden age of the poets" as Spinoza puts it in a text to
which we shall return.[8] The aporia, then, is part of the tradition we are
reading, and the traditional ways of trying to resolve or pass through that
aporia seem often dogmatic and unsatisfactory, and thereby most often
generate what I call "moralism," that seems to me to be endemic in contemporary discussion of politics, and to be itself a significant symptom of

6. Plato, *The Republic*, 2.368c–370c. I quote *The Republic* primarily in the translation by Tom Griffith (Cambridge: Cambridge University Press, 2000), with reference to earlier versions by Paul Shorey and Benjamin Jowett, and to the recent
version by Chris Emlyn-Jones and William Preddy (Cambridge, MA: Harvard
University Press, 2013).

7. As in Kant's famous 1793 essay "On the Common Saying: 'This May Be
True in Theory, but It Does Not Apply in Practice," trans. H. B. Nisbet, in *Kant:
Political Writings*, ed. H. Reiss, 2nd ed. (Cambridge: Cambridge University Press,
1991), 61–92.

8. Spinoza, *Tractatus Politicus*, trans. R. H. M. Elwes, in *A Theologico-Political
Treatise and A Political Treatise* (Mineola, NY: Dover Publications, 1951), 287.

the aporia I am identifying. *Scatter 2* attempts, often with some discomfort, to dwell with and in that aporia, to read some of its instantiations, but certainly does not claim to resolve it, and still less to issue prescriptions as to how we should conduct our political affairs.

At the beginning of the tradition we will be reading, there is already what amounts to a preemptive attempt to resolve the question of the relationship between politics and philosophy once and for all. This too is an extremely "well-known" moment that is perhaps more often mentioned than actually read, accepted as the cliché it has become. As will often be the case in what follows, and in the interests of what I was just calling "reading," I give a lengthy quotation rather than a summary, in this case with some salient Greek terms and a few interspersed comments: my wager in this case is that "everybody knows" the Platonic proposal or fantasy of the "philosopher king," but for just that reason I imagine pretty much everybody has stopped reading it, and forgotten, for example, contextual or "co-textual" features involving, among other things, humiliation, laughter, and violence (not to mention the really quite minimally "dialogic" quality of the exchanges here, with Socrates's poor interlocutor reduced largely to tendentially monosyllabic assent):

> "It wasn't our aim to demonstrate that these things were possible."
> "True enough."
> "Suppose a painter paints a picture which is a model of the outstandingly beautiful man. Suppose he renders every detail of his painting perfectly, but is unable to show that it is possible for such a man to exist. Do you think that makes him any the worse a painter?"
> "Good heavens, no."
> "Then what about us? Aren't we in the same position? Can't we claim to have been constructing a theoretical model of a good city [a model or paradigm in words: *paradeigma epoioumen logō agathēs poleōs*]?"
> "We certainly can." . . .
> "In which case, do you think our inability to show that it is possible to found a city in the way we have described makes what we have to say any less valid?"
> "No," he said.
> "Well, that's how things are. So if you want me, as a favor to you, to do my best to show how, exactly, and under what circumstances, it would be most possible, then you in return, for the purposes of this demonstration, must make the same allowances for me."
> "What allowances?"

"Is it possible for anything to be put into practice exactly as it is described? Or is it natural for practice [*praxin*] to have less hold on truth than theory [*lexeōs*] has? I don't care what some people may think. What about you? Do you agree, or not?"

"I agree," he said. (472d–473a)

In this passage, there is first a defense of theoretical or speculative thinking, of words rather than deeds, independent of any considerations of realizability whatsoever. But then the divide between what the translator here has (in perhaps slightly anachronistic terms) as "theory" and "practice" is shifted or narrowed: the slightly different point now is to say that all we need for the theoretical speculation to be justifiable is for there to be *some* possible practical *approximation* to the ideal city or "city of words" (in the first part of the argument we didn't care if any of this were possible at all, but now we want it to be at least partially possible):

"Then don't keep trying to compel me to demonstrate that the sort of thing we have described in a theoretical way [*to logō*] can also be fully realized in practice [*to ergō*]. If we turn out to be capable of finding how a city can be run in a way pretty close to what we have described, then you can say that we have discovered how what you are asking for can be put into practice. Or won't you be satisfied with that? I know I would."

"So would I." (473a)

And now we try to find the point of difference between the "theoretical" model (the talk, as it were) and actual instantiations (the walk), and use the model or the theory to identify what improvements might be made to the practice. So whereas the model originally had no responsibility to any possible practical realization, now the suggested improvement has to be at least possible, and thus bridge the apparent gulf just opened up between the theoretical and the practical. The bridge between those two domains (which we might call the metaphysical and the political) will be just that, a bridging suggestion that yokes the two together in one unifying figure:

"The next step, apparently, is for us to try to discover, and point out, what the failings are in cities nowadays, which stop them being run in this way, and what is the minimum change which could help a city arrive at political arrangements of this kind. Ideally a single change. Failing that, two. And failing that, as few as possible in number and as small as possible in impact."

"Absolutely," he said.

"All right, then. There is one change which I think would allow us
to show that things could be different. It is not a small change or an
easy one, but it is possible." (473b)

The single change to be proposed (and part of the bravura of Socrates's
coming proposal is that it *is* single, that there really only needs to be one,
albeit radical, change)—a change that involves a complex twist whereby
the yoking of the philosophical and the political will itself be not just
theoretically proposed but proposed as needing to be practically imposed
and enforced—is in fact so outrageous that it will be ridiculed and its pro-
ponent will possibly be the object of physical attack by what is, not coinci-
dentally, presented as an angry mob:

"What is it?"
"We've been using the analogy of waves. Well, now I'm coming to
the largest wave. But I'll make my suggestion anyway, even if it is
literally the laughter of the waves which is going to engulf me in
ridicule and humiliation. Listen carefully to what I am about to say.'
"Tell me."
"There is no end to suffering, Glaucon, for our cities, and none,
I suspect, for the human race, unless either philosophers become
kings in our cities, or the people who are now called kings and rulers
become real, true philosophers—unless there is this amalgamation of
political power and philosophy, with all those people whose inclina-
tion is to pursue one or other exclusively being forcibly prevented from
doing so. Otherwise there is not the remotest chance of the political
arrangements we have described coming about—to the extent that
they can—or seeing the light of day. This is the claim which I was
so hesitant about putting forward, because I could see what an extremely
startling claim it would be. It is hard for people to see that this is the
only possible route to happiness, whether in private life or public
life."
And Glaucon said, "Really, Socrates! Here's what you can expect after
a suggestion like that. You're facing a large and ugly crowd. The cloaks
come off—practically hurled off. They're stripped for action. All that's
needed is a weapon, any weapon, and they'll have launched themselves at
you, bent on mayhem. Can you hold them off, find an argument to
escape by? If you can't, you'll get what you deserve: utter humiliation."
"It's your fault. You got me into this." (473c–474a)

The moment at which the fusion of philosophy and politics is supposed to
occur (still hypothetically, though not thereby merely theoretically) is, we

might say, a quite explosive moment, one at which the supposedly serene domain of metaphysics is drawn by force (by the pull of praxis) into the confrontational and potentially violent zone of politics. The resulting space, cleared by that explosion and littered with its debris and fallout, might just be the space of what I call "scatter."

The effort to negotiate the tradition from which we inevitably inherit here chooses, then, the concept of politics as a promising concept through which that inheritance might be critically examined, *read*, and possibly resisted. But of course philosophy has already put in place all manner of safeguards that, as it were, resist our resistance in this domain, especially in the form of the slightly shady subdiscipline of philosophy called "political philosophy." We will soon enough be exploiting ambiguities in the name of that subdiscipline: for the purposes of this introductory sketch, suffice it to say that within political philosophy the greatest metaphysical pull, as it were, and the greatest resistance to the type of reading I hope to carry out, will be exercised by the concept of *sovereignty*, and the most promising zone of resistance to *that* concept will be given by the concept of *democracy*. We will regularly—often, although not agreeing in all the details, in the company of Jacques Derrida—identify democracy as a place where trouble (indeed what I call scatter) is happening. On an initial approach, this may appear to be simply because of the traditional opposition or antagonism between the One and the Many. But a crucial supplementary feature that "scatter" is attempting to capture is that the "one" and the "many" in play here are not merely numerical terms: as we shall see, the concept of the One is struck by an ambiguity between (at least) a numerically adjectival ("only one") sense and a qualitatively adjectival ("at one (with itself), unified") sense (the concept of God will most often be charged with, yes, *uniting* those two senses into one); and conversely, that the "many" in play in and around democracy is not just a numerical multiplicity, but a manifold, a multiplicity not just multitudinous but multifarious, a many that is not made up simply of a large number of countable *units*, but a many that is intrinsically diverse, variable and variegated, *motley*, not readily graspable in terms of any form of identity at all.

To read the complications of the One, especially in its annexation by the (otherwise unmanageably voluminous) Christian tradition,[9] I will follow

---

9. For an impressive scholarly account of some of this history, see Gwenaëlle Aubry, *Dieu sans la puissance:* Dunamis *et* Energeia *chez Aristote et chez Plotin* (*Archéologie de la puissance I*) (Paris: Vrin, 2006), and *Genèse du dieu souverain* (*Archéologie de la puissance II*) (Paris: Vrin, 2018).

the guiding thread provided by the afterlife of a line from Homer's *Iliad* twice quoted by Aristotle—once quite famously, once much less so. For the complications of the variegated, scattered many, we will regularly encounter invocations of the biblical episode of the Tower of Babel, Babel being an exemplary story of scatter and scattering,[10] and I will also often appeal to a term, or a family of terms, often used with a negative connotation by Plato, namely *poikilos, poikilia,* or *to poikilon.* In its fullest extension, *to poikilon* denotes not only what is multicolored, variegated or diverse, but it also communicates, with its connotations of indirection, slyness and cunning, with what in the first volume of this work I termed "the politics of politics," namely an irreducibly indirect and even devious aspect of politics, usually held at bay by metaphysics with the help of terms such as rhetoric, oratory, and sophistry. I believe that this "politics of politics," which in *Scatter 1* I argued is co-originary with politics, such that there is no conceivable politics unaffected by the politics of politics, ought to disallow—though not at all in a spirit of relativism—the kinds of appeal to the concept of truth rather differently proposed by Foucault or Badiou, and so also disallow the moralism still today endemic in political philosophy (and indeed in political discourse more generally).

The effort to read the tradition in this way will, then, involve at least the following elements: (1) an effort to track something of the internal construction of that very tradition itself as metaphysics of presence or as ontotheology; (2) an effort to show how politics, even as relatively contained by metaphysics in the terms of "political philosophy," has a number of disruptive effects in that construction (most notably via the concept of democracy); (3) an effort to show (or at least enact, perform) how the type of reading undertaken here itself produces, intrinsically as it were, political effects (for example, within the eminently metaphysical institution of the university and the disciplinary boundaries that currently define the study of philosophy, literature, and history); and (4) a suggestion that the effect of a deconstructive approach to the tradition might be said to operate a more general and radical "politicization" of metaphysics itself, via the irreducible and originary relation to alterity that Derrida variously calls by the nicknames "trace," "différance," "arche-writing," or (the one at least apparently closest to "scatter"), "dissemination." This last suggestion will at least implicitly contest the current dominance of historicism in the humanities and the recent return in force of "ontology" as an object of ap-

---

10. See Derrida's exemplary reading of this episode in "Des tours de Babel," PSY 203–237.

parently widespread philosophical and political desire. At least insofar as it continues to put unanswered questions to these two tendencies, deconstruction, which is nowadays often—with a surprising degree of bad faith and indulgence in circular argument—written off to history, as, for example, "what they used to do back in the 1980s," remains as topical and vital as ever, whatever the vagaries of intellectual fashion.

PART I

Politics, Metaphysics, Sovereignty

CHAPTER I

Bios Theōrētikos, Bios Politikos

Philosophy has always had the greatest difficulty with its relation to politics. From the beginnings of Western thinking up to thinkers such as Leo Strauss, Hannah Arendt, Jacques Rancière and Alain Badiou, philosophy and politics have maintained what Badiou calls an "enigmatic" relation,[1] one that Rancière describes as a *mésentente*, more than a mere "disagreement," as the English translation has it, almost "bad blood," a deep-seated failure of understanding, a conflict, perhaps of the order of what Jean-François Lyotard had earlier called a *différend*, a dispute that cannot be resolved equitably for want of a criterion applicable to both sides.[2] Throughout this history, philosophy has repeatedly tried to assert its grasp of politics—and repeatedly failed. The Western tradition is tormented by this conflict,

---

1. Alain Badiou, *La relation énigmatique entre philosophie et politique* (Paris: Germina, 2011).

2. Jacques Rancière, *La mésentente* (Paris: Galilée, 1995); trans. Julia Rose, *Disagreement: Politics and Philosophy* (Minneapolis: University of Minnesota Press, 1999). Rancière wants to distinguish his *mésentente* from Lyotard's *différend*, but it seems more plausible to me to see in the former a specific case of the latter.

mismatch, or misunderstanding, whereby—in spite of appearances—
philosophy itself cannot ever finally and convincingly conclude that the
bios theōrētikos, the philosophical or contemplative life, really is superior to
the *bios politikos*, the political or active life.

In the Socratic dialogue *Gorgias*, trying to talk down Callicles, Socrates
separates out these two possibilities, which subsequently become canonical in Aristotle:[3]

> For you see that our debate is upon a question which has the highest
> conceivable claims to the serious interest even of a person who has
> but little intelligence—namely, what course of life is best; whether it
> should be that to which you invite me, with all those manly pursuits of
> speaking in Assembly and practicing rhetoric and going in for politics
> after the fashion of you modern politicians [*retorikēn askounta kai
> politeuomenon touton ton tropon, on umeis nun politeuesthe*], or this life of
> philosophy [*ton bion ton en philosophia*]; and what makes the difference
> between these two.[4]

The remainder of the dialogue is devoted to urging the superiority of the
"life of philosophy."

Aristotle might at first seem to take this same Platonic line, when in
what came to be called the *Metaphysics* he claims that the supreme science
(of wisdom, *sophia*) is "the theoretical science of first principles and first
causes [*tōn prōtōn archōn kai aitiōn einai theōretikēn*]" (982b9). But that statement is immediately preceded by the idea that "The highest science, which
is superior to every subordinate science, is the one that knows in view of
what end each thing must be done. And this end is the good of each being
and, in a general manner, the supreme good in nature as a whole" (982b3–7):
and this slight indeterminacy, between "principles" and "causes" on the one
hand, and "ends" and "goods" on the other, between archeo-logy and teleology, between what will later be clearly demarcated as the "theoretical" and
the "practical," allows what can look like a contradictory claim at the beginning of *The Nichomachean Ethics* as to the priority of politics:

> So if what is done has some end that we want for its own sake, and
> everything else we want is for the sake of this end; and if we do not
> choose everything for the sake of something else (because this would
> lead to an infinite progression, making our desire fruitless and vain),

3. *Nichomachean Ethics*, 1095b17–18.
4. *Gorgias*, in Plato, *Lysis, Symposium, Gorgias*, trans. W. R. M. Lamb (Cambridge, MA: Harvard University Press, 1925), 500c.

then clearly this will be the good, indeed the chief good [*heis tagathon kai to ariston*].[5] Surely, then, knowledge of the good must be very important for our lives? And if, like archers, we have a target [*skopos*], are we not more likely to hit the right mark? If so, we must try at least roughly to comprehend what it is and which science or faculty is concerned with it.

Knowledge of the good would seem to be the concern of the most authoritative science, the highest master science [*tēs kuriōtates kai malista arkitektonikēs*]. And this is obviously the science of politics, because it lays down which of the sciences there should be in cities, and which each class of person should learn and up to what level. And we see that even the most honourable of faculties, such as military science, domestic economy, and rhetoric, come under it. Since political science employs the other sciences, and also lays down laws about what we should do and refrain from, its end will include the ends of the others, and will therefore be the human good [*anthrōpinon agathon*]. For even if the good is the same for an individual as for a city, that of the city is obviously a greater and more complete thing to obtain and preserve. For while the good of an individual is a desirable thing, what is good for a people or for cities is a nobler and more godlike thing [*kallion de kai theioteron ethnei kai polesin*]. Our enquiry, then, is a kind of political science, since these are the ends it is aiming at.[6]

Apparently resolving this contradiction, or showing it to be merely apparent, Aristotle has most often been taken to be resorting to a stable distinction between a hierarchically superior "theoretical science," in the form of what subsequently comes to be called "metaphysics," and a clearly subordinated "practical science" (teleologically directed to and by the science of politics). This is, for example, the position taken by Aquinas in the prologue to his *Commentary on Aristotle's Politics* (though a close reading of

---

5. See also *Metaphysics* 994b for this argument (still a central tenet of Kant's "teleological judgment"), whereby teleology always entails that there be one supreme or final end that "finalizes" all others.

6. *Nicomachean Ethics*, trans. and ed. Roger Crisp (Cambridge: Cambridge University Press, 2000), 1094a18–1094b7. I have also consulted the translations by W. D. Ross (as revised by J.O Urmson in *The Complete Works of Aristotle: The Revised Oxford Translation*, ed. Jonathan Barnes, 2 vols. (Princeton, NJ: Princeton University Press, 1984); by Hugh Tredennick (Cambridge, MA: Harvard University Press, 1933); by C. D. C. Reeve (Indianapolis: Hackett, 2014); and the French translation by Jules Tricot (Paris: Vrin, 1990).

that text might well show that position to be less secure than it at first appears).[7] But the assumption of such a distinction rather begs the questions raised here: from the point of view of metaphysics, it seems clear that the *bios theōrētikos* is superior (see for example *Metaphysics*, Lambda, 1072b22–23). But I will be claiming that once the *bios politikos* comes into play in such a way that the decision in favor of the *bios theōrētikos* is no longer *simply* a theoretical or metaphysical decision, then a fundamental tension emerges that complicates not only what is usually taken to be the clear subordination of politics (which is at best an art or a practical science) to *sophia* or first philosophy (which is a purely theoretical science), but also thereby what is often taken to be Aristotle's own unambiguous endorsement of the superiority of the *bios theōrētikos* over the *bios politikos*. Here is how the problem is initially set up in the *Politics*:

> Now it is evident that the form of government is best in which every man, whoever he is, can act best and live happily. But even those who agree in thinking that the life of virtue is the most eligible raise a question, whether the life of business and politics [*bion airetōtaton poteron o politikos kai praktikos*] is or is not more eligible than one which is wholly independent of external goods, I mean than a contemplative life [*bios . . . theōrētikos*], which by some is maintained to be the only one worthy of a philosopher. For these two lives—the life of the philosopher and the life of the statesman [more literally "the political and the philosophical"]—appear to have been preferred by those who have been most keen in the pursuit of virtue, both in our own and in

7. Aquinas states in his prologue that "the whole that is the political community is superior to all the other wholes that human reason can know or constitute." Thomas Aquinas, *Commentary on Aristotle's* Politics, trans. Richard J. Regan (Indianapolis: Hackett, 2007), 2. Aquinas then asserts that "we distinguish practical from theoretical sciences in that the latter are directed only to the knowledge of truth, while the former are directed to action. Therefore, politics is necessarily included in practical philosophy . . ." (ibid.). But according to a potentially fractal structure that will be precious to us, politics is nonetheless on the theoretical side, as it were, of the practical, the "moral" as opposed to the "mechanical" branch of the practical in general. Hannah Arendt also appears to accept that this is a fairly straightforward distinction in Aristotle (and Plato), albeit one with the unfortunate effect that politics is "deprived of all dignity" and that the "end of politics" is, paradoxically, the withdrawal from politics into, precisely, the *bios theōrētikos*. See, for example, the essay "The End of Tradition" in *The Promise of Politics*, ed. Jerome Kohn (New York: Schocken Books, 2005), 81–84.

other ages. Which is the better is a question of no small moment; for
the wise man, like the wise state, will necessarily regulate his life
according to the best end.[8] (1324a22–32)

It is hard, however, not to think that Aristotle's proposed resolution of this
"question of no small moment"—which involves claiming a measure of activity for contemplation itself, so that a revised version of the "political
life" allowing for that now active contemplation should be chosen—rather
complicates this apparently simple distinction, or at least leaves a degree
of tension unresolved, perhaps inviting deconstruction. Here is how Aristotle puts it, with a telling final reference to a theological principle:

> If we are right in our view, and happiness is assumed to be virtuous
> activity, the active life will be the best, both for every city collectively,
> and for individuals. Not that a life of action must necessarily have
> relation to others, as some persons think, nor are those ideas only to
> be regarded as practical which are pursued for the sake of practical
> results, but much more the thoughts and contemplations which are
> independent and complete in themselves; since virtuous activity, and
> therefore a certain kind of action, is an end, and even in the case of
> external actions the directing mind is most truly said to act. Neither,
> again, is it necessary that states which are cut off from others and
> choose to live alone should be inactive; for activity, as well as other
> things, may take place by sections; there are many ways in which the
> sections of a state act upon one another. The same thing is equally
> true of every individual. If this were otherwise, God and the universe,
> who have no external actions over and above their own energies, would
> be far enough from perfection. Hence it is evident that the same life is
> best for each individual, and for states and for mankind collectively.
> (1325b14–32)

In some now classical reflections on this issue in Aristotle, Leo Strauss is
also suspicious of this supposed resolution of the politics/philosophy relation, and has to work quite hard in his readings to ground the possibility
of political philosophy in the maintenance of the very distinction Aristotle is here apparently trying to overcome, and in a clear hierarchization of
the relation between the *bios theōrētikos* and the *bios politikos*. For example,

---

8. Trans. Benjamin Jowett, in *The Complete Works of Aristotle*. I have also consulted the translations by H. Rackham (Cambridge, MA: Harvard University
Press, 1932), as well as Reeve's and Jules Tricot's (see note 6).

in *The City and Man* (1964), Strauss summarizes Aristotle's position as follows:

> Prudence and moral virtue united and as it were fused enable a man to lead a good life or the noble life which seems to be the natural end of man. The best life is the life devoted to understanding or contemplation as distinguished from the practical or political life. Therefore practical wisdom is lower in rank than theoretical wisdom which is concerned with the divine things or the *kosmos*, and subservient to it—but in such a way that within its sphere, the sphere of all human things as such, prudence is supreme. The sphere ruled by prudence is closed since the principles of prudence—the ends in the light of which prudence guides man—are known independently of theoretical science. Because Aristotle held that art is inferior to law or to prudence, that prudence is inferior to theoretical wisdom, and that theoretical wisdom . . . is available, he could found political science as an independent discipline among a number of disciplines.[9]

But this apparently clearly hierarchized position is then interestingly complicated by Strauss, whose Aristotle also recognizes that the pursuit of the theoretical life entails some essentially political conditions:

> In order to grasp the ground of Aristotle's procedure, one must start from the facts that according to him the highest end of man by nature is theoretical understanding or philosophy and this perfection does not require moral virtue as moral virtue, i.e., just and noble deeds as choiceworthy for their own sake. It goes without saying that man's highest end cannot be achieved without actions resembling moral actions proper, but the actions in question are intended by the philosopher as mere means toward his end. That end also calls for prudence, for the philosopher must deliberate about how he can secure the conditions for his philosophizing here and now. (26–27)

This means that the attempted resolution of the dilemma is not straightforward and that it depends on what is merely an "analogy":

> Aristotle . . . bases his thematic discussion of the best regime on the principle that the highest end of man, happiness, is the same for the individual and the city . . . The difficulty arises from the fact that the highest end of the individual is contemplation. He seems to solve the

---

9. Leo Strauss, *The City and Man* (Chicago: University of Chicago Press, 1964), 25.

difficulty by asserting that the city is as capable of the contemplative life as the individual. Yet it is obvious that the city is capable at best only of an analogue of the contemplative life. (49)

As Strauss puts it in the essay "On Classical Political Philosophy," this situation means that although theoretical philosophy may well be man's highest pursuit, it needs to give itself a political justification or alibi in order to secure its own possibility. There has to be, as it were, a practical or active presentation of the theoretical or contemplative, and just this gives rise to "political philosophy" as such, now defined less by its specific object and more by its mode of presentation, whereby the philosopher convinces the politician or citizen, politically rather than philosophically, of the superiority of philosophy:

> From this point of view the adjective "political" in the expression
> "political philosophy" designates not so much a subject matter as a
> manner of treatment; from this point of view, I say, "political philoso-
> phy" means primarily not the philosophic treatment of politics, but
> the political, or popular, treatment of philosophy, or the political
> introduction to philosophy—the attempt to lead the qualified citizens,
> or rather their qualified sons, from the political life to the philosophic
> life.[10]

This is why, in the eponymous essay "What is Political Philosophy," Strauss can say "Political philosophy is that branch of philosophy which is closest to political life, to non-philosophic life, to human life" (10). Only subsequently, says Strauss, could anything like an academic discipline of "political philosophy" be established: "Classical political philosophy is characterized by the fact that it was related to political life directly. It was only after the classical philosophers had done their work that political philosophy became definitely 'established' and thus acquired a certain remoteness from political life. . . . It was its direct relation to political life which determined the orientation and scope of classical political philosophy."[11] My suggestion is that the frontier between philosophy and politics, the border-zone occupied by political philosophy, is certainly complex, and best thought of in nonlinear, fractal terms (so that the closer we look at the supposed dividing line the more it divides, as in a "Newton

---

10. Leo Strauss, "On Classical Political Philosophy," in *What Is Political Philosophy? And Other Studies* (Glencoe, IL: Free Press, 1959), 78–94, at 93–94.

11. Ibid., 78.

Basin"), and that the problems raised cannot be satisfactorily resolved by any attempt to draw a hard boundary, nor indeed by giving in to the almost inevitable temptation to make predictions, issue specific political recommendations, or propose a general political program from this complex frontier space.[12] One upshot of this is that however far we go toward the "theoretical" extreme of the supposed divide our position will always have a "political side" (just as New York City is far to the east but still has a West Side), and however far we try to go toward the political extreme our position will have a theoretical side (Los Angeles is far to the west but has an East Side): part of the point of *Scatter* is to negotiate this space without entirely accepting the traditional ways it has been understood.[13]

At the beginning of an as-yet unpublished seminar dating from 1970–71, Derrida lays out some of the general issues here, wondering whether in general putting the question of textuality, of its "material inscription" to philosophy is a "political strategy":

> And in such a question what does "political" mean? . . . From the Aristotelian roots of such a division [between *metaphysica generalis* and *metaphysica specialis*] up to Husserl's distinction and hierarchy between

12. So *Scatter 2* will not, for example, aim to follow either the philosophical proposals for a workable democracy made by Joshua Ober in *Demopolis: Democracy before Liberalism in Theory and Practice* (Cambridge: Cambridge University Press, 2017), nor the more popularizing defense of an Athenian model of direct democracy in Roslyn Fuller, *Beasts and Gods: How Democracy Changed Its Meaning and Lost Its Purpose* (London: Zed Books, 2015), nor other often admirable and disquieting books convincingly diagnosing shortcomings or crises in current democratic politics, such as Sheldon S. Wolin, *Democracy Inc.: Managed Democracy and the Specter of Inverted Totalitarianism* (Princeton, NJ: Princeton University Press, 2008), Wendy Brown, *Undoing the Demos: Neoliberalism's Stealth Revolution* (New York: Zone Books, 2017), and Bonnie Honig, *Public Things: Democracy in Disrepair* (New York: Fordham University Press, 2017), and other still more recent books, by historians or political scientists, with titles like *How Democracies Die* (New York: Crown Publishing, 2018), by Steven Levitsky and Daniel Ziblatt, or *How Democracy Ends* (New York: Basic Books, 2018), by David Runciman.

13. For a preliminary attempt to understand this kind of space on the basis of Derrida's reading of Rousseau's construal of the relation between north and south, and notably my suggestion that the "horn torus" might be an interesting figure for thinking polar but nonoppositional structures, see my "Fractal Geography," in *Reading Of Grammatology*, ed. Sean Gaston and Ian McLachlan (London: Continuum Books, 2011), 137–145.

formal ontology and regional ontology, up to Heidegger's question of
the meaning of being in general . . . going via Hegel's *Logic* as Science
of sciences, the determination of the political as such has always
appeared to constitute an extremely narrow, dependent, and derivative
specificity. The text of political philosophy, when it appeared under
this title, always appeared to be *deduced* on the basis of ontological,
metaphysical, or moral positions [*instances*], of a knowledge or a will in
themselves non-political. In this sense, we can say that the project and
the text of political philosophy have been *inscribed*—in the sense of a
figure comprehended within a more powerful figure in the text of
philosophy, without this inscription or this architectonic derivation
being interrogated for itself.[14]

This complexity in the relation between philosophy and politics has arguably never been satisfactorily resolved, and it allows Giorgio Agamben,
for example, who has his own quite obscure reading of the relation between the active and the contemplative,[15] to refer to the "most tenuous
and uncertain discipline among the many taught in our universities: political philosophy."[16] Whence also Jacques Rancière's attempt to identify
what in the French is more than a "disagreement," or Alain Badiou's more
recent location of a "relation énigmatique entre philosophie et politique,"
and Michel Foucault's attempt (which I criticize at length in the first
chapter of *Scatter 1*) to formulate the appropriate relation of philosophy to
politics as one of a truth-telling, a *parrhesia*, that does not, however, involve the attempt to tell politicians what to do: "it does not tell the truth
of political action, it does not tell the truth for political action, it tells the

---

14. *Théorie du discours philosophique II: La forme du texte philosophique: les conditions d'inscription du texte de philosophie politique* (*l'exemple du matérialisme*), Session I,
5. I am grateful to Thomas Clément Mercier, who drew this seminar (later
parts of which contribute significantly to Derrida's 1987 text *Khôra*) to my
attention.

15. "Opposing the contemplative life to the political as 'two *bioi*' . . . Aristotle deflected politics and philosophy from their trajectory . . . The political is neither a *bios* nor a *zōē*, but the dimension that the inoperativity of contemplation . . .
ceaselessly opens and assigns to the living." *The Kingdom and the Glory: For a Theological Genealogy of Economy and Government*, trans. Lorenzo Chiesa with Matteo
Mandarini (Stanford: Stanford University Press, 2011), 251.

16. Giorgio Agamben, *Stasis: Civil War as a Political Paradigm* (*Homo Sacer II, 2*),
trans. Nicholas Heron (Stanford: Stanford University Press, 2015), 27.

truth in relation to the practice of politics, in relation to the political personage."[17]

On the other side of a different philosophical frontier, John Rawls's solution to the relation between politics and metaphysics, in "Justice as Fairness" (1985), seems at least as problematic.[18] Rawls is attempting to provide a philosophically presented political solution to a problem he believes simply cannot be solved philosophically in a "constitutional democracy." Just because there will (by definition) be a diversity of philosophical opinions, and such diversity must be respected if we are to remain within the terms of democracy, then philosophy cannot provide an answer (because any such answer would then merely be one opinion among others):

> Thus, the aim of justice as fairness as a political conception is practical, and not metaphysical or epistemological. That is, it presents itself not as a conception of justice that is true, but one that can serve as a basis of informed and willing political agreement between citizens viewed as free and equal persons. This agreement when securely founded in public political and social attitudes sustains the goods of all persons and associations within a just democratic regime. To secure this agreement we try, so far as we can, to avoid disputed philosophical, as well as disputed moral and religious, questions. We do this not because these questions are unimportant or regarded with indifference, but because we think them too important and recognize that there is no way to resolve them politically. The only alternative to a principle of toleration is the autocratic use of state power. Thus, justice as fairness deliberately stays on the surface, philosophically speaking. Given the profound differences in belief and conceptions of the good at least since the Reformation, we must recognize that, just as on questions of religious and moral doctrine, public agreement on

17. Michel Foucault, *Le gouvernement de soi et les autres: Cours au Collège de France, 1982–3*, ed. François Ewald and Alessandro Fontana (Paris: Seuil, 2008), 265; *The Government of Self and Others: Lectures at the Collège de France, 1982–1983*, trans. Graham Burchell (London: Palgrave/Macmillan, 2010), 288.

18. John Rawls, "Justice as Fairness: Political not Metaphysical," *Philosophy and Public Affairs* 14, no. 3 (Summer 1985): 223–251. In general, given our stress on reading, the Anglo-American tradition is always likely to be less germane to our endeavor than the continental (for reasons that are at least akin to those we pursue later in Hobbes). For an exceptionally happy bridging of those two traditions, however, see Simon Glendinning's forthcoming work *Europe: A Philosophical History*.

the basic questions of philosophy cannot be obtained without the state's infringement of basic liberties. Philosophy as the search for truth about an independent metaphysical and moral order cannot, I believe, provide a workable and shared basis for a political conception of justice in a democratic society. (230)

Recommending his notion of "justice as fairness" as a good way to proceed in this situation, Rawls recognizes what he calls "certain hazards" which in his view rest on a misunderstanding of his famous "original position" and "veil of ignorance" argument:

> As a device of representation the original position is likely to seem somewhat abstract and hence open to misunderstanding. The description of the parties may seem to presuppose some metaphysical conception of the person, for example, that the essential nature of persons is independent of and prior to their contingent attributes, including their final ends and attachments, and indeed, their character as a whole. But this is an illusion caused by not seeing the original position as a device of representation. The veil of ignorance, to mention one prominent feature of that position, has no metaphysical implications concerning the nature of the self; it does not imply that the self is ontologically prior to the facts about persons that the parties are excluded from knowing. (238)

This is all a "simulation" (239), from which, however, all "deception and fraud, and so on, must be excluded" (235: we might think that the force of the "must be excluded" is already a problem). As long as we recognize this non-fraudulent nature of the simulation, and exercise the principle of tolerance ("we must apply the principle of toleration to philosophy itself" [231]), as a "method of avoidance" (ibid.), then we are not unduly foisting our deep metaphysical views on others. Unless, of course, worries Rawls in a funny footnote, the fact that "there is no accepted understanding of what a metaphysical doctrine is" *already* compromises our earnest and liberal attempt to avoid such doctrines, if only because the principle of tolerance and the method of avoidance, and thus the whole "justice as fairness" proposal might *themselves* be already metaphysical:

> One might say, as Paul Hoffman has suggested to me, that to develop a political conception of justice without presupposing, or explicitly using, a metaphysical doctrine, for example, some particular metaphysical conception of the person, is already to presuppose a metaphysical thesis: namely, that no particular metaphysical doctrine is required for this purpose. (240n22)

And so

> One might also say that our everyday conception of persons as the
> basic units of deliberation and responsibility presupposes, or in some
> way involves, certain metaphysical theses about the nature of persons
> as moral or political agents. Following the method of avoidance, I
> should not want to deny these claims. What should be said is the
> following. If we look at the presentation of justice as fairness and note
> how it is set up, and note the ideas and conceptions it uses, no particu-
> lar metaphysical doctrine about the nature of persons, distinctive and
> opposed to other metaphysical doctrines, appears among its premises,
> or seems required by its argument. If metaphysical presuppositions are
> involved, perhaps they are so general that they would not distinguish
> between the distinctive metaphysical views—Cartesian, Leibnizian, or
> Kantian; realist, idealist, or materialist—with which philosophy
> traditionally has been concerned. In this case, they would not appear
> to be relevant for the structure and content of a political conception of
> justice one way or the other. (240n22)

"No particular metaphysical doctrine," perhaps, but certainly a very general metaphysical presupposition (so general that it is not indeed opposed
by any of the views Rawls mentions), the presupposition of metaphysics
itself as metaphysics of presence (and more specifically of what Heidegger
would call "subjectity").

As is also the case with Habermas, the politely liberal values of discussion and tolerance presuppose "some consensus" on the basis of which we
address our disagreements, including presumably the consensus that "existing differences between contending political views can at least be mod-
erated, even if not entirely removed" (231). Such that, as always, liberalism
is extremely tolerant, but only really of liberalism itself, thereby in equal
measure anxious and self-satisfied, and any "toleration" of apparent differences, divergencies and disputes is at best negative and condescending.[19]

19. Rawls does not think that his version of liberalism tolerates (or should
tolerate) only liberalism; in his later *The Law of Peoples* (Cambridge, MA: Harvard
University Press, 1999), he thinks that liberal peoples should also tolerate what
he calls "decent peoples" (who need not be liberal to qualify as "decent"), but it
is quite clear that (quite apart from the—I prefer to imagine unconscious—
condescension implied by the use of the evaluation "decent") this is still being
thought with a telos of liberalism, as for example in "Liberal peoples must try to
encourage decent peoples and not frustrate their vitality by coercively insisting
that all societies be liberal. Moreover, if a liberal constitutional democracy is, in

A quick way of formulating the upshot of all this is that it would spell the end of politics as essentially and irreducible conflictual, *and* the end of philosophy, as we are too concerned to avoid dispute to pursue our deeper metaphysical issues (which are presumably now to be left to professional philosophers to discuss more or less acrimoniously in the safety of their departments). Jean-François Lyotard's apparently scandalous suggestion at the end of *The Postmodern Condition* that consensus is only a local, unstable *state* of discussion, and that the *end* of discussion is to sharpen and accentuate differences rather than overcome them, can stand for now as the "continental" response—still undertaken in the name of justice—to Rawls's arguments.[20] As we shall see as we develop the thought of scatter, Lyotard's rather terse suggestion cannot be taken to be proposing a *telos* of absolute disagreement or dissensus as a substitute for the traditional *telos* of consensus and agreement (which for Lyotard is represented by Habermas), but must instead be seen to disrupt the whole teleological setup still implicitly governing Rawls's arguments, rather than simply advancing a—quite unthinkable—telos of absolute disagreement. In Lyotard's wake, *Scatter* does not advance the absurd idea that the more we disagree the better, but seeks a way of thinking about disagreement (and indeed about difference in general) that is not committed, even ideally, to seeing the end of disagreement in assent, consensus, or, as the currently fashionable idiom has it, "coming together." Our (local and unstable, of course often

---

fact, superior to other forms of society, as I believe it to be, a liberal people should have confidence in their convictions and suppose that a decent society, when offered due respect by liberal peoples, may be more likely, over time, to recognize the advantages of liberal institutions and take steps toward becoming more liberal on its own" (62: Rawls goes on to describe a "hypothetical decent hierarchical people . . . an idealized Islamic people named 'Kazanistan'"). See Derrida's comments on the essentially Christian (and in his view intrinsically condescending) value of "tolerance" (not explicitly with reference to Rawls), in Jacques Derrida and Jürgen Habermas, *Philosophy in a Time of Terror* (Chicago: University of Chicago Press, 2003), 124–130; *Le "concept" du 11 septembre: Dialogues à New York (octobre-décembre 2001) avec Giovanna Borradori* (Paris: Galilée, 2004), 183–189, and Habermas's measured defense of the concept (40–42/75–78). See also FS, 36–37.

20. Jean-François Lyotard, *La condition postmoderne* (Paris: Minuit, 1979), 106; trans. Geoffrey Bennington and Brian Massumi as *The Postmodern Condition* (Minneapolis: University of Minnesota Press, 1984), 65–66: "I have shown . . . that consensus is only a particular state of discussion, not its end. Its end, on the contrary, is paralogy . . . search for dissent."

precious) agreements also remain preciously *precarious* in a more general milieu that never resolves difference into sameness: and this maintenance of difference against its (even ideal) teleological resolution holds to a principle of general disruption and dispute, not necessarily manageable by dialectics in any sense, as underlying argumentative practices. As I shall go on to suggest, only this type of very general disruption (what I am calling scatter, then) can do justice to the thought of democracy, even as that thought has been, tendentially, repressed in the Western tradition of political philosophy. *Scatter* will be picking up the—scattered—traces of a different thinking of democracy that I shall argue can most promisingly be formulated in deconstructive terms. The maximal claim of this volume is not that politics has to be deconstructed, or that deconstruction has to be introduced into politics, but that politics as such has to be thought *in deconstruction* from the start, which is another way of saying that it has to be *read*.

This development of a thinking of difference and dissensus involves suspicion not merely of liberal and more generally metaphysical teleological schemas, but of a more pervasive pattern of thinking about difference in general, whereby politics has always been conceptualized in view of its *end*, in both senses of the word. The concept of politics as we inherit it from the tradition is always the concept of politics *ending*, coming to an end by realizing its end (however that end be specified: the good life, justice, liberty, prosperity, happiness, the classless society . . .). One pervasive and persuasive way in which such schemas have worked is essentially Kantian: ends are proposed in terms of Ideas of Reason toward which we are enjoined to make progress, in the sober realization that the end will never be fully realized in fact. With some help from Aristotle, later we will see that this way of presenting the situation is more complicated than it appears, in that the full realization of the end proposed is not only empirically out of reach, but would in fact be catastrophic—which then, as I have argued in detail elsewhere,[21] complicates any progressive construal of the structure in question and indeed is the internal ruin of the teleological schema as such. Another powerful way in which this schema has been, as it were, enforced (provoked at least in part by an at least partial perception of the problem just mentioned) is exemplified in the Hegelian dialectic, which has the immense philosophical advantage over the relatively straightforward teleological schemas we have mentioned thus far of apparently allowing

---

21. See my *Kant on the Frontier: Philosophy, Politics, and the Ends of the Earth* (New York: Fordham University Press, 2017).

for a thoroughgoing admission into thought of negativity in general as the very motor of its possible advance. The Hegelian operator of sublation (*Aufhebung*) is, as it were, fueled by the very negativity it is always already destined eventually to overcome or redeem, and the supposedly logically secured horizon of that overcoming then allows for an indefinite and apparently attractive ability to dwell at great length, to "tarry," with difference, dissensus, and antagonism, and indeed to exacerbate them into the at least apparently more conflictual forms of opposition and contradiction. It can easily seem as though contradiction must be the height of dissensus (and as we shall see in a moment, Hegel thinks it is, logically, the only way to think through difference in general).

First, let us note in Hegel a transformed but recognizable version of the problematic relation between *bios theōrētikos* and *bios politikos* we have been following. As is well known, in the general shape of Hegel's encyclopedic "system," "ethical life [*Sittlichkeit*]" (which includes what we would call politics) appears at the end of what Hegel calls "Objective Spirit," which is the second major part of the third top-level division (philosophy of spirit) of the system. We might represent that place as follows in a simplified schema of the system as a whole:

[I. Logic (Spirit in and of itself); II. Philosophy of Nature (Spirit as other than itself); III Philosophy of Spirit [1. Subjective Spirit; 2. Objective Spirit [a. Abstract Right; b. Morality; c. Ethical Life]; 3. Absolute Spirit [a. Art; b. Religion; c. Philosophy]]].

According to a persistent pattern in Hegel,[22] "political philosophy" can be located in two places: as *philosophy* it comes as part of the very end of the system (as indeed does the entire system itself), at its place as the culmination of Absolute Spirit as philosophy; but as *political* philosophy it is elaborated around its other place, as the culmination of Objective Spirit. What is more, the possibility of *doing* philosophy (of living the *bios theōrētikos*) is given by concrete developments at the level of objective spirit, namely the

---

22. This is perhaps most dramatically illustrated by the initially puzzling place of the *Phenomenology of Spirit*, which "occupies a double position in the encyclopedia-system: In a certain way the phenomenology is a foundational part for the system while being at the same time an affiliated component *within* the system." See Heidegger's illuminating discussion in the 1931–32 lecture course *Hegel's Phenomenology of Spirit* (GA 32), trans. Parvis Emad and Kenneth Maly (Bloomington: Indiana University Press, 1988); the quotation is at 9.

realization of the State. Here is a helpful account of this double position-
ing as given by Herbert Marcuse in *Reason and Revolution*:

> One question still to be answered affects the whole structure of
> Hegel's system. The historical world, in so far as it is built, organized,
> and shaped by the conscious activity of thinking subjects, is a realm
> of [spirit]. But [spirit] is fully realized and exists in its true form only
> when it indulges in its proper activity, namely, in art, religion, and
> philosophy. These domains of culture are, then, the final reality, the
> province of ultimate truth. And this is precisely Hegel's conviction:
> absolute [spirit] lives only in art, religion, and philosophy. All three
> have the same content in a different form: Art apprehends the truth
> by mere intuition (*Anschauung*), in a tangible and therefore limited
> form; Religion perceives it free of such limitation, but only as mere
> "assertion" and belief; Philosophy comprehends it through knowledge
> and possesses it as its inalienable property. On the other hand, these
> spheres of culture exist only in the historical development of mankind,
> and the state is the final stage of this development. What, then, is the
> relation between the state and the realm of absolute [spirit]? Does the
> rule of the state extend over art, religion, and philosophy, or is it
> rather limited by them?[23]

Various versions of this tension or duplicity show up explicitly in Hegel
himself, notably perhaps in the Preface to the second edition (1831) of the
Science of Logic, which, preciously for us given what awaits us, involves a
reference to Aristotle's *Metaphysics*:

> "Only after almost everything which is necessary to life, and pertains
> to its comfort and sociability, was made available," says Aristotle, "did
> man begin to trouble himself with philosophical knowledge." "In
> Egypt," he had previously remarked, "there was an early development
> of the mathematical sciences because there the priestly caste were
> brought early to a state of leisure." Indeed, the need to occupy oneself
> with pure thoughts [i.e., Logic] presupposes a long road that the human
> spirit must have traversed; it is the need, one may say, of having already
> attained the satisfaction of necessary need, the need of freedom from
> need [*das Bedürfnis des schon befriedigten Bedürfnisses der Notwendigkeit,
> der Bedürfnislosigkeit*], of abstraction from the material of intuition,

---

23. Herbert Marcuse, *Reason and Revolution: Hegel and the Rise of Social Theory*, 2nd ed. (London: Routledge, 2000), 86–87. I have taken the liberty of substi-
tuting "spirit" where Marcuse uses "mind" for Hegelian *Geist*.

imagination, and so forth; from the material of the concrete interests
of desire, impulse, will, in which the determinations of thought hide
as if behind a veil. In the silent regions of thought that has come to
itself and communes only with itself, the interests that move the life
of peoples and individuals are hushed. "In so many respects," says
Aristotle in the same context, "is human nature in bondage; but this
science, which is not pursued for any utility, is alone free in and for
itself, and for this reason it appears not to be a human possession."[24]

It may be, of course, that this "need of freedom from need" is never quite
satisfied, and that the very "modern life" that allows Hegel the freedom to
occupy himself with pure thoughts also regularly intrudes in the form of
"external necessity" on that freedom and strikes the work with necessary
contingencies and imperfections, which provokes an interesting comparison with Plato (and perhaps not entirely contingently, the Plato of the *Republic*), and indeed a reference to scatter:

> Anyone who in our times labors at erecting anew an independent
> edifice of philosophical sciences may be reminded, thinking of how
> Plato expounded his, of the story that he reworked his *Republic* seven
> times over. The reminder of this, any comparison, such as may seem
> implied in it, should only serve to incite ever stronger the wish that for
> a work which, as belonging to the modern world, is confronted by a
> profounder principle, a more difficult subject matter and a material of
> greater compass, the unfettered leisure had been afforded of rework-
> ing it seven and seventy times over. But the author, in face of the
> magnitude of the task, had to content himself with what could
> be made of it in circumstances of external necessity [*unter den
> Umständen einer äußerlichen Notwendigkeit*], of the inevitable distraction
> [*Zerstreuung*, dispersion, scatter] caused by the magnitude and multi-
> tude [*Vielseitigkeit*: multifacetedness, multifariousness] of contemporary
> interests, all the while in doubt whether the noisy clamor of the
> day and the deafening chatter of a conceit that takes pride in confining
> itself to just these interests, might still leave room for partaking in
> the dispassionate calm of a knowledge dedicated to thought alone.
> (21–22)

If the need to be free of needs cannot be realized, then one imagines that
the speculative dialectic will always be (at least contingently, but by a kind

24. G. W. F. Hegel, *The Science of Logic*, trans. and ed. George di Giovanni
(Cambridge: Cambridge University Press, 2010), 14.

of necessary contingency) falling short of its entire self-inwardizing as Spirit *bei sich*, and it thus leaves traces ("material" traces, in a sense to be specified) in the form of Hegel's always insufficiently revised written texts, which are then open to the further contingency of potential misreading. The famous Marxist claim, made explicitly in a text by Friedrich Engels,[25] to set the Hegelian dialectic on its feet again is of course important, but that corrective inversion does not escape the formal problem recognized here, and that shows up most saliently in Marxism as the tension between

25. See Engels, *Ludwig Feuerbach and the End of Classical German Philosophy*: "Hegel was not simply put aside. On the contrary, a start was made from his revolutionary side, described above, from the dialectical method. But in its Hegelian form, this method was unusable. According to Hegel, dialectics is the self-development of the concept. The absolute concept does not only exist—unknown where—from eternity, it is also the actual living soul of the whole existing world. It develops into itself through all the preliminary stages which are treated at length in the *Logic* and which are all included in it. Then it 'alienates' itself by changing into nature, where, unconscious of itself, disguised as a natural necessity, it goes through a new development and finally returns as man's consciousness of himself. This self-consciousness then elaborates itself again in history in the crude form until finally the absolute concept again comes to itself completely in the Hegelian philosophy. According to Hegel, therefore, the dialectical development apparent in nature and history—that is, the causal interconnection of the progressive movement from the lower to the higher, which asserts itself through all zigzag movements and temporary retrogression—is only a copy [*Abklatsch*] of the self-movement of the concept going on from eternity, no one knows where, but at all events independently of any thinking human brain. This ideological perversion had to be done away with. We again took a materialistic view of the thoughts in our heads, regarding them as images [*Abbilder*] of real things instead of regarding real things as images of this or that stage of the absolute concept. Thus dialectics reduced itself to the science of the general laws of motion, both of the external world and of human thought—two sets of laws which are identical in substance, but differ in their expression in so far as the human mind can apply them consciously, while in nature and also up to now for the most part in human history, these laws assert themselves unconsciously, in the form of external necessity, in the midst of an endless series of seeming accidents. Thereby the dialectic of concepts itself became merely the conscious reflex of the dialectical motion of the real world and thus the dialectic of Hegel was turned over; or rather, turned off its head, on which it was standing, and placed upon its feet."

"theory" and "practice" (or "interpreting the world" and "changing it") which remain philosophical concepts through and through.[26]

More specifically, the whole effort to think scatter in nonteleological and nondialectical terms involves asserting, not exactly *contra* Hegel—for any such contradiction plays into the dialectic—but *otherwise than* Hegel (and in the wake of Heidegger and more than one modern French philosopher) that it is at least *possible* for difference as such to be thought without its necessarily resolving itself dialectically into opposition, contradiction and sublation, as Hegel argues it must in the long account in *The Science of Logic* (361ff), including the claims that "Difference in itself is the difference that refers itself to itself; thus it is the negativity of itself, the difference not from another but *of itself from itself*; it is not itself but its other. What is different from difference, however, is identity [already treating difference as opposition, then]. Difference is, therefore, itself and identity"; that difference becomes diversity and that "diversity . . . is opposition" (365); and that "difference as such is already *implicitly* [*an sich*] contradiction" (374)). Or again, the more concisely quotable version from the *Encyclopedia Logic* (Part II, "The doctrine of essence," Section A "Essence as Ground of Existence," subsection a. "The pure determinations of reflection," subsubsection beta, "Difference [*Der Unterschied*]"[27]:

> §117 Difference is (1) *immediate* difference, *diversity* [*die Verschieden-heit*], in which each of the different [terms] *is* what it is *on its own account* and each is indifferent vis-à-vis its relation to the other, so that

---

26. See Derrida's seminar on *Theory and Practice*, trans. David Wills (Chicago: University of Chicago Press, 2019).

27. G. W. F. Hegel, *The Encyclopedia Logic: Part I of the Encyclopaedia of Philosophical Sciences with the Zusätze*, trans. T. F. Geraets, W. A. Suchting, and H. S. Harris (Indianapolis: Hackett, 1991). Throughout I have substituted the traditional rendering of *Unterschied* as "difference" for the term "distinction" used in the translation. In view of our earlier remarks on polar structures, it is interesting that in his remarks and additions to these paragraphs Hegel does indeed discuss magnetic polarity: see too Lyotard's repeated reference to a moment in Marx's *Critique of Hegel's Doctrine of the State*, where Marx argues that "real extremes" would not answer to Hegel's interpretation of difference: "true, real extremes, would be a pole as opposed to a non-pole, a human as opposed to a *non-human* sex." Karl Marx, *Early Writings*, trans. Rodney Livingstone and Gregor Benton (Harmondsworth: Penguin Books, 1975), 134, discussed by Lyotard in *Discours, figure* (Paris: Klincksieck, 1971), 138–141. See my "Figure, Discourse," *Contemporary French Civilization* 35, no. 1 (2011): 53–72.

the relation is an external one for it. Because of the indifference of the diverse [terms] with regard to their difference, the difference falls outside of them in a third, that *makes the comparison*. As identity of those that are related, this external difference is *equality* [*die Gleichheit*], as their nonidentity it is *inequality*.

§118 Equality is only an identity of [terms] that are *not the same*, not identical with one another—and inequality is the *relation* between unequal [terms]. So equality and inequality do not indifferently fall apart into diverse sides or aspects but each is a shining into the other [*ein Scheinen in die andere*]. Hence diversity is difference of reflection, or *difference that is in its own self, determinate* difference.

§119 (2) Difference *in its own self* [*an sich*] is essential [difference], the *positive* and the *negative*: the positive is the identical relation to self in such a way that it is *not* the negative, while the negative is what is different on its own account in such a way that it is *not* the positive. Since each of them is on its own account only in virtue of *not being the other one*, each *shines* within the other, and is only insofar as the other is. Hence, the difference of essence is *opposition* [*Entgegensetzung*] through which what is different does not have an *other in general*, but *its own other* facing it; that is to say, each has its own determination only in its relation to the other: it is only inwardly reflected insofar as it is reflected into the other, and the other likewise; thus each is the other's *own* other . . .

Addition 2 . . . Generally speaking, it is contradiction that moves the world, and it is ridiculous to say that contradiction cannot be thought. What is correct in this assertion is just that contradiction is not all there is to it, and that contradiction sublates itself by its own doing. Sublated contradiction, however, is not abstract identity, for that is itself only one side of the antithesis. The proximate result of opposition posited as contradiction is the *ground*, which contains within itself both identity and difference as sublated and reduced to merely ideal moments.

As Lyotard analyzes it in *Le différend*, this means that Hegel is already presupposing at the beginning of his discussion of difference that it will indeed resolve into diversity, opposition, and contradiction: our claim against this (with Lyotard, and in a slightly different way also with Derrida or Deleuze) is that it is at least *possible* to hold difference short of this resolution (and possibility is all we need here, as Hegel needs the sequence to be *necessary*), and that difference thought in this way (what Derrida calls *différance*, what

I am here calling scatter) cannot be presumed to give rise, via opposition and contradiction, to sublation. Another way of putting this is that in order to operate the dialectical resolution, Hegel has to apply to difference the notion of the absolute: *absolute* difference indeed resolves into diversity, opposition, and contradiction. But *différance* or scatter hold short of absolutizing in this way, and can be thought of as names (among others, for there will of necessity be a scatter of names for "scatter") for a non-absolutizability of difference, a holding back of difference *as* difference that inhibits or impedes its dialectical resolution.[28] As Derrida put it in *Positions*, "If there were a definition of différance, it would be precisely the limit, the interruption, the destruction of Hegelian sublation *everywhere* it operates."[29]

Although these passages in Hegel are, perhaps surprisingly, never the object of detailed published commentary by Derrida, on at least two occasions he states very clearly the importance of this moment. First in a very general context in the third interview collected in *Positions* (where he is being interviewed by dialectical materialists):

> I tried to distinguish *différance* . . . from Hegelian difference. At precisely the point where Hegel, in the *Greater Logic*, determines difference as contradiction* only in order to resolve, interiorize, sublate it, according to the syllogistic process of the speculative dialectic, into the self-presence of an onto-theological or onto-teleological synthesis.
>
> *[Derrida's note, presumably added after the interview:] Difference as such is already *implicitly* contradiction . . . (*Der Unterschied überhaupt ist*

28. This "holding short" or "holding back" can seem to bring Derrida's *différance* close to the Pauline *catechon*, "the restrainer," who or which holds back both the coming of the Antichrist and the second coming of the Messiah. This motif has been more or less persuasively deployed in political thinking, notably by Paulo Virno, Roberto Esposito, and Peter Szendy, and is something to which we will return elsewhere.

29. POS, 55/40–41. Given this very trenchant statement, it is striking that in her claim that everything has now been "definitively" deconstructed and that it is time to move on to something else, Catherine Malabou can suggest imperturbably that the replacement of the notion of *différance* by her own concept of plasticity—qua putative "motor scheme" of our time and the very thing we therefore need to move on to—should be thought of precisely as a "dialectical sublation" of *différance*, thus rather disarmingly showing that her own position at least has *not* in fact yet been deconstructed. See her "Postface" to the second edition of *L'avenir de Hegel: Plasticité, temporalité, dialectique* (Paris: Vrin, 2012), 264–265.

schon der Widerspruch an sich.) In no longer allowing itself to be simply subsumed under the generality of *logical* contradiction, *différance* (*process* of differentiation) allows one to take differentiating account of heterogeneous modes of conflictuality or, if you like, contradictions. If I have more often spoken of conflicts of forces than of contradiction, this is first of all through critical suspicion of the Hegelian concept of contradiction (*Widerspruch*) which, moreover, as its name suggests, is designed to be resolved within dialectical *discourse*, in the immanence of a concept capable of its own exteriority, and capable of having its outside-itself close to itself. (POS 59–60/44 and 101n13)

And in the other reading—or reconstruction—of this moment in Hegel, in the more specific—but probably decisive[30]—context of the determination of *sexual* difference as opposition, in *Glas:*

> Sexual difference is *overcome* when the brother leaves, and the other (sister and wife) remains. There is no longer any sexual difference *as natural difference.* "The sexes overcome their natural difference." Once overcome, sexual difference will have been merely a natural diversity. The opposition between difference and qualitative diversity is a hinge of the *Greater Logic.* Diversity is a moment of difference, an indifferent difference, an external difference, without opposition. While the two moments of difference (identity and difference, since identity differs, as identity) relate only to themselves and not to the other, while identity is not opposed to difference nor difference to identity, there is diversity. Diversity is, then, a moment of both difference and of identity, it being understood, quite explicitly, that difference is the whole *and* its own moment. Which is true too, then, of sexual difference: it is identity, identity is difference, itself the whole and its own moment.

30. See the initially surprising suggestion by Alain Badiou (after a number of almost equally surprising suggestions about Plato, Hegel, and Nietzsche): "Derrida transformed the classical approach to rigid metaphysical oppositions to a large extent because of the growing and irreducible importance, in our experiences, of their feminine dimension." *La relation énigmatique entre philosophie et politique* (Paris: Germina, 2011), 26 (my translation). See below some further remarks about sexual difference in Aristotle and Arendt; see also Emanuela Bianchi, *The Feminine Symptom: Aleatory Matter in the Aristotelian Cosmos* (New York: Fordham University Press, 2014).

In overcoming natural difference *as diversity* of the sexes, one moves to difference *as opposition*. In *Sittlichkeit*, sexual difference finally becomes a true opposition: which it was, moreover, *called*, destined to be.[31]

The "resistance" of difference to dialectical treatment has, *ex hypothesi*, an indefinite, diverse, or scattered number of possible names, and incalculable consequences. I believe that the names "democracy" and "matter" can help us to think through some of them. I want to say that in the area of political philosophy, "democracy" uneasily names something of the order of multiplicity, dispersion, or what I shall often prefer to term simply *scatter*. And *scatter* will sometimes best be thought of in terms of *matter*. "Scatter," I shall argue, in what I will suggest is a more Aristotelian spirit than Derrida recognizes, is at one and the same time the possibility of the political (the political bond always gathers a dispersion, on pain of not being political) and, simultaneously, the necessary possibility of its end (the dispersion constantly unbinds the bond and scatters, otherwise the political would become absorbed by the One and cease being political).

Although, as we shall see, this (muted, modest) stress on difference cannot be reduced simply to the motif of numerical multiplicity or plurality, of the Many (still less the Two) as opposed to the One (for scatter, as we said, will turn out to involve a multitudinous but also always a multifarious or variegated multiplicity), the simple fact of plurality does give us some initial opening onto the political aspect of our exploration. Here is a typically trenchant statement from Hannah Arendt from the opening page of her unfinished work *Was ist Politik?*:

> Politics is based on the fact of human plurality. God created *man*, but *men* are a human, earthly product, the product of human nature. Because philosophy and theology are always concerned with *man*, because all their pronouncements would be correct if there were only one or two men or only identical men, they have found no valid philosophical answer to the question: What is politics?

In Arendt's diagnosis, this means that "even in Plato" the great thinkers' political philosophies never reach the same depth as the rest of their works because of a failure to "sense the depths in which politics is anchored" (*Der*

---

31. GL 189a; English from the new translation by Geoffrey Bennington and David Wills, *Clang* (Minneapolis: University of Minnesota Press, forthcoming).

fehlende Tiefsinn ist ja nichts anderes als der fehlende Sinn für die Tiefe, in der Politik verankert ist).[32]

We might suspect that this slightly dismissive comment about political philosophy is itself part of the problem Arendt is trying to diagnose. Compare, especially for the "even in Plato," the more judicious assessment proposed by Derrida near the beginning of an as yet unpublished seminar from 1970–71:

> It is not simply true that philosophy has always made the political object into a particular object inscribed in the broader field of ontology or morality. Or rather that gesture, that narrow determination has a history in which we shall need to find our bearings. Since, as everybody knows, it is as pro- and explicitly political that philosophy opened itself with Plato, since philosophy was initially one with [*confondue avec*] politics or the political [*la ou le politique*] as such, something must have become organized, some determinate process must have been instituted such that the political came later to occupy only a specific and derivative domain in ontology or the Encyclopedia. Plato's *Politeia* is a book of general ontology. . . . Aristotle's *Politics* is already a specialized treatise. This discrepancy does not necessarily have to be interpreted in terms of an evolution. There has no doubt always been a double register for reading the political in philosophy, for reading political philosophy in philosophy. On the one hand, in the philosopher's very consciousness, the task of philosophy has always been, consubstantially, congenitally and coextensively, a political task *in the broad sense*, the program of an ideal organization of the city. That's an invariable that can also be followed from Plato to Husserl. And in this sense it is not a subversive proposition but one in conformity with most traditional philosophical consciousness to say that philosophy is political through and through.[33]

Granted the complications this would bring to Arendt's rather high-handed dismissal of the general quality of political philosophy, let us recognize her intriguing passing comment that will be precious for our attempt to think through scatter, in which Arendt asserts that "Men [*sic*] organize themselves politically according to certain essential commonalities found within or abstracted from an absolute chaos of differences [*in einem abso-*

---

32. "Introduction *into* Politics," in *The Promise of Politics*, 93. German text in *Was ist Politik?*, ed. Ursula Ludz (Munich: Piper Verlag, 2017), 9.
33. *Théorie du Discours Philosophique*, session I, 6.

luten Chaos oder aus einem absoluten Chaos der Differenzen]" This "chaos of differences," prior to (as it were) the "abstraction of commonalities" will certainly resonate with our notion of scatter. After a brief excursus on how unhelpful it is to try to think politics on the basis of family and kinship (to which we will return later), Arendt offers two principal, perhaps contradictory reasons for the supposed general failure of political philosophy, and again both of these reasons will resonate with our analyses, and, given the complication introduced by the Derrida seminar comments, will have broader effects on philosophy in general that Arendt intended:

> There are two good reasons why philosophy has never found a place where politics can take shape. The first is the assumption that there is something political *in* man that belongs to his essence.[34] This is simply not so; *man* is apolitical. Politics arises *between men* [*in dem Zwischenden-Menschen*], and so quite *outside* of *man*. There is therefore no real political substance. Politics arises in what lies *between men* and is established as relationships [*als der Bezug*]. Hobbes understood this.
>
> The second is the monotheistic concept of God, in whose likeness man is said to have been created. On that basis there can, of course, be only *man*, while *men* become a more or less successful repetition of the same. (95)

The issue of monotheism will indeed be detaining us at length soon enough. For now, let's pursue a little the thought that politics emerges from plurality (or more radically from the "chaos of differences"). The claim that this originary plurality or scatter communicates with the notion of democracy (as we shall see) brings us close, on this point at least, to some assertions by Jacques Rancière, who also interestingly relates it to the metaphysical desire we have already identified to bring politics to an end, to think politics as politics on the way to its end (both *finis* and *telos*):

> The art of politics is the art that consists in suppressing the political. It is an operation of self-subtraction. Perhaps the "end of politics" is then merely its fulfilment, the ever young fulfilment of its agedness. And it is perhaps this duplicity of the *techne politike* that philosophy has never ceased theorizing, beyond the opposition of the "ancients" and

---

34. The German text reads: "Der erste ist: I) Zoon politikon: als ob es *im* Menschen etwas Politisches gäbe, das zu seinder Essenz gehöre," more accurately translated as: "The first is: I) zoon politikon: as though there were *in* man something political, that belonged to his essence."

the "moderns." It is this ever-young end that it has always placed close
to the thought of foundation.

And just a little later:

> To designate, with Leo Strauss, the *Republic* or the *Politics* as works and
> paradigms of political philosophy, is perhaps to erase the originary
> tension of the relation between philosophy and politics: the coinciding
> of the desire to "do in truth the things of politics" claimed by the
> *Gorgias* and the desire to put an end to politics, to hear nothing more
> about it. In any case to put an end to the political as it presents itself,
> in its spontaneous, democratic state: the anarchic self-regulation of
> the multiple by majority decision.[35]

35. Jacques Rancière, *Aux bords du politique* (1992) (Gallimard, Folio Essais,
2004), 3; trans. Liz Heron as *On the Shores of Politics* (London: Verso Books, 1995),
11–12. See too, from the slightly later "Dix thèses sur la politique" (1996), not included in the English volume: "Democracy is the specific situation in which it is
the absence of entitlement that entitles the exercise of the *arkhé*. . . . But this situation of exception is identical to the very condition of any specificity of the political in general. . . . Democracy is thus in no way a political regime. . . . Democracy
is the very institution of politics. . . . The whole of politics . . . is at stake in the
interpretation of democratic 'anarchy.'" *Aux bords du politique*, 231 and 248. Rancière is perhaps remembering Marx's trenchant and much-debated claim in his
early *Critique of Hegel's Doctrine of the State* that "democracy is the *essence of all
political* constitutions." In Marx, *Early Writings*, 88. As for Badiou, whose hostility to democracy is well known, it is interesting to track a shift in his thinking
from *Peut-on penser la politique?* (Paris: Seuil, 1985), in which he aligns political
judgment—as do Lyotard and others—with the Kantian reflective judgment (75–
76), to *Abrégé de métapolitique* (Paris: Seuil, 1998), in which the idea that politics
comes under the reflective rather than the determinative judgment is attributed
(26) to a now vilified liberal parliamentarian position that views politics as the
domain of opinion (in Platonic fashion tarred with the brush of sophistry [ibid.,
23]), rather than (as increasingly with Badiou) with truth, the concept of which
here subsumes the concept of justice (ibid., 111). Compare Derrida's position on
this issue as discussed in *Scatter 1* (New York: Fordham University Press, 2016),
5–6 and 158–166. By the time of *Eloge de la politique* (Paris: Flammarion, 2017),
politics for Badiou is reduced to a quite simple and scarcely even dialectical opposition between capitalism and communism, which are supposedly now the only
two possibilities (22–23). The final explicit "éloge" of politics-as-communism in
the book is striking both for its humanism and its religious quality: "Of all the
enterprises—artistic, scientific, amorous or political—that humanity has proved
to be capable of, communism is no doubt the most ambitious, the most global,

These are precious comments, but still fall short of what is at stake here, and notably of what I proposed in the first volume of this work to call "the politics of politics." At least insofar as it is under the sway of theory, of *theōrein*, and is the product not in fact of the *bios politikos* but of the *bios theōrētikos* (as Spinoza sardonically points in a remark at the opening of the *Tractatus politicus* to which we shall be returning in due course), political philosophy attempts to reduce the politics out of politics, and it does this almost inevitably by trying to treat politics as the object of a theory (rather than the object of a politics). The failure (already in Plato) of this attempt to be purely theoretical would, on my hypothesis, already mark political philosophy as itself political, but perhaps no longer simply as philosophy (Machiavelli is the most obvious proper name to attach to this problem). This failure involves an *exposure* of political philosophy to politics (I am going to claim that this is a kind of *transcendental* exposure), an exposure that my "politics of politics" doublet is attempting to capture, and which will resonate in due course with what Derrida calls "autoimmunity." Neither Arendt nor Rancière really comes close to what I have called "the politics of politics," the somewhat diabolical doubling whereby, among other things, any political *philosophy* is (also) *political* philosophy. This does not simply make it the least philosophical and most "everyday life" kind of philosophy, as Strauss thought, but as it were infects philosophy, like a virus, with the necessary possibilities of what philosophy from its Platonic inception needs always to eliminate and expel as sophistry and rhetoric. This "politics of politics" resonates with another slogan I have often used, namely that, in the conceptual schemas of political philosophy,

---

and the one that will radiantly raise the human race above the laws of competition, of survival at any price, of private interest, of constant hostile distrust of others, which are all laws of raw life, animal laws, natural laws. The new communism . . . is, finally, the exit from humanity's stone age. . . . Every truth, that of a theorem finally clearly understood, like that of a successful and promising political meeting, is a work of eternity, an eternity the affect of which is a shared kind of beatitude" (139–140, my translation). In general, Badiou is perhaps rashly confident that he can unproblematically detach the "fabular content" from metaphysical and Christian sources and continue to use the same vocabulary without detriment to his thinking: see *Saint Paul: La fondation de l'universalisme I* (Paris: PUF, 1999), 6; and *Second manifeste pour la philosophie* (Paris: Flammarion, 2010), 122–123n4 on his attachment to religious concepts (or concept-names), and 119–120: "Descartes spoke of the 'creation of eternal truths.' I take up the same program without the help of God."

"the end of politics is the end of politics." The (not entirely philosophical) "politics of politics" works against the (very philosophical) "end of politics" by interfering with the teleological structures that are endemic in political philosophy. The politics of politics is both a condition of possibility and a condition of impossibility of politics: it is what endlessly prevents politics from reaching its end(s),[36] maintains politics *as* politics, endlessly (though as we shall see, not entirely aimlessly: *skopos* need not be the same as *telos*).

The thought that politics is always already engaged in the politics of politics also distinguishes *Scatter 2* from the interesting and compelling but insufficiently thought through (insufficiently deconstructed) positions of Foucault and, in his wake, Agamben, both of whom want to displace the focus of political thought away from the theme of sovereignty toward that of what Foucault calls "governmentality," and what Agamben (for once recognizing the problems in Foucault's periodizing) tracks throughout the tradition in terms of *economia* and *dispositio*. Foucault's position is clear and, shall we say, trenchant:

> I wonder if this [the view of power as dividing those possessing it from those subjected to it, *mutatis mutandis* the "repressive hypothesis"] is not linked to the institution of monarchy. . . . Political theory has remained obsessed by the person of the sovereign. All these theories are still posing the problem of sovereignty. What we need is a political philosophy that is not constructed around the problem of sovereignty, and therefore of law, and therefore of interdiction; we have to cut off the king's head and this has not yet been done in political theory.[37]

36. To this extent, "the politics of politics" is close to what Chantal Mouffe calls "the democratic paradox," and would certainly agree with her claim that "To imagine that pluralist democracy could ever be perfectly instantiated is to transform it into a self-refuting ideal, since the condition of possibility of a pluralist democracy is at the same time the condition of impossibility of its perfect implementation." Chantal Mouffe, *The Democratic Paradox* (London: Verso Books, 2000), 16. See also, as part of her critique of Rawls, 32: "pluralist democracy becomes a 'self-refuting ideal' because the very moment of its realization would coincide with its disintegration." I think that this logic of "self-refuting ideals" is much more broadly generalizable, and that it is in fact inscribed in the very logic of Ideas in the Kantian sense.

37. "Entretien avec Michel Foucault," in *Dits et écrits* (Paris: Gallimard, 2001), 2:150 (my translation).

Agamben's learned genealogical complication of this, especially in the volume *The Kingdom and the Glory* (the most interesting and least dogmatic of his *Homo Sacer* series) leads to a conclusion he puts more bluntly in the collective volume *Democracy in What State?*, summarizing *The Kingdom and the Glory*:

> In a recent book I tried to show that the central mystery of politics is not sovereignty but government; not God but his angels; not the king but his minister; not the law but the police—or rather, the governmental machine they form and propel.
>
> Our Western political system results from the coupling of two heterogeneous elements, a politico-juridical rationality and an economic-governmental rationality, a "form of constitution" and a "form of government." Incommensurable they may be, but they legitimate and confer mutual consistency on each other. Why does the *politieia* get trapped in this ambiguity? What is it that gives the sovereign, the *kyrion*, the power to ensure and guarantee the legitimacy of their union? What if it were just a fiction, a screen set up to hide the fact that there is a void at the center, that no articulation is possible between these two elements, these two rationalities? What if the task at hand were to disarticulate them and force into the open this "ungovernable" that is simultaneously the source and the vanishing point of any and all politics?[38]

Assuming that this is even intelligible (but let's concede that what seems unintelligible here—a legitimating incommensurability—comes from the tradition Agamben is exploring rather than from his analysis of it), and that Agamben has correctly identified something like an aporia affecting the whole tradition, we might reasonably suspect that simply "cutting off the king's head," as Foucault wishes or fantasizes, would be part of the problem rather than its solution (we shall see that sovereignty in fact always entails a certain "paregisuicide," that means that the severed head of the sovereign is, as it were, part of the logic of sovereignty itself and certainly not its overcoming), and that its displaced version in Agamben (tearing down the screen, exposing the fiction, showing that the Wizard of Oz is no wizard at all or perhaps more pertinently that the Emperor has no clothes) is a rather simplistic and pious approach to what is a more intractable aporia than can be dealt with in these brisk terms of a "task at hand."

38. Giorgio Agamben, Alain Badiou, et al., *Democracy in What State?*, trans. William McCuaig (New York: Columbia University Press, 2011), 4.

We shall see in the course of our own readings that in Rousseau, for example (a major figure in the elaboration of Agamben's conclusion), something of this tension (between sovereign and government) is in fact clearly "articulated" in terms of a quite lucid logic of supplementation, usurpation and, indeed, *execution*. And, again as we shall see, we might say the same for Aristotle's complex analysis of the figure of the One Best Man or Absolute Monarch which, like its counterpart in a radical form of Absolute Democracy, already quite lucidly shows up "the source and the vanishing point of any and all politics."

The politics of politics bespeaks, in the language of the always-already,[39] what metaphysics can only apprehend as a fall or a corruption. This language of a purity subsequently corrupted or infected, a language which is metaphysical through and through, survives in many contemporary discussions, and no doubt always goes along with an inadequate understanding of temporality and historicity. To put it crudely, the tensions between metaphysics and politics we have been following thus far might be at least in part produced by the fact that the theoretical or contemplative time of metaphysics is, tendentially, of the order of eternity (as Badiou would confirm) or some phantasy of infinite time—philosophy in principle demands all the time in the world, even if in practice it (luckily) never has that time available to it—whereas political time is the time of decision and action, of finding the right time or *kairos*, an always finite time that draws metaphysics down and away from its lofty aspirations and back into the realm of politics. Like Hegel interrupted by the surrounding clamor of life and thus unable to revise his book as much as a strictly philosophical approach would demand, philosophy in general finds itself short of time and therefore back in a context that is always at least in part political.

As an example of the persistence of this type of metaphysical schema in recent—and otherwise politically sympathetic—thinking about politics, Michael Hardt and Antonio Negri assert in their *Multitude* that by going "back to the eighteenth century" we can find a time when "the concept of

---

39. See Derrida's precious clarification of this pervasive deconstructive motif in *Heidegger: The Question of Being and History*, trans. Geoffrey Bennington (Chicago: University of Chicago Press, 2016), 42: "The signification of 'always already' is the historical translation or rather the historical foundation of the signification 'a priori.' The *always* modifies the *already* in such a way that the already does not depend on this or that contingent situation, but has a value of unconditioned universality. The always wrests the historicity of the *already* from empiricity."

democracy was not corrupted as it is now."[40] One page later, however, we are told that "we have to find a way to free ourselves of the tenacious ghosts of the past that haunt the present and cripple our imagination," (308), and then one page later again, "As the Federalists said in the eighteenth century, the new times require a 'new science' of society and politics. . . . A new science of global democracy would not simply restore our political vocabulary from the corruptions it has suffered" (309). A little later still: "Now, with the cold war over and the first experiments of global order completed, we cannot help but recognize the planet as a sick body and the global crisis of democracy as a symptom of corruption and disorder . . . the corruption of life in its entirety" (352–353).[41] One of the points of scatter is that there was no time before the "corruption," and there can be no time after it. This does not mean that all politics is *equally* corrupt or that there is no point fighting against corruption in the narrower sense, simply that there is no horizon of purity or noncorruption to be aimed for. This means that the superficially attractive claim that "sovereignty in all its forms inevitably poses power as a rule of the one and undermines the possibility of a full and absolute democracy" (353) itself repeats the problem it is claiming to address by the adoption of a language of sovereignty ("full and absolute") in the attempt to contest that same language.

40. Michael Hardt and Antonio Negri, *Multitude: War and Democracy in the Age of Empire* (New York: Penguin Press, 2004), 307. Subsequent page references will be given in the text.

41. In their earlier *Empire* (Cambridge, MA: Harvard University Press, 2000), Hardt and Negri had argued for a nonmoral use of the term "corruption" (although they recognize that current usage of the term has itself become corrupt compared to an older usage). There, they claim that "It is important to make clear that we in no way intend our definition of imperial sovereignty as corruption to be a moral charge. In its contemporary and modern usage, corruption has indeed become a poor concept for our purposes. It now commonly refers only to the perverted, that which strays from the moral, the good, the pure. We intend the concept rather to refer to a more general process of decomposition or mutation with none of the moral overtones, drawing on an ancient usage that has been largely lost. . . . We have to forget all the commonplace images that come to mind when we refer to imperial decadence, corruption, and degeneration. Such moralism is completely misplaced here" (201–202). Quite apart from the fact that it is quite impossible to wish moralism away by trying to stipulate the content of an inherited concept in this way, it seems clear that the way "corruption" is being used in the final pages of *Multitude* does not obey the strictures enounced here in *Empire*.

In any case, the tension we are pursuing is certainly not resolved by Hardt and Negri, who are still trying to develop a "new science" that reflects a "new ontology" (312). The "mosaic" they promise (xvii), which might sound like a version of scatter, is still too ontological, too beholden to a metaphysical notion of truth.[42] Their proposal to "combine Madison and Lenin" (355) dreams that it can combine a revolutionary abolition of sovereignty with "institutional procedures that guard against dramatic reversals and suicidal errors" (355). But that promise of truth is in fact, quite traditionally, the end of politics. Further, their invocation of the *kairos* as "the moment when the arrow is shot by the bowstring, the moment when a decision of action is made" (357), cannot, as they think, be coordinated with the thought that "the constituent power of the multitude has matured to such an extent that it is becoming able, through its networks of communication and cooperation, through its production of the common, to sustain an alternative democratic society on its own" (ibid.). The motif of "maturing" precisely presupposes the "linear accumulation of Chronos" to which they want (but fail) to *oppose* the thought of *kairos*. This temporal configuration then becomes straightforwardly Pauline, and the cutting, interruptive potential of *kairos* is blunted by the thought of a "fullness of time." So the authors' (rather loose) philosophical ambition for their work ("This is a philosophical book . . . Our primary aim is to work out the conceptual bases on which a new project of democracy can stand" [xvi–xvii]) remains in thrall to just the kind of "tenacious ghosts of the past that haunt the present and cripple our imagination" that we saw them warn against. Whatever the sympathy and solidarity one may feel for their political ambitions, the "conceptual bases" they are working on are not new at all, but metaphysical, teleological,[43] and thus condemned in spite of themselves to moralism.

42. See too the more recent *Assembly* (Oxford: Oxford University Press, 2017), which not only reaffirms its commitment to ontology (their word for "the world as it is" [xviii]) and truth ("truth is not given but constructed, not substance but subject" [ibid.; the reference to Hegel is explicit at xiii]), but is happy to project (with an implicit reference to Gramsci) a "new Prince . . . emerging on the horizon, a Prince born of the passions of the multitude," and then tries, quite characteristically, to have its metaphysical cake and eat it too: "This Prince thus appears as a swarm, a multitude moving in coherent formation" (xxi).

43. In *Empire*, Hardt and Negri lay explicit claim to a "new materialist teleology," drawing initially on Althusser's reading of Machiavelli (*Empire*, 63–64) and clarify their position on this in a much later note at 368: "Obviously when we

As it happens, Hardt and Negri open the main text of their most recent book, *Assembly*, with an epigraph from Homer that they proceed to ignore in the body of their text, as though it were self-explanatory. As we shall now go on to see, this line from Homer has a long and distinguished afterlife in the Western tradition from Aristotle onward, and indeed it will provide the principal guiding thread for the rest of the *Scatter 2*.

---

speak about a materialist telos we are speaking about a telos that is constructed by subjects, constituted by the multitude in action. This involves a materialist reading of history which recognizes that the institutions of society are formed through the encounter and conflict of social forces themselves. The telos in this case in not predetermined but constructed in the process. Materialist historians such as Thucydides and Machiavelli, like the great materialist philosophers such as Epicurus, Lucretius, and Spinoza, have never negated a telos constructed by human actions. As Marx wrote in the introduction to the *Grundrisse*, it is not the anatomy of the ape that explains that of humans but, vice versa, the anatomy of humans that explains that of the ape (105). The telos appears only afterwards, as a result of the actions of history" (*Empire*, 470). *Scatter* thinks that this account of teleology is still perfectly Hegelian, and that a more careful reading of the Marx passage would in fact provide for something more complicated than that "the telos appears only afterwards." Marx goes on to qualify the sense of the anatomy argument: "Although it is true, therefore, that the categories of bourgeois economics possess a truth for all other forms of society, this is to be taken only with a grain of salt. They can contain them in a developed, or stunted, or caricatured form etc., but always with an essential difference. The so-called historical presentation of development is founded, as a rule, on the fact that the latest form regards the previous ones as steps leading up to itself, and, since it is only rarely and only under quite specific conditions able to criticize itself—leaving aside, of course, the historical periods which appear to themselves as times of decadence—it always conceives them one-sidedly." Karl Marx, *Grundrisse: Foundations of the Critique of Political Economy*, trans. Martin Nicolaus (London: Penguin Books, 1973), 106.

CHAPTER 2

Polykoiranie I (Derrida, Homer, Aristotle, Xenophanes)

At the very end of Book Lambda (12) of the *Metaphysics*, often referred to as his "theology,"[1] Aristotle famously quotes a line from Homer's *Iliad*:

> And those who say mathematical number is first and go on to generate one kind of substance after another and give different principles for each, make the substance of the universe a series of episodes (for one substance has no influence on another by its existence or non-existence), and they give us many principles; but the world must not be governed badly.
>
> "The rule of many is not good; let there be one ruler [*ouk agathon polykoiranie. heis koiranos esto*]." (1075b37–1076a3)

As we shall see, this line from Homer, and more especially Aristotle's quotation of it here, has an immense afterlife in the tradition we often call

---

1. For a measured account of this very traditional assessment, see Fabienne Baghdassarian's Introduction to her new French translation, *Aristote: Métaphysique Lambda* (Paris: Vrin, 2019).

"Western metaphysics," from Philo Judaeus, via early Christian apologists, through Dante, Bodin and La Boétie, and up to Erik Peterson and Carl Schmitt, Jacques Derrida, and beyond. The apparent promise it implies, of some convergence or harmonization of metaphysics, theology and politics—and even aesthetics, if we relate the "series of episodes" remark here to an almost equally famous remark from a different book of the *Metaphysics*, to the effect that "nature is not a series of episodes, like a bad tragedy" (1090b20)—has made this ending, and especially this closing, quoted, line, irresistible to a great many different authors across the entire timespan from Aristotle to our own day.[2] As we shall go on to see, it is most often invoked (often enough as though it were a direct statement by Aristotle rather than a quotation from Homer) in support of a monotheistic view of theology and a monarchistic view of sovereignty, which it is most often read as opposing to some form of democracy. The poles of sovereignty on the one hand and democracy on the other will indeed provide the general framework of this book.

Let me begin with a recent invocation of the line from Homer, by Jacques Derrida in *Rogues*. In the first numbered section of the first of two texts in that book, "The Right of the Strongest (Are There Rogue States?)," Derrida has been allusively putting in place many of the elements he will

2. "With confident blows of the hammer he chisels magnificent sentences, which even today we involuntarily read aloud, in spite of the abbreviated nature of notes made for oral delivery. 'The creative activity of thought is life.' 'All things are ordered towards an end.' 'On this principle hang the heavens and nature.' The conclusion, where he addresses the Platonic dualists in the words of Odysseus ('the rule of many is not good, one ruler let there be [*Niemals frommt Vielherrschaft im Volk; nur einer sei Herrscher, Einer König allein*]'), is positively stirring in effect. It is a document unique of its kind, for here, and here alone in his lectures, Aristotle boldly sketches his picture of the universe in its totality, disregarding all questions of detail." Werner Jaeger, *Aristotle: Fundamentals of the History of His Development*, trans. Richard Robinson, 2nd ed. (Oxford: Oxford University Press, 1948), 219. It seems that Jaeger does not, however, mention this line in his later work *Paideia*, which was suspected of Nazi sympathies in its depiction of the "strong leader" Pericles and is the object of oblique criticism in Heidegger's 1942 seminar, nominally on Hölderlin's Hymn "Der Ister," but with an extended central section around Sophocles, in the course of which Heidegger is critical of those who would present the Ancient Greeks as "the true National Socialists." We return below to the possible resonances Homer's line might have in the context of National Socialism.

go on to develop in his discussion of democracy and sovereignty, of democratic sovereignty, of sovereign "ipseity" and the "rotundity" and even "sphericity" associated with that ipseity. After quoting Tocqueville from *Democracy in America*, to the effect that in American democracy power resides intrinsically in the social body (and not outside or above it), Derrida uses a theologico-political analogy in Tocqueville to transition to his quotation from Aristotle:

> [Tocqueville] then gives what he considers to be a demonstrative description of the organization of executive and legislative powers, before concluding the chapter with the trope of a theological figure that he believes to be conventional and purely rhetorical but whose necessity seems to me much more serious and important: "The people," he concludes, "reign over the American political world as God rules over the universe. It is the cause and the end of all things; everything rises out of it and is absorbed back into it." (34/14)

This is part of Derrida's setting up of the question he goes on to explore (and to which we will be returning often), namely the troubled and troubling relationship between democracy and sovereignty:

> I will perhaps have to confess that what tortures me, the question that is putting me to the question, might just be related to what structures a particular axiomatics of a certain democracy, namely, the turn, the return to self of the circle and the sphere, and thus the ipseity of the One, the *autos* of autonomy, symmetry, the homogeneous, the same, the like, the similar, and even, finally, God, in other words everything that remains incompatible with, even clashes with, another truth of the democratic, namely, the truth of the other, the heterogeneous, the heteronomic, the dissymmetric, disseminal multiplicity, the anonymous "anyone," the "no matter who," the indeterminate "each one." (V 35/14–15)

And this setup leads directly to the reference to Aristotle and the quotation from Homer we are approaching:

> For the democratic God of which Tocqueville speaks, this sovereign cause of itself and end for itself, would also resemble—and this resemblance has not ceased provoking us to think—pure Actuality, the *energeia* of Aristotle's Prime Mover (*to proton kinoun*). Without moving itself or being moved, the actuality of this pure energy sets everything in motion, a motion of return to self, a circular motion, Aristotle specifies, because the first motion is always cyclical. (V 35/15)

After some remarks about life, desire and enjoyment, Derrida quotes Aristotle's claim that "the unmovable first mover is one both according to the *logos* [conventionally translated as "in formula"] and in number; therefore also that which is moved always and continuously is one alone; therefore there is one heaven alone" (1074a35–38).

In the quite complex rhetoric of Derrida's presentation, this whole invocation of Aristotle in the wake of Tocqueville is now explicitly motivated by the fact of Aristotle's ending this book of the *Metaphysics* with the quotation from Homer from which we began. Unlike most of the authors we shall see quoting this line (he does not mention any, perhaps for once unaware of the long tradition to which he is contributing here), Derrida characteristically does a certain amount of work to recontextualize the line Aristotle quotes,[3] and, to the best of my knowledge unlike any of the other authors who quote it, sees it as Aristotle's own almost submissive invocation of the sovereign authority of Homer himself. Here is the initial gloss leading to Derrida's quotation of Aristotle's quotation:

> If . . . I refer in this way to Aristotle's *Metaphysics* before turning to his *Politics*, it is because the final sentence of this book proposes a political analogy. Aristotle quotes the *Iliad* (2.204). The end of this book 12 (Lambda) thus seems written under, or underwritten [*signee, soussignée*] by the sovereign authority of Homer, of his words and his verdict, in a place where Homer himself is citing a word of sovereign authority. Present on the scene are Athena, daughter of Zeus, and an Odysseus who is compared to Zeus. The saying is elliptical and thus sententious. It cites a verdict and is thus placed under the guard of a sovereign authority. What does it say? It declares, declares itself by declaring the One and the sovereignty of the One, of the One and Only [*Unique*], above and beyond the dispersion of the plural. These lines caution against the government of many, against *polykoirania*. Aristotle excerpts them, then, from a long tirade. After having reprimanded the man of the people (*demou andra*), warning him, "In no wise shall we Achaeans all be kings here," the two lines pronounce a sententious, performative, and jussive sentence: "No good thing is a multitude of lords; let there be one lord, one king [*ouk agathon polykoiranie. heis koiranos esto, heis basileus*]." (V 36–37/16. In fact Aristotle breaks off his

---

3. In spite of common misapprehensions, deconstruction, which indeed affirms the necessary possibility of escape from any given context as a condition of readability, often enough uses careful recontextualization as providing deconstructive purchase on a given text.

quotation before the last two words, omitting the *heis basileus*, thus making the line even more elliptical and sententious.)

Without, a little strangely perhaps, making it entirely clear to the reader that in the *Iliad* these lines are in fact spoken by Odysseus (Erik Peterson, whose work in general is marked by an almost extravagant erudition, surprisingly misattributes the line to Agamemnon, as we shall see later), nor indeed registering the fact that Aristotle does not explicitly refer this line to Homer by name at all (nor, one can only assume, would he have used quotation marks, not available in Ancient Greek), which might be taken to complicate slightly any supposed appeal to "the sovereign authority of Homer," Derrida goes on to give the whole of what he calls the "tirade" from which the line is taken, and which I quote first in the venerable translation by A. T. Murray, as used by the translators of *Rogues*:

> "Fool [*daimoni*], sit thou still, and hearken to the words of others that are better men than thou; whereas thou art unwarlike and a weakling, neither to be counted in war nor in counsel [*boulē*: deliberative assembly]. In no wise shall we Achaeans all be kings here. No good thing is a multitude of lords; let there be one lord, one king, to whom the son of crooked-counselling Cronos hath vouchsafed the scepter and judgments, that he may take counsel for his people." (*Iliad* 2.200–206)

Compare with the more recent blank verse translation by Robert Fagles:

> You *fool*—sit still! Obey the commands of others,
> your superiors—you, you deserter, rank coward,
> you count for nothing, neither in war nor council.
> How can all Achaeans be masters here in Troy?
> Too many kings can ruin an army—mob rule!
> Let there be one commander, one master only,
> endowed by the son of crooked-minded Cronus
> with kingly scepter and royal rights of custom:
> whatever one man needs to lead his people well.[4]

4. Homer, *The Iliad*, trans. Robert Fagles (Harmondsworth: Penguin Books, 1990), 106. Compare Alexander Pope's verse translation, which foregrounds the proper name of Zeus and shifts slightly the sententious force of the proposition a little to the negative evaluation of *polykoiranie*, which is given greater political scope than the text really warrants: "Be silent, wretch, and think not here allow'd / That worst of tyrants, an usurping crowd. / To one sole monarch Jove

Before pursuing Derrida a little further in his reading of the indirect reference to Zeus and his lineage, let's pause on this textual scene from Homer from which Aristotle takes the line that we will be following. From what Derrida calls this "tirade," Aristotle, as we saw, takes only the words "*ouk agathon polykoiranie. heis koiranos esto*," "no good thing is a multitude of lords; let there be one lord" in the Murray translation, "Too many kings can ruin an army—mob rule! Let there be one commander . . ." in Fagles's much more active version, which might seem to buy its fluency at the cost of potentially confusing the reader by specifying that the problem is really only a military one (the words "ruin an army" do not correspond to anything in the Greek), then taking the *koiranos* root of *polykoiranie* to refer to "kings" ("too many kings"), but the word *koiranos* itself to mean "commander," presumably in a military sense. This is further complicated by the fact that either side of the line quoted by Aristotle, Fagles translates the Greek *basileus* as "master," whereas that word might normally be a better candidate for translation as "king."

Murray's rather dated version at least has the advantage of consistency here: he indeed translates *basileus* as "king," and *koiranos* as "lord." Still, it remains a little unclear how to construe the different "leadership" terms in play here, and to decide whether Odysseus is making a general ("political") claim, or more narrowly one to do with military discipline.[5] This leads to two further issues the reader of this book of the *Iliad* faces. One is that *basileus* and *koiranos* are far from being the only two "leadership" terms in play (here and indeed throughout Homer and beyond): the other is that it is difficult to understand exactly what we might call the pragmatics of the scene, in which Odysseus is urging the case for, not of course his own, but Agamemnon's monarchy (or at least mono-archy, sole authority)

---

commits the sway; His are the laws, and him let all obey." George Chapman's famous 1611 Keats-inspiring translation: "'Stay, wretch, be still/And heare thy betters. Thou art base, and both in power and skill/Poore and unworthie, without name in counsel or in warre./We must not all be kings. The rule is most irregularre/Where many rule. One Lord, one king propose to thee; and he/To whom wise Saturn's sonne hath given both law and Emperie/To rule the publicke is that king.'"

5. See Filippomaria Pontani, "What Is Polykoiranie? Aristotle and Aristarchus on Il. 2, 204," *Hyperboreus* 18, no. 1 (2012): 75–86, at 77. When Aristotle uses the analogy of an army and its general at *Metaphysics* 1075a14, he uses the term *stratēgos* (which also appears regularly in the *Nichomachean Ethics* and the *Politics*)—a term that does not appear in Homer.

over the Achaeans, but in doing so is addressing not other potentially bothersome candidates for such a role, but the common soldiers who, one imagines, have no kind of say in the matter anyway.

On the first of these questions, it is striking to take note of Homer's rich and varied vocabulary of leadership. Alongside *koiranos* and *basileus*, which we have encountered so far, the terms *anax, archos, hēgemōn,* and *kreiōn* all appear, and Agamemnon is also regularly described as *poimena laon*, which Fagles in his militarily-inclined way usually renders as "field marshal" and Murray consistently and a little more literally as "shepherd of the host."[6] These terms are not simply synonyms—and *poimena laon* is a figurative expression on a slightly different level, literally "shepherd of the people"[7]—and they are not all treated as such in the Fagles translation (*hēgemōn* is consistently "captain," *archos* is "leader"), but a good number of them (*anax, kreiōn, basileus, koiranos*) are often plausibly enough translated as "king." For now, let us simply register this plurality of terms and the slightly awkward way they sit with the stress on the One: Odysseus (in the fuller version of the quotation, a little beyond what Aristotle actually quotes), says that there should be one . . . what exactly? One King, one Lord, one ruler or leader, and he says so perhaps in a general political sense, but perhaps also in a more restricted military context: it might not, for example, be implausible to hold both that *military polykoiranie* is a bad idea, and that some sort of nonunitary exercise of leadership in *political* life might be a good idea: Fagles's bold use of "mob rule" in this context seems as though it might foster misapprehension of this possibility. (In due course, we will see that in the other place in the *corpus aristotelicum* where this same line of Homer is quoted, in the *Politics*, to which Derrida is announcing a transition but in which he does not seem to have noticed the return of the

6. See the note to this line in G. S. Kirk, ed., *The Iliad: a Commentary: Volume I, Books 1–4* (Cambridge: Cambridge University Press, 1985), 137: "*Koiranos* is an evidently ancient word, occurring only occasionally in Homer and later poetry, for a leader in war (usually) or peace. It was probably superseded in general use by *anax* and *basileus*, both common in the Linear B tablets, as they became more and less specialized respectively."

7. On this very common figure, see Roger Brock, *Greek Political Imagery from Homer to Aristotle* (London: Bloomsbury Academic, 2013), chap. 3, "The Shepherd of the People," and more especially Michael Naas's incisive critique of Foucault's reading of the motif of "pastoral power" in Plato in "Plato's State of Exception: Foucault's Exclusion of Pastoral Power from the Dialogues," *theory@ buffalo* 15 (2011): 49–76.

Homer quote, Aristotle *himself* notes an ambiguity in the Homeric formulation that will not fail to be of interest to us.)

The multiplicity of leadership terms is not the only slightly perplexing feature of the passage in which the condemnation of *polykoiranie* occurs. The second issue mentioned above involves what we might call the pragmatics of the scene. In this second book of the *Iliad*, Agamemnon is encouraged in a dream sent by Zeus to marshal his armies for the final assault on Troy. In what we might think is not the most obviously kingly or masterful exercise of his own *koiranie*, he decides to test the mettle of his troops by in fact ordering them to board their ships and prepare to sail away without victory over Troy. This test seems to fail quite spectacularly, as the troops are all too keen to obey and make for home. Spurred on by Athena, Odysseus is charged with winning over the soldiers with his *aganois epēessin*, his "gentle words" (Murray) or "winning words" (Fagles), and making them stay and prepare for battle in spite of Agamemnon's explicit, but tricky, order to take to the ships. To do so, Odysseus first takes Agamemnon's scepter (possession of which perhaps marking the current chief, lord, king, or leader: Murray has him simply "receiving" the scepter from Agamemnon's hand; Fagles has him "relieving" Agamemnon of the scepter). He is then described in an iterative way as making two kinds of speech to the troops (who one imagines now to be quite confused about what they are supposed to do).

Before reading these speeches or "tirades," we might spend a moment on the scepter which recapitulates a genealogy that goes back to the gods, and more specifically to Zeus. Here too there is some tension between the one and the many: Agamemnon, rising from his dream and making his way to address first his council and then the troops as a whole, takes up the *skeptron patroion aphthiton aiei*, "the scepter of his fathers, imperishable ever" (Murray) and goes first to announce his plan to the council, which itself consists of *skeptrouchoi basilees*, scepter-bearing kings. As the troops gather, heralds tell them to listen to the kings (in the plural): then *kreiōn Agamemnon*, "King Agamemnon" (Fagles) or "lord Agamemnon" (Murray), rises, holding what Homer now unpacks as the very special scepter that is Agamemnon's and that Odysseus will take or receive from him before his iterative speeches to which we are coming shortly. This is no ordinary scepter, but:

> Hephaestus made [it] with all his strength and skill.
> Hephaestus give it to Cronus' son, Father Zeus,
> and Zeus gave it to Hermes, the giant-killing Guide

and Hermes gave it to Pelops, that fine charioteer.
Pelops gave it to Atreus, marshal of fighting men,
who died and passed it on to Thyestes rich in flocks
and he in turn bestowed it on Agamemnon, to bear on high
as he ruled the many islands and lorded mainland Argos.

Holding this scepter among scepters, then, Odysseus first harangues (with those "winning" or "gentle" words) *tina basilēa kai exochon andra kicheie*, "whomsoever he met that was a chieftain or man of note" (Murray), "some man of rank, a king" (Fagles). Here is how Odysseus addresses the nobles, in the Fagles translation:

> "My *friend*—it's wrong to threaten you like a coward,
> but you stand fast, you keep your men in check!
> It's too soon to see Agamemnon's purpose clearly.
> Now he's testing us, soon he'll bear down hard.
> Didn't we all hear his plan in secret council?
> God forbid his anger destroy the army he commands.
> The rage of kings is strong, they're nursed by the gods,
> their honor comes from Zeus—
> they're dear to Zeus, the god who rules the world."[8]

Whereas, as we saw, the "tirade" to the common soldiers whom he finds "shouting out" (I imagine "mouthing off" might also be a reasonable translation: Murray has "brawling," either from a misprint for "bawling" or a more active interpretation) begins "You *fool*—sit still . . .": the friend/fool alternative in fact trying to capture a nuance in the Greek where the term of address is actually the same in both cases, *daimonie*, here not directly to do with gods or daemons, and usually something like "good sir," but open to ironic or antiphrastic uses.

The parallelism between this speech to the "man of note," and the harangue to the common soldier we saw above and will quote again shortly, is emphatic: but there can seem something puzzling about Odysseus' choosing to make his apparently "political" and monarchical point when talking, precisely not to the "men of note," whom one imagines might have some issues with the overall command of Agamemnon, for whose absolute authority Odysseus is arguing, whereas the common soldiers presum-

---

8. "The god who rules the world" is a rather free translation of *metieta Zeus*, which Murray translates as "god of counsel," but the root of which is *metis*, a term to which we return shortly.

ably represent no genuine threat to that command structure. And indeed this puzzlement went so far as already to motivate Aristarchus of Samothrace, one of the earliest scholars of Homer, to suggest in the 2nd century BCE, that the lines including the "verdict" are simply misplaced where they stand, and should in fact be moved to the *earlier* harangue to the "men of note," replacing the lines in which Odysseus expresses concern over Agamemnon's anger.[9]

Without yet pursuing the way in which the *polykoiranie* line was indeed very often subsequently taken up and quoted in both pagan and Christian authors, let us for now simply note a further complication in what I have been calling the pragmatics of the scene. The speaker here, as is often forgotten when the line becomes a self-standing adage or maxim, is Odysseus, the one whose "winning words" are most often associated not with truth, sincerity, and reliability, but with indirection, deviousness, lying, and manipulation. (This does not at all exclude Odysseus from being himself a leader or a king: immediately after the second tirade, he is described as *koiraneon*, masterfully managing the army.) As Détienne and Vernant put it in their classic study of the notion of *metis* in Ancient Greece, Odysseus, the *aner polytropos* of the opening line of the *Odyssey*,[10] is *metis* incarnate, the very embodiment of ruse and trickery.[11] And further, the authority that is being constantly invoked throughout, including in this very speech, namely that of Zeus, whose scepter confers authority on Odysseus, is itself shot through with a comparable uncertainty and unreliability As Derrida does spend some time in *Rogues* discussing these references to Zeus, let us look a little more closely at this aspect of the text.

9. On this suggestion by Aristarchus, see Kirk's commentary at 137 ("This is clearly wrong—Aristarchus at his weakest and most subjective"), and Pontani, who is more sympathetic to Aristarchus's position: "Aristarchus' main argument, taken at face value regardless of the overall rhetorical strategy pursued by Homer (through his character), is not absurd: why should Odysseus remind a group of simple privates the principles presiding over the sphere of political power, to which they will never have direct access (democracy remaining, even in *Iliad* II, conspicuously remote from Homer's political horizon)?" "What Is *Polykoiranie?*" 77.

10. "Many-sided hero" (Butler); "The man of twists and turns" (Fagles); "a complicated man" (Wilson).

11. Marcel Détienne and Jean-Pierre Vernant, *Les ruses de l'intelligence: La mètis des grecs* (Paris: Flammarion, 1978).

Derrida quotes the "tirade" just after announcing that he will later, "in the margins of Plato, Aristotle, and Rousseau," speak of "One God, of the One God or of the God who is One" [*d'Un Dieu, de l'Un Dieu ou du Dieu Un*]"—and we will indeed pursue him at length in that later discussion. After the quotation of the tirade, Derrida immediately picks up on the indirect reference to Zeus which is made right after the line that Aristotle quotes, and goes on to make a characteristically bold and dense set of claims:

> "No good thing is a multitude of lords; let there be one lord, one king, to whom the son of crooked-counselling Cronos hath vouchsafed the scepter and judgments, that he may take counsel for his people." (*Iliad* 2.200–206)

An allusion to Zeus, from whom issue the kings. And Zeus is a son. There is a lineage [*souche*] here. The defeat of the father, the putting to death of the *Urvater*, as Freud would say, parricide and regicide, are not without relation to a certain genealogical, filial, and especially fraternalistic interpretation of democratic equality (liberty, equality, fraternity): a reading of the egalitarian contract established between rival sons and brothers, in the succession of the father, for the sharing of *kratos* in the *demos*. Zeus is first of all a son, a male child and a descendent who, by means of ruse (*metis*), but also with the help of his mother, escapes from time. He thus wins out over [*a raison de*] his father, Cronos, who himself had won out over, having in his turn emasculated him, his own father, Ouranos. It is by winning out over time, by putting an end to the infinite order of time, so to speak, that he asserts his sovereignty. One might take this formula to the extreme, to the point where it touches the end of time, touches the finitude or the finity of time, touches sovereignty as the instant of a decision that, at the indivisible point of its act, puts an end to time, as well as to language (and we will see what's at stake here later).

Through this parricidal theogony there rages a political struggle over monarchic sovereignty, the intent of Cronos being to prevent one of his sons from taking up in his stead, as Hesiod puts it, "the kingly office amongst the deathless gods." Among the guardians of his son Zeus, himself a combination of ruse and force, are *Kratos* and *Bia* (*Bie*), power and violent force. Whether or not this theogonic mythology of sovereignty is inaugural, it belongs to, if it does not actually inaugurate, a long cycle of political theology that is at once paternalistic and patriarchal, and thus masculine, in the filiation father-son-brother. I would also call it ipsocentric. This political theogony or theology gets revived or relayed (despite claims to the contrary by experts on Bodin and Hobbes, whom I cannot treat here) by the so-called modern political theology of monarchic sovereignty and even by the unavowed political theology—itself just as phallocentric, phallo-paterno-filio-fraterno-ipsocentric—of the sovereignty of the people, that is, of democratic sovereignty. The attribute "ipsocentric" intersects and links with a single trait all the others (those of the phallus, of the father, of the husband, of the son or the brother). *Ipsocentric* could even be replaced by *ipsocratic*, were that not a pleonasm, for the idea of force (*kratos*), of power, and of mastery, is analytically included in the concept of ipseity. (V 37–38/16–17)

There is much more in this passage than we can hope to address immediately, and indeed in some ways in lays out a whole program of reading and reflection that *Scatter II* hopes modestly to advance. What is of interest immediately is that this elaboration of the reference to Zeus in the immediate context of our line about *polykoiranie* opens what I would call a typical Derridean scenario, whereby Derrida first reads the texts of the tradition according to their main and most explicit lines of force, according to what his earlier work would call their "propos déclaré" or simply what they "declare," and subsequently (but of necessity never exhaustively) explores other possibilities, their "autre geste," or what they—in spite of themselves and their best intentions, perhaps—*describe* rather than what they *declare*.[12] Texts in general (at least texts of sufficient complexity) always propose readings of themselves. As Derrida puts it at the end of the *Grammatology*, they say "A," and immediately interpret "A" as meaning "B," whereas "A" harbors other resources, to be read, that may stand in some relation of tension and even contradiction with "B." On a Derridean construal, we are not really reading if we only read "A" as "B," taking the text's word for it, as it were, but nor are we reading if we fail to register that "A" is being interpreted as "B" by the text, and simply rush off to some other reading of "A" that happens to please us more. Deconstructive "double reading" involves the more or less respectful recognition or reconstruction of how the text proposes to read "A" as "B," as well as the exploitation of those "other resources," that the text in question has "preferred to cut short."[13]

12. The terms "propos déclaré" and "autre geste" are used in the reading of Saussure in *De la grammatologie* (45); the distinction between declaration and description is used repeatedly of Rousseau, for example at 310–311 and 326.

13. "Rousseau says A, then, for reasons we must determine, he interprets A as B. A, which was already an interpretation, is reinterpreted as B. After taking

It is, then, entirely predictable that in cases where, for reasons about which we might speculate, Derrida foregrounds the first part of that double gesture, and *himself* stabilizes a text around its *propos déclaré*, there should be potential for other readings of the *autre geste*, of the undeclared-but-described aspects or strata of texts. This means that the most Derridean gesture in reading Derrida, and in reading Derrida's readings, is to recognize and respect Derrida's own declarations (already quite a difficult task that is far from complete), but then also to pursue other possibilities that he has, for one reason or another, not exploited. (The standard way that this has been done, which consists in more or less indignantly defending this or that author—most typically Hegel—against Derrida on the grounds that they are "already saying" what Derrida is taken to be claiming in his own name, is based on a misapprehension of this structure.) In the most general terms, this means that the text of "Western metaphysics" as metaphysics of presence, is also from the start shot through with other possibilities that are not completely under control and are not exhausted by their "official" metaphysical presentation. If, then, we throughout this book propose readings that do not always literally agree with Derrida's own, this is done in what we might reasonably call a "Derridean spirit," in the hopes of making a modest contribution to the ongoing deconstruction of the tradition. (It is perhaps no accident that these preliminary "methodological" reflections were provoked by a passage about inheritance and lineage, fathers, sons, and parricide. The point in rereading these scenes and their like in what I just called a Derridean spirit is to try to displace—and indeed deconstruct—the alternatives of simple repetitive or commemorative filial piety on the one hand, and on the other of more or less ill-concealed Oedipal rage and rejection that can be discerned in the recent work of some of Derrida's erstwhile students and commentators.)

We can return to the long passage from *Rogues* and begin to open it up along these eminently deconstructive lines by noting Derrida's own passing reference to Zeus's exercise of *metis* in overthrowing his father Cronos. Odysseus's "tirade" closes on a reference to Zeus as confirming or authenticating the claim of Agamemnon to what it is indeed tempting to call sovereignty over the Achaeans. In reference to line 197, from Odys-

---

note of that fact, we can, without; leaving Rousseau's text, isolate A from its interpretation as B and find in it possibilities, resources of meaning that indeed belong to Rousseau's text, but which have not been produced or exploited by it, but which, for reasons that are themselves readable, and by a gesture that is neither conscious nor unconscious, he *preferred to cut short*" (G 434).

seus's first tirade to the "men of note"—"Proud is the heart of kings, fostered of heaven; for their honour is from Zeus, and Zeus, god of counsel, loveth them" (Murray); "The rage of kings is strong, they're nursed by the gods,/their honor comes from Zeus/they're dear to Zeus, the god who rules the world" (Fagles)—Allen Rogers Benner states confidently and rather anachronistically in his notes dating from 1903: "Note the emphasis continually laid on the belief that the Homeric king rules by divine right." But in the habitual exercise of *metis*, Zeus is opened to what Détienne and Vernant brilliantly diagnose in their account of "the myths of sovereignty." Whether it be in Hesiod's *Theogony*, as here appealed to by Derrida, or in Aeschylus's *Prometheus Bound*, Zeus gets to be king by ruse and trickery, and will himself, as a result, eventually and inevitably be brought down by ruse and trickery. Sovereignty (and therefore, if we follow Derrida, "ipseity" in general) is simultaneously secured and undermined by ruse and trickery, by *metis*: we are not far from what Derrida increasingly in his later work called "autoimmunity."

Given the "genealogy" explicitly presented in the *Iliad*, this will lead to some redoubtable complications as we try to read the line we are following. The scenario of Book II opens with an insomniac Zeus sending an *oulon oneiron* ("murderous dream," Fagles; "a baneful dream," Murray) to trick Agamemnon into believing he can conquer Troy that very day. As we have seen, Agamemnon announces the dream to his council (where Nestor says that "If any other Achaean had told us of this dream/we'd call it false [*pseudos*]") along with his "cunning plan" to test his men by lying to them about the dream and claiming that Zeus is ordering them all to return home without victory. The levels of lying are hard to stay on top of here: Zeus is lying because he wants Agamemnon to suffer and get the Greeks "slaughtered against their ships"; to achieve this he tells him that he will in fact win victory by attacking Troy that day; Agamemnon, believing that lying prediction, in turn lies about it to his men by telling them they should pack up and return home as a way of testing their morale and obedience and thereby supposedly indirectly preparing them for a triumphant attack on Troy. Here is Agamemnon's lying speech in the Murray translation:

> My friends, Danaan warriors, squires of Ares, great Zeus, son of
> Cronos, hath ensnared me in grievous blindness of heart, cruel god!
> seeing that of old he promised me, and bowed his head thereto, that
> not until I had sacked well-walled *Ilios* should I get me home; but now
> hath he planned cruel deceit, and bids me return inglorious to *Argos*,

when I have lost much people. So, I ween, must be the good pleasure of Zeus, supreme in might, who hath laid low the heads of many cities, yea, and shall yet lay low, for his power is above all. A shameful thing is this even for the hearing of men that are yet to be, how that thus vainly so goodly and so great a host of the Achaeans warred a bootless war, and fought with men fewer than they, and no end thereof hath as yet been seen. For should we be minded, both Achaeans and Trojans, to swear a solemn oath with sacrifice, and to number ourselves, and should the Trojans be gathered together, even all they that have dwellings in the city, and we Achaeans be marshalled by tens, and choose, each company of us, a man of the Trojans to pour our wine, then would many tens lack a cup-bearer; so far, I deem, do the sons of the Achaeans outnumber the Trojans that dwell in the city. But allies there be out of many cities, men that wield the spear, who hinder me mightily, and for all that I am fain, suffer me not to sack the well-peopled citadel of *Ilios.* Already have nine years of great Zeus gone by, and lo, our ships' timbers are rotted, and the tackling loosed; and our wives, I ween, and little children sit in our halls awaiting us; yet is our task wholly unaccomplished in furtherance whereof we came hither. Nay, come, even as I shall bid, let us all obey: let us flee with our ships to our dear native land; for no more is there hope that we shall take broad-wayed *Troy.*

And in the terms of the narrative, it appears that the Greeks would indeed have sailed away (thus failing Agamemnon's risky test, but also in their own way thwarting Zeus's altogether bloodier plan for them), had not the goddess Athena been alerted by the goddess Hera and herself (in disguise) appealed to an Odysseus here explicitly compared by the narrator to Zeus in terms precisely of *metis* (he is described at II, 169, as *dii metin atalanton,* "a mastermind like Zeus," Fagles; "the peer of Zeus in counsel," Murray; also the peer of Zeus in *metis,* cunning), addressing him not only as "sprung from Zeus," but as *polymechanos,* resourceful, literally the man of many machinations, and leading directly to the first of the two "tirades" we have been discussing.

So the tagline quoted by Aristotle, from which our adventure begins, is to say the least complicated when read in its immediate context or co-text. Whether or not Derrida is really justified in saying that in quoting this line Aristotle is appealing to Homer's "sovereign authority," we can easily see that any such authority is not simple. The line is spoken by a dubiously sovereign character (Odysseus is a "king," perhaps, and often referred to as such, but not The One King, even as he seems to speak for that One

King), a dubiously sovereign character the major characteristics of whom are ruse, indirection, manipulation, and lying, in a pragmatically confusing circumstance, with an authority from a "king of the gods" himself characterized by those same *metis*-related qualities, and the more especially as part of a sequence of downright lies extending from the dream Zeus sends to Agamemnon, to Agamemnon's lying about it to his men, and in so doing unwittingly furthering Zeus's treacherous plan. What there might be of sovereignty here seems, to say the least, somewhat complicated by these contextual features.

Needless to say, however, and for essential reasons, such complications never stopped a line escaping from its context—and a good thing too, because without the possibility of such escape, reading would become impossible, and we would at best be condemned to doing history.[14] And that necessarily possible escape from context is the more evident in the case of a sententious line such as this, the aphoristic structure of which already suggests a cut from any context (*aphorizein*, to separate off, to set apart), and invites what long ago I called an "anthologizing reading," which eagerly separates out the sententious utterance and sets it somewhere different, perhaps in a list or a dictionary of gems or pearls of wisdom. So when this line shows up in the *Characters* of Theophrastus, for example, who may perhaps have picked it out from Aristotle's quoting it in the *Metaphysics*,[15] it is the "one and only line of Homer's" that the Oligarch or authoritarian knows,[16] and the very possibility of that "one and only [*hen monon*]," that "one-liner" quality of the line seems inscribed in the line itself in at least a double way: first in that *any* sententious proposition tends to present itself as a "one and only," to stand proud of its contexts and invite repetition elsewhere,[17] and a second time in that the line is in this case explicitly *about* a "one and only" being better than

---

14. It would be easy to show that the possibility of "doing history" is itself dependent on a prior escape from context, even as the historian strives more or less successfully to put things back into the context from which they have escaped: history starts only after the fact of that escape and always somewhat in denial of it.

15. Theophrastus was Aristotle's immediate successor as head of the Lyceum.

16. Theophrastus, *Characters*, edited and translated by Jeffrey Rusten and I. C. Cunningham (Cambridge, MA: Harvard University Press, 2003), 126–127.

17. Kirk in his commentary refers to "the noble-sounding generalization of 204 (*ouk agathon polykoiranie*), perhaps a traditional poetic epigram suitable for several different kinds of occasion" (137). See my analysis of this feature of aphorisms

a "many." Our tagline capitalizes on the thematic of the One implicitly to urge its *own* special Oneness, thus making it plausible that the Oligarch (but more still, as we shall be going on to see, the Monarch) need indeed know no other line of Homer—or perhaps of anybody else—at all. In spite of all the complications we have pointed to in Homer's text, and the ways they can, and perhaps should, undermine the sententious authority of this line, its standing as a *sententia maxima*, it tends to rise imperturbably above those complications and asserts itself, asserts its own assertion, almost tautologously asserts in formally sovereign fashion the superiority of the One superior, the superiority of the Sovereign. Whatever complications we detected in the multiplicity of "leadership" terms in the *Iliad* rapidly recede as this line is allowed to stand alone and make its sovereign claim. To that extent Derrida (who first energetically taught us that possible "escape from context" is a necessary feature of marks in general) is not wrong to suggest that in quoting this line Aristotle is appealing to something like a sovereign authority, and indeed beginning to take on some of that authority: later appeals to this same line will often forget that it is taken from Homer and attribute its authority to that of The Philosopher himself, whose thought will then over a period of centuries and a complex process of interpretation and appropriation, parts of which we shall be following, become increasingly aligned with a different Sovereign, Lord of All, King of Kings. To that extent, this single line will allow for and convey the single *trait* of ipsocentrism as Derrida diagnoses it in the passage we quoted following the genealogy back through Zeus, and in so doing its fate will be, as it were, a key witness to the construction of what we have come, after Heidegger, to call ontotheology or the metaphysics of presence. And to the same extent, this line puts what Derrida in *Rogues* might have called a "torturing question" to our capacities as readers: for if we take what there really is every reason to call its *declaration* seriously, then we risk becoming unable to read it in any strong sense at all. In declaring the superiority of the One, the line does what it can to preclude anything other than one meaning for itself ("not good is a multiplicity of meanings: let there be one meaning!"), and this implicit claim to monosemia cannot but tend to repress all efforts to read it otherwise. And there is nothing surprising about this: the very tradition we are trying to read differently is very committed to

---

and maxims in *Sententiousness and the Novel* (Cambridge: Cambridge University Press, 1985), 55–63.

reading itself in general as One and the Same, and to construing meaning in general in terms of One.

As we saw, Derrida, reading Aristotle's *Metaphysics* in the wake of his reference to Tocqueville, stresses the thought that sovereign ipseity is in a meaningful sense circular or spherical. "The return to self of the circle and the sphere . . . Everything is cyclical, circular, and spherical in what the *energeia* of the Prime Mover puts in motion, the incorruptibility of substance being linked to the circular eternity of motion" (V 35–36/14–15). Just before quoting our line from Homer, Derrida concludes his summary of book Lambda thus:

> After long historical considerations about the number of spheres
> and heavens thus put in motion, Aristotle concludes that "the Prime
> Mover, which is immovable, is one both in formula [in *logos*] and in
> number [*hen ara kai logō kai arithmō to prōton kinoun akinēton on*];
> and therefore so also is that which is eternally and continuously in
> motion [*kai to kinoumenon ara aei kai sunekhōs*]." (*Metaphysics* 12.1074a).
> (V 36/15–16)

This type of circular or spherical figure does not originate with Aristotle, and may have come to him from pre-Socratic sources. Of these, we might take a moment to reference Xenophanes of Colophon (c. 570–c. 478 BCE), "the first Greek thinker to offer a complex and at least partially systematic account of the divine nature" (Stanford Encyclopedia of Philosophy), often presented as the teacher of Parmenides, who has, at least as reported by "pseudo-Aristotle," a rather charming argument[18] that runs as follows:

---

18. For a serious (if rather eccentric) attempt at a positive reconstruction of Xenophanes' "natural theology," see the chapter "The Divine Philosophy of Xenophanes" in Jonathan Barnes, *The Presocratic Philosophers* (London: Routledge, 1982 [1979]), 82–99. I call Barnes's chapter "eccentric" in part on the basis of the juxtaposition of quite hard analytic-style reconstruction of arguments with sentences such as the following, redolent of that strange academic object called "Oxford" (Barnes is arguing against an interpretation held by Nietzsche among others, to the effect that Xenophanes was a mystic): "If that is true, then Xenophanes is the progenitor of that pestilential tribe of theological irrationalists, whose loudest member is Martin Luther and whose recent aspirations to philosophical respectability have been encouraged from the grave by the palsied shade of the late Wittgenstein" (85). More generally, Barnes imperturbably, and without explanation, organizes his encyclopedic book into three main sections, entitled respectively "Eden," "The Serpent," and "Paradise Regained," and leaves it

Further, [Xenophanes] says that if God is the most powerful of all
[*apanton kratiston*, the most powerful of all, we might be tempted to say
sovereign], He must be one. For if there were two or more gods, He
would no longer be the most powerful and best [*beltiston*] of them all.
For each of the many being a god would also share His characteristics.
For the essence of God and of His power is to rule and not to be ruled,
and to be the most powerful of all. In so far then as He is not most
powerful He is not God. But supposing that there are many gods in
some respects more powerful than each other, and in other respects
less so, they would not be gods; for it is the essential nature of God not
to be subject to any control. Supposing that there were equal gods
none of them would have the nature of gods; for God by nature must
be most powerful of all; but that which is equal is neither better nor
worse than that to which it is equal. If then God exists, and such is
His character, God must be one alone. If this were not so, God could
not do whatever He wished. He could not if there were more gods:
therefore God must be one. But being one He must be similar in
every direction, both having power to see and to hear and all the
other senses in every part. For otherwise different parts of God would
control and be controlled by each other; which is impossible. Again,
Xenophanes says that being alike in all parts He must be spherical;
for He cannot be of such a kind in one direction and not in another,
but must be of that kind in every part. But being eternal, and one,
and spherical He must be neither limited nor unlimited . . .
(977a14–977b4)[19]

On this argument, which pseudo-Aristotle finds unimpressive, the Oneness of God (in what we will see is a crucially double sense—there is only
one, and that one is utterly one, unified, thoroughgoingly one with itself—
this double sense of "One" will return many times in what follows) entails
the sphericity we saw Derrida associate with the circular and cyclical character of ipseity more generally.

Some commentators have, apparently, been less inclined than Jonathan
Barnes to view Xenophanes's positions as rational and coherent. Notably

---

to the reader to decide what to make of that juxtaposition of the Presocratic and
the Christian.

19. (Pseudo-)Aristotle, in Aristotle, *Minor Works*, trans. W. S. Hett (Cambridge, MA: Harvard University Press, 1936), 482–483.

on the basis of Diels-Kranz fragment B23,[20] the first line of which reads
"*heis theos, hen te theiosi kai anthrōpoisi megistos*" [most obviously translated
as "[There is] one god, one greatest among gods and men"], there can seem
to be an elementary contradiction between the apparent monotheism of
the "there is one god," and the apparent polytheism implied by the "among
gods." As Barnes points out, the reading that would have "one greatest god
among gods and men" seems to gesture toward a Homeric-type polytheism, "a hierarchy of divinities ruled by a greatest god, as the Homeric Zeus
rules, with uncertain sway, the Olympian pantheon" (89–90). Interestingly
enough, as we prepare to follow Derrida in his passage from Aristotle's
Metaphysics to his *Politics*, a related suspicion might hang over our understanding of the line from Homer we are following. For the very concept
of *polykoiranie* being criticized by Odysseus might plausibly be taken to
mean two slightly different things: it could mean that it is a bad thing for
there to be more than one leader/lord/king (perhaps equals disputing
among themselves for *primus inter pares* status: this would perhaps be the
thought that motivated Aristarchus's editorial suggestion mentioned
earlier): but it could also mean that it is a bad thing for there to be effectively *no* leader, or a leadership exercised collectively by many at once (an
equally plausible interpretation of the term *polykoiranie*, or "mob rule" as we
saw Fagles translate it), namely democracy, "ochlocracy," or perhaps anarchy. And if we turn to the only other invocation of our tag line in the
corpus aristotelicum, which is indeed in the *Politics* (Derrida does not mention it and perhaps overlooked it), then what emerges is that Aristotle
himself is very aware of that ambiguity. In a discussion in book 4 of the
different types of democracy, the logic of which will detain us at length
later, Aristotle comes to a fifth type, apparently a radical democracy in
which the assembled people make decisions on all things by decree, rather
than by appeal to any established law, and ends his discussion by
remarking:

> Another kind of democracy is where all the other regulations are the
> same, but the multitude is sovereign [*kurion*: Jowett has "supreme
> power"] and not the law; and this comes about when the decrees of

20. This corresponds to Xenophanes fragment 35 in *The Texts of Early Greek
Philosophy: The Complete Fragments and Selected Testimonies of the Major Presocratics*,
trans. and ed. Daniel W. Graham (Cambridge: Cambridge University Press,
2010), 1:110.

the assembly over-ride the law. This state of things is brought about by the demagogues; for in the states under democratic government guided by law a demagogue does not arise, but the best classes of citizens are in the most prominent position; but where the laws are not sovereign [*oi nomoi mē eisi kurioi*], then demagogues arise; for the common people become a single composite monarch, since the many are sovereign not as individuals but collectively [*monarchos gar o dēmos ginetai synthetos heis ek pollōn, oi gar polloi kurioi eisin ouk os ekatos alla pantes*].[21] Yet what kind of democracy Homer means by the words 'no blessing is the lordship of the many'—whether he means this kind or when those who rule as individuals are more numerous, is not clear. (*Politics* 1292a4–15; trans. Rackham)

This lack of clarity here detected by Aristotle in our line from Homer, to do with "the many in one" will, arguably at least, complicate our understanding of Aristotle himself: both of the *Politics* and its understanding of monarchy on the one hand and democracy on the other, but also, in return as it were, of the *Metaphysics* and the nature of the One and of God.

In one of Derrida's many later returns to Aristotle in *Rogues*, the question of the Oneness of God reemerges as a crucial element in the analysis of sovereign ipseity more generally. Derrida is impressed by an apparently incidental or merely rhetorical feature of Rousseau's account of democracy (of which much more later), when Rousseau says that democracy would be the appropriate form of political regime for a "people of gods," but cannot work for humans. Here is Derrida:

The plural that then affects the word *gods*, the dissemination by which it is literally taken into account (the gods, yes, but how many, and will they be as equal as they are free?), this *more than one* [*plus d'un*] announces democracy, or at least some democracy, beyond government and democratic sovereignty. This "more than one" affects God with divisibility where sovereignty, that is, force, *cracy*, does not however suffer division, where the force of the One God, single and sovereign [*du Dieu unique, un et souverain*], *qua* power of political sovereignty, will have been called single, one and indivisible [*une,*

21. Jowett has "For the people becomes a monarch, and is many in one; and the many have the power in their hand, not as individuals, but collectively"; C. D. C. Reeve's recent translation (Indianapolis: Hackett, 2017), producing a clever rhetorical effect not strictly corresponding to the Greek, gives "For the people become a monarch, one monarch composed of many people, since the many are in control not as individuals but all together."

unique et indivisible] by all those who have conceived of sovereignty, from Plato and Aristotle to Bodin, Hobbes, and Rousseau.

These last three even, literally, used the word *indivisible* to qualify the essence of sovereignty, of sovereign government. As for Plato and Aristotle, each time in treating democracy as a government, and thus as a political regime, as a paradigm or constitution, they named God, it was always by attributing to him an exceptional and indivisible oneness [*unicité*]. This political salute to the One God signs, by turns, the *Politikōs* and the *Politikon*, that is, the *Statesman* of Plato (303a–b) and the *Politics* of Aristotle (3.1283b.8, 13–15). (V 110–111/75–76)

Derrida's quite insistent placing of Plato and Aristotle as essentially equivalent in this respect is a fairly consistent feature of his work: Plato-and-Aristotle, even more than Socrates and Plato,[22] seem to form the founding couple of Western metaphysics as metaphysics of presence and as ontotheology, here centered, as it were, on the Oneness of the One God as the very figure of sovereign ipseity in general.

As we began to suspect with Aristotle's lesser-known invocation of our Homeric tagline in the *Politics*, however, that Oneness, the oneness of the One, does not have to wait until Rousseau to find itself pluralized and "disseminated." We might even want to say that the "One" [*to hen*] is *itself* not at all so self-evidently One, if only because it seems to be trying to gather up the subtly different valences that Derrida's text marks without quite thematizing: namely the One as single (but perhaps just one among others); the One as unique (the only one), and the One as unified or indivisible ([at] one with itself). As Aristotle explicitly recognizes in a different book of the *Metaphysics* (Book Iota is devoted to the question), *to hen*, the one, is a *pollachos legomenon*, the One is said in many ways (as is, most famously but not at all uniquely, Being, *to on*, to which *to hen* is ambiguously assimilated). One of the suspicions we will be pursuing is that Aristotle's quite acute awareness of this complication in our understanding of the One (this intrinsic plurality or not-quite-oneness of the One, we might want to say) opens onto possibilities of deconstructive reading that are not quite registered in Derrida's gesture whereby Aristotle is here (and indeed most often) placed alongside Plato in their supposed "salut politique au Dieu Un."

22. As famously read by Derrida in the "Envois" section of *La carte postale*.

CHAPTER 3

Polykoiranie II (Philo Judaeus, Early Christian Apologists, Pseudo-Dionysius)

The fragment from Xenophanes that some suspected of inconsistency between an affirmation of monotheism and an implication of polytheism in spite of itself, is attested only on the basis of a quotation by Clement of Alexandria, often considered to be the first Christian philosopher, in a work perversely enough entitled *Stromata*, usually translated as *Miscellanies*, but which we might almost be tempted to translate as "scatterings." In that work (5.14), Clement is arguing that the Greeks essentially plagiarized their philosophy from the Jews, and more especially from the Bible and its presumed author, Moses. This is not an entirely new theory in the second century CE, when Clement is writing: as early as the second century BCE, Jewish authors had already made similar claims, with Aristobulus of Alexandria suggesting (at least as reported by Clement himself, as in turn reported by Eusebius of Caesarea) that the Greeks had read the Hebrew Bible in a translation that predated that of the Seventy,[1] and that Homer

---

1. On evidence of Greek versions of scripture antedating the Seventy, see also Maren R. Niehoff, *Jewish Exegesis and Homeric Scholarship in Alexandria* (Cambridge: Cambridge University Press, 2011), 31–32.

and Orpheus, among others, had plagiarized that text in their poetry. A century or two centuries later respectively, the most famous of the Alexandrian Jewish authors, first Flavius Josephus and then Philo Judaeus, provided a good deal of material subsequently drawn on by the second century CE Christian apologists (including Clement of Alexandria himself), who try to show not only that Christianity has its roots in ancient Judaism, but that Plato and the pagan poets directly plagiarized Moses. Whatever the complex historico-political details of these claims,[2] and whatever their value in establishing some priority of "Judeo-Christianism" over Hellenism, it is striking that they bring their authors into proximity with the Ancient Greeks and involve an abundant practice of citation.[3] And in Philo Judeaeus's often very bold and even rather wild allegorical interpretations of texts, we see one of the earliest examples after Aristotle of our line from Homer being quoted.

In a work preciously for us entitled *On the Confusion of Tongues*, which is essentially an allegorical reading of the story of the Tower of Babel, Philo has an interesting and unusual defense of democracy, at least in the "allegorical" sense in which the individual soul can be described in terms of a political regime (this Platonic parallelism between state and individual will be detaining us at length later on):[4]

2. In tracking down these early quotations of the line from Homer, I am indebted to the learned work of Nicole Zeegers-Vander Vorst, *Les citations des poètes grecs chez les apologistes chrétiens du IIe siècle* (Louvain: Université de Louvain Recueil des Travaux d'Histoire et de Philologie, 1972), at 180–186. Zeegers-Vander Vorst is herself indebted for several of these references to Erik Peterson's almost extravagantly erudite tractate "Monotheism as a Political Problem," to which we shall return later.

3. See, much later (early fifth century CE), the judgment of St. Jerome: "To prove the antiquity of the Jewish people Josephus wrote two books against Appio a grammarian of Alexandria; and in these he brings forward so many quotations from secular writers as to make me marvel how a Hebrew brought up from his childhood to read the sacred scriptures could also have perused the whole library of the Greeks. Need I speak of Philo whom critics call the second or the Jewish Plato?" (Letter LXX, To Magnus, an Orator of Rome).

4. Philo's support for democracy is not simply or merely allegorical, however, as appears from a remark in his work *On the Unchangeableness of God*, part of a sequence stressing what we might call the world-historical mutability of human affairs: "Greece was once at its zenith, but the Macedonians took away its power. Macedonia flourished in its turn, but when it was divided into portions it weakened till it was utterly extinguished. Before the Macedonians fortune smiled on the Persians, but

The words, "Come, let us build for ourselves a city and a tower whose head shall be unto heaven," suggest such thoughts as these. The lawgiver thinks that besides those cities which are built by men's hands upon the earth, of which the materials are stones and timber, there are others, even those which men carry about established in their souls. Naturally these last are models or archetypes, for the workmanship bestowed upon them is of a more divine kind, while the former are copies composed of perishing material. Of the soul-city there are two kinds, one better, the other worse. The better adopts as its constitution democracy, which honors equality and has law and justice for its rulers—such a one is as a melody which sings God's praises. The worse, which corrupts and adulterates the better, as the false counterfeit coin corrupts the currency, is mob-rule [*ochlocratia*], which takes inequality for its ideal, and in it injustice and lawlessness are paramount.[5]

On Philo's reading, itself clearly quite close to Platonic motifs in several respects, it is the "ochlocratic" organization that takes on the Babelian ambition to build a tower and "make a name" for itself: "Let a tower be built as a citadel, as a royal and impregnable castle for the despot [*tyrannos*] vice. Let its feet walk upon the earth and its head reach to heaven, carried by our vaulting ambition to that vast height." (§§112–113). Those who have

a single day destroyed their vast and mighty empire, and now Parthians rule over Persians, the former subjects over their masters of yesterday. The breath that blew from Egypt of old was clear and strong for many a long year, yet like a cloud its great prosperity passed away. What of the Ethiopians, what of Carthage, and the parts towards Libya? What of the kings of Pontus? What of Europe and Asia, and in a word the whole civilized world? Is it not tossed up and down and kept in turmoil like ships at sea, subject now to prosperous, now to adverse winds? For circlewise moves the revolution of that divine plan which most call fortune. Presently in its ceaseless flux it makes distribution city by city, nation by nation, country by country. What these had once, those have now. What all had, all have. Only from time to time is the ownership changed by its agency, to the end that the whole of our world should be as a single state, enjoying that best of constitutions, democracy" (173–176; Loeb 3, 95–97). The editors of the Loeb volume provide a helpful note (at 489) with further references to Philo's positive characterization of democracy, and they point out that this does not seem to come to him from either Plato or Aristotle.

5. Philo, "On the Confusion of Tongues," translated by F. H. Colson, in *Philo IV* (Cambridge, MA: Harvard University Press, 1932), 23, §§107–109, 69.

such an ambition, proceeds Philo, have the "monstrous and extravagant shamelessness" to want to "make themselves a name":

> What sort of name, then, do you desire? Is it the name that best befits your deeds? Is it one name only? One general name perhaps, but a thousand specific ones, which you will hear from the lips of others even if your own are silent. Recklessness with shamelessness, insolence with violence, violence with murder, seductions with adulteries, unbridled lust with unmeasured pleasures, desperation with foolhardiness, injustice with knavery, thefts with robbery, perjuries with falsehoods, impieties with law-breakings, these and the like are the names for such deeds as yours. It is indeed a fine cause for pride and boasting, when you pursue so eagerly the repute which these names give, names at which you should in all reason hide your heads for shame. (§§117–118)

And yet, continues Philo as he pursues his reading, these aspirant name-makers have at least a presentiment of their fate, which is precisely the fate of scattering, "Though perhaps they have not merely a presentiment, but a clear foresight of their own destruction. For they say, 'before we are dispersed [*prin diasparenai*]' (Gen. xi. 4)."[6] After tracing back to Cain the evil embodied by the Babelian tower-builders, making links with other examples of towers in the Bible, establishing that "the Lord came down to see the city and the tower" cannot be taken literally—God does not move, so Moses "the lawgiver" (supposed by Philo to be the author of the biblical text) is "applying human terms to the superhuman God" (§135)—glossing at length the sense in which the tower of Babel was built by "the sons of men,"[7] providing a rather feverish reading of God's "behold there is one

---

6. Philo glosses the biblical verb *diasparenai* (which is the Seventy's translation for the Hebrew term meaning "we be scattered abroad," and which yields the relatively undramatic *dividamur* in the Vulgate) with the more graphic *skedasthēsesthe ginōskete*, to become scattered, picked up a few lines later with *skedasthēsontai*. He may be misconstruing the tenses or moods here, however: the KJV has, not "before," but "*lest* we become scattered," maintained in Robert Alter's new translation: *The Hebrew Bible*, 3 vols. (New York: Norton, 2019) and supported by the word-for-word interlinear translation in *The Hebrew-English Interlinear ESV Old Testament* (Wheaton, IL: Crossway, 2014), 21. (The online version of the LXX text at https://bit.ly/3bOo543 has "before we are scattered," but a slightly different Greek text: *pro tou diaspharēnai hēmas epi prosōpou pasēs tēs gēs.*)

7. The apparent triviality of the point that the tower was built by the sons of men and not some other beings provokes, as often in Philo, a parallel "methodological"

race and one lip of them all" as identifying a special kind of harmony among
the wicked who build the allegorical tower,[8] and offering a demonstration
that the tower could not possibly have been completed, Philo finally
comes to the occasion for citing the line from Homer we are following.
Curiously enough, the reference is called up not directly in terms of the
many figures of scattering and multiplicity we have noted thus far, but by
the fact (in the narrative attributed to Moses) of God's use of a plural pronoun in talking about himself: "Come and let us go down and confuse their
tongue there" (Gn 11:7). Philo appears quite troubled by this hint of plurality in God's self-presentation, and continues:

----

justification for his reading and method of reading: "the phrase which follows,
'which the sons of men built' (Gen. xi. 5), is no idle addition, though perhaps
some profane person might say with a sneer, 'a novel piece of information this
which the lawgiver here imparts to us, namely that it is the sons of men and not
some other beings who build cities and towers.' 'Who,' he would continue, 'even
among those who are far gone in insanity, does not know facts so obvious and
conspicuous?' But you must suppose that it is not this obvious and hackneyed fact
which is recorded for us in our most holy oracles, but the hidden truth which can
be traced under the surface meaning of the words. What then is this truth? Those
who ascribe to existing things a multitude of fathers as it were and by introducing
their miscellany of deities have flooded everything with ignorance and confusion,
or have assigned to pleasure the function of being the aim and end of the soul,
have become in very truth builders of the city of our text and of its acropolis.
They pile up as in an edifice all that serves to produce that aim or end and thus
differ not a whit to my mind from the harlot's offspring, whom the law has ban-
ished from God's congregation with the words 'he that is born of a harlot shall
not enter the congregation of the Lord' (Deut. xxiii. 2). For like bowmen, whose
shots roam from mark to mark and who never take a skilful aim at any single
point, they assume a multitude of what they falsely call sources and causes to account for the origin of the existing world and have no knowledge of the one
Maker and Father of all. But they who live in the knowledge of the One are
rightly called 'Sons of God,' as Moses also acknowledges when he says, 'Ye are
sons of the Lord God' (Deut. xiv. 1), and 'God who begat thee' (ibid, xxxii. 18),
and 'Is not He Himself thy father?' (ibid. 6)" (§§142–145).
   8. "All have the same harmony and fellowship of voice; there is none whose
mind is a stranger to the other nor his voice discordant. It is so also with men who
have no gift of music. Sometimes their vocal organ, though every note is entirely
tuneless and highly unmelodious, is supremely harmonized to produce disharmony, with a consonance which it turns to mere dissonance [*pros anarmostian
akrōs hērmosmenon kai pros to asymphōnon symphōnian monon agon*]. And the same
studied regularity may be noticed in fever."

For it is clear that He is conversing with some persons whom He treats as His fellow-workers, and we find the same in an earlier passage of the formation of man. Here we have "The Lord God said 'let us make man in our own image and likeness'" (Gen, i. 26); where the words "let us make" [*poiēsōmen*] imply plurality [*plēthos*]. And once more, "God said, 'behold Adam has become as one of us by knowing good and evil'" (Gen. iii. 22); here the "us" in "as one of us" is said not of one, but of more than one [*pleionōn*].

Philo swiftly and emphatically interrupts any sense of a becoming-plural of God, and here finally is the quotation from Homer, now explicitly re-ferred to a monotheological sense beyond its obvious political (or perhaps just military) point:

Now we must first lay down that no existing thing is of equal honour to God and that there is only one sovereign and ruler and king [*heis archōn kai hēgemōn kai basileus*], who alone may direct and dispose of all things. For the lines:

It is not well that many lords should rule;
Be there but one, one king,

could be said with more justice of the world and of God than of cities and men. For being one it must needs have one maker and father and master [*henos gar hena poētēn te kai patera palin kai despotēn anagkaion einai*]. (§§170–171; the triad or trinity "*poētēs/pater/despotēs*" apparently mapping onto the earlier "*archōn/hegemōn/basileus.*")

Philo will go on to justify what plurality he had recognized in terms of a plurality of God's "potencies" (*dynameis*) and more especially angels. But as we have rather laboriously seen, Philo takes up Homer's line (without referencing Aristotle directly, and indeed quoting the "*heis basileus*" part that Aristotle does not include in his quotation in the *Metaphysics*) and quite readily transfers it, via its obvious political reference, to the context of Judaic monotheism.

Our line is also quoted by pagan authors, both Greek and Latin, such as Cornelius Nepos (first century BCE), whose *Life of Dion* has Dion quoting the line in a military context,[9] and Dio Chrysostom (first century CE) in

---

9. Cornelius Nepos, *On Great Generals/On Historians*, translated by J. C. Rolfe (Cambridge, MA: Harvard University Press, 1929), 118–119: "Next, dissension arose between him and Heraclides, who, unwilling to yield the first place to

his *Third Discourse on Kingship*,[10] in which Dio, addressing his discourse to the emperor Trajan, and purportedly glossing the views of Socrates and Aristotle, uses Odysseus's line not, as one might expect, to argue against democracy—in the context of which we saw Aristotle himself pick out an ambiguity in Homer's line—which Dio seems to think is simply unworkable as: "possibly the most impracticable one of all, the one that expects by the self-control and virtue of the common people some day to find an equitable constitution based on law. Men call it 'democracy'—a specious and inoffensive name, if the thing were but practicable [*epieikes onoma kai praon, eiper hēn dynaton*]." Rather, Dio wields the line against aristocracy, having already announced the superiority of what he calls (as in his title) "Kingship [*Basileia*]," defined not as a situation in which the King's will is law (as in Plato's *Statesman*), but—again simplifying Aristotle, as we will see—as a lawful regime, "a city, or a number of peoples, or the whole world, well ordered by one good man's judgment and virtue":

> the so-called "aristocracy," where not one man, nor a considerable number of men, but a few, and they the best, are in control—a form of government, at length, far from being either practicable or expedient. It seems to me that Homer too had this in mind when he said:
>
> "The rule
>
> Of the many is not well. One must be chief
>
> In war, and one the king, to whom the son
>
> Of Cronus, crafty in counsel, the sceptre doth give." (124–125)[11]

Dion, formed a party against him. Heraclides had no less influence with the aristocrats than Dion, and by them he was unanimously chosen to command the fleet, while Dion retained the land forces. This situation Dion could not bear with patience, but quoted the well-known verse of Homer from his second book, of which the purport is, that a state cannot be well governed when there are many in authority [*in quo haec sententia est: non posse bene geri rem publicam multorum imperiis*]. This saying of his, since it seemed to show that he aimed at supreme power, excited great dissatisfaction, a dissatisfaction which he did not try to lessen by mildness, but to crush out by severity; and when Heraclides had come to Syracuse, he contrived to have him assassinated."

    10. Dio Chrysostom, *Discourses 1–11*, trans. J. W. Cohoon (Cambridge, MA: Harvard University Press, 1932), 126–127.

    11. Dio gives Homer's Greek accurately, so the translation "chief in war" seems to be based on a tendentious decision by the translator (the translator of

A quite general cultural familiarity with the line is suggested by a passage in Plutarch's *Life of Antony* (first century CE), when Plutarch recounts the fate of Caesarion, "who was said to be Cleopatra's son by Julius Caesar" and who was persuaded to return to Egypt on Caesar's invitation, provoking his assassination on the grounds of a witticism attributed to Areius, namely that "*ouk agathon polykaisarie*," it is not good that there be many Caesars, or, as the Loeb translation has it, "Not a good thing were a Caesar too many."[12] Other pagan thinkers also quote the line (at least partially). For example, Maximus of Tyre, writing in the late second century CE, invokes it twice in his "dissertations" or "orations": first in a text entitled "Virtue and Science," where the monarchical burden of the line is slightly (one imagines unconsciously) displaced in that the authority for the "one ruler" argument is shifted away from either Homer or Aristotle (and indeed away from Odysseus) onto Zeus: "Do you want knowledge to rule over a well-lived life? Let it do so. Do you want reason to rule? Let it indeed be sole ruler, 'since cunning Cronus' son granted it this rank,'" and second as part of an attack on what he takes to be the Epicurean promotion of pleasure over good as the *telos* of philosophy. Our tagline sits a little awkwardly in the essentially Platonic argument in that the "one king" to whom Maximus is appealing is not being opposed to a *polykoiranie* at all (that part of the line is indeed not quoted), but to a different "one king" (who will turn out to be a tyrant), namely Pleasure.[13]

Dio is relying on an 1870 version of the *Iliad* by William Cullen Bryant). In Dio's *First Discourse on Kingship*, a truncated version of the same quotation appears as "to whom the son / Of Saturn gives the scepter, making him / The lawgiver, that he may rule the rest" (8–9), where "the lawgiver, that he may rule the rest" seems to overtranslate the Greek. Murray has, less committally, "to whom the son of crooked-counselling Cronos hath vouchsafed the sceptre and judgments, that he may take counsel for his people."

12. Plutarch, *Lives*, trans. Bernadotte Perrin (Cambridge, MA: Harvard University Press, 1920), 9:320–321. As Pontani points out, a reference to this line reappears at the end of C. P. Cavafy's poem "Caesarion."

13. Maximus's works are variously ordered and titled. I refer to the edition entitled *The Philosophical Orations*, trans. M. B. Trapp (Oxford: Clarendon Press, 1997), first to Oration 27, "Virtue and Science," and Oration 33, here given the title "The True End of Life: Virtue or Pleasure," but often in different editions numbered differently and referred to by the Greek title *ti telos philosophias*.

These pagan appropriations notwithstanding,[14] the movement from
Philo Judaeus to early Christianity is of particular interest to us here, in
that it prepares the way for the early apologists to take up our tagline in
an explicitly Christian way.[15] We saw that part of that movement involved
suggesting a priority of biblical texts (or at least of the Pentateuch) over
those of the ancient Greeks, so that the Greeks could be accused, notably
by Tatian, Pseudo-Justin, and Theophilus of Antioch in the second century

14. Such appropriations can also occur in more straightforward commentar-
ies on Aristotle: so Simplicius's celebrated sixth-century CE commentary on the
Physics, for example, appeals to Aristotle's use of it more than once to clarify arguments in that text (though not always with obvious perspicuity); so, for example,
commenting on *Physics* I, 192a16–25, he writes, "Now if matter strives for form
and privation is contrary to form, the difference between the two will be great.
But how is privation contrary to the first form since nothing is contrary to it (as
Aristotle says, 'The rule of many is not good') and since everything which exists
in any way strives for it?" A little later, commenting on 192a29–34, he again
explicitly appeals to the line to answer those who might suspect that if matter
does not come to be or perish it might be a first principle in the same way that god
is: "However, [Aristotle] is the person who proclaims that the rule of many is not
good." Simplicius, *On Aristotle, Physics 1.5–9*, trans. Han Baltussen, Michael
Share, Michael Atkinson, and Ian Mueller (London: Bloomsbury, 2012), 135 and
140. Later, examining Aristotle's claim at *Physics* 259a8–13 that "we should believe
that there is one [prime mover] rather than many," Simplicius writes, "He declares it more reasonable for the primary mover to be "one" cause "rather than
many." For the rule of many is not a good thing, as he proclaims in Homeric
language when treating this issue in the *Metaphysics*." Simplicius, *On Aristotle's
Physics 8.6–10*, trans. Richard McKirahan (Ithaca, NY: Cornell University Press,
2001), 20. In fact, Aristotle's argument at this point in the *Physics* is appealing to a
kind of Occam's razor principle, namely that "when the consequences are the
same, we must always take the limited number."

15. I am not qualified to pursue the Arabic commentators, but we might note
Ibn Rushd (Averroes)'s gloss: "On the whole, the world is one because [it has] one
principle, otherwise its unity would be accidental or it would follow that it does
not exist [at all]. In sum, the disposition of the world is similar to that of the city-
state ruled by an aristocracy, for although its leadership is multiple, it forms one
leadership directed towards one end; otherwise it would not be one. As the con-
tinuance of the city-state depends on this [leadership], so is the case with the
world. For that reason household city-states [a note by the editor indicates that
this means democracies] are easily perishable because their unity is only somehow accidental." Averroes, *On Aristotle's Metaphysics: An Annotated Translation of
the So-called "Epitome,"* ed. Rüdiger Arnzen (Berlin: De Gruyter, 2010), 156–157.

CE, of borrowing or even plagiarizing from those sources. As an example of this type of argument, Tatian's *Address to the Greeks* (usually known by its Latin title, *Oratio ad Graecos*), 31, opens as follows:

> But now it seems proper for me to demonstrate that our philosophy is older than the systems of the Greeks. Moses and Homer shall be our limits, each of them being of great antiquity; the one being the oldest of poets and historians, and the other the founder of all barbarian wisdom. Let us, then, institute a comparison between them; and we shall find that our doctrines are older, not only than those of the Greeks, but than the invention of letters. And I will not bring forward witnesses from among ourselves, but rather have recourse to Greeks.[16]

In that demonstration, a recurring concern is to argue that Moses (presumed author of the Bible), came much earlier than Homer, even if Homer is thought to be contemporaneous with the Trojan War.[17]

16. *The Writings of Tatian and Theophilus; and the Clementine Recognitions*, trans. B. P. Pratten, Marcus Dods, and Thomas Smith (Edinburgh: T&T Clark, 1867), 35.

17. This line of argument is not entirely confined to the period covered in Zeegers-Vander Vorst's meticulous study. See already Flavius Josephus's *Against Apion*, or a little later in Origen of Alexandria's *Against Celsus* (*contra Celsum*), trans. Frederick Crombie (n.p.: Ex Fontibus, 2015): "Seeing that [Celsus] imagines, however, that Moses, who wrote the account of the tower, and the confusion of tongues, has perverted the story of the sons of Aloeus [see the *Odyssey*, 11.315–318, also discussed in Philo's *Confusion of Tongues* §4], and referred it to the tower, we must remark that I do not think any one prior to the time of Homer has mentioned the sons of Aloeus, while I am persuaded that what is related about the tower has been recorded by Moses as being much older not only than Homer, but even than the invention of letters among the Greeks. Who, then, are the perverters of each other's narratives? Whether do they who relate the story of the Aloadae pervert the history of the time, or he who wrote the account of the tower and the confusion of tongues the story of the Aloadae? Now to impartial hearers Moses appears to be more ancient than Homer. The destruction by fire, moreover, of Sodom and Gomorrah on account of their sins, related by Moses in Genesis, is compared by Celsus to the story of Phaethon—all these statements of his resulting from one blunder, viz., his not attending to the (greater) antiquity of Moses. For they who relate the story of Phaethon seem to be younger even than Homer, who, again, is much younger than Moses" (4.21, 282). See, too, 6.7, 443–444: "There might also be found in the writings of Moses and the prophets, who are older not only than Plato, but even than Homer and the invention of letters among the Greeks, passages worthy of the grace of God bestowed upon them,

Nicole Zeegers-Vander Vorst marshals a good deal of evidence for the existence of an anthology of quotations used in the attempt to make the case for that plagiarism: given its eminently "anthologizable" form, as pointed out earlier, and the frequency with which it is quoted by the apologists, one imagines that the tagline from Homer would have found its place, perhaps indeed pride of place, in such an anthology, as indeed it was to find its place in later anthologies, from Stobaeus's in the fifth century CE, to Erasmus's *Adages* in the early sixteenth century, to Georg Büchmann's *Geflügelte Worte* in the nineteenth.[18] Part of that operation, as undertaken by pseudo-Justin, for example, involves the demonstration that Homer, supposedly borrowing from or plagiarizing Moses, was in fact *himself* really a monotheist. Justin tries to give some external plausibility to his claims by suggesting in the wake of Diodorus of Sicily[19] that Homer (among others) traveled to Egypt where he encountered both Egyptian science and Hebrew Scripture,[20] but also, notably in the text usually known by its Latin title as *Cohortatio ad Graecos*, adduces textual evidence to show that the Greek authors were in fact—or became after this supposed exposure to Scripture—monotheists. After chapters devoted

---

and filled with great thoughts, to which they gave utterance, but not because they understood Plato imperfectly, as Celsus imagines." As far as I am able to tell, this type of argument disappears from the work of the Church Fathers after the third century CE.

18. Stobaeus, *Anthologion*, ed. Thomas Gaisford (Oxford: E Typographeo Clarendoniano, 1822), 2:293. The line from Homer is the first entry in the subsection "oti kalliston e monarchia," "that the most beautiful is monarchy," under the section on *arkhe* in the general section on politics. Erasmus, *Adages*, 2.7, 7. We will return to Büchmann later.

19. See Diodorus Siculus, *The Library of History*, trans. C. H. Oldfather (Cambridge, MA: Harvard University Press, 1933), 1.12, esp. 44–45; and: "despite the fact that . . . strangers found it difficult in early times to enter the country, it was nevertheless eagerly visited by Orpheus and the poet Homer in the earliest times and in later times by many others, such as Pythagoras of Samos and Solon the lawgiver" (239).

20. "For I think that some of you, when you read even carelessly the history of Diodorus, and of those others who wrote of these things, cannot fail to see that both Orpheus, and Homer, and Solon, who wrote the laws of the Athenians, and Pythagoras, and Plato, and some others, when they had been in Egypt, and had taken advantage of the history of Moses, afterwards published doctrines concerning the gods quite contrary to those which formerly they had erroneously promulgated." *Cohortatio ad Graecos*, chap. 14, Kindle ed., loc. 10542.

to Orpheus and the Sybil (and before chapters on Sophocles, Pythagoras, and Plato), Justin turns to Homer and, perhaps not surprisingly, quotes our tagline as his best evidence for Homer's monotheism. Here is the entire chapter:

Chapter XVII

Testimony of Homer

And the poet Homer, using the license of poetry, and rivalling the original opinion of Orpheus regarding the plurality of the gods, mentions, indeed, several gods in a mythical style, lest he should seem to sing in a different strain from the poem of Orpheus, which he so distinctly proposed to rival, that even in the first line of his poem he indicated the relation he held to him. For as Orpheus in the beginning of his poem had said, "O goddess, sing the wrath of Demeter, who brings the goodly fruit," Homer began thus, "O goddess, sing the wrath of Achilles, son of Peleus," preferring, as it seems to me, even to violate the poetical metre in his first line, than that he should seem not to have remembered before all else the names of the gods. But shortly after he also clearly and explicitly presents his own opinion regarding one God only, somewhere saying to Achilles by the mouth of Phoenix, "Not though God Himself [*theos autos*] were to promise that He would peel off my old age, and give me the rigor of my youth," where he indicates by the pronoun the real and true God. And somewhere he makes Ulysses address the host of the Greeks thus: "The rule of many is not a good thing; let there be one ruler." And that the rule of many is not a good thing, but on the contrary an evil, he proposed to evince by fact, recounting the wars which took place on account of the multitude of rulers, and the fights and factions, and their mutual counterplots. For monarchy is free from contention [*ten gar monarchian amakon einai symbainei*]. So far the poet Homer.

On this view, and despite the near-absurdity of the claims (for Homer's polytheism in general does not inhibit his quite habitual use of the singular term "God" to refer to Zeus as chief among gods) the whole of the *Iliad* can be invoked as evidence in favor of Homer's monotheism, and our tagline is the best evidence for that. Note, too, the brief remark to the effect that "monarchy is free from contention," which also repoliticizes Homer's quote at the very moment it is being theologized. We might want to see here something it would probably be unwise to call an "origin" of political theology as it will subsequently unfold across the tradition. But the two-way nature of the communication here between the theological claim to monotheism and the political claim to monarchy might also make us wary of Schmitt's famous claim to the effect that "all significant concepts of the modern theory of the state are secularized theological concepts," which, despite Schmitt's rapid attempt to say that this must be understood in structural as well as historical terms, probably concedes too much to a priority of the theological over the political.[21] It may be that this is what makes Schmitt's position at least *somewhat* vulnerable to Erik Peterson's arguments against him: as we shall see in due course, this dispute itself saliently invokes our tagline from Homer and a particular interpretation of the concept of "monarchy."

As Zeegers-Vander Vorst also shows, Clement of Alexandria could point to parallelisms between biblical and ancient Greek wisdom without always needing to invoke anything as crude as direct plagiarism. For Clement, who does indeed argue, often with elaborate chronologies, that the Greeks learned their wisdom from the Jews or the "barbarians,"[22] the parallelism can also be explained by the fact that all humans are illuminated by the same Logos. Early in the *Stromata*, for example, Clement describes philosophy (by which he specifically means Greek thinking) as "the clear image of truth, a divine gift to the Greeks," and a little later: "Perchance, too, philosophy was given to the Greeks directly and primarily, till the Lord should call the Greeks. For this was a school master to bring 'the Hellenic mind' as the law, the Hebrews, 'to Christ.' Philosophy, therefore, was a preparation, paving the way for him who is perfected in Christ," and in *Stromata* 1.19: "By reflection and direct vision, those among the Greeks who have philosophized accurately, see God." And this can allow him to state, for example, that "Plato in *The Statesman* says that the Lawgiver is one; and in *The Laws*, that he who shall understand music is one; teaching by these words that the Word is one, and God is one" (1.29).

This quite complex appropriation of the Greek philosophical tradition, via Judaism, by the nascent Christian theology of the second century CE saliently includes both the motif of lordship or leadership, and the motif

21. Carl Schmitt, *Political Theology: Four Chapters on the Concept of Sovereignty*, trans. George Schwab (Chicago: University of Chicago Press, 1985), 36.

22. See, for example, *Stromata*, 1.15, entitled (by the translator) "The Greek philosophy derived in great part from the barbarians," or 5.14, "Greek Plagiarism from the Hebrews." For an example of the use of chronology in the argument, see *Stromata* 1, 21, "The Jewish institutions and laws of far higher antiquity than the philosophy of the Greeks."

of oneness so strongly—if, as we saw, ambiguously—linked to it in our Homeric tagline. Eusebius of Caesarea, writing a century or so after Clement
of Alexandria, might be said to complete the outflanking maneuver begun
by the apologists in the second century. They placed Judaism and especially Moses earlier than the Greeks; Eusebius reaches back even earlier,
to Abraham, and generously extends the term "Christian" that far (and in
so doing both acknowledges and, as it were, sublates into Christianity the
Mosaic law in its relation both to the Greeks and to the Jews). Here is his
reading of God's appearance to Abraham recounted in Genesis 12 and
again in Genesis 18, with its breezy conclusion linking the originary, the
one, and the true:

> So that it must clearly be held that the announcement to all the Gen-
> tiles, recently made through the teaching of Christ, is the very first and
> most ancient and antique discovery of true religion by Abraham and
> those lovers of God who followed him . . .
>
> And to him, just as he was, before circumcision, was the oracle
> given by the God who showed himself to him (and this was the Christ
> himself, the word of God),[23] concerning those who in time to come
> would be justified in the same manner as himself, in the following
> promise, "And in thee shall all the tribes of the earth be blessed,"
> and, "It shall be a great and numerous nation, and all the nations
> of the earth shall be blessed in it." Now this is obviously intelligible
> as fulfilled in us; for it was by faith towards the Logos of God, the
> Christ who had appeared to him, that he was justified, and gave up the
> superstition of his fathers, and his former erroneous life, and confessed
> the God who is over all to be one; and him he served by virtuous deeds,
> not by the worship of the law of Moses, who came later. To him, just
> as he was then, was it said that all the tribes of the earth and all the
> nations will be blessed in him; and more clearly than any words do
> facts show that at the present moment it is only among Christians
> throughout the whole world that the manner of religion which was
> Abraham's can actually be found in practice. What objection then can
> there be to admitting that the life and pious conduct of us, who belong
> to Christ, and of the God-loving men of old is one and the same?
> Thus we have demonstrated that the practice of piety handed down
> by the teaching of Christ is not new or strange, but, if one must speak

23. See the much more nuanced and inconclusive discussion of this incident
in Augustine's *De Trinitate*, 2.11–12.

truthfully, is primitive, unique, and true [*prōtēn hyparchein kai monēn kai alēthē*]. And let this suffice.[24]

It is not entirely a surprise that this language of appropriation should go along with an insistent use in Eusebius of the vocabulary of leadership and lordship. For example, still near the beginning of the *Ecclesiastical History*, unpacking what Eusebius presents as the "twofold [*dittou*]" nature of Christ:

> the living Logos who was, in the beginning, God by the side of the Father, the first and only offspring of God, before all creation and fabrication, both visible and invisible, the captain [*archistrategon*, perhaps "commander-in-chief"] of the spiritual and immortal host of heaven, the angel of great counsel [*megalēs boulēs angelon*], the minister of the ineffable plan of the Father, the fabricator of all things along with the Father, the true and only begotten child of God, the Lord and God and King [*kurion kai theon kai basilea*] of all begotten, who has received lordship and might, together with deity itself, and power and honour from the Father [*to kyros homou kai to kratos autē theotēti kai dynamei kai timē para tou patros hypodedegmenon*]. (1, 2)

Christ may be twofold, and indeed part of the Trinity (the concept of which will much later be invoked by Peterson in his attempted refutation of Schmitt, as we shall see), but this language of lordship and kingship and even military leadership is still not far from our Homeric line. So it does not come as a surprise when, not indeed in the *Ecclesiastical History* but at the very opening of his work on *The Martyrs of Palestine*, our line returns, Eusebius quoting the first martyr Procopius. This is the opening of chapter 1 of Eusebius's text:

> The first of the martyrs of Palestine was Procopius, who, before he had received the trial of imprisonment, immediately on his first appearance before the governor's tribunal, having been ordered to sacrifice to the so-called gods, declared that he knew only one to whom it was proper to sacrifice, as he himself wills. But when he was commanded to offer libations to the four emperors, having quoted a sentence which displeased them, he was immediately beheaded. The quotation was from the poet: "The rule of many is not good; let there be one ruler and one king."

24. Eusebius of Caesarea, *Ecclesiastical History*, trans. Kirsopp Lake (Cambridge, MA: Harvard University Press, 1926), 1.4, 42–45.

Origen too, writing in the third century CE, makes indirect use of our line in his celebrated *Contra Celsum*, where, near the end of this voluminous work, Celsus is reported as quoting the Homer line, and Origen attempts to refute his understanding of it by using the appeal to crooked or crafty Zeus to undermine the Godlike qualities of that particular God:

> Celsus goes on to say: We must not disobey the ancient writer, who said long ago, "Let one be king, whom the son of crafty Saturn appointed"; and adds: If you set aside this maxim, you will deservedly suffer for it at the hands of the king. For if all were to do the same as you, there would be nothing to prevent his being left in utter solitude and desertion, and the affairs of the earth would fall into the hands of the wildest and most lawless barbarians; and then there would no longer remain among men any of the glory of your religion or of the true wisdom. If, then, there shall be one lord, one king, he must be, not the man whom the son of crafty Saturn appointed, but the man to whom He gave the power, who removeth kings and setteth up kings [Daniel 2:21], and who raiseth up the useful man in time of need upon earth. [Ecclesiastes 10:4] For kings are not appointed by that son of Saturn, who, according to Grecian fable, hurled his father from his throne, and sent him down to Tartarus (whatever interpretation may be given to this allegory), but by God, who governs all things, and who wisely arranges whatever belongs to the appointment of kings. We therefore do set aside the maxim contained in the line, "Whom the son of crafty Saturn appointed"; for we know that no god or father of a god ever devises anything crooked or crafty. But we are far from setting aside the notion of a providence, and of things happening directly or indirectly through the agency of providence. And the king will not inflict deserved punishment upon us, if we say that not the son of crafty Saturn gave him his kingdom, but He who removes and sets up kings. And would that all were to follow my example in rejecting the maxim of Homer, maintaining the divine origin of the kingdom, and observing the precept to honor the king! In these circumstances the king will not be left in utter solitude and desertion, neither will the affairs of the world fall into the hands of the most impious and wild barbarians. For if, in the words of Celsus, they do as I do, then it is evident that even the barbarians, when they yield obedience to the word of God, will become most obedient to the law, and most humane; and every form of worship will be destroyed except the religion of Christ, which will alone prevail. And indeed it will one day triumph,

as its principles take possession of the minds of men more and more every day.[25]

This direct confrontation of the "pagan" reading of Homer's text by Celsus (which is in a trivial sense clearly the more accurate reading) and the Christian retrieval of it by Origen, might stand for us as emblematic of the process we have begun observing, whereby on the one hand a blatant polytheism is being monotheized, and on the other the Oneness of the One is being, as it were, reinforced (along lines the logic of which Xenophanes would have recognized). These maneuvers from the start clearly have rhetorical components that it is tempting to attribute to the logic of the One itself: once in its gravitational pull, as it were (on the way to what Derrida calls sovereign ipseity), then, as we shall increasingly see, paralogisms proliferate and orthodoxies are established in which sound argument is subordinated to the sheer authority of the One, theology and politics become intertwined, heresies are denounced and the prospect of excommunication is never far away. There are many other examples that display a remarkable consistency, perhaps lending support to Zeegers-Vander Vorst's hypothesis of the existence of an anthology or crib-sheet of quotations that could be used in arguing the case for Christianity. So for example, Epiphanius of Cyprus's *Ancoratus* (late fourth century CE) quotes the line from Homer as part of an attack on polytheism,[26] and in what has been described as the last (and even the best) of the Christian apologies,[27] Theodoret of Cyrus entitles the third Discourse of his *Cure for Pagan Maladies* (early fifth century CE) "On Angels, So-Called Gods, and Maleficent Demons," and opens with a section on "The origin of Polytheism," which both quotes our line from Homer and echoes an earlier formulation from Gregory of Nazianzus that will be central to our reading of the exchange between Peterson and Schmitt:

---

25. Origen, *Against Celsus (contra Celsum)*, 8.68, 648–649.

26. St. Epiphanius of Cyprus, *Ancoratus*, translated by Young Richard Kim (Washington D.C.: The Catholic University of America Press, 2014), 104, 203. Epiphanius was a notorious anti-Origenist and "heresy-hunter" more generally. We are less interested in the historical detail of such disputes within Christianity and more in the way that monotheism in general generates both orthodoxies and heresies.

27. J. Quasten, quoted in the Introduction to Theodoret of Cyrus, *A Cure for Pagan Maladies*, usually referred to by its Latin title, *Graecarum Affectionum Curatio*, trans. Thomas Halton (New York: Newman Press, 2013), 1.

While condemning anarchy and polyarchy as pernicious, we admire monarchy, and we approve the sentiment of Homer who introduces this law:

It is not good that many govern;

Let there be one chief, one king. (70)

Which appeal to Homer does not prevent Theodoret, who is keen to attack "not merely those that deny the existence of God but also those who have promoted a multiplicity of gods," from immediately including Homer in a list of "atheists," alongside Hesiod and "the schools of philosophers who in their fables invented hosts of gods and presented them as enslaved to human passions" (70–71).

I do not propose to follow here the detail of how Plotinus's thinking of the One plays a role in this complex process,[28] but its becoming-Christian can quite rapidly be illustrated from the work of pseudo-Dionysius the Areopagite, active in the fifth–sixth centuries CE, whose work *The Divine Names* is a precious resource for us here. For example, in the chapter of his work immediately preceding the one that discusses the divine name "One" as such, the pseudo-Dionysius picks up the "leadership" vocabulary we were following in Homer, and provides a complex account of how that vocabu-

---

28. See especially for our context *Ennead*, 5.5: "The Supreme in its progress could never be borne forward upon some soulless vehicle nor even directly upon the Soul: it will be heralded by some ineffable beauty: before the great King in his progress there comes first the minor train, than rank by rank the greater and more exalted, closer to the King the kinglier; next his own honored company until, last among all these grandeurs, suddenly appears the Supreme Monarch himself, and all—unless indeed for those who have contented themselves with the great spectacle before his coming and gone away—prostrate themselves and hail him./In that royal progress the King is of another order from those that go before him, but the King in the Supreme is no ruler over externs; he holds that most just of governances, rooted in nature, the veritable kingship, for he is King of Truth, holding sway by all reason over a dense offspring his own, a host that shares his divinity, King over a king and over kings and even more justly called father of Gods./Zeus (universal soul) is in this a symbol of him, Zeus who is not content with the contemplation of his father (Kronos, divine Intellect) but looks to that father's father (to Ouranos, the Transcendent) as what may be called the divine energy working to the establishment of real being." *The Enneads*, trans. Stephen McKenna (Burdett, NY: Larson, 1992), 466–467. See the classic account in Arthur O. Lovejoy, *The Great Chain of Being: A Study in the History of an Idea* (Cambridge, MA: Harvard University Press, 1964), 61–66.

lary is doubled up in Scripture, into the names "King of Kings [*basilea tōn basileuontōn*]," "Lord of Lords [*kyrion tōn kyriōn*]," and "God of Gods [*theon tōn theōn*]." For Dionysius, these formulas are also linked to the name "Holy of Holies" (*agion agiōn*) in a way that adds to the predicates of sovereign ipseity that of purity or untaintedness, what Derrida will call the immune:

> In my way of speaking, holiness [*agiotes*] is freedom from all defilement [*e pantos agous eleuthera*].[29] Kingship [*basileia*] is the power to arrange every border, realm, law and order. Lordship [*kuriotes*] is not merely a matter of being superior with respect to inferiors but a complete possession of all that is beautiful and good, and is furthermore a true and unshakeable stability. The word is derived from the idea of "lording," "having the capacity to lord" and "actually lording" [*Dio kai kyriotēs para to kyros kai to kyrion kai to kyrieuon*]. And as for deity, this is the Providence which sees all things and which in its utter goodness makes the round of all things, holding them together, filling them with itself, transcending all the things that enjoy the benefit of its providence.[30]

These names are being absolutized by the doubling formulas, and in so doing referred to a single and unified transcendent cause described as "a preeminent holiness and lordship, a supreme kingship and a totally simple divinity" (*aploustaton theoteta*). And this preeminence, supremacy and simplicity allow Dionysius to have these different terms converge upwards, as it were, with a series of terms in *hyper-*, on the One, from which multiplicity and diversity can supposedly be granted without compromising the posited unicity of that One:

> Since the Cause of all things is himself overflowing [*hyperplērēs*] with them in one transcendent excess of all [*kata mian tēn pantōn hyperechousan hyperbolēn*], he is called "Holy of Holies [*agios agiōn*]" and all those other names. For he is, you might say, brimming causality and supreme transcendence [*hyperblyzousan aitian kai exērēmenēn hyperochēn*]. Just as there are things which are surpassed [*hyperechousi*] by being, holiness,

29. A note to the English translation here: "The author acknowledges his fondness for puns, such as this one: 'Holiness is hole-less.' But not far away is a further potential pun linking *agios* [holy], *agos* [pollution, taint, what the English translator's note is trying to capture here with "hole"] and *agós*, a leader or chieftain."

30. In Pseudo-Dionysius, *The Complete Works*, trans. Colm Luibheid (New York: Paulist Press, 1987), 126.

divinity and kingship, just as the things sharing in these attributes are inferior to the attributes themselves, so it is that the things which have being are surpassed by the One who is beyond them all. Scripture gives the name of "holy ones," "kings," "lords," and "gods" to the primary ranks in themselves, through whom the secondary ones receive from God the gifts they possess, pluralizing the simplicity of their portion in terms of their differentiations [*tēs ekeinōn diadoseōs haplotēta peri tas heautōn diaphoras plēthyousin*]. And the very first ranks in their providential godlike activity draw this variegation [*poikilia*] into the unity of their own being.

However obscure some of this remains, the important point for us is the way in which talk of lord, king, and god gives rise (rather literally) to a pure or holy One which is a principle of gathering of whatever is multiple or, as Dionysius says here with a term that will detain us later, variegated, *poikilia*. Although to my knowledge Dionysius never quotes the line from Homer that Aristotle uses to round off his own "theology," *The Divine Names* can only confirm the movement we have been observing. And it is no accident that this movement should now come on, in the work's final chapter, to the two "last" names of God, namely "Perfect" (*teleion*) and "One" (*to hen*).[31] Let me skip over the perfect and come to the One, which is, then, the last name of God, which will then yield to the thought that God is essentially nameless.[32]

31. See the editor's footnote 261 on page 127 for a summary of the various ways in which the structure of *The Divine Names*, and more especially the ordering of the names has been variously interpreted by commentators beginning with Aquinas.

32. See too, already a century or two earlier, the dialogic text of Marcus Minucius Felix, *Octavius*, 18: "Neither must you ask a name for God. God is His name [*deus nomen est*: this could of course be translated in many different ways, for example, "God is the name; 'God' is a name; His name is God," and so on.] We have need of names when a multitude is to be separated into individuals by the special characteristics of names; to God, who is alone, the name God is the whole./If I were to call Him Father, you would judge Him to be earthly; if a King, you would suspect Him to be carnal; if a Lord, you will certainly understand Him to be mortal. Take away the additions of names, and you will behold His glory. What! is it not true that I have in this matter the consent of all men? I hear the common people, when they lift their hands to heaven, say nothing else but Oh God, and God is great, and God is true, and if God shall permit. Is this the natural discourse of the common people, or is it the prayer of a confessing Christian? And they who speak of Jupiter as the chief [*principem*], are mistaken in

In a couple of remarkable paragraphs, Dionysius lays out very precisely the onto-monotheological structure that our own thought of scatter is hoping to contest in both metaphysical and political terms. We have just seen how scatter itself (variegation, *poikilia*) is drawn back toward unity. The argument now claims not simply that existent multiplicity is drawn back toward the One, but that multiplicity *as such* cannot be thought except as *caused by* the One, as flowing from the One before returning to it (that movement of departure and return also, according to Aquinas, defining the very structure of *The Divine Names* itself):

> The One cause of all things is not one of the many things in the world but actually precedes oneness and multiplicity [*to plethos*] and indeed defines oneness and multiplicity. For multiplicity cannot exist without some participation in the One. . . . Without the One there is no multiplicity, but there can still be the One when there is no multiplicity, just as one precedes all multiplied number. . . . If you take away the One, there will survive neither whole nor part nor anything else in creation. . . . Hence scripture describes the entire thearchy, the Cause of everything, as the One. Furthermore, "there is one God the father and one Lord Jesus Christ" and "one and the same Spirit." (128–129)

Allow me to sidestep for now the relation (to which Dionysius immediately goes on to refer) between this One and the doctrine of the Trinity, which will reappear as a crux of the argument between Schmitt and Peterson to which I have already alluded, and to which we shall return in due course. For now, let us simply register the force of the argument here presented, which might reasonably be said, at least in its formal structure, to put in place all the essential elements of the tradition to come, at least as far as Hegel, and therefore also beyond. The relation between the One and the *variegated* many will be at the heart of everything we will go on to discuss. Our argument will be that the principle of *poikilia* or variegation introduces a crucial complication into what I am tempted to call a *simple* notion of multiplicity or the many: what I am calling scatter is not just many or multiple, but multiply multiple, manifoldly many, multifariously multitudi-

---

the name indeed, but they are in agreement about the unity of the power." On grounds of perspicuity, I have preferred the translation by Robert Ernest Wallis available at http://www.documentacatholicaomnia.eu to that of Gerald H. Rendall in the Loeb Classical Library (Cambridge, MA: Harvard University Press, 1931), here at 365.

nous, *motley*, and so, or so I shall be arguing, endlessly resistant to being gathered back into the One.

This Christianizing appropriation of Plato and Aristotle, even via the Hebrew Bible, is not entirely implausible given what we might think of as an intrinsic monotheistic concern with God as the One God. Famously in Deuteronomy 6: 4, still today part of the most basic prayer of Judaism, the *Shema Israel*, with its quite striking echo (or prediction, if we were to believe the apologists) of the tagline from Homer that is our guiding thread here: "Hear, O Israel, the Lord our God is one Lord" (*Shema, Yisra'eil Adonai Eloheinu Adonai echad*), translated by the Seventy as *kyrios ho theos hēmōn kyrios heis estin*. The identical Greek appears in the Gospel of Mark (12:29), when Jesus has been answering questions in the Temple in Jerusalem, and regularly confounding his interlocutors. The last question he is asked by a scribe, a *grammateus*, is simply "Which is the first commandment of all?," to which Jesus, showing off his knowledge of orthodox judaeology, replies with a direct and literal quotation of Deuteronomy 6:4.[33] But it is one thing for Jesus to repeat the canonical Judaic formula, and another for us to know how subsequently to factor in the enunciatory role of Jesus himself in that very repetition. Some of the delicacy of the issue here can be sensed from I Corinthians 8:4–6 ("As concerning therefore the eating of those things that are offered in sacrifice unto idols, we know that an idol *is* nothing in the world, and that *there is* none other God but one. For though there be that are called gods, whether in heaven or in earth, (as there be gods many, and lords many [*theoi polloi kai kyrioi polloi*]), But to us *there is but* one God, the Father, of whom *are* all things, and we in him; and one Lord Jesus Christ, by whom *are* all things, and we by him"), where Paul, presumably agreeing with his Corinthian correspon-

---

33. In the version of this same exchange as reported in Matthew 22:35–38, Jesus is reported as replying to the scribe's question with what in Deuteronomy immediately follows the commandment reported in Mark: "Then one of them, *which was* a lawyer, asked *him a question*, tempting him, saying, Master, which *is* the great commandment in the law? Jesus said unto him, Thou shalt love the Lord they God with all thy heart [*cardia*], and with all thy soul [*psychē*], and with all thy mind [*dianoia*]. This is the first and great commandment." For helpful commentary on the exchange in Mark, with reference also to rabbinic understanding of the place of this commandment among the 613 listed in the five books of Moses, see R. T. France, *The Gospel of Mark: A Commentary on the Greek Text* (Grand Rapids, MI: Eerdmans, 2002), 476–482.

dents that "there is none other God but God" (8:4), and that "to us there
is but one God" (8:6), wants to draw out a difference with Jewish monotheism precisely by invoking Christ: as one commentator puts it,

> The Jewish Shema . . . is here split apart into a statement about *God*,
> the creator of the world and goal of salvation, and a matching state-
> ment about *the Lord*, now taken to mean Jesus Christ, the medium of
> creation and redemption. The two are clearly distinguished (cf. 3:23;
> 11:3; 15:27–28) but the way in which Paul reads them both out of the
> Jewish declaration of monotheism is suggestive of the way in which
> Christian theology will struggle to define Christ's exalted status
> without falling into ditheism.[34]

In both Hebrew and Greek (and indeed in English), there is room for some
ambiguity in the understanding of the term "one," which can function as
a number word (in both Hebrew and Greek it is the first cardinal number), and as an adjective of quality. It seems clear that monotheism as such
demands the first usage, which seems prescribed by the recurrent formulas such as "no God beside me" (Isaiah 45:21) or in the opening of the ten
commandments from which the *shema Israel* is derived (see for example
Exodus 20:2–3, "I am the Lord thy God . . . Thou shalt have no other gods
before me [*egō eimi Kyrios ho Theos sou . . . ouk esontai soi theoi heteroi plēn
emou*]," as well as in explicit usages of the word *heis* (as in Zechariah 14:9:
"And the LORD shall be king over all the earth: in that day shall there be
one LORD, and his name one [*kai estai Kyrios eis basilea epi pasan tēn gēn; en
tē hēmera ekeinē estai Kyrios heis kai to onoma autou hen*]." In this more
straightforwardly monotheistic sense in which God is (self-)declared to be
the one (and only) god, similar statements can also be found throughout
the Quran. For example, Surah Al-Baqarah (The Cow), 163: "And your
God is One God: there is no god but He . . . ," 255: "Allah! There is no god

---

34. John Barclay, in *The Pauline Epistles*, ed. John Muddiman and John Bar-
ton (Oxford: Oxford University Press, 2001), 109. See, too, James D. G. Dunn, in
The Theology of Paul the Apostle (Grand Rapids, MI: Eerdmans, 1998), 253: "In an
astonishing adaptation of the *Shema* . . . Paul attributes the lordship of the one
God to Jesus Christ. And yet his confession of God as one is still affirmed. Evidently the lordship of Christ was not thought of as any usurpation or replacement
of God's authority, but expressive of it. The one Lord attests the one God." For a
measured overview of the significant complications involved in the interpretation
of this passage, see Anthony C. Thiselton, *The First Epistle to the Corinthians: A
Commentary on the Greek Text* (Grand Rapids, MI: Eerdmans, 2000), 628–638.

but He . . ."; and this formula "there is no god but he" is repeated many times.

The second, adjectival sense of "one" can seem more elusive: God may be quantitatively (or exclusively) one, as it were, but He is also qualitatively one, not merely one God among others or the only God, but a God who is (at) one with Himself, thoroughly unified in his oneness. (This will of course engage with the whole mystery of the Trinity, as we shall see later.) This slightly different sense opens up a space within the One, and that this space is working here can be shown by consulting different translations of the encounter in Mark: in Latin ("Iesus autem respondit ei quia primum omnium mandatum est audi Israhel Dominus Deus noster Deus unus est"), as in English, the ambiguity between the two senses of "one" need not be resolved, but in French at least two possibilities offer themselves, and it seems that a weighty decision must be taken: in the 1923 Crampon translation, the line becomes: "Jésus répondit: Le premier, c'est: Ecoute Israël: le Seigneur notre Dieu, le Seigneur est un," which tends toward the adjectival reading of *heis* or *echad*, but the Louis Segond version (1910) clearly opts for the numerical sense: "Jésus répondit: Voici le premier: Écoute, Israël, le Seigneur, notre Dieu, est l'unique Seigneur."[35] This is also true of the Italian Giovanni Diodati Bibbia version of 1649. Luther's 1545 German has in both Deuteronomy and Mark "Höre, Israel, der Herr, unser Gott, ist ein einiger Gott," where the doubling up in the formula "ein einiger" perhaps captures both senses if we take the "ein" in the sense of "one" rather than just as an indefinite article. In Derrida's own favorite Bible translation, that of André Chouraqui, the version in both Deuteronomy and Mark respects the fact that in the Hebrew this is a nominal sentence, and maintains the ambiguity in the sense of "one": "Entends, Israël, IHVH-Adonaï, notre Elohîms, IHVH-Adonaï un."

In Islam, the concept of *Tawhid* appears to work with the same ambiguity, as brought out quite clearly in a passage from the Prophet Ali:

> To know God is to know his oneness. To say that God is one has four meanings: two of them are false and two are correct. As for the two meanings that are false, one is that a person should say "God is one"

---

35. Interestingly enough, Segond translates Deuteronomy 6:4 a little differently, perhaps implicitly criticizing the Greek of the Seventy: "Ecoute, Israël! L'Éternel, notre Dieu, est le seul Éternel." In both cases the translation is almost identical to that of the 1707 Martin version—in both cases, however, Martin and Segond clearly prefer the numerical to the adjectival sense of "one."

and be thinking of a number and counting. This is false because that which has no second cannot enter into the category of number. Do you not see that those who say that God is a third of a trinity fall into this infidelity? Another meaning is to say, "So-and-So is one of his people," namely, a species of this genus or a member of this species. This meaning is also false when applied to God, because it implies likening something to God, whereas God is above all likeness. As to the two meanings that are correct when applied to God, one is that it should be said that "God is one" in the sense that there is no likeness to him among things. Another is to say that "God is one" in the sense that there is no multiplicity or division conceivable in Him, neither outwardly, nor in the mind, nor in the imagination. God alone possesses such a unity.[36]

That these (at least two) understandings of "one" are not the same can, interestingly enough, also be brought out in a different way by looking at Derrida's own writing, where there is repeated, but to my knowledge never thematized, use of formulas that draw attention to the same type of ambiguity, paradigmatically in the form "un X (qui soit) un," sometimes complicated with a "qui en soit un." This occurs not merely in discussions *of* the One, as in the passage quoted earlier from *Rogues*, speaking of "One God, of the One God or of the God who is One" [*d'Un Dieu, de l'Un Dieu ou du Dieu Un*]." For example:

quelque chose comme la philosophie, s'il y en a et qui soit une
something like philosophy, if there is any and [if so, one] that is one
      (DP 56/31)

le lieu de passage d'un *sens* et d'un sens *un*
the site of passage of a *meaning*, and of a meaning that is *one* (M 367/309)

notre histoire, notre mémoire, notre culture, s'il en est une et qui soit *une*
our history, our memory, our culture, if there is one and if it is *one*
      (PA 98/79)

s'il existe un tel paradigme, *s'il en est un*, qui en soit un (un modèle ou un
      artefact *exemplaire*) et qui soit *un*

36. Quoted in Vincent Cornell, "God in Islam," in *The Encyclopedia of Religion*, 2nd ed., ed. Lindsay Jones (New York: Macmillan, 2005), 5:3560–3567, 9:3561. Cornell goes on to explain, "Most simply, *tawhid* means that God is one, unique, and not divisible into hypostatic entities or incarnated manifestations." Ibid., 9:3562.

whether there is such a paradigm—*if it is one*—which would be an
  example of one (an *exemplary* model or artifact) and would be *one*
  (PA 204/180)

pour commencer à penser les portées multiples du mot "représentation"
  et l'histoire, s'il en est une et qui soit une, de la *Vorgestelltheit* . . .
to begin to think the multiple bearings of the word "representation"
  and the history, if there is one that really is one, of *Vorgestelltheit* . . .
  (PSY 125/110)

l'histoire de la philosophie, de la langue et de la langue philosophique
  française. Y en a-t-il une, et qui soit une?
The history of philosophy, of language, and of French philosophical
  language. Is there such a language, and is it one language?
  (PSY 132/118)

Autrement dit, y a-t-il un concept de la paix? Et qui soit *un*, indestructible
  dans son identité?
In other words, is there a concept of peace? One that would be *one*,
  indestructible in its identity? (AEL 152/85)

Est-ce un animal, la chimère, un animal qui en soit un, et un animal qui
  soit un?
Is it an animal, this chimera, an animal that can be defined as one, and
  only one? (ADS 43/23)

un exemple de mot, si c'en est un et qui soit un, unique, seul, le mot
  relevant . . .
an example of a word, if it is one and one that is one, unique, sole, the
  word "relevant"
(TR 562, my translation)

L'Europe aujourd'hui se trouve à un moment de son histoire (*si* elle en a
  une et qui soit *une*, identifiable), de l'histoire de sa culture (si elle peut
  jamais s'identifier comme une . . .)
Europe today . . . is at a moment in its history (*if* it has one, and indeed
  is *one*, i.e. identifiable), in the history of its culture (if it can ever be
  identified as one . . .)
(AC 21/16)

D'un concept de l'archive qui en soit un? Qui soit un concept et dont
  l'unité soit assurée?
A concept of the archive which deserves this name? which is one and
  whose unity is assured? (MA 55/33)

Faisons provisoirement comme s'il y avait une *psychanalyse* et qui soit *une*.
Let us . . . provisionally assume that there is indeed a psychoanalysis that
   is a single whole. (RES 100/76)

Dans la langue française, s'il y en a qui soit une . . .
In the French language, if there is one that is one (VEP 10–11/6)

   . . . la question se posant ici de savoir ce que pourrait être un texte un et si
   quelque chose de tel existe plus qu'une unicorne
   . . . the question being posed here asks what *a* text *alone* [un *texte* un]
   could be and whether such a thing exists more than a unicorn
   (GL, 190b/169b)

As the different versions suggest, such formulas are often not so easy to
translate into English, in part because "un" in French is the masculine indefinite article and well as the first cardinal numeral, and in part because,
especially when positioned after the noun, it has primarily the adjectival
sense of unity and self-identity (in the entry for "un" in Littré's dictionary, this second sense ("simple, qui n'admet point de pluralité [simple, ad-
mitting no plurality]") is immediately illustrated by "La religion est une.
La foi est une [religion is one, faith is one]," and a little later "la vérité est
toujours une, elle n'est jamais contraire à elle-même [truth is always one,
it is never contrary to itself]").

   This gesture in Derrida, which we might think is little more than a sty-
listic tic, seems to imply doubts about both the numerical identity or
uniqueness and the self-identity or unity of the phenomena in question.
In many cases, Derrida's conditional *if*s suggest a doubt as to whether
there really is a unified X, and therefore one X, at all.[37] This is true of
one of the biggest X's of all, namely what Derrida calls "Western metaphysics." He has often been criticized for his use of this notion, on the
grounds that it homogenizes or "makes everything the same" the better
to criticize and perhaps reject it. This is a mistake: Derrida is resolutely
unconvinced that there is anything unified and identifiable under the
name "Western metaphysics"; his point rather is that it is the tradition

---

37. My use of the algebraic "X" here provisionally ignores, in the interest of
clarity, Derrida's repeated insistence that concepts "are not algebraic Xs," that
could then be the object of stipulations as to their names or meanings (see for
example HQE 176/115; M 302, 304/253, and 254). This of course follows from the
inheritance argument from which we began, and more generally from the *différance* account of meaning.

under scrutiny that habitually identified itself in the terms of unity and identity that he is carefully suspending, among other ways by returning to the "if there is one that is *one*" type formulas I was just listing.[38] As in our earlier remarks about reading, and reading Derrida's readings, it is in part his recognizing the irreducibility of inheritance from the tradition and the tradition's self-understanding (along eminently ipsocentric lines— or circles) that makes possible the deconstructive work undertaken by him, and after him by us, and it is part of our inheritance from him that we are able on occasion to put more pressure on some aspects of that tradition (for us, here, saliently Aristotle) as part of our efforts to receive and read that inheritance.

This is one of the things that distinguishes our efforts here from the ill-conceived remarks about Derrida and Aristotle to be found in, for example, Giorgio Agamben. Agamben's typically broad and confident claim in *What Is Philosophy?* is that "the Derridean critique of metaphysics is . . . founded on an insufficient reading of Aristotle" (20). Agamben wants to argue that Derrida's quotation of the opening of the *De Interpretatione* near the beginning of the *Grammatology* to establish the thenceforth classical metaphysical assumption of a proximity of voice and soul fails to register the fact that the voice Aristotle has in mind is one that, qua *logos* or *dialektos*, is distinguished from the mere *phonē* of other animals by its being *articulated*, and that such articulation involves an originary presence within *logos* of *grammata*, letters, such that Aristotle is *already* advancing a grammatology from the start rather than laying down any canonical phono-logocentrism. As in so many readings critical of Derrida, Agamben here is doing no more than projecting back onto the text being read (here the *De Interpretatione*)—in this case doing so with help from later (but unnamed) "ancient grammarians"—a relationship between articulation and writing that is derived from Derrida himself, as Agamben all but recognizes in an earlier version of this same text (in *Infancy and History*), where Derrida is not criticized, and on the contrary is at least parenthetically credited with "opportunely" (the English

---

38. See, for example, in *Positions:* "the 'closure of metaphysics' cannot have the form of a *line*, that is, the form in which philosophy recognizes it, in which philosophy recognizes itself. The closure of metaphysics is above all not a circle surrounding a homogeneous field, homogeneous with itself on its inside, and whose outside would therefore be homogeneous too. The limit has the form of always different faults, of splits of which all the texts of philosophy bear the mark or the scar" (POS 77/57).

translation has "fortuitously"),[39] pointing out something along these lines—derived from Derrida himself and then attributed unambiguously to the author in question, here Aristotle.[40]

We can formalize this maneuver, more or less blatant examples of which can be found throughout the reception of Derrida's work, according to a schema Derrida himself lays out later in the *Grammatology*, discussing what Rousseau says about the *fête*, and that we mentioned earlier. The text we are reading says "A," and then interprets "A" as "B." This would then be what the Saussure chapter calls the text's *propos déclaré*—what the Rousseau readings call the text's *declaration*, its own understanding of what it means or wants to say—a declaration that our reading has at least to recognize and register if it is to be a reading at all. Our reading, however, can also find other resources in "A," that the text in question's own reading and understanding of itself has left unexplored or unexploited (in this case, some Bataillean resonances of the *fête*): such resources constitute what the Saussure reading calls "another gesture" in the text, what the Rousseau readings call what the text *describes* but does not *declare*, or what it says without saying or meaning to say, or what it does without saying so. Although Derrida does not put it quite like this, let us call this other possibility or set of possibilities "C." The text says "A," declares "A" to mean "B," and we find that "A" also, alongside or underneath "B," allows for "C." The move often made in the reception of Derrida's work, then, is to point to "C" and treat it as though the text in question *declared* that possibility already, as it were independently of any subsequent reading by Derrida or anyone else. By this logic, *all* results of deconstructive reading can always be credited to the primary texts being read (and the question of reading is thereby shut down): "you see, what Derrida says is *already in* Plato, or Aristotle, or Kant, or Hegel, or Lacan—so who needs Derrida?" This gesture symptomatically, and in the mode of denial, shows up something of

---

39. The earlier version of Agamben's text, entitled "Experimentum linguae," was written for the French edition of *Enfance et histoire* (Paris: Payot, 2002): "La voix ne s'est jamais écrite dans le langage; et le gramme (comme l'a opportunément montré Derrida) n'est que la forme même de la présupposition de soi et de la puissance" (17); the English edition, trans. Liz Heron (London: Verso Books, 1993), gives "(as Derrida fortuitously demonstrated)" (9). The Italian original ("il pensiero di Derrida è venuto per tempo a mostrarlo") at least seems to concede that Derrida's thinking was timely in this regard.

40. See Francesco Vitale's incisive criticisms of Agamben on this point in "Flatus vocis," *Atque* 20 (2017): 63–80.

what Derrida calls "textuality" (so that in a certain sense it is not simply *false* to say that the possibility of "C" is granted by "A"). But grasping what is thus shown up, as Derrida says in "The White Mythology," would require "a new delimitation of corpuses and a new problematic of signatures" (M 274/231). In Agamben's case, perhaps more blatantly than in others, this reattribution of "C" to the author of "A" is doubled by a surplus benefit accruing to Agamben himself (in a gesture Derrida identifies in *Beast and Sovereign I*)—namely that he, Agamben, emerges quite heroically as the first to point out that Aristotle was already pointing to an originary implication of writing in the voice, and that surplus credit is then used to authorize all manner of pronouncements (which in the case in question go along with other massive and dogmatic simplifications of the relations between, for example, language and discourse, semantics and semiotics, philosophy and politics), not just consigning grammatology to metaphysics, but assigning to philosophy its proper task as that of fulfilling Agamben's own program for our future, namely thinking about the voice *not* thus grammatized.

CHAPTER 4

Polykoiranie III (John of Salisbury, Aquinas, Dante, Marsilius of Padua)

Our tagline from Homer sits relatively unread for centuries until the "recovery" of Aristotle's works in the late Middle Ages, and more especially the thirteenth-century translations, most famously by William of Moerbeke, thought to have been encouraged or commissioned by Aquinas himself.[1] The difference this work of translation makes is hard to overstate, given a culture in which learned people did not as a matter of course read Greek (already in the fifth century CE, Augustine notoriously struggled with it).[2] In our case, it is striking, for example, that Aristotle scarcely figures in the mid-twelfth-century *Policraticus* by John of Salisbury (and

---

1. For a detailed account of "Latin Aristotle," with valuable further references, see Robert Pasnau, "The Latin Aristotle," in *The Oxford Handbook of Aristotle*, ed. Christopher Shields (Oxford: Oxford University Press, 2012), 665–689.

2. See *Confessions* 1.14 for the difficulty in learning Greek, and the preface to Book 3 of the *De Trinitate*: "nor are we so familiar with Greek, as to be in any way capable of reading and understanding such books on these subjects in that language." Saint Augustine, *On The Trinity*, trans. Stephen McKenna (Washington, DC: Catholic University of America Press, 1963), 95.

when he does, only in anecdote or in reference to the *Organon*, which had been translated into Latin by Boethius in the fourth century CE and is the object of extensive commentary in John's other *magnum opus*, the *Metalogicon*).[3]

And yet the *Policraticus*, reputedly "the first extended work of political theory to be written in the Latin Middle Ages,"[4] contains some valuable reflections for our purposes, as we await Aristotle's return in (Latin) force. The book's epistolary Prologue is a celebration of reading and writing, of Letters, and indeed is not far short of a description of the structures of inheritance as we laid them out earlier on the basis of Derrida. The pursuit of letters, writes John, "excludes all annoyances stemming from differences of time and place. . . . Arts would have perished, laws would have disappeared, faith and all religious duties would have shattered [*corruerant*], and even the correct use of eloquence would have declined, save that divine compassion granted to mortals the use of letters as a remedy for human infirmity" (3). Only writing (in books, but also, say, in the form of inscriptions on triumphal arches) allows for the preservation of glory or its opposite: "The reputation of the fool and the emperor is the same after a moderate period of time except where the memory of either is prolonged by the beneficence of writers" (ibid.) As John goes on to specify, this is not just a matter for the edification of individual readers or the preservation of the deeds and words of the famous or the infamous, but more particularly applies to the Prince who "is to be proficient in letters, and . . . is to receive counsel from men of letters" (41). This place of letters involves a quite complex understanding of the Hebrew Bible account of the first and second versions of the law, which John is striving to make consistent with the Pauline opposition of spirit and letter—an essential element in the supposed overcoming of Judaism in Christianity. Here is the opening of John's chapter:

3. *The Metalogicon of John of Salisbury: A Twelfth-Century Defense of the Verbal and Logical Arts of the Trivium*, trans. Daniel D. McGarry (Mansfield Centre, CT: Martino Publishing, 2015).

4. John of Salisbury, *Policraticus: of the Frivolities of Courtiers and the Footprints of Philosophers*, ed. and trans. Cary J. Nederman (Cambridge: Cambridge University Press, 1990). On the back cover, the "first extended work" becomes the "first complete work." For the Latin: *Ioannis Saresberiensis episcopi Carnotensis Policratici sive De nugis curialium et vestigiis philosophorum libri 8*, ed. Clemens C. I. Webb, 2 vols. (Oxford: E Typographeo Clarendoniano, 1909).

"When he sits upon the throne of his kingdom, he will write for
himself a copy of this law of Deuteronomy in a book." See that the
prince must not be ignorant of law and, although he takes pleasure in
many privileges, he is not permitted to be ignorant of the laws of God
on the pretext of the martial spirit. The law of Deuteronomy, that is,
the second law, is therefore to be written in the book of his heart [*in
volumine cordis*] so that the first law, which is impressed upon the page,
corresponds to the second, which is recognized by the mystical
intellect. The first could be written on stone tablets; but the second
was not imprinted, except upon a purer intelligence of mind [*puriore
intelligentia mentis*]. And the prince properly writes Deuteronomy in a
book [now a literal book again, then, and not "the book of his heart"]
because he may thus reflect upon the law in his reason without the
letter disappearing from before his eyes. And hence, the letter of the
law is followed in such a fashion that there is no divergence at all from
the purity of its spirit [*Et sic quidem insistit litterae ut nequaquam ab
intellectus discordet puritate*]. For in fact the letter destroys, while the
spirit confers life . . . (41)

So it seems that the literality of the law, the fact that it is essentially *written*, is not so much an obstacle as a prerequisite for the correct (spiritual)
appropriation of it through reading. This means that although the letter
killeth and the spirit giveth life, the spirit does so—at least in the political
sphere—essentially via the letter: the prince shall read the law all the days
of his life, as specified in the Bible,[5] and this is, as it were, a literal reading
that is a (literal) condition of the life in question:

It indeed seems too little to have the law in one's purse [*in mantica*],
unless it is also faithfully protected in one's soul. It is to be read,
therefore, all the days of his life. As a result of this, it is clearly
accepted that it is necessary for princes, who are commanded to reflect

5. Deuteronomy 17:18–10: "And it shall be, when he sitteth upon the throne of
his kingdom, that he shall write him a copy of this law in a book out of *that which
is* before the priests the Levites: And it shall be with him, and he shall read therein
all the days of his life: that he may learn to fear the LORD his God, to keep all
the words of this law and these statutes, to do them: That his heart be not lifted
up above his brethren, and that he turn not aside from the commandment, *to the*
right hand, or *to* the left: to the end that he may prolong *his* days in his kingdom,
he, and his children, in the midst of Israel."

daily upon the text of the divine law, to be proficient in letters.[6] And
perhaps you do not commonly find that priests are commanded to read
the law daily. Yet the prince is to read it each and every day of his life
because the day that the law is not read is not a day of his life, but the
day of his death. (43–44)

This complex relation to reading also affects John's project as such: he reads
in Deuteronomy that the prince must read the law every day of his life,
and in the more general pursuit of his arguments he is also essentially reading, even when he does not make that obvious to *his* reader, be that reader
the nominal addressee of his work or the common, "ignorant" reader of
the time or, we must presume on the basis of the opening of the prologue,
of our time now. Reading John, we are enjoined to more reading, to more
"assiduity" in reading, if only to try to separate out what is his and what he
has taken from his own many readings,[7] what is statement and what is
quotation. And this seems to precede the issue of whether what is advanced
is even true:

> I have helped the case by bringing in pertinent material from diverse
> authors insofar as they contribute or support the concerns that have
> been introduced, occasionally making no mention of the names of the
> authors, not only because your experience in letters is a sign that for
> the most part you will recognize the bulk of them, but also so that the
> ignorant may be incited to more assiduous reading. If anything here
> departs extensively from true faith I am confident that you shall
> indulge me, since I am not promising that all which has been written
> here is true, but that, whether it is true or false, it will serve the reader
> as useful. (6)

This possibility of untruth still being "useful" appears to apply less to
downright falsehood and more to fiction and fable:

> I am not so silly as to ascribe truth to the tale that the winged bird was
> once spoken to by the tortoise or that the country mouse accepted into
> his poor house the city mouse, and so on: but I do not doubt that these
> fictions of ours are of service to instruction. (6)

---

6. In a later chapter John professes particular—and hyperbolic—admiration
for Julius Caesar in this respect: "He was so diligent in literary matters that he
would dictate four letters simultaneously" (79).

7. "The scope of John's learning has often earned him the designation of the
best read man of the twelfth century" (xx).

These two issues (what is true and what is borrowed or cited from others) then communicate with the possibility that the borrowings are not accurate anyway. In an obscure and allusive paragraph invoking a certain "enemy," "I agree that I have told lies," writes John (but with a disarming scriptural reference to the fact that "every man is a liar" [Psalms 116:11]): but then "should he refute my reason and my fictional authorities, the words of the enemy shall not deter me from making amends. Indeed I shall call friend whoever may correct my errors" (7). And in any case, "if it is discovered that what is written somewhere is other than its author's words," this does not demonstrate that I am being deceptive: I have followed historians who disagree among themselves, and, more important for us, "in philosophy I am a devotee of Academic dispute, which measures by reason that which presents itself as more probable. I am not ashamed of the declarations of the Academics, so that I do not recede from their footprints [*ab eorum vestigiis non recedo*] in those matters about which wise men have doubts" (7: remember the full subtitle of John's work is "of the frivolities of courtiers and the footprints of philosophers [*de nugis curialium et vestigiis philosophorum*]"). Much later, in the prologue and chapter 1 of book 7 of the work, John returns to these issues about reading, quoting, fiction and lying, again in the context of the Academic philosophers.

> You, faithful reader [including—iterability *oblige*—us, here, today] will heed not the meaning which the words at first sight designate but the origin of their meaning and the meaning for which they are created. For frivolous matters thus are intermingled with the serious and false matters with the true so that everything may concentrate upon the purpose of cultivating the supreme truth. Do not be disturbed if some of the things which are written here may be found differently elsewhere, since even historical occurrences themselves are discovered to contradict each other in different historical accounts, but they are profitable for the fruits of utility and honour. For I do not hazard to establish the truth myself; but without malice I propose to import for the utility of readers what I have read among various authorities. For even the Apostle does not assert "Whatever is written is true," but: "Whatever is written is written for the sake of our learning [*ad nostrum doctrinam*]," although the entirety of those matters about which he speaks can be reduced to only those which are written in the law of the prophets, about the truth of which no one doubts except those who do not agree with the catholic faith. (147)

Yet there are things I do not find in the authorities, says John, and in those cases my spirit of investigation is closer to that of the Academics than to that of other ancient schools, "so that in the examination of truth each person reserves to himself freedom of judgment and the authority of writers is to be considered useless whenever it is subdued by a better argument" (148). The modesty this entails sets them apart from other ancient philosophers, whose success in the measurement and explanation of natural phenomena led to an overweening "rashness," such that "as if conveyed by the might of giants and strengthened by a prowess no longer human, they puffed up and proclaimed war against the grace of God by means of the vigor of their reason and reliance upon free will":

> And so they were hurled down as often as they were raised up, and by calling themselves wise they were made to be fools, and their unwise heart was darkened, so that those who became fully acquainted with almost everything were the most perniciously in error about most things. In the distraction of their various opinions they were ignorant about even the least of matters. (148–149)

This logic, which subsequently appears to be wielded even against the Academics (who are, however, being described as "preferable to others for imitation" because of their commitment to the pursuit of [a certain] truth), erupts in a rather extraordinary paragraph in which it is genuinely hard to disentangle John's "own" position, and in which the tissue of quotations and allusions tightens as we come to a certain crisis-point in his text.[8] It exacerbates the "distraction" generated by earnest, and in many ways admirable, philosophical debate into scattering. And as if by chance, and perhaps remembering the Prologue's general remarks about fiction and fable, the paragraph turns to the myth of Babel:

> Yet if there are those who vilify the tools of fiction (although the soul of the wise man does not refuse to learn even from the enemy, since the special people of God glitter in the golden clothing and silver ornaments of all the Egyptians); if the fictions of the gentiles, I say, are evil, then a confusion of tongues was caused by God, hurling it down from on high while the impious were constructing the foundations of Babylon on the Plain of Shinar and while they were erecting

8. The editor of the Latin text points to more or less explicit references and allusions to Saint Paul, Ovid, Isidore of Seville, Deuteronomy, Genesis, Exodus, and the Gospel of John in this short passage.

the tower of exaltation and the scaffolding of opposition to God [*dum turris elationis et contradictionis machina in celum erigitur*]; and the withdrawal of impious verbal intercourse was of necessity followed by the dispersal of the population [*subtractoque impiis uerbi commercio ex necessitate secuta est secessio populorum*]. (149; trans. slightly modified)

Which dispersal calls up what for John is an unusually vehement—and, we might suspect, somewhat denegatory—affirmation of the One. He continues:

> Thus, while the genius of the philosophers erected their scaffolding on high to generate a sort of plot against God, the unity of the really immutable and unfailing truth was denied to them, and, covered up by the cloud of their ignorance, they were completely lost to the greatest knowledge of those things which are true on the basis of the one and only Truth. They were convicted by their own works of being given to false beliefs, and just as their guide (namely, the spirit of truth) vanished, so they were scattered into various factions of erroneous and crazy falsehoods [*dispergerentur in uarias sectas erroris et insanias falsas*]. (149; trans. slightly modified)

From this scatter the Truth will have to be more or less laboriously gathered again, with help from the now available translations of Aristotle.

After Moerbeke's and other translations, notably for our purposes of the *Politics, Rhetoric,* and *Metaphysics,* Aristotle is, just a few decades after the *Polycraticus,* never far from discussions of political philosophy, and our Homeric tagline begins to reappear. Not surprisingly in the case of Aquinas's monumental *Commentary* on the *Metaphysics* (1266–72?), which in fact ends on book 12 (Lambda) and therefore on the quotation from Homer that closes that book (although Aquinas does not comment on the fact of the quotation, nor does he mention Homer). Aquinas's lesson 12 on book 12 is, relative to the lines covered (1075a11–1076a4), much the shortest in the whole eight-hundred-plus-page *Commentary,* and it ends the whole huge work as follows:

> 2663: But many rulers [*pluralitas principatuum*] are not good. For example, it would not be good for different families which shared nothing in common to live in a single home. Hence it follows that the whole universe is like one principality and one kingdom [*totum universum est sicut unus principatus et unum regnum*], and must therefore be governed by one ruler [*ab uno gubernatore*]. Aristotle's conclusion is that there is one ruler [*unus princeps*] of the whole universe, the first

mover, and one first intelligible object, and one first good, whom above he called God (1074:C 2544), who is blessed for ever and ever. Amen.[9]

But it is in Aquinas's explicitly political writing that we can observe most clearly the often dogmatic yoking of Aristotle and the Bible. Aquinas's treatise *On Kingship* (*De Regno*), for example,[10] opens with what is essentially a summary, often simply a direct translation (but never presented as such) of the opening of the *Politics*, as can rapidly be judged from the following selections:

> It is natural for a human to be a social and political animal, to live in a multitude, even more than other animals as the necessity of his nature demonstrates. For other animals, nature has prepared food, a covering of hair, teeth, horns, and claws as a means of defence, or failing that, speed in flight. Humanity, on the other hand, was created without any such natural provisions, but instead of these it was endowed with reason, through which one could prepare these things oneself by the service of one's hands . . . This is, further, most clearly evidenced by the fact that the use of speech is more closely related to humanity, through which one person is able to express conceptions to others. Other animals, it is true, express their feelings to each other in a general way, as when a dog expresses anger by barking, and other animals demonstrate their feelings in like fashion. So human beings communicate with their own kind at a higher level than any other animal which is known to be gregarious, such as the crane, the ant, and the bee.[11]

---

9. Compare the anonymous translation of the *Metaphysics* known as the "translatio media," which has simply: "Nec bonum plures dominates. Unus ergo dominatus." (From the online *Aristoteles Latinus Database*. Latin text at https://bit .ly/38P67PY.)

10. See a brief but characteristically bracing summary of Aquinas's text by Michel Foucault in the 1977–78 course *Sécurité, Population, Territoire* (Paris: Gallimard/Seuil, 2004), 238–240. Foucault takes Aquinas to be exemplary of a view of sovereignty that will culminate in the late sixteenth and early seventeenth centuries, at the time of what Foucault still here calls the "very foundation of the classical *épistémè*" (242), according to the very questionable historical schema of *Les mots et les choses*.

11. I quote the *De regno* from the extracts provided in Cary J. Nederman and Kate Langdon Forhan, eds., *Readings in Medieval Political Theory 1100–1400* (Indianapolis: Hackett, 1993), at 99–100, and have consulted the Latin text available online at https://bit.ly/38PN9sj (last accessed March 5, 2019).

But Aquinas also intersperses quotations from Scripture, directly attributed as such (whereas he never so much as refers to Aristotle here, neither by name nor, as often in his work, as "The Philosopher") often enough prepared by arguments that are not straightforwardly to be found in Aristotle,[12] so that, for example, the "more political" nature of humans which in Aristotle flows from possession of *logos* (already in the passage quoted earlier separated out by Aquinas into "reason" and "language," as is not explicitly the case in Aristotle's text) leads immediately to the following monarchical argument that is not strictly Aristotelian at all, and that is haunted by the threat of scatter, even in what becomes a strangely inverted exploitation of the standard analogy between the state and the individual body:

> Therefore, Solomon says in Ecclesiastes 4:9: "It is better to be two than one. For they have the advantages of mutual company." If, therefore, it is natural for human beings to live in the society of many, it is necessary that there exist among them some means by which the common people may be governed. For where there are many people together, and each one is looking out for his own interests, the multitude would be scattered and broken apart [*multitudo in diversa dispergeretur*] unless there was someone from its number to take care of what extends to the good of the multitude; in like manner, the body of a human being or any other animal would disintegrate [*deflueret*] unless there were some general regulating force within the body which would extend to the common good of all the members. With this in mind, Solomon says (Proverbs 11:14): "When there is no governor, the people shall be scattered."[13] (100)

12. Compare Aquinas's unfinished *Commentary on Aristotle's Politics*, which stays much closer to the letter of Aristotle's text.

13. Aquinas quotes Proverbs in Latin: "ubi non est gubernator, dissipabitur populus," interestingly (and interestedly) cutting the quotation just before a positive reference to a "multiplicity of counsellors." The Septuagint gives *hois mē hyparchei kybernēsis, piptousin hōper phylla, sōtēria de hyparchei en pollē boulē*. The Vulgate has "ubi non est gubernator populus corruet salus autem ubi multa consilia." The KJV gives "Where no counsel is, the people fall: but in the multitude of counsellors there is safety." Robert Alter's new translation has: "For want of designs a people falls,/but there is rescue through many councilors." Aquinas is quietly truncating the quotation to avoid the element of multiplicity in *pollē boulē* in the interests of his monarchical argument. Chouraqui has "Sans stratégies, un peuple tombe; le salut est dans la multitude des conseillers." We shall see in due

Although Aquinas does not here explicitly quote from the end of Book Lambda of the *Metaphysics*, it is certainly not far away as he generalizes from this political mix of Aristotle and Scripture so that formally the same teleological schema applies analogically to individual, state, and universe. Note the strictly paralogical "therefore" introducing what is supposed to follow from the analogies—this type of maneuver, perhaps at the limit of intellectual honesty ("Angelic Doctor" notwithstanding), will return shortly in Dante.

> In all things that are governed according to a single end, something
> is found which rules the rest. In the corporeal universe, for example,
> other bodies are regulated according to a certain order of divine
> providence by the first body, namely, a celestial body, and all bodies
> are controlled by a rational creature. Likewise, in the individual human
> being, the soul rules over the body, and among the parts of the soul,
> the passions and desires are ruled by reason. And thus also, among the
> members of the body, one is principal and moves all the others, such
> as the heart or head. Therefore, in every multitude it is proper to have
> some governing power [*aliquod regitivum*].

With this much established, Aquinas can continue his mix of Aristotle and Scripture, splicing his undeclared summary of Aristotle's view of "correct" and "incorrect" or "perverse" governments with quotations from Ezekiel, and leading up to a version of Aristotle's *autarchia* as definitive of the properly political body of the *polis*, now redirected toward a monarchical principle and indeed extended by the notion of "province" to a proto-imperial structure:

> If a just government is extended to one person alone, he is properly
> called king; for this reason, the Lord says through Ezekiel (37:24):
> "My servant, David, will be king over all, and all of them will have one
> shepherd." From this it is clearly shown that, concerning the idea of
> the king, he will be one who excels and he will be a shepherd, seeking
> the common good of the multitude and not his own advantage. Still,
> since human beings must live in a multitude because, if they remain
> solitary, they would not in themselves be sufficient with regard to the
> necessities of life, it follows that the society of a multitude will be
> more perfect to the extent that it is more sufficient in itself with regard
> to the necessities of life.

---

course how the issue of a multitude of counsellors causes a lot of trouble in Hobbes.

Some degree of self-sufficiency exists at the level of household or village, says Aquinas still following Aristotle closely; however, "it exists in a city, which is a perfect community, with regard to all the necessities of life," and now extending Aristotle in scope (Aristotle does not go beyond the city in his initial account in the *Politics*), in the implication that monarchy somehow flows naturally from the earlier descriptions, and the suggestion that there is a continuity between fatherhood and kingship (which Aristotle explicitly contests):

> But still more in one province, because of the need to fight together and to help one another mutually against enemies. Thus, he who rules the perfect community, that is, a city or province, is called a king; but he who rules a home is called head of household, not king. Nevertheless, he has a certain resemblance to a king, on account of which kings are sometimes called the fathers of the people.
>
> It is plain from what is said, therefore, that a king is one who rules over the multitude of a city of province, and rules on account of the common good. For this reason, Solomon says in Ecclesiastes 5:8: "The king rules over a land subject to him." (102)

This is still not Aquinas's direct justification of monarchy, which is addressed in chapter 2[14] of *On Kingship*, entitled "That it is more useful that a multitude of human beings living together be ruled by one person rather than by many." The argument here involves exploiting the equivocation around the concept of One that we have already noted, as Aquinas slides from "one" in the adjectival sense of unity (the political, or indeed theologico-political unit at one with itself, united or unified) to "one" in the numerical sense of single (one and only one leader), making use of an intermediary concept of "peace," and a notion of usefulness or efficiency. Here are the essential moments of this argument, with the often very dubious "logical" articulations highlighted:

> The aim of any ruler should be directed so that he secures the welfare of those whose government he undertakes. . . . **Now**, the welfare and safety of a multitude formed into a society are that its unity, which is called peace [*unitas . . . quae dicitur pax*], may be preserved, since if unity is removed, the advantage of social life is lost and moreover the

---

14. There is some variation in the way *De Regno* is divided into chapters: chapter 2 in the *Readings* volume corresponds to chapter 3 in the online version (see note 11) and in the *Political Writings*, ed. and trans. R. W. Dyson (Cambridge: Cambridge University Press, 2002).

multitude, disputing within itself [*multitudo dissentiens*], becomes a
burden to itself. **Therefore** [*hoc igitur est*], the ruler of a multitude
ought to uphold the most important concern, so that he should attend
to the unity of peace. . . . **Therefore** [*propterea*], the Apostle, having
commended the unity of the faithful people, says (Ephesians 4:3):
"Be careful to protect the unity of the spirit in the bond of peace."[15]
Accordingly [*igitur*], the more effective [*efficacius*] the government is
with regard to protecting the unity of peace [*unitatem pacis*], the more
useful [*utilius*] it will be. **For** [*hoc enim*] that which leads better to the
end we call "useful." And **now it is clear that** [*manifestum est*] what is
itself singular is more able to bring about unity than several things,
just as [*sicut*] the most effective cause of heat is that which is hot in
itself. **Therefore** [*igitur*], the rule of one person is more useful than
the rule of many. (103)

All of which prepares for the corporeal-cosmotheological parallel, itself
involving dogmatic claims about nature, and about the relative priority of
multiplicity and oneness:

> **Once again** [*adhuc*], that which is in accord with nature is best: **for**
> [*enim*] all things function by nature in the best way; **thus** [*enim*] every
> government by nature is by one man. **Indeed** [*enim*] in the multitude
> of bodily members, there is one which moves them all, namely the
> heart; and among the parts of the soul, one power commands them in
> chief, namely, reason. Even among bees there is one king, and in the
> whole universe there is one God, creator and Ruler of all. And this is
> reasonable. **For every multitude is derived from unity** [*omnis enim
> multitudo derivatur ab uno*]. **For this reason** [*quare si*] natural things
> are imitated by a work of art, and since a work of art is better insofar as
> it attains a closer likeness to what is in nature, **it necessarily follows
> that** [*necesse est*] in a human multitude it is best to be ruled by one
> person. (103)

15. It is perhaps a little surprising that Aquinas does not quote a little more
from the immediate context of this verse from Ephesians 4:3–6, which makes repeated use of the motif of the One, in the masculine [*heis*], feminine [*mia*] and
neuter [*hen*] forms: "Endeavouring to keep the unity of the Spirit [*henotēta tou
pneumatos*] in the bond of peace. *There is* one body, and one Spirit [*hen sōma kai hen
pneuma*], even as ye are called in one hope [*mia elpidi*] of your calling; One Lord,
one faith, one baptism [*heis kyrios, mia pistis, hen baptisma*] One God and Father of
all, who *is* above all, and through all, and in you all [*heis theos kai patēr pantōn, ho
epi pantōn kai dia pantōn kai en pasin*]."

Often enough, these late medieval discussions are concerned not just with the apparent convergence, and relative position, of metaphysics, politics and theology, but with a new object of concern, namely the political organization of the church itself, especially in its relation to secular political structures, and more especially the relationship between the Pope and the Holy Roman Emperor. In the early fourteenth century these concerns are acute, and the possible analogies and differences between secular politics and ecclesiastical politics are explored in some memorable work—in the space of just a few years, Marsilius of Padua's remarkable *Defender of the Peace* (1324), William of Ockham's *Dialogus* (early 1330s), and (intellectually speaking much less impressive, and indeed often reading like a parody of scholastic writing), Dante Alighieri's treatise *De monarchia* (1314–21?).[16]

Dante, not far from Aquinas in this, determines that "universal peace" is the end of political action (which concerns temporally finite issues), so that mankind can develop its full, essentially intellectual, potential: the *bios theōrētikos* is, classically, the telos of the *bios politikos*. Dante's task will then be to urge the need for a monarch as a prerequisite for the realization of that end. Again appealing explicitly to the Aristotle (always referred to in Aquinian vein simply as "the Philosopher") of the opening of the *Politics* (and again distorting Aristotle's argument), Dante claims that just as the individual should be guided by the intellectual faculty ("it is the intellectual faculty which guides and directs all the others [*vis ipsa intellectualis est regulatrix et rectrix omnium aliarum*]"), in a household "there must be one person who guides and directs, who is called the *pater familias* or his representative, in line with the Philosopher's observation that 'every household is governed by the eldest,' and his role, as Homer says, is to guide everyone and impose rules on the others [*regulare omnes et leges imponere aliis*]."[17]

The earlier part of the quotation, attributed to Aristotle, is in fact already taken from Homer (*Odyssey* 9.114), as quoted by Aristotle in *Politics* 1252b20. (It appears Dante had no direct knowledge of Homer, and indeed may not actually have read Aristotle's *Politics*).[18] As we have seen to be also

16. All three argued against papal political authority over the Holy Roman Emperor: Marsilius was condemned by the Pope in 1327, and William was excommunicated in 1328. For a much more sympathetic and emphatically "humanist" reading of Dante's *Monarchia*, see Ernst Kantorowicz, *The King's Two Bodies* (Princeton: Princeton University Press, 1957), chap. 8.

17. Dante, *Monarchy*, ed. and trans. Prue Shaw (Cambridge: Cambridge University Press, 1996), 10. I have consulted the Latin text at https://bit.ly /32erxDL (last accessed May 26, 2019).

18. Ibid., 8n9.

the case with our tagline (which will shortly reappear), putting this line back into its immediate context somewhat mitigates its generalizing sententious force and somewhat undermines Dante's purpose in quoting it. Aristotle has in fact by this point of the opening of the *Politics* already advanced beyond the household [*oikos*] formed by the association of male and female (and slave or ox) to consideration of the village [*kome*], something like an extended family, a "colony" linked by kinship to the household from which it emerges:

> The village according to the most natural account seems to be a colony
> from a household, formed of those whom some people speak of as
> "fellow-nurslings [*homogalaktas*]," sons and sons' sons. It is owing
> to this that our cities were at first under royal sway [*ebasileuonto*] and
> that foreign races are so still, because they were made up of parts that
> were under royal rule [*basileuomenon*] for every household is under the
> royal rule [*basileuetai*] of its eldest member, so that colonies from the
> household were too, because of the kinship of their members. And this
> is what Homer means: "And each one giveth law / To sons and eke to
> spouses"—for his Cyclopes live in scattered families; and that is the
> way in which people used to live in early times. Also this explains why
> all races speak of the gods as ruled by a king, because they themselves
> too are some of them actually now so ruled and in other cases used to
> be of old; and as men imagine the gods in human form, so also they
> suppose their manner of life to be like their own. (1252b16–27)

Not only will Aristotle go on explicitly, and importantly for his differences with Plato, to contest the homology between the type of rule involved in household and village and the type of rule involved in the *polis*, but the context here, explicitly one concerning barbarians (and even the exacerbated form of barbarian represented by the Cyclopes, who do not work the land, do not have assemblies or laws—Homer in fact goes on immediately to add the words *oud allelon alegousin*, "they reck nothing of one another" (Murray), "not a care in the world for any neighbor" (Fagles), "without concern for what the others think" (Wilson)) hardly provides support for the type of analogy Dante wants to claim, the more so still as Aristotle also then uses this pre-political organization to provide a breezy anthropological debunking of the theological use of the language of kingship, which rather undermines the authority of the argument Dante is reaching for here.[19]

---

19. As it turns out, the particular Cyclops whom Odysseus goes on to encounter, Polyphemus, seems to be even more of a barbarian, even less political in

Unperturbed, Dante goes on to extend what he thinks is a workable continuity from household through village to city (following Aristotle's sequence) and, following Aquinas, beyond that to "kingdom [*regnum*]" (where the choice of term for this supra-polis political unit rather begs the question as to its appropriate organization) emphasizing the parallels he is finding by repeated use of the formula "if we consider [*si consideremus*]" with which he had already introduced the question of the household:

> **If we consider** a small community [*vicum unum*] whose purpose is neighbourly support in relation both to people and to goods, there must be one person who guides the others [*unum oportet esse aliorum regulatorem*], either appointed by someone from outside or emerging as leader from among their number with the agreement of the others; otherwise not only will they fail to achieve that neighbourly collaboration, but sometimes, if a number of people contest the leadership, the whole community is destroyed [*sed aliquando, pluribus preheminere volentibus, vicinia tota destruitur*]. **If we consider a city,** whose purpose is to be self-sufficient in living the good life, there must be one ruling body [*unum oportet esse regimen*], and this is so [now appealing to Aristotle's famous distinction between correct and deviant forms] not only in just government, but in perverted forms of government as well; if this should not be the case, not only is the purpose of political life [*vite civilis*] thwarted, but the city itself ceases to be what it was. Lastly, **if we consider** an individual kingdom—and the purpose of a kingdom is the same as that of a city, but with greater confidence that peace can be maintained—there must be one king who rules and governs [*oportet esse regem unum qui regat atque gubernet*]; otherwise not only do those who live in the kingdom not achieve that purpose, but the kingdom itself falls to ruin [*sed etiam regnum in interitum labitur*]. (10)

This quasi-Aristotelian teleology, which in Aristotle himself culminates at the level of the *polis* and its all-but self-sufficiency, is now fearlessly extended even further by Dante, to mankind taken as a whole:

> Now it is agreed that the whole of mankind is ordered to one goal . . . there must therefore be one person who directs and rules mankind, and he is properly called "Monarch" or "Emperor" [*ergo unum oportet esse regulans sive regens, et hoc 'Monarcha' sive 'Imperator' dici debet*] (11)

Aristotle's sense, than the usual Cyclops: he "mingled not with others, but lived apart, with his heart set on lawlessness," the very figure of the naturally non-political beastly and/or godly man we will discuss in some detail later.

Having established this much, Dante, like Aquinas before him, wants to relate it to the divine order of the cosmos. This he does by arguing that parts of wholes relate primarily not among themselves, but to the whole of which they are a part, which whole gives the part its *telos*. This initially (in 1.6) is taken to confirm the point just made: "thus the parts we have enumerated which are lower than kingdoms, and those kingdoms themselves, must be ordered to one ruler or one rule, that is to a monarch or monarchy." But the argument by parts and wholes now allows the desired theological extension: the human race is the whole that orders its parts, but it is itself merely a part of the whole universe, teleologically ordered by God: "absolutely speaking it [the human race] too is well adapted to the universe (or to its ruler, who is God and Monarch) in relation to a single principle, i.e., one ruler. And thus it follows that monarchy is necessary to the well-being of the world." The God who rules the universe as Monarch (explicitly described as prime mover, *primi agentis*) wishes every created thing to be in His likeness to the extent that it can. So mankind "is in a good (indeed, ideal) state when, to the extent that its nature allows, it resembles God." And now a further sequence of paralogisms, including a reference to the Oneness of God in the formulation we read in Deuteronomy and again in Mark:

> But mankind most resembles God when it is most a unity, since the true measure of unity is in him alone; and for this reason it is written "hear, O Israel, the Lord thy God is one [*Audi, Israel, Dominus Deus tuus unus est*]."[20] But mankind is most a unity when it is drawn together to form a single entity, and this can only come about when it is ruled as one whole by one ruler, as is self-evident. Therefore mankind is most like God when it is ruled by one ruler, and consequently is most in harmony with God's intention. (13)

If this is not convincing enough, the ninth section offers a slightly different version of the same argument, this time starting from a dogmatic statement of the paternal metaphor:

> Every son is in a good (indeed ideal) state when he follows in the footsteps of a perfect father, insofar as his own nature allows. Mankind is the son of heaven, which is quite perfect in all its working. . . . Therefore mankind is in its ideal state when it follows the footsteps of

---

20. The Vulgate actually translates the *shema Israel* as "Dominus Deus noster Deus unus est."

heaven, insofar as its nature allows. And since the whole sphere of
heaven is guided by a single movement (i.e., that of the Primum
Mobile) . . . then if our argument is sound, mankind is in an ideal state
when it is guided by a single ruler. . . . Hence it is clear that monarchy
(or that undivided rule which is called "empire") is necessary to the
well-being of the world.

All of which prepares a sequence which derives the necessity of the monarch along lines that are also reminiscent of Xenophanes, and that culminate in Odysseus's line, now simply attributed directly to Aristotle. Here
is the whole of chapter 10 of the first part of *De Monarchia*:

> Now wherever there can be conflict [*litigium*] there must be judgment
> to resolve it, otherwise there would be an imperfection without its
> proper corrective; and this is impossible, since God and nature never
> fail in matters of necessity. There is always the possibility of conflict
> between two rulers where one is not subject to the other's control;
> such conflict may come about either through their own fault or the
> fault of their subjects (the point is self-evident); therefore there must
> be judgment between them. And since neither is judge of the other
> (since neither is under the other's control, and an equal has no power
> over an equal) there must be a third party of wider jurisdiction who
> rules over both of them by right. And this person will either be the
> Monarch or not. If he is, then our point is proved; if he is not, he in his
> turn will have an equal who is outside the sphere of *his* jurisdiction,
> and then it will once again be necessary to have recourse to a third
> party. And so either this procedure will continue *ad infinitum*, which is
> not possible, or else we must come to a first and supreme judge, whose
> judgment resolves all disputes either directly or indirectly; and this
> man will be the Monarch or the Emperor. Thus monarchy is neces-
> sary to the world. And the Philosopher saw this reason when he said:
> "Things do not wish to be badly ordered; a plurality of reigns is bad;
> therefore let there be one ruler [*Entia nolunt male disponi; malum autem
> pluralitas principatuum: unus ergo princeps*]." (14–15)

Further "logical" arguments, which Dante proudly describes in terms of
syllogisms and prosyllogisms ("this prosyllogism is of the second figure
with intrinsic negation") and even some formal features ("all B is A; only
C is A; therefore only C is B") follow to establish the superiority of monarchy in other ways. In chapter 11, "the world is ordered in the best possible way when justice is at its strongest in it. . . . The more powerful a just
man is, the more effectively will justice be brought about by his actions. . . .

Only the monarch is such a subject; therefore justice is at its strongest in the world when it is located in the monarch alone" (17). In chapter 12, "living under a monarch [the human race] is supremely free" in that it exists for its own sake: "Mankind exists for its own sake and not for the sake of something else only when it is under the rule of a monarch, for only then are perverted forms of government (i.e., democracies, oligarchies and tyrannies), which force mankind into slavery, set right . . . for since the monarch loves men most . . . he wants all men to become good; and this cannot happen under perverted forms of government" (21). As these arguments proceed more or less compellingly, there is a striking drift toward the thematic of the One and of multiplicity, which are reminiscent of some of the things we saw in the pseudo-Dionysius, but that also, given Dante's almost parodic logicism, bring out the more sharply some of the implications of those arguments. So in chapter 14, Dante argues that "what can be brought about by a single agent is better done by a single agent than by more than one," and rather hilariously formalizes the argument as follows:

> Let there be one agent (A) by which something can be brought about, and let there be several agents (A and B) by which it can equally be brought about; now if that same thing which can be brought about by means of A and B can be brought about by A alone, then B is introduced unnecessarily, because nothing is achieved by the introduction of B, since that same thing was already achieved by means of A alone.

Which can perhaps seem anodyne enough, except that Dante immediately and confidently pushes the argument toward questions of good and evil. Introducing B in the preceding example is "unnecessary and pointless"; such things are "displeasing to God and to nature, and everything which is displeasing to God and to nature is evil [*malum*] (as is self-evident)." It follows "that not only is it better that something be brought about by a single agent, where that is possible, rather than by several, but that being brought about by a single agent is good, by more than one in absolute terms bad." The chapter concludes on a rather stunning argument whereby the comparative judgement "is better" can be converted to a superlative by an absolutizing claim whereby, when supposedly only two things (that is, one and more-than-one) are being compared, the better simply *is* the best:

> Therefore it is better for mankind to be ruled by one person than by several, and thus by a monarch who is the only ruler; and if this is better, then it is more acceptable to God, since God always wills what is better. And since when there are only two things being compared, the better *is* the best, it follows that when the choice is between "one"

and "more than one," not only is the first of these more acceptable [*acceptabilius*] to God, but it is entirely acceptable [*acceptabilissimum*; most acceptable]. It follows from this that mankind is in its ideal state when it is ruled by one person; and thus monarchy is necessary to the well-being of the world. (25)

The formal political implications of these arguments are clear enough: but Dante is ambitious enough in chapter 15 to advance into deeper metaphysical and theological waters, again relying on the convergence of Aristotelian and scriptural motifs. According to a pedantically marked sense of "priority" (the fifth of the twelve senses Aristotle advances in the *Categories*), Dante argues for the priority of being [*ens*] over unity [*unum*], and the priority of *unum* over goodness [*bonum*], such that "the further removed something is from perfect being, the further it is from being one and consequently from being good" (26).[21] By hallucinating the value of *bonum* alongside *to on* and *to hen* into Aristotle's *Metaphysics*,[22] Dante can align anything more than one with sin, no less, thus apparently accomplishing a metaphysical confirmation of the familiar Augustinian association of vice and evil with multiplicity and variegation.[23] "This is how it comes about," says Dante, "that unity seems to be the root of what it is to be good, and

21. These are the three *transcendentalia* of Scholastic philosophy. I will return elsewhere to the difficulties posed by the fact that, according to Aristotle, they are all *pollacha legomena*, "said in many ways."

22. The editor of the Cambridge University Press edition of Dante's *Monarchia* (26n2) provides references to book *Iota*, which is indeed the book of "the one," but those references (to 1053b20–28 and 1054a9–14) say nothing about the good.

23. See, for example, the opening of book 2 of the *Confessions* (edited and translated by Carolyn J-B. Hammond, 2 vols. (Cambridge, MA: Harvard University Press, 2014–16): "pulling me back together from the disintegration in which I was being shattered and torn apart, when I turned away from you who are unity and dispersed into the multiplicity that is oblivion [*conligens me a dispersio, in qua frustatim discissus sum dum ab uno te aveersos in multa evanui*]" (1:61). See too, from book 4: "I loved the peace that is found in virtue, so likewise I hated the discord that attaches to vice. In the one I remarked its unity, in the other a kind of disunity [*divisionem*]" (1:173) and from book 10, famously, "Through continence . . . we are joined together and restored to wholeness, from which we trickled away into multiplicity [*a quo in multa defluximus*]" (2:139), and "another kind of temptation, far more dangerous in its diversity [*alia forma temptationis multiplicius periculosa*]" (2:161). See *Scatter 1* (New York: Fordham University Press, 2016), 125–126, for the survival of this motif in Heidegger.

plurality the root of what it is to be evil"; and now a reference to Pythagoras, who Dante claims "placed unity on the side of goodness and plurality
on the side of evil," pretending that this is supported by Aristotle in Book
A of the *Metaphysics*, where Aristotle is in fact criticizing rather than endorsing the Pythagorean position—which in any case does not, at least in
Aristotle's presentation of it, concern good and evil at all. On the basis of
this evidence, "it can be seen that to sin is nothing other than to spurn
unity and move towards plurality" (26), and this marks the conclusion to
this "theoretical" part of the work, and allows Dante to go on to claim in
chapter 16 (the last chapter of part I) that the kind of good universal monarchy which he has been attempting to derive from first principles in fact
existed in the reign of Caesar Augustus, which happened to coincide with
the life of Christ, and which Dante does not hesitate to assimilate to the
Pauline "fullness of time." For now, let us take the final paragraph of chapter 15 as a kind of culmination of the tradition of "reading" our tagline
that we have been following:

> Having made these preliminary points in order to clarify the proposi-
> tion to be advanced for our purposes, we may reason as follows: all
> concord depends on the unity which is in wills; mankind in its ideal
> state represents a kind of concord; for just as one man in his ideal state
> spiritually and physically is a kind of concord (and the same holds true
> of a household, a city, and a kingdom), so is the whole of mankind; thus
> the whole of mankind in its ideal state depends on the unity which is
> in men's wills. But this cannot be unless there is one will which controls
> and directs all the others towards one goal, since the wills of mortals
> require guidance on account of the seductive pleasures of youth, as
> Aristotle teaches at the end of the *Ethics*.[24] Nor can such a single will
> exist, unless there is one ruler who rules over everybody, whose will
> can control and guide all the other wills. Now if all the above conclu-
> sions are true—as they are—for mankind to be in its ideal state there
> must be a monarch in the world, and consequently the well-being of
> the world requires a monarchy. (27)

24. The reference, to 1179b32 and following, is typically imprecise: Aristotle
does indeed say that "to live temperately and hardily is not pleasant to most
people, especially when they are young," but his main point is that the difficulties
that ensue are not limited to the young, so our laws need to cover the whole of
life, and not just youth.

A century later, a clear allusion to our tagline appears in Nicholas of Cusa, who also uses the "court of final appeal" argument used by Dante:

> There are many reasons why there should only be one ruler, even if the government is made up of several leading men united in agreement. Otherwise confusion would arise when several compete in ruling and good order would be destroyed when the subjects do not know whom to obey. It is bad to have many rulers, for there should be one to whom a final appeal can be made with certainty.[25]

But in this Book III of his work, Nicholas is in fact drawing quite extensively not on the *De monarchia*, but on a work almost exactly contemporaneous with Dante's, namely Marsilius of Padua's *Defender of the Peace* (1324), famous for arguing against the view that the Pope should hold sway over the temporal political authorities. Marsilius, like Dante (the main point of whose book is in fact to claim that the Pope does not have authority over the Emperor, whose authority comes directly from God), attributes our line (or at least the thought behind it) directly to Aristotle, and alludes to it twice in his work. In chapter 16 of the first discourse of the book, Marsilius, not simply or straightforwardly a monarchist,[26] unlike Dante, and explicitly dubious of the One Best Man argument we shall be discussing in due course (see especially Discourse 1, chapter 11), is wondering whether, given monarchy, it is better for it to be elected or hereditary.[27] His final

---

25. Nicholas of Cusa, *The Catholic Concordance*, ed. and trans. Paul E. Sigmund (Cambridge: Cambridge University Press, 2003), 210.

26. Marsilius of Padua, *The Defender of the Faith*, ed. and trans. Annabel Brett (Cambridge: Cambridge University Press, 2005); Latin, ed. C. W. Previté-Orton (Cambridge: Cambridge University Press, 1928). As the editor of the translation points out in a note at 114: "Dante put forward a series of arguments concerning unity in his *Monarchy*. . . . But all of these saw the argument for the unity of government as an argument for the unity of one single governor, i.e., for monarchy, whereas Marsilius makes it clear that these are two different arguments: so long as the principate is a unity, there can be several exercising the function of prince at the same time."

27. Some variation of this problem will return again and again in discussions of monarchy: the problem arises because the monarch is mortal, and we might suspect that the whole later construction of the doctrine of the "king's two bodies" emerges from it—later we will see Hobbes with characteristic truculence half-admitting that in this respect alone democratic sovereignty might have an advantage over monarchy.

argument (§10) in favor of the latter solution is cosmological or theologico-metaphysical in scope:

> Finally, because the principate of a monarch who succeeds on the basis of heredity is more similar to the governance or principate of the entire universe, since in the universe it is always one alone who exists unchangeably, as in *Metaphysics* XII, last chapter: "One prince, therefore, because beings do not wish to be badly arranged." But this is what seems to happen where the son succeeds the father to the principate, because of the unity of the family and also because the father is judged to be almost the same person as the son. (103)

Just a little later, in chapter 17, Marsilius argues directly for the "numerical unity of the principate or the prince [*unitate numerali principates aut principantis*]: "we wish to establish for certain that either the principate or prince is only one in number in a city or a realm, or that if there are several, the one that is supreme over them all is only one in number and not more [*aut si plures, supremum omnium esse unicum tantum numero*]" (17, 3 [115]). As was also the case in Dante, this logic generates an almost automatic link between plurality as such and evil:

> If there were more than one principate in a city or realm, and they were not reduced[28] or ordered towards any one supreme [*non reducti seu ordinari sub aliquo uno supremo*], then the judgement, command and execution of what is advantageous and just would fail, and the result . . . would be fighting, disintegration [*separatio*] and ultimately the destruction of the city or realm. Now this consequence is an evil most of all to be avoided; that it follows from the given antecedent, sc. a plurality of principates, can be plainly shown. (115–116)

The "demonstration," which is not immediately convincing, goes as follows: someone who transgresses the laws needs to appear before the prince: if there is more than one principate that does not ultimately reduce to one, then no such appearance could be satisfactory (how could one appear at the same time before more than one prince? Suppose different princes of equal rank—not "reduced to one"—made different findings and imposed different penalties?) This will inevitably lead to contradiction and impossibility. Conclusion: "A plurality of such principates, not ranked in

---

28. On the *reductio ad unum*, see the helpful note 3 at 114–115, which derives it from the pseudo-Dionysius and points out that it could be used to argue for papal sovereignty as well as for secular monarchy.

respect of each other, is therefore an impossibility for a city or realm if what is just and advantageous in civil terms is to be safeguarded." (17, 3 [117]). There follow several other similar arguments (suppose several princes convene the citizens in different places at the same time, or different times at the same place, and propose different things to those gatherings (§4); the citizens would split into warring factions depending on which prince they chose to obey (§5); "Again, if we suppose this kind of plurality, there will be something redundant and superfluous in one of the greatest products of reason and art, since whatever civil profit could be had from several principates can perfectly well be had from one, or one supreme, without the evils that result from a plurality of them" (§6). This is prelude to the fuller argument that, absent a single supreme principate, the city or realm will not be *one*, and once this not-oneness occurs, there is, apparently immediately, an unmasterable profusion or scatter of evils (that scatter being itself evil, according to the Augustinian association we also saw in Dante):

> Furthermore, supposing a plurality of principates in this way, no realm or city will be one. For realms and cities are said to be one on account of the unity of the principate, towards which and for the sake of which the remaining parts of the city are ordered. . . . And again there will be no order in the parts of the city or realm, since they are not ordered to any first part if they are not bound to be subject to any one . . . and so they and the whole city will be in confusion: for every man will choose for himself the office he wants, one or more, without anyone to regulate them or separate them out. So many more evils would follow from this that it is not easy or even possible to enumerate them. (§7)

After a traditional comparison in this regard between the city and an animal body (a well-ordered city is like a well-formed animal), Marsilius again alludes to Aristotle's use of our tagline to give his argument its ontologico-metaphysical authority: "since it is in the nature of beings that the primary principle should be one in number, not more, because 'beings do not wish to be badly arranged,' as is maintained in *Metaphysics*; therefore the primary principate established according to the reason and art of men will also be only one in number" (§9, 119).

The nature of the oneness, the "numerical unity" is then further specified as a teleological principle: the state or city is not one in the "formal" sense because (as we shall see in our reading of Aristotle, who is taking his distance from Plato in this respect and opening thereby the very space of politics as such: the point is not to argue plurality away but to "order" it toward a unity that is its *telos*):

the numerical unity of a city or realm is . . . not a unity simply speaking but a plurality of elements, called one or said to be one thing in
number. This is not because they are formally one in number through
the existence of some form, but rather they are truly said to be one in
number because they are spoken of in relation to something that is one
in number, sc. the principate: towards which and for the sake of which
they are ordered and governed [*sed unum numero vere dicuntur, propterea quod ad unum numero dicuntur, scilicet principatum, ad quem &
propter quem ordinantur & gubernantur.*] . . . In the same sort of way the
world is said to be one in number and not several worlds. All beings
are said to be one world not because of some numerically unique form
that inheres formally in the universe of beings, but because of the
numerical unity of the first being, since every being naturally inclines
towards and depends upon the first being [*quoniam entium quodcunque
naturaliter inclinator, & pendet ab ente primo*]. Hence the predication by
which all beings are said to be one world in number is not a formal
predication of some numerical unity in all of them, nor of some universal
predicated in consequence of one thing; rather, it is a plurality of certain
elements that is said to be one because it is towards and for the sake of
one. So too the men of one city or province are said to be one city or
realm, because their will is for one single principate [*quia volunt unum
numero principatum*]. (§11)

This cosmo-ontologico-metaphysical justification of the sense in which the
city (or realm, or animal body politic) is one, itself opens further difficulties. For if the plurality of beings can be unified by teleological reference
to the primary being toward which that plurality is organized, and if that
principle justifies the sense in which the city is one, then might we not extend that principle to the world as a whole, in a kind of cosmopolitical
gesture à la Dante? Here Marsilius, treading carefully on difficult theological ground,[29] anticipates an argument more familiar from Kant, who
allows a certain interruption of his own teleological notion of "perpetual
peace" on the (Babelian) grounds that "nature wisely separates the nations"

---

29. See note 12 at 120, which points out that such a hypothesis would have
been associated with the so-called Averroist reading of Aristotle, which had been
the subject of a famous condemnation by the Bishop of Paris in 1277. See, too, the
helpful introduction to and translation of the text of that condemnation in *Medieval Political Philosophy: A Sourcebook*, ed. Joshua Parens and Joseph C. Macfarland,
2nd ed. (Ithaca, NY: Cornell University Press, 2011), 320–332.

to avoid the unhappy consequences of too rapid or complete a unification
of the world as a whole.[30]

> As to whether it is appropriate for the universal body of those who
> live a civil life throughout the whole world [*utrum autem universitati
> civiliter viventium & in orbe totali unico numero supremum omnium
> principatum habere conveniat*], to have a single principate that is supreme
> over all [as we might have been tempted to think given the drift of
> Marsilius's argument thus far] or whether at any one time it is appro-
> priate to have different such principates in different reaches of the
> world, separated almost of necessity by their geographical situation,
> and particularly in those which do not share a language and are very
> far apart in manners and custom; this being perhaps propelled by a
> celestial cause, to avoid the over-propagation of humanity [*ne hominum
> superflua propagatio fiat*]; this is a topic for rational examination, but a
> different one from the present inquiry. For it might perhaps occur to
> someone that nature, by means of battles and epidemics, has put a
> check on the propagation pf men and the other animals, so that the
> land should suffice for their development. (§10)

"Almost of necessity. . . ." Perhaps nature limits the scattering propagation
of humanity by encouraging the maintenance of a *certain* scatter of principates, each no doubt internally "one" according to the arguments we have
rehearsed, but only doubtfully to be unified on a "higher" international or
cosmopolitical plane. As is regularly the case throughout the history of political thought, trouble begins once "the state" (the habitual object of political philosophy) has to be seen in the context of more-than-one-state, and
therefore has to encounter the perhaps intractable issue of the frontier.

---

30. See my *Kant on the Frontier*, 77–78.

Polykoiranie IV (Bodin, La Boétie)

The afterlife of our tagline continues beyond its explicit fourteenth-century iterations in Dante and Marsilius, and at least indirectly in William of Ockham's contemporaneous *Short Discourse on Tyrannical Government* (1334–47) and in other works.[1] It is at least alluded to in Francisco Suárez's

---

1. "For according to Aristotle in *The Politics*, kingship is the best constitution, and therefore unless one head has lordship of the whole world the best mode of ruling the world will be lacking. He is therefore not a true lover of the common good who does not desire and work as much as is permissible in his station to make the whole world subject to one monarch," translated by John Kilcullen in *A Short Discourse on Tyrannical Government*, ed. A. S. McGrade (Cambridge: Cambridge University Press, 1992), 128–129. See, too, in Ockham's slightly earlier *Dialogus*, "It is beneficial for the community of the faithful to be governed in matters relating to the Christian religion under the form of government that most resembles the best secular constitution. But the best secular constitution is kingship, as Aristotle testifies." William of Ockham, *A Letter to the Friars Minor and Other Writings*, trans. John Kilcullen, ed. A. S. McGrade (Cambridge: Cambridge University Press, 1995), 127.

Commentary on Aristotle's Metaphysics in the late sixteenth or early seventeenth century,[2] and—more importantly for our purposes—around the same time it reappears to very different effect in two famous works both first published in 1576, namely Jean Bodin's *Six livres de la république* and Etienne de la Boétie's *De la servitude volontaire*. Bodin is of course widely credited with being among the first to formulate a "modern" concept of sovereignty, which he names as such in Book I, Chapter VIII of his work. It would probably be unwise to overemphasize the modern or innovative quality of Bodin's definitions, if only in that he explicitly presents "la souveraineté" as the equivalent of ancient terms in other languages, as though the concept itself existed before Bodin's work, albeit ill- or undefined:

> Sovereignty is the absolute and perpetual power of a commonwealth, which the Latins call *maiestas*, the Greeks [using terms most of which we already saw in Homer] *akra exousia, kurion arche*, and *kurion politeuma* . . . while the Hebrews call it *tomech shévet*—that is, the highest power of command.[3]

Derrida comments quite briefly on these opening sentences of the sovereignty chapter in *La bête et le souverain I* (79–80/47–48), in preparation for a longer discussion of Hobbes, and names Bodin a handful of times in *Rogues*. We have already mentioned in passing one of those references, in which Derrida is making his transition from the plural "peuple de dieux"

2. Francisco Suárez, *A Commentary on Aristotle's Metaphysics*, trans. John P. Doyle (Milwaukee: Marquette University Press, 2004), who entitles his commentary on *Lambda* X, "There is one Prince and Governor of the Universe," and suggests that Aristotle is proposing a syllogism with a major premise ("The good of the universe consists in the appropriate order of its parts, in such a way that this good is a kind of intrinsic good which inheres in the universe itself"), a minor premise ("it cannot have a good of this kind unless there is in it someone who is its Governor, who is at the same time outside it and its ultimate end, from whom it emanates and to whom it returns as the extrinsic good of the universe"), and a conclusion ("Therefore, one supreme Prince and Governor is necessary in the universe"). The conclusion to *Lambda* X is then presented as a "proof" of the minor premise: "A plurality of governing principles is not good, and it does not contribute to good government: 'but beings are unwilling to be governed badly'; therefore, let there be one Prince" (216–217).

3. Where possible, I quote Bodin from the abridged edition entitled *On Sovereignty*, ed. and trans. Julian H. Franklin (Cambridge: Cambridge University Press, 1992), at 1. For passages not included in this translation, I have translated from a 1579 fourth edition published by Jacques du Puys in Paris.

remark that interests him in Rousseau, to the "salut politique au Dieu Un" that he sees in Plato and Aristotle: the plurality of "gods," on Derrida's reading, opens a protodemocratic space or division in what has traditionally been seen as the *indivisibility* of the sovereign. Elsewhere in *Rogues*, that indivisibility is related to the temporality of sovereignty, to the sovereign decision or exception that happens instantaneously. Reserving for now direct discussion of Derrida's analysis of the tensions between democracy and sovereignty in this section of *Rogues*, and of the role of language and silence in those tensions, let's simply note this temporal claim (and the "s'il y en a . . ." motif again):

> Sovereignty itself (if there is one and if it is pure) always keeps quiet in the very ipseity of the moment proper to it, a moment that can only be the stigmatic point of an indivisible instant. A pure sovereignty is indivisible or it is not at all, as all the theoreticians of sovereignty have rightly recognized, and that is what links it to the decisionist exceptionality spoken of by Schmitt. . . . In a certain way, then, sovereignty is ahistorical; it is the contract contracted with a history that retracts in the instantaneous event of the deciding exception, an event that is without any temporal or historical thickness. (V 143–144/100–101)

The time of the sovereign, as we shall have occasion to verify with reference to Rousseau (and indeed Bataille), is a time of pure instants, "without temporal thickness," as Derrida says, though here conceived not interruptively, but as a time each time full of itself, pure presence of the will to itself, without relation to any other instant, instantaneous and thereby also eternal presence. Any sovereignty "worthy of the name" must thus be punctual but also eternal. Now perpetuity is indeed the first characteristic of the sovereign established by Bodin in the *Six Books of the Republic*: and even if Bodin, who also recognizes the punctuality of sovereignty in that the sovereign is not subject to the laws he pronounces (this will become Schmitt's famous "exception"[4])—even if Bodin will end up understanding

---

4. Etienne Balibar contests this. He suggests that Schmitt misreads Bodin on this point. Cf. "Prolégomènes à la souveraineté: La frontière, l'État, le peuple," *Les Temps modernes* 610 (September–November 2000): 47–75. See Derrida's comments on this in *La bête et le souverain I* (80–81/48–49): "Balibar thinks that Bodin's whole doctrine belies this '[Schmittian] primacy of the exception.' And in support of his thesis, Balibar affirms that Schmitt's interpretation amounts to 'distorting the sense of Bodin's construction, which considers the state of exception precisely as an exception, the status and treatment of which depend on the

"perpetuity" in terms of the natural life of the sovereign, the very logic of this perpetuity will push him almost mechanically into preferring heredi- tary monarchy to other forms of government, given that, as he says, "The King never dies."[5]

Bodin negotiates the difficult relation between the perpetuity and in- stantaneity of sovereignty in terms of *promise* and *perjury*. According to a very tortuous argument, the sovereign, so as not to commit perjury, *must not* promise (promise to subject himself to existing laws, or even to main- tain them in place), for what is proper to sovereignty is clearly to be able to make the law, but also to change it: if the first "true mark" of sovereignty is "the power to give law to all in general, and each in particular" (56), this power is immediately "power to give *and* [literally] *break* the law [*puissance de donner & casser la loy*]" (58, my emphasis; *casser* less literally in this con- text means to quash or rescind), and therefore to change the laws (the civil laws, that is, since Bodin will say that the Prince, above the laws he gives and breaks at one and the same time, is nonetheless obliged to recognize the laws of God and nature). More simply still: "absolute power is nothing other than derogation of civil laws" (39). In the sovereign instant, the law that is given breaks or replaces the existing law. By the very fact that the word of the sovereign has immediate force of law, it immediately and radi- cally contains an illegal or alegal moment. A sovereign who promised to maintain the existing civil laws would therefore either be less than sover- eign, or else in perjury just because of his sovereignty; having shown that the King of Denmark is not truly sovereign, because the nobility obliged him to promise to respect certain of their rights, Bodin continues:

> But it has to be one way or the other. The prince who swears to keep
> the civil laws either is not sovereign or else becomes a perjurer if he

---

constituted norm.' No doubt. But does Schmitt say anything different? The ex- ception is the exception, it must remain the exception, it is not the norm even if it appears as exception only with respect to the norm. Schmitt has not said that the exception is normal, which would be absurd, any more than sovereignty is nor- mal, even if he has said that the exception is more interesting and decisive than the norm."

5. "Car il est certain que le Roy ne meurt jamais, comme lon dit, ains si tost que l'vn est decedé, le plus proche masle de son estoc est saisi du Royaume, & en possession d'iceluy au parauant qu'il soit couronné. [For it is certain that the King never dies, as they say, because as soon as one is deceased, the closest male of his stock takes over the Kingdom, and is in possession of it before being crowned.]" *Les six livres de la république* (Paris: Jacques du Puys, 1579) 1.8, 160.

violates his oath, which a sovereign prince will have to do in order to
annul [*casser*], change, or correct the laws according to the exigencies
of situations, times, and persons. Or else, if we say that the prince,
without ceasing to be sovereign, is still bound to take the advice of the
Senate or the people, he will also have to be dispensed by his subjects
from the oath he took to keep the laws inviolate; and the subjects who
are bound and obligated to the laws, both individually and collectively,
will also need a dispensation from the prince on pain of being per-
jured. Sovereignty will be tossed up and back between two parties
[*la souveraineté sera jouée à deux parties*], and sometimes the people,
sometimes the prince will be the master—which are egregious
absurdities and utterly incompatible with absolute sovereignty, as well
as contrary to the laws and to natural reason. (27)

The sovereign must promise nothing, on pain of inevitable perjury: and
the sovereign must not be a perjurer, for he is, even *qua* sovereign, obliged
to respect and impose respect for the laws of God ("who is the absolute
sovereign of all the Princes in the world"). The sovereign must not promise, not simply because he would be free not to keep his promises, but
because he must guarantee the sanctity of the promise in general. If he
must not promise, this is because the sovereign is *even less* allowed than
anyone else to be a perjurer: "a sovereign prince is bound by the contracts
he has made, whether with his subject or with a foreigner. For since he is
the guarantor to his subjects of the agreements and mutual obligations that
they have entered with one another, *a fortiori* he is duty bound to justice
in his own affairs [*à plus forte raison est-il debiteur de justice en son faict*]" (35),
and there are two reasons for this:

> For the obligation is twofold. It arises on the one hand from natural
> equity, which requires that agreements and promises be kept and, on
> the other, from the prince's good faith, which he ought to honor even
> if he suffers loss, because he is the formal guarantor to all his subjects
> of good faith among themselves: and because there is no crime more
> detestable in a prince than perjury. That is why the sovereign Prince
> must always be less tolerated by justice than his subjects when a
> promise is at stake . . . the prince is so obliged by agreements that he
> makes with his subjects, be they merely of civil right, that with all his
> absolute power he cannot break them . . . seeing as God himself, as the
> master of Sentences says, is bound to his promise. (35–36)

This dimension of faith (not simply faith in God, but something like faith
in God's [good] faith, faith that God himself is obliged by his promise) can

alone prevent sovereignty from becoming mere violence, prevent its absolute power becoming what Bodin calls a "career" of absolute *criminal* power
(39). In other terms, sovereignty may indeed be in itself "derogation of civil
laws," but this power of derogation is only sovereign to the extent that it is
exercised in the name of the law, of the law of law, the being-law of the
law, so to speak, which is that the law indeed be law, be worthy of faith as
the law that it is. Even "breaking" the laws, the sovereign makes the law,
cannot but make the law: the sovereign is even more obliged to the law
that his subjects, more subject than his subjects to the law of the law, i.e.,
faith in the promise. Simple derogation of laws renders the sovereign less
than sovereign: sovereign is only he who makes the law itself at every instant, absolutely, while breaking the existing law in the same blow.

It follows that the sovereign, in order to be sovereign, in order to be
worthy of his name, cannot simply hold himself at the point of the sovereign instant itself, even though that instant defines him as sovereign. Like
it or not, the sovereign, breaking the law each time, makes the law each
time, cannot, as it were, prevent himself from making the law, and thus
promising, on pain of not being sovereign. A law that did not promise would
not be a law: every word of the sovereign is law and therefore promise. The
sovereign must not promise, and yet promises at every moment.

The definition of the sovereign as simultaneously making and breaking the law, and the prospect of a potentially criminal "career" that follows from that definition, means that the traditional question of tyranny,
a focus of political thought at least since Plato, takes on a slightly different
cast and urgency. Bodin recognizes a certain continuity between sovereign
and tyrant ("the tyrant is nonetheless a sovereign" [6]), and we might even
be tempted to think that the tyrant on Bodin's definition is merely an extension or doubling down of the logic of sovereignty: if a tyrant is "someone who makes himself into a sovereign prince by his own authority" (110),
we might think that such a tyrant would be the epitome of sovereignty itself. Anticipating arguments that will return in Hobbes and Kant, Bodin
will accept a consequence of this continuity: for after initially (in Book II,
Chapter 5) arguing that if "a subject seeks, by whatever means, to invade
the state and steal it from his king or, in a democracy or aristocracy, to
turn himself from a fellow-citizen into lord and master, he deserves to be
put to death," (110) he progressively weakens this position (initially "a tyrant . . . may be justly killed without form or shape of trial" [111]), such that
it really only applies in cases where the sovereign is "not absolutely sovereign, or is properly speaking not a sovereign" (114: "absolutely sovereign"
is strictly speaking a pleonasm in Bodin's terms). In cases where the sovereign really is, absolutely, sovereign,

as are the genuine monarchs of France, Spain, England, Scotland, Ethiopia, Turkey, Persia, and Moscovy—whose power has never been called into question and whose sovereignty has never been shared with subjects—then it is not the part of any subject individually, or all of them in general, to make an attempt on the honor or the life of the monarch, either by way of force or by way of law, even if he has committed all the misdeeds, impieties, and cruelties that one could mention. . . . I conclude then that it is never permissible for a subject to attempt anything against a sovereign prince, no matter how wicked and cruel a tyrant he may be. (115, 120)

The implied becoming-criminal of the sovereign (which we shall explore later in terms of a counter-reading of the "One Best Man" argument in Aristotle, where the Absolute King's separation from the polis, his movement to the heights like a god or to the depths like a beast, already entails this possibility), means that it is not a surprise to see a return of our Homeric tagline in Bodin. This occurs in the context in which Bodin is establishing the fundamental feature of the sovereign, that of breaking and making the law, and in principle avoiding any promise or oath to keep any law. Against an apparent exception (the Emperor Trajan's swearing to a consul to keep the law), Bodin first argues that in fact "the early Roman emperors were not sovereign" and the form of state was that of a *principatus*. But in spite of appearances ("the emperor's only prerogative was to be the first in dignity, honor, and precedence"), "in fact the majority of emperors were tyrants" (and therefore, according to Bodin's own logic, sovereign), as is apparently shown by the example of Caligula:

Indeed, one day, when some foreign kings were arguing about their nobility and grandeur at his table, Caligula quoted the verse from Homer, *Ouk agathon hē polukiraniē eis koiranos esto basileus . . .* [*sic*]. And he was not very far, says Suetonius, from taking the diadem and changing the form of the state, which was a principate, into a kingdom. (25)

And in fact, in Suetonius himself (first century CE), this quotation is part of a longer sequence that nicely illustrates the becoming-criminal of the sovereign that we are tracking in Bodin.[6] In Suetonius's narrative, indeed,

---

6. The convergence between the sovereign and the figure of the *grand criminal* is a leitmotif of Derrida's *Beast and Sovereign* seminars: see especially BS I, 38/17: "Beast, criminal, and sovereign have a troubling resemblance: they call on each other and recall each other, from one to the other; there is between sovereign, criminal, and beast a sort of obscure and fascinating complicity, or even a worrying mutual

this incident marks a turning point in the story, or in the attitude of its narrator, in that at the beginning of chapter 22, in which the anecdote is recounted, Suetonius writes: "So much for Caligula as emperor; we must now tell of his career as a monster [*Hactenus quasi de principe, reliqua ut de monstro narranda sunt*]."[7] He goes on with the continuous extension of sovereignty from becoming-king to becoming-god to becoming-criminal:

> After he had assumed various surnames (for he was called "Pious," "Child of the Camp," "Father of the Armies," and "Greatest and Best of Caesars"), chancing to overhear some kings, who had come to Rome to pay their respects to him, disputing at dinner about the nobility of their descent, he cried:
>
> Let there be one Lord, one King.[8]
>
> And he came near assuming a crown at once and changing the semblance of a principate into the form of a monarchy. But on being reminded that he had risen above the elevation both of princes and kings, he began from that time on to lay claim to divine majesty; for after giving orders that such statues of the gods as were especially famous for their sanctity or their artistic merit, including that of Jupiter of Olympia, should be brought from Greece, in order to remove their heads and put his own in their place, he built out a part of the Palace as far as the Forum, and making the temple of Castor and Pollux its vestibule, he often took his place between the divine brothers, and exhibited himself there to be worshipped by those who presented themselves; and some hailed him as Jupiter Latiaris. He also set up a special temple to his own godhead, with priests and with victims of the choicest kind. In this temple was a life-sized statue of the emperor in gold, which was dressed each day in clothing such as he wore himself. The richest citizens used all their influence to secure the priesthoods of his cult and bid high for the honor. The victims were flamingoes, peacocks, black grouse, guinea-hens and pheasants, offered day by day each after its own kind. At night he used constantly to invite the full and

---

attraction, a worrying familiarity, an *unheimlich*, uncanny reciprocal haunting. Both of them, all three of them, the animal, the criminal, and the sovereign, are outside the law, at a distance from or above the laws: criminal, beast, and sovereign strangely resemble each other while seeming to be situated at the antipodes, at each other's antipodes."

7. Suetonius, *Lives of the Caesars, Volume I*, trans. J. C. Rolfe (Cambridge, MA: Harvard University Press, 1914), 447.

8. Suetonius gives the familiar quotation in Greek: *heis koiranos esto, heis basileus*.

radiant moon to his embraces and his bed, while in the daytime he would talk confidentially with Jupiter Capitolinus, now whispering and then in turn putting his ear to the mouth of the god, now in louder and even angry language; for he was heard to make the threat: "Lift me up, or I'll lift you."[9] But finally won by entreaties, as he reported, and even invited to live with the god, he built a bridge over the temple of the Deified Augustus, and thus joined his Palace to the Capitol.[10] (447–451)

It is arguably this "necessary possibility," as Derrida would say, namely the becoming-criminal of the sovereign, that motivates La Boétie's almost exactly contemporaneous quotation of our tagline. Indeed, La Boétie chooses to open his famous *De la servitude volontaire* with this quotation, which then stands as the sign under which the whole discourse is elaborated.[11] But unlike any other reader of whom I am aware, La Boétie reads the line at least partially against the grain: where Odysseus is saying that *polykoiranie* is "not good" and that "mono-koiranie" is good, La Boétie chooses to agree with the first part of the line, but dispute the second, such that having many masters is bad, *but so is having even one master*, and so Odysseus would have done better to cut his remark short. Here is the very opening of the *Discourse*, where the French translation of Homer quoted by La Boétie uses three distinct terms (*seigneur*, *maître*, and *Roi*) for Homer's two-term *koiranos* and *basileus*:

> I see no good in having several lords:
> Let one, not more, be master, and one alone be king.

9. Suetonius again gives a quote in Greek: *hē m'anaeir', hē egō se*, which also comes from the *Iliad* (XXIII, 724), where Ajax is challenging Odysseus to end their long wrestling match. See my essay "Crying Out Loud" (forthcoming in *Down to Dust*) for a reading of the Odysseus/Ajax relation as emblematic of a certain birth of politics as politics of politics.

10. The narrative of the "criminal career" continues at some length and in some detail.

11. For a reading quite germane to what I will be suggesting here, see Richard Regosin, "'Mais o bon Dieu, Que peut estre cela?': La Boétie's *La Servitude Volontaire* and the Rhetoric of Political Perplexity," in *Etienne de la Boétie: Sage révolutionnaire et poète périgourdin*, ed. Marcel Tetel (Paris: Champion, 2004), 241–260, which begins with some discussion of the Homer quotation. The same volume also includes an essay by Lawrence Kritzman that reads La Boétie in relation to Derrida's *Politiques de l'amitié*, and pieces by Claude Gilbert-Dubois (317–331) and Jamil Chaker (349–362) that analyze La Boétie's use of numbers and numerals, to which we will attend.

Thus said Homer's Ulysses, speaking in public. Had he said nothing more than

I see no good in having several lords,

it would have been just as well said, with nothing else. But instead of saying, reasonably, that domination by several masters could not be good since the power of one alone, once he takes this title of "master," is harsh and unreasonable, he went on to add, getting it backwards [*tout au rebours*]:

Let one, no more, be master, and one only be King.[12]

Maybe Odysseus was somewhat justified by the circumstances of his speech (he needed to calm down the rebellious troops), but in truth it is an extreme misfortune to have one master and, on this first approach, having many masters is just a multiplication of the misfortune of having one. La Boétie's argument, much more bluntly than Bodin's, follows a little somnambulistically what Derrida would call a logic of autoimmunity: just because it is a—necessary—possibility of the master, even if a good one, to become bad when he wishes ("il est toujours en sa puissance d'être mauvais quand il voudra"), power is ipso facto the power to be bad. But the logic of this argument will mean that in fact, and contrary to these initial appearances, *polykoiranie*, however onerous, might *not* in fact be quite as bad as single kingship or lordship, monarchy.

La Boétie explicitly avoids entering into the classical debate in political philosophy as to the ranking of the different types of regime, but in so doing suggests in passing that monarchy might have no rank at all, just because (a little as in the case of the One Best Man hypothesis), "before questioning what rank monarchy should have among republics, I should like to know whether it should have any, since it is hard to believe that there is anything 'public' in this government, where everything belongs to one [*ce gouvernement où tout est à un*]" (33/2). But, as Montaigne informs us when he discusses his (now deceased) great friend La Boétie's text in the *Essais*— where he claims it had been his intention to publish the whole *Discours* as a kind of centerpiece—people who did not know the title of the work had a good name for it. I am like a painter, says Montaigne at the opening of the famous *Essai* on friendship, but only insofar as having chosen the best

---

12. *Discours de la servitude volontaire*, ed. André Tournon (Paris: Vrin, 2014), 31; trans. James B Atkinson and David Sices (Indianapolis: Hackett, 2012), 1. I have often retranslated the text in the interests of literal accuracy.

place for my paintings, I have filled the empty space around that place with "antike Boscage or Crotesko works; which are fantasticall pictures, having no grace, but in the strangenesse of them [*crotesques, qui sont peintures fantasques, n'ayans grace qu'en la varieté et estrangeté*]"; that's what my *Essais* are, then, "antike works, and monstrous bodies, patched and hudled up together of divers members, without any certaine or well ordered figure, having neither order, dependencie, or proportion, but casuall and framed by chance [*crotesques et corps monstrueux, rappiecez de divers members, sans figure, n'ayants ordre, suite, ny proportion que fortuite*]."[13] But I cannot produce a work "rich, polished, and according to true skill [*un tableau riche, poly et formé selon l'art*]," so I had planned to borrow such a picture from La Boétie, in the form of his *Discours*, to be the central piece of my work. (In fact, Montaigne did not follow through on this plan, for conjunctural political reasons: so reasons perhaps justifiable "more by the time than by the truth," as La Boétie himself concessively describes Odysseus's claim.) "It is a discourse he entitled 'Voluntary Servitude,' but those who have not knowne him, have since very properly rebaptized the same, 'The against one' [*le Contre-un*]" (190/197). If Montaigne is right in the claim that this odd expression[14] is a "quite proper" name for La Boétie's text, then perhaps we have to assume after all that the *polykoiranie* denounced by Odysseus is not, as a first approach to La Boétie's text justifiably thought, simply a kind of multiplication of the misfortune of the lordship of One.

And it is striking that La Boétie's best figure of voluntary servitude is indeed servitude of many to One, to a monarch who (as per the autoimmune logic just pointed out), is always tendentially a tyrant. So even if I reserve for another occasion the discussion of the relative merits of the different regimes and whether monarchy even *is* a regime, says La Boétie, the question to which I am drawing your attention is:

> How it can happen that so many men, so many towns, so many cities, so many nations at times endure a single tyrant, whose only power is the power they give him; who has power to harm them only so long as they have the will to endure him; who can harm them not at all, except when they prefer to suffer him than contradict him. (33/2)

---

13. Michel de Montaigne, *Les Essais*, ed. Jean Balsamo, Michel Magnien, and Catherine Magnien-Simonin (Paris: Gallimard, 2007), 1.27, "De l'amitié," 189; translated by John Florio [1613] (Edinburgh: T. and A. Constable, 1892), 196.

14. "Contr'un" is not a readily available syntagma for modern French, and today would function almost exclusively as a proper name of La Boétie's discourse.

So it seems that it is not just that because mastery or lordship are bad per se, having many lords is at least worse than having only one (which is what La Boétie initially says, so that Odysseus would at least be right as to the *relative* merits of having many lords and having one lord, if not the absolute merit of monarchy itself), but that by a logical twist that in fact carries the entire weight of the "voluntary servitude" argument, the One really is the problem, and the question of the discourse is that of knowing why the many (and La Boétie will stress just how many the many are by regularly invoking large numbers to make his point—here it will soon be one million) do indeed submit voluntarily to a lordship which is indeed best represented as the lordship of one lord, against which, *contr'un*, then, he is calling for resistance, if not exactly for revolt and revolution. The function of the motif of the One here is not merely to accentuate the disparity of numbers, but to begin an explanation of the otherwise incomprehensible tendency to voluntary servitude:

> To see a million men serving miserably, with their neck beneath the yoke, not constrained by a greater force, but as it were (or so it seems) enchanted and charmed by the name alone of one [*par le nom seul d'un*, perhaps even, stretching the reading a little, "by the name 'one' alone"], of whom they must neither fear the power, since he is alone, nor love the qualities since he is with respect to them inhuman and savage. (33–34/2–3)

The argument in this early (and quite tightly argued) part of the text now goes as follows: we often have to give in to a greater force and wait patiently for things to get better; and so it is at least understandable, if not necessarily wise, to promote to a position of lordship someone who at least *looks* rather like Aristotle's One Best Man:

> If the inhabitants of a country have found some great personage who has shown them by test foresight in protecting them, great boldness in defending them, great care in governing them: if from then on they get used to obeying him, and trust him to the point of granting him some privileges, I do not know if it would be wise, given that they are taking him from a place where he was doing good to promote him to a place where he can do evil; but certainly there could not fail to be goodness in not fearing ill from him from who one has received only good. (34–35/3)

But now imagine the more common situation, in which many (we will see the numbers mount up) accept subjugation to one who is *not even close* to being the One Best Man: What do we even call such a situation? Here is La Boétie's splendid (if rather virilist) indignation:

> But oh good God, what can this be? What shall we say that this is called? What misfortune is this, what vice, or rather what unhappy vice, to see an infinite number of people, not obey but serve; not be governed but be tyrannized, having neither goods, nor parents, wives and children, not even their life itself be theirs, suffer the pillaging, lechery, cruelties, not of an army, not of a barbarians' camp before which one should lose one's blood and one's life, but of one alone; not a Hercules or a Samson [candidates for the One Best Man partial exemption granted above], but one sole little man, most often the most cowardly and effeminate of the nation; not accustomed to the dust of battles but scarcely even the sand of tourneys; not one who can by force command men, but unable even to service vilely the least little lady: will we call that cowardice? (35–36/4)

Fascination with the name of one, or the name "one," itself defies naming. We cannot really call this nameless thing cowardice, because of a kind of numerical disproportion, almost of the order of Kant's mathematical sublime in the mode of the *monstrous*, such that the affect involved escapes one's grasp and ability to name:

> Will we call that cowardice? Will we say that those who serve are cowards and toadies? If two, if three, if four do not defend themselves against one, that is strange, but nonetheless possible: one can in that case say quite rightly that it is for lack of heart. But if one hundred, one thousand endure from one alone, will we not say that they do not want to, not that they dare not, take him on, and that it is, not cowardice, but rather scorn or disdain? If one sees not one hundred, not one thousand men, but one hundred countries, one thousand cities, one million men not attack a single one, from whom the best treated of all of them receives the evil of being a serf and a slave, how can we name that? Is it cowardice? (36/4)

Not cowardice, says La Boétie firmly, because of what now seems like a quasi-Aristotelian argument about the scale and limits of virtues and vices. There is no possible measure or moderation here, whence the monstrous namelessness of subjection to the One:

> Now there is in all vices naturally some limit, beyond which they cannot go: two, and possibly three, can fear one; but a thousand, but a million, but a thousand cities [*mille villes*], if they do not defend

themselves against one, that is not cowardice, it does not go that far, any more than valiance extends to one man scaling a fortress, or assailing an army, or conquering a kingdom. So what monster of vice is this, which does not yet merit the title of cowardice, which finds no name base enough, that nature disavows having made, and that language refuses to name? (36–37/4)

You might think, continues La Boétie, that freedom would be a powerful motivator: in a battle between equal forces, for example, where one side is fighting to preserve its freedom and the other to take that freedom away, we think that those defending themselves have the greater motivation (because if they win, they get the great benefit of keeping what they have enjoyed: if the others win, as their own freedom was not in question, they get only the minimal surplus satisfaction of dominating the others), and indeed this seems to explain some famous ancient Greek victories over the Persians (La Boétie alludes to the battles of Marathon, Thermopylae, and Salamis). It is *étrange* (perhaps wonderful rather than strange) to hear tell these stories of the power of freedom to motivate courage: but who would even believe it if you tried to tell them that *everybody*, in *every* country, *every* day, allowed a *single* person to abuse a hundred thousand and take away their freedom? If people were told that these stories were true of far-flung foreign lands, who would not think that such stories were made up, fictions, and not true at all?

And the worst of it is that, just as we are off the measurable scale of virtue and vice in this domain (which is all the more scandalous because the situation is universal and omnitemporal [*ce qui se fait en tous pays, par tous les hommes, tous les jours*] [39/5]), we do not even need to fight to put an end to it. Servitude to the One is easily overcome: "And there is no need to combat this lone tyrant, there is no need to undo him: he is by himself undone so long as the country does not consent to its servitude; not need to take anything away from him, simply not to give him anything; no need for the country to go to the effort to do anything for itself, so long as it does nothing against itself" (39/5–6). This means that in fact the servitude in question is not even servitude to a tyrant after all. The people are in servitude to themselves; they are their own tyrant:

So it is the peoples themselves who let themselves be, or rather get themselves, abused, because in ceasing to serve they would be done with it; it is the people that enslaves itself, which cuts its own throat, which, given the choice of being slaves or being free, gives up its freedom and puts on the yoke: which consents in its ill, or rather chases after it. (39–40/6)

No effort is required to throw off that yoke: all that is needed is not to desire it. Just as a fire dies out if you do not keep feeding it, so tyrants are undone, not by any active resistance, but by simple nonobedience: "if one does not obey them, without fighting against them, without striking, they remain naked and undone, and are no longer anything" (41/6). So that freedom is achieved simply through the desire for freedom which, paradoxically, means that this one good (which gives savor to all others), this one desire that is itself its own fulfilment, is in general *not* an object of desire, too easy perhaps, or perhaps (though La Boétie does not put it like this), it is a desire like no other, a desire that simply leaves nothing to be desired. But the slightly magical quality of this self-fulfilling desire is matched, still according to the logic of autoimmunity, by a slightly magical self-destruction of the (inner) tyrant to whom we are all enslaved: "only be resolved no longer to serve, and you are free; I do not want you to push or shake it, but simply no longer hold it up, and you will see it, like a great colossus whose base has been taken away, collapse under its own weight and break up" (44/8). At this point the formal argument, as it were, is complete: servitude, however habitual it has become, is bad, and in principle is easily overcome by natural freedom and the natural desire for freedom: and in overcoming servitude, man can return from bestiality to humanity, "de bête revenir homme," escaping from the quasi-natural condition of beasts for the truly natural condition of man, which is a condition of freedom.

After his rousing apostrophe to the people urging them to throw off the yoke and retrieve their natural freedom, though, La Boétie recognizes a complication, at least in the rhetorical gesture of his text, and shifts, via an introductory "but . . ." from what was a bracingly direct political and ethical register into one of "conjecture" which will, however, seriously complicate and perhaps contradict what we have seen thus far. La Boétie draws back a little, or steps down from his soapbox and adopts a rather different tone:

> But of course doctors rightly counsel not to touch incurable wounds;
> and I am not being wise in wanting to preach about this to the people,
> who long ago lost all consciousness of it, and of whom, since it no
> longer feels its pain, this shows clearly enough that its malady is fatal.
> Let us then seek by conjecture, if we can find out how this stubborn
> will to serve became so deeply-rooted that it seems now as though the
> very love of freedom were not as natural as it. (44–45/8)

The first conjecture, which over two or three pages will lead to the conclusion that freedom is indeed natural (in spite of present-day appearances), begins rather disconcertingly by seeking to establish first that if servitude is not natural, obedience is, alongside rationality, and secondly that nature herself has tended to make humans on the model of the One. This strange sequence, which reads a little like a counterversion of the opening of Aristotle's *Politics*, makes the following claims:

1. If we lived in accordance with natural rights, we would be
   a) obedient to our parents, b) subject to reason, and c) slaves to nobody;
   a. We all intuitively feel this natural obedience
   b. We at least have some seeds of reason that can develop if appropriately nurtured;
   c. There is nothing so clear and undeniable about nature as that we are destined to live together.

The evidence for (c) is that nature, God's (feminine) minister (*la ministre de Dieu*) and man's tutor (*gouverneur*), has made us all from the same mold so we can recognize each other as companions or, better, brothers. Even the disparities between men in terms of natural endowments seem designed to bring us together, so that not only do we develop fraternal affection, but Nature has also followed the same pattern with all of us, "so that each can look and as it were recognize the one in the other," and more than that,

> If she has given us all this great gift of voice and speech so we can get to know each other and fraternize better, and make by the common and mutual declaration of our thoughts a communion of our wills; and if she has tried by all means to tighten and squeeze so hard the knot of our alliance and society; if she has shown in all things that she wanted less to make us all united than all one . . . [*si elle a montré en toutes choses qu'elle ne voulait pas tant nous faire tous unis que tous uns*]. (47/9)

It is this tightly bound fraternity and mutual recognition that for La Boétie (who of course has not read his Hegel) confirms our natural freedom by the fact of that companionship, company, and oneness:

> One cannot doubt that we are all naturally free, since we are all companions; and it cannot occur to anyone that nature placed anyone in servitude, having placed us all in company. (47/9)

But in any case, adds La Boétie, now with a rather desperate and tendentially circular argument, there is no point debating whether freedom is natural, because no one can be held in servitude without doing them a wrong, and nothing is so contrary to nature as such a wrong, given that nature is entirely rational. So, by apagogic argument, all that remains for freedom to be is to be natural, and this also explains that we equally naturally have a propensity to defend it. And if you are so benighted or degenerate as to doubt it, my best argument in its favor is to have the beasts tell you ex cathedra that even animals, if men are not deaf to them, cry "long live freedom." Remove that freedom and either they die (like fish out of water), or defend themselves tooth and nail, then languish in captivity or, like the elephant, try *in extremis* to buy their freedom by breaking off their own tusks. All of which proves that even the beasts, who of course are *not* naturally free (for they are "made for the service of humans" [50/10]) suffer from their subjection and seek their freedom: and so, if even those who were not made to be free would like to be free, says La Boétie (who needs the animals to be naturally not free but naturally desirous of freedom), how denatured must humans be if they no longer desire that freedom which, in their case, *is* natural?

This complication in the value of the natural leads to increasingly precarious arguments. Nature is nature, but it is not as powerful as custom, and custom is at its strongest when it provokes us ("unbelievably") into a radical forgetting of nature itself in the form of freedom (54–55/13): in spite of everything (including the testimony of the animals), custom (nurture, *la nourriture*) trumps nature (however powerful nature nonetheless is), "because nature, however good, is lost if not sustained, and nurture always makes us in its fashion, whatever that be, in spite of nature"(56/13). It turns out after all that nature is weak and feeble, its seeds "so tiny and slippery" that they succumb immediately to any contrary nurture. La Boétie's retreat from the inconclusive animal realm to that of plants shows us not really nature but still artifice, grafting of fruit trees onto other stock, or simply variation due to climate or horticulture, such that the plant one has seen in one place one cannot recognize in another, just as someone seeing on the one hand the Venetians so attached to their natural freedoms and on the other the subjects of the Ottoman Empire one might not think their nature was the same (the One from which this whole development started), or else (now completely scrambling the use of analogies from the natural world) would rather think "that leaving a city of men he had entered into a park of beasts"(or a zoo: 56/14).

This priority of "nourriture" over nature can itself, confusingly enough, be related not to servitude as the custom-driven loss of natural freedom, but to an attachment to freedom itself: a sequence of anecdotes and episodes involving Sparta and Rome shows at least the possibility that an indefectible attachment to freedom may in fact arise *not* from nature but from education, and this subordination of nature *is itself natural*. This natural status of custom drives La Boétie to make a further distinction or fold that further complicates the nature/nurture divide by identifying a nature prior to the nature that we have thus far been opposing to nurture. *In extremis*, this earlier value of "simple and unadulterated" nature can be associated with freedom, and so servitude can still be assigned to custom, even if that custom is, as we have just seen, natural:

> The nature of man is indeed to be free and to want to be free; but his nature is also such that naturally he takes the bent that nurture gives him. So let's say that to man all things are as though natural to which he is nurtured and accustomed, but what is alone native [*naif*] to him is that to which his simple and unadulterated nature calls him; and so the primary reason for voluntary servitude is custom. (63/17)

And now the animals (in this case horses), who before were invoked to show how they did *not* give up their taste for freedom, return as examples of how they *do* get used to training and become proud of their fancy harness.

Having at any rate saved the value of nature for his purposes, La Boétie can spend the rest of his text examining how the mechanisms of tyranny operate (by generating little tyrants subordinated to the One [87/31]) and how tyrants are in fact unhappy in their tyranny (close here to Plato). It seems possible to say that in this broad and quite striking picture, La Boétie is exploiting possibilities in the relation between One and many that were already in play in the opening quotation from Homer. It looked there at first as though La Boétie were committed to the view that, as any lordship is an evil, lordship of many (*polykoiranie*, then) was indeed worse that lordship by one (or by One), and to that extent La Boétie was actually agreeing with Odysseus. As we saw, though, through the quite complex play of oneness and multiplicity, the tyrant, or perhaps better tyranny "itself," is always best figured by the One (whence the propriety of the title "Contr-Un" as described by Montaigne). This gives rise to "autoimmune" structures (such that, for example, it is natural for nature to be undone or overcome by custom), which in the end make it difficult to identify with confidence the relative positions of freedom and tyranny, whence the (potentially infinite) appeal to a nature prior to the nature that naturally allows itself to be outdone by custom.

Once it is natural for nature to be stifled by custom, and for that custom at least possibly to strive for what is natural, then we no longer really know what is natural and what is not. La Boétie spends a good deal of time with anecdotes about how tyrants soften their people up to accept the custom of servitude (by bread and circuses, for example), or by tricks to have the people believe that the tyrant is divine, but these tricks are essentially autoimmune disorders generated by the fundamental confusion of nature and custom, so that "always the stupid people itself makes up the lies it will later believe" (79/26). Or a little later, demonstrating a kind of propagation of tyranny such that the tyrant needs only a handful of people close to him who each control a group of others, all of whom control still others, so that (returning finally to the much earlier thought that the people is its own tyrant), and producing an almost perfect image of the autoimmune confusion of denaturing nature: "Thus the tyrant enslaves the subjects by means of other subjects, and is protected by those who, if they were worth their salt, he would need to protect himself against: and as they say, to split wood he makes wedges of the wood itself (88/32)."

So La Boétie's *Discourse* ends up with, in one direction, as it were, a potentially infinite regress in its appeal to nature, as he attempts to find the "pure and unadulterated" state that *never should have* become corrupted by the custom of servitude (even though his starting point is that it manifestly has, quite scandalously and unbelievably, become quite generally and even transhistorically corrupted in this way), and in the other direction a call to liberation that supposedly can happen quasi-automatically, in that the mere desire for freedom is supposed already to be freedom and give rise to the inner collapse of the colossus. The problem is that the truth of that true nature is based on a figure of the One (nature, remember, has made us one rather than merely united), and involves a supposedly natural obedience to parents that manifestly already prepares for the servitude to come. The whole system obeys a logic that La Boétie is in no position to understand explicitly: whence the symptomatic inconsistencies in, for example, the appeal to animal analogies throughout the text. Once we grasp the ("autoimmune") logic at work here, then (as will become clearer when we read Hobbes, Spinoza, and Rousseau) the value of nature is compromised, and we have therefore to be suspicious of the stirring appeal to the value of what I have tended to translate as "freedom," but that a whole tradition in the reception of La Boétie would probably prefer to call "liberty." Once the mutually supporting values of nature and liberty are compromised in this way, then probably there is no alternative than to return to the more strictly political analysis that La Boétie set aside at the beginning of his *Discourse*:

So I do not wish for now to debate this thorny question as to whether the other kinds of republic are better than monarchy: and I would wish to know, before placing in doubt the rank that monarchy should have among the republics if it should have any, because it is difficult to believe that there is anything public in this government where everything belongs to one; but this question is reserved for another time and would indeed require a separate treatise, or rather would bring with it all political disputes. (32–3/2)

The strength and appeal of the *Discours de la servitude volontaire* is, perhaps, that it is itself not really political at all, but rather leaves the political question entire as it sits on the threshold of the political, trying as best it can to trace a secure boundary between nature and custom. The extreme difficulty of knowing how to think of that threshold and that boundary will inevitably bring the question of democracy into greater prominence, as the very question of the political itself, always tendentially encouraging the collapse of the sovereign colossus, and its scattering into dust.

PART II

(Proto)Democracy

CHAPTER 6

To Poikilon (Plato, Alfarabi, Aristotle)

We have tracked a certain fate of the "One Lord," culminating in a doctrine of sovereignty that, just as it establishes itself, shows itself to be always already failing, or falling from the sovereign heights, allowing for a continuity of sovereign and criminal tyrant. One persistent figure of the difficulties of sovereignty thought of as monarchy is, precisely, a form of polyarchy most often called democracy. Democracy does not in general find favor in the tradition of political philosophy, the metaphysical character of which almost predestines it to preference for the One. But that same tradition not only most often prefers monarchy, but expends not inconsiderable energy criticizing and even vilifying democracy, which gathers to itself all the features of plurality, diversity, difference, and variegation—in a word, *scatter*—which we have already seen associated, at least in the Christian tradition, with vice and evil.

The association of democracy and a multicolored, variegated diversity begins very early, paradigmatically in book 8 of Plato's *Republic*, which displays a striking exuberance in its sarcastic depictions both of the democratic regime and the corresponding "democratic man." Here is Socrates's initial and famous description:

Possibly, said I, this is the most beautiful of polities; as a garment of many colours [*poikilon*], embroidered with all kinds of hues [*pepoikilmenon*], so this, decked and diversified [*pepoikilmene*] with every type of character, would appear the most beautiful. And perhaps many would judge it to be the most beautiful, like boys and women when they see bright-coloured things [*ta poikila*]. (557c)

In his discussion of this moment in Plato in *Rogues* (and indeed already in earlier references in the essay "Plato's Pharmacy"),[1] Derrida emphasizes Socrates's characterization of democracy as superficially attractive and seductive:

1. "One could compare the case against writing with the case against democracy prosecuted in the Republic. In a democratic society, there is no concern for competence: responsibilities are given to anyone at all. Magistracies are decided by lots (557a). Equality is equally dispensed to equal and unequal alike (558c). Excess, anarchy; the democratic man, with no concern for hierarchy, 'Putting all his pleasures on an equal footing, he grants power over himself to the pleasure of the moment, as if it were a magistrate chosen by lot. And when he has had his fill of it, he surrenders himself in turn to another pleasure. He rejects none of them, but gives sustenance to all alike. . . . If someone tells him that some pleasures are the result of fine and good desires, others of evil desires, and that he should follow and value the first, and punish and hold in subjection the second, he does not admit this truth, or allow it into the fortress. He shakes his head at any claims of this sort, saying that all desires are equal, and must be valued equally' (561b–c). This errant democrat, wandering like a desire or like a signifier freed from the logos, this individual who is not even perverse in a regular way, who is ready to do anything, who lends himself to anyone, who gives himself equally to all pleasures, to all activities—perhaps even to politics or philosophy ('sometimes he passes the time in what he calls philosophy. Much of his time is spent in politics, where he leaps to his feet and says and does whatever comes into his head' [561d]). This adventurer, like the one in the *Phaedrus*, simulates everything at random and is in truth nothing. Swept off by every stream, he belongs to the masses; he has no essence, no truth, no patronym, no constitution of his own. Moreover, democracy is no more a constitution than the democrat has a character of his own: 'I take it to be a variegated life, full of all sorts of characteristics. This democratic man is elegant and colorful, just like the democratic city. Many men and women might envy him his life, with all the examples of regimes and characters it contains within it' (561e). Democracy is orgy, debauchery, flea market, fair, 'a bazaar (*pantopolion*) of constitutions where one can choose the one to make one's own'" (557d). (D 166–167/144–145)

Insofar as each person in this democracy can lead the life (*bion*) he
chooses, one will find in this regime, this *politeia*—which, as we will
see, is not a regime, nor a constitution nor an authentic *politeia*—all
sorts of people, a greater variety than anywhere else. Whence the
multicolored [*bigarée*] beauty of democracy. Plato insists as much on
the beauty as on the medley of colors [*bariolage*]. Democracy *seems*—
and this is its appearing, if not its appearance and its simulacrum—the
most beautiful (*kalliste*), the most seductive of constitutions (*politeion*)
(557c). Its beauty resembles that of a multi- and brightly colored
(*poikilon*) garment. The seduction matters here; it provokes; it is
provocative in this "milieu" of sexual difference where *roués* and
voyous roam about. The key word *poikilon* comes up more than once.
It means, in painting but also in the weaving of garments—and
this no doubt explains the allusion to women that soon follows—
"multicolored," "brightly colored," "speckled," "dappled." The same
attribute defines at once vivid color and the diversity, a changing,
variable, whimsical character, complicated, sometimes obscure,
ambiguous. Like the fanning [*la roue*] of a peacock, irresistible to
women. For this multicolored beauty, Plato notes, and this is politically significant, arouses particularly the curiosity of women and
children. All those who resemble women and children consider it the
most beautiful. And so, because of this freedom and the multicoloredness, one would seek in vain a single constitution or *politeia* within this
democracy peopled by such a diversity of men. Given over to freedom,
to *exousia* this time, democracy contains all the different kinds of
constitutions, of regimes or states (*panta gene politeion*) (557d). If one
wants to found a state, all one has to do is go to a democracy to pick
out and acquire the paradigm of one's choice. As in a market, there is
no shortage of *paradeigmata*. This market resembles a bazaar (*pantopolion*), a *souk* where one can find whatever one wants in the way of
constitutions (*politeia*). (V 48–49/26)

Derrida is certainly correct to pick out *to poikilon* (the neuter noun formed
from the adjective *poikilos*) as the key term in this passage, and to relate it
not only to strictly visual characteristics,[2] but also to variability, whimsy,
and inconstancy. The term and its cognates appear in fact quite often elsewhere in Plato, and several times in the *Republic* itself, often at quite tell-

2. The Septuagint uses the same word to describe Joseph's coat of many colors in Genesis 37:3, 23, and 31.

ing moments. So for example, in the discussion of injustice in book 9, Socrates proposes an image of the soul in terms of a mythical beast:

> An ideal image of the soul, like the composite creations of ancient mythology, such as the Chimera or Scylla or Cerberus, and there are many others in which two or more different natures are said to grow into one.
>
> There are said to have been such unions.
>
> Then do you now model the form of a multitudinous, many-headed monster [*theriou poikilou kai polukethalou*], having a ring of heads of all manner of beasts, tame and wild, which he is able to generate and metamorphose at will.
>
> You suppose marvellous powers in the artist; but, as language is more pliable than wax or any similar substance, let there be such a model as you propose.
>
> Suppose now that you make a second form as of a lion, and a third of a man, the second smaller than the first, and the third smaller than the second.
>
> That, he said, is an easier task; and I have made them as you say.
>
> And now join them, and let the three grow into one.
>
> That has been accomplished.
>
> Next fashion the outside of them into a single image, as of a man, so that he who is not able to look within, and sees only the outer hull, may believe the beast to be a single human creature. I have done so, he said.
>
> And now, to him who maintains that it is profitable for the human creature to be unjust, and unprofitable to be just, let us reply that, if he be right, it is profitable for this creature to feast the multitudinous monster [this time *pantodapon thurion*] and strengthen the lion and the lion-like qualities, but to starve and weaken the man, who is consequently liable to be dragged about at the mercy of either of the other two; and he is not to attempt to familiarize or harmonize them with one another—he ought rather to suffer them to fight and bite and devour one another. (588c–589a)

And in the famous critique of mimeticism in book 10, one of the arguments put forward is that mimetic poetry will typically take as its object the "fitful," "rebellious," or manifold, tendentially feminine and childish part of the soul, rather than the rational and law-abiding part, and *to poikilon* appears twice in this context, associated, as in the democracy passage, with the diverse and promiscuous crowd. The law of rationality, says Socrates, suggests we should bear misfortune with fortitude and restraint, rather than bawling like children, whereas the other, nonrational principle,

> which inclines us to recollection of our troubles and to lamentation, and can never have enough of them, we may call irrational, useless, and cowardly?
>
> Indeed, we may.
>
> And does not the latter—I mean the rebellious principle—furnish a great variety of materials for imitation [*pollēn mimēsin kai poikilēn echei*]? Whereas the wise and calm temperament, being always nearly equable, is not easy to imitate or to appreciate when imitated, especially at a public festival when a promiscuous crowd [*pantodapois anthrōpois*] is assembled in a theatre. For the feeling represented is one to which they are strangers.
>
> Certainly.
>
> Then the imitative poet who aims at being popular is not by nature made, nor is his art intended, to please or to affect the rational principle in the soul; but he will prefer the passionate and fitful temper [*poikilon ēthos*], which is easily imitated?
>
> Clearly. (604e–605a)

See too *Republic* 365c, describing the fox in the fable by Archilochus, "shifty and bent on gain" (*kerdalean kai poikilēn*);[3] 399e describing an undesirable variety of rhythms in music (*mē poikilous autous diōkein mēde pantodapas baseis*: "we should not pursue complexity, nor do we want all kinds of metres:" Plato often links *poikilon* and *pantodapon*); 426a describing a variety of fake remedies (*plēn ge poikilōtera kai meizō poiousi ta nosēmata*; "Their medical treatment achieves nothing, except to increase the complications and severity of their ailments"); 568d describing the bodyguard of the tyrant (*to kalon te kai poly kai poikilon kai oudepote tauton*; "that fine, large, varied and ever-changing army"); and 616e (the only not clearly pejorative use of the term in the work) describing the "spangled" rim of one of the cosmic circles (*kai ton men tou megistou poikilon*; "the rim of the largest whorl is spangled").

---

3. The reference is to Archilochus's fable of the fox and the hedgehog, according to which "the fox knows many things, the hedgehog one big thing," giving the title to a famous book by Isaiah Berlin. This wily fox would take us all the way to Machiavelli's famous fox in chap. 18 of *The Prince*: see Derrida's commentary in BS I 129–133/88–91.

The dictionary entry for the adjective *poikilos* from the Liddell-Scott lexicon includes the following senses: many-colored, spotted, pied, dappled; tattooed; wrought in various colors (of woven or embroidered stuffs); cunningly wrought (in bronze); intricate; complicated; changeful, diversified, manifold; a song of changeful strain or full of diverse art; (of abstruse knowledge), intricate, complex; (of persons and things), subtle, artful, wily; changeable, unstable. So *to poikilon* is not merely multi- or particolored, but also intricate and labyrinthine, both superficial and deep, complex and changeable, cunning and shifty. Odysseus, the speaker of the tagline from Homer that we have followed, can himself be described as *poikilos*: cunning, foxy, wily, *polytropos*, if not in Homer himself, then in Euripides, where the qualification is again associated with the crowd or the mob.[4] We might venture to say that *to poikilon* is a quality of all that Plato most obviously stands against, and indeed what philosophy more generally from Plato to Heidegger stands against.[5] The One, as we have tracked it in the progressive Christianizing of Greek thought, is most emphatically not *poikilon*.

Back with the description of democracy in the *Republic*, we can say that it is, at the least, a mix, a collection, a farrago of different things. And this is what gives it its curious status among different sorts of regime: democracy is not just one regime among others, because in a sense it *includes* all others within itself. In an abyssal or fractal logic of "self-similarity," democracy is a *mix* of all regimes, *including itself*. Plato continues:

> Yes, said I, and it is the fit place, my good friend, in which to look for a constitution.
>
> Why so?
>
> Because, owing to this license, in includes all kinds, and it seems likely that anyone who wishes to organize a state, as we were just now doing, must find his way to a democratic city and select the model that pleases him, as if in a bazaar of constitutions, and after making his choice, establish his own. (557d)

So if democracy is a bazaar, or catalogue, or supermarket of different constitutions, providing within its shimmering surface some version of *any*

---

4. In an exchange between Agamemnon and Menelaus in *Iphigeneia in Aulis*: Agamemnon, "He was ever shifty by nature, siding with the mob [*poikilos aie pethuke tout t'oklou meta*]:" Menelaus, "True, he is enslaved by the love of popularity, a fearful evil [*philotimia men eneketai, deino kako*]."

5. See Chapter 4 note 23.

constitution the prospective founder of a state might look to in order to decide which model to choose, this is because it both is and is not itself— on this account, democracy is itself to the extent that it is anything *but* itself, or everything *including* itself. Democracy is one among the list of possible constitutions, but is set apart from the other members of the list in that it just *is* the list of which it is also a part. This double position generates paradoxical and sarcastic formulations:

> Then there's the tolerance of this city. No pedantic insistence on detail, but an utter contempt for the things we showed such respect for when we were founding our city . . . How magnificently the city tramples all this underfoot, paying no attention to what kind of life someone led before he entered political life! All anyone has to do to win favour is to say he is a friend of the people.
>
> Ah, yes, that's true nobility!
>
> These and related qualities will be the ones possessed by democracy. You'd expect it to be an enjoyable kind of regime—anarchic, colorful [*anarchos kai poikilē*], and granting equality of a sort to equals and unequals alike. (558b–c)

And this double quality extends to the corresponding character type that Socrates derives: the democratic man "is a manifold man stuffed with most excellent differences, and . . . like that city he is the fair and many-coloured [*poikilon*] one whom many a man and woman would count fortunate in his life, as containing within himself the greatest number of patterns [*paradeigmata*] of constitutions and qualities." This means that democracy is both political and beyond or above politics: just as democracy is both one constitution and the whole list of constitutions, so the democratic man is both one and many, goes in for all sorts of activities, following his nose or his desire, and politics is just one of those activities, as is philosophy:

> And so he lives out his life from day to day, gratifying the desire of the moment. One days he drinks himself under the table to the sound of the pipes, the next day he is on a diet of plain water. Now he is taking exercise, but at other times he is lazing around and taking no interest in anything. And sometimes he passes the time in what he calls philosophy . . . (561c–d)

This reference to philosophy (or at least "what he calls philosophy") as one of the things indulged by the democratic man raises an obvious question that is entertained among others by Leo Strauss, though it does not seem quite to justify his reading of it:

Democracy itself is characterized by freedom which includes the right to say and do whatever one wishes: everyone can follow the way of life which pleases him most. Hence democracy is the regime which fosters the greatest variety: every way of life, every regime can be found in it. Hence, we must understand, democracy is the only regime other than the best in which the philosopher can lead his peculiar way of life without being disturbed. . . . Since democracy, in contradistinction to the three other bad regimes, is both bad and permissive, it is that regime in which the frank quest for the best regime is at home: the action of the *Republic* takes place under a democracy. . . . *One is thus led to wonder why Socrates did not assign to democracy the highest place among the inferior regimes or rather the highest place simply, seeing that the best regime is not possible* [my emphasis]. One could say that he showed his preference for democracy by deed: by spending his whole life in democratic Athens, by fighting for her in her ways and by dying in obedience to her laws. However this may be, he surely did not prefer democracy to all other regimes in speech. The reason is that, being a just man in more than one sense, he thought of the well-being not merely of the philosophers but of the non-philosophers as well, and he held that democracy is not designed for inducing the non-philosophers to attempt to become as good as they possibly can. . . . One could say that, adapting himself to his subject matter, he abandons all restraint when speaking of the regime that loathes restraint. . . . The exaggerated blame of democracy reminds us again of the disharmony between philosophy and the people. (*The City and Man*, 131–133)

So on the one hand democracy is the regime most friendly to the philosopher, but on the other a proof of the disharmony of philosophy and the *demos*. This contradiction is Strauss's reading is of course symptomatic of the genuine issue we are tracking in Plato.

Socrates continues with his description of the democratic man:

and frequently he goes in for politics and bounces up and says and does whatever enters into his head. And if military men excite his emulation, thither he rushes, and if moneyed men, to that he turns, and there is no order or compulsion in his existence, but he calls this life of his the life of pleasure and freedom and happiness and cleaves to it to the end. (561c–e)

The exuberance of Socrates's descriptions here, quite unusually in Plato, goes to almost absurdist lengths as he describes the supposedly inevitable transition from democracy to anarchy, and how that transition turns all apparently self-evident hierarchies upside down: the anarchy of the democratic city and man is "bound to make its way into private households," "until finally it starts appearing among dumb animals"; not only is the order of generations inverted ("A father, for example, gets used to being like a child, and being afraid of his sons. A son gets used to being like his father. He feels no respect of fear for his parents" [562e–563a]), but the relations of the citizen, the foreigner [*xenon*] and the resident alien [*metoikon*] are muddled; teachers are afraid of their pupils; the young challenge and infantilize their elders; slaves are as free as their owners and, apparently worst of all, allowing Socrates, as Strauss pointed out, a kind of mimetic license in his own speech:

> "As for the relationship of women to men and men to women, I all but forgot to mention the extent of the legal equality and liberty between them."
>
> "Shall we then, borrowing a phrase from Aeschylus, say whatever it was that 'came to our lips' just now?"
>
> "By all means," I said. "It's certainly what *I'm* going to do. You wouldn't believe, without seeing it for yourself, how much more free domestic animals are here than in other cities. Dogs really *are* like the women who own them, as the proverb says. And horses and donkeys are in the habit of wandering the streets with total freedom, noses in the air, barging into any passer-by who fails to get out of their way. It's all like that—all full of freedom."

This strange discursive effect, whereby supposed democratic license seems to license in its turn a lack of restraint in the discourse commenting on it—as though there were an effect of contagion between the democratic man's freedom of speech and that of Socrates, who finds himself saying anything that comes to his lips—seems to extend beyond Socrates and Plato to commentators on these passages who do not make Strauss's point explicitly. So for example, in a note to his 1969 Loeb translation, after some learned cross-references to other Plato texts, a comparison of these remarks to passages in Arnold, Ruskin, and Carlyle, and an otherwise rather gratuitous quotation from Goethe,[6] Paul Shorey feels moved to add the quite unscholarly and strangely stuffy remark: "Similar phenomena may be ob-

---

6. "[Plato] would agree with Goethe (Eckermann i. 219, Jan. 18, 1827) "Nicht das macht frei, das wir nichts über uns erkennen wollen, sondern eben, dass wir etwas verehren, das über uns ist." (What makes us free is not that we want to know nothing above us, but rather that we worship something that is above us.)

served in an American city street or Pullman club car." And even supposedly serious philosophers are curiously drawn into the sarcasm, which here does not seem to stay within the classical bounds of "Socratic irony." So Jacques Rancière can write, apparently approving of Plato's description of the democratic individual:

> We could easily translate this portrait into modern terms: this democratic man, moving from politics to dieting or from the gym to philosophy, bears a fair resemblance to what is described to us as the postmodern individual. Plato draws for us in advance the portrait of this schizophrenic individual of consumer society people are keen to tell us is the ruin or debasement of democracy but who, in his caricature looks to Plato like its perfect embodiment. (*Aux bords du politique*, 79/42)

And less surprisingly, perhaps, that description has been picked up and retranslated by that avowed Platonist Alain Badiou, who, like Rancière, uses it to sarcastic and moralistic effect in his "translation" of *The Republic*.[7] So for example in a short piece entitled "The Democratic Emblem," gathered in *Democracy in What State?*, Badiou dismisses Plato's positive suggestions for the ideal state on the plausible grounds that they represent an aristocratic "nostalgia for something that never existed" (9), but nonetheless endorses Plato's critique both of the democratic state and, perhaps especially, of the democratic individual, again with an explicit gesture toward his own lack of verbal restraint:

> Not to mince words [here comes the parrhesiast saying "whatever comes to his lips"], the crucial traits of the democratic type are egoism and desire for petty enjoyments . . . the only thing that constitutes the

---

7. It is unclear to me, moralism and ingrained anti-*poikilon* prejudice apart, exactly where the distinction would be drawn between this Platonic picture of democracy and the one famously offered by Marx of man under communism in *The German Ideology* where he writes: "In communist society, where nobody has one exclusive sphere of activity but each can become accomplished in any branch he wishes, society regulates the general production and thus makes it possible for me to do one thing today and another tomorrow, to hunt in the morning, fish in the afternoon, rear cattle in the evening, criticize after dinner, just as I have a mind, without ever becoming hunter, fisherman, herdsman or critic." See too Arendt's comment, "the image of a 'classless society' [is] strikingly oriented around the ideals of leisure and free time as realized in the Greek polis" (*The Promise of Politics*, 77).

> democratic subject is pleasure or, more precisely, pleasure-seeking
> behavior . . . There is something essentially juvenile about the demo-
> cratic ethos, something that feels like universal puerilization . . .
> "Have fun" is the universal maxim . . . hence the profound stupidity
> of contemporary democratic societies. (9–12)

And this effect of contagion extends to Badiou's excerpt in this short essay
from his then forthcoming "hypertranslation" (121n1) of the whole *Republic*, "rendered with a certain liberty" (12), and itself, in its (relative) exuberance, clearly "having fun" under cover of its exceedingly serious overall
claim that "we will only ever be true democrats . . . when we are commu-
nists again" (15). Teaching experience tells me that it is indeed quite hard
for readers to resist the drive to identify with this sneering moralism faced
with a passage such as the one Badiou proudly chooses to provide here:

> Democratic man lives only for the pure present, transient desire is
> his only law. Today he regales himself with a four course dinner
> and vintage wine, tomorrow he is all about Buddha, ascetic fasting,
> streams of crystal-clear water, and sustainable development. Monday
> he tries to get back in shape by pedalling for hours on a stationary
> bicycle; Tuesday he sleeps all day, then smokes and gorges again in the
> evening. Wednesday he declares that he is going to read some phi-
> losophy, but prefers doing nothing in the end. At Thursday's dinner
> party he crackles with zeal for politics, fumes indignantly at the next
> person's opinion, and heatedly denounces the society of consumption
> and spectacle. That evening he goes to see a Ridley Scott blockbuster
> about medieval warriors. Back home, he falls to sleep and dreams of
> liberating oppressed peoples by force of arms. Next morning he goes
> to work, feeling distinctly seedy, and tries without success to seduce
> the secretary from the office next door. He's been turning things over
> and has made up his mind to get into real estate and go for the big
> money. But now the weekend has arrived, and this economic crisis isn't
> going away, so next week will be soon enough for all that. There you
> have a life, or lifestyle, or lifeworld, or whatever you want to call it: no
> order, no ideas, but nothing too disagreeable or distressing either. It is
> as free as it is unsignifying, and insignificance isn't too high a price to
> pay for freedom.[8]

8. This passage does not, however, appear as such in the full "hypertranslation" of the *Republic*, as subsequently translated from the French by Susan Spitzer
(New York: Columbia University Press, 2012), where the parallel passages do display, however, a similar exuberance.

This contagious effect of Socrates's descriptions, is, we might be tempted to think, itself "good for democracy," and certainly seems more appealing in its affinity with the *poikilon* it is describing and denouncing than some of the more doctrinal pronouncements of the same thinkers.[9]

The root of the reason for Plato's complex ironic hostility to democracy, his repeated sarcastic use of the motif of multicoloredness or motley, is no doubt his insistence on the motif of *unity* in the context of the State, and his perception that democracy cannot easily be reduced to this value of unity, or that it threatens this value of unity more persistently and thoroughly than other types of regime. We can perhaps bring this out more clearly by looking at an important and striking appropriation of Plato's descriptions, which often enough resorts to almost verbatim borrowings, but which also presents some fascinating divergences. This is Alfarabi's discussion of the democratic state in *The Political Regime*. In Alfarabi's classification, which owes something to Aristotle as well as a lot to Plato,[10] the

9. Plato's depiction of democracy may be unusual in eliciting these excessive reactions, but it might be that democracy itself provokes the worst in the scholar: see for example Jules Tricot's not-so-scholarly diatribe in a note to his French translation of Aristotle, which, as the French might say, *se passe de commentaire*: "[Aristotle] believes that an assembled crowd is capable of manifesting a wisdom that none of its members is in a position to reach. But that is an optimistic view that history belies at every step. Experience has taught us that the progress of the human race depends on the quality and the influence of its elites, and that crowds, through their impulsiveness, their lack of reasoning and the ease with which they let themselves be led, can exercise only a destructive role. Aristotle has a sense of this. . . . Athenian democracy has only the name in common with our modern democracies, in which senseless legislation and mores allow, in the management of public affairs, equal participation to millions of individuals, men and women, without wishing to give any consideration to the differences of every kind that divide us." Aristotle, *La politique* (Paris: Vrin, 1989), 214n2 (my translation).

10. In *Rogues*, Derrida points to the fact that Aristotle's *Politics* was not readily available to the Arab philosophers as relevant to the different status of democracy in the Islamic tradition (V 55/31–32). See too the measured discussion in the general introduction to *Medieval Political Philosophy: A Sourcebook*, ed. Joshua Parens and Joseph C. Macfarland, 2nd ed. (Ithaca, NY: Cornell University Press, 2011), to which volume references to Alfarabi here refer, in which the authors point out that Islamic (and Jewish) understanding of religion in terms of law and jurisprudence rather than theology, coupled with Islamic focus on the figure of the legislator, perhaps means that Alfarabi's limited knowledge of the *Politics* not be so much to do with historical accidents in the transmission of Aristotle, but

democratic city is one of the "ignorant" cities (as opposed to the "virtu-ous" city), and is not to that extent being extolled or recommended. On the one hand, Alfarabi provides, on the basis of an explicitly monotheistic starting point, a more clearly and rigorously hierarchized ontotheological structure than is the case in Plato, with the pinnacle occupied by a figure who is in proximity to the deity, more legislator than king (32–33), or equivalently legislator, philosopher, and king:[11] but on the other hand, somewhat along the lines of the "best of the worst" logic we will shortly be following in Aristotle, democracy emerges looking quite a lot better than was the case in Plato himself.

Democracy is an "ignorant" city, which is already the higher class of all cities opposed to the "virtuous" city, (the essential difference seems to be that in the virtuous city a true leader with an essential link to an originary revelation guides the people toward true happiness, whereas in the igno-rant cities the people think they know what they need for their happiness and choose the leader they think can deliver it). Although the relationship between the different types of "ignorant" city (the necessary city, the plu-tocratic, hedonistic, timocratic, and despotic cities),[12] and what Alfarabi calls "immoral" and "errant" cities is not entirely perspicuous, it does ap-pear that, of the ignorant cities, what the translator renders as "the demo-cratic city" (while explaining in a note (46n18) that *al-madina al-jamā 'iyya* is more literally translated as "the associational city") has some advantages

---

that "one begins to wonder whether the *Politics* was rarely commented upon because medieval political philosophers in Islam had few reasons to be interested in the text" (4).

11. See "The Attainment of Happiness," ibid., 70: "So let it be clear to you that the idea of the Philosopher, Supreme Ruler, Prince, Legislator, and Imam is but a single idea." It is instructive to compare Alfarabi's account with the later arguments of Maimonides. For example, in chapter 40 of part II of *The Guide of the Perplexed*, humans are political by nature but also diverse by nature; this means that the political community can only be realized by a (single) ruler through whom "the natural diversity is hidden through the multiple points of conven-tional accord." "It was part of the wisdom of the deity with regard to the continu-ance of this species, that He put it into its nature (when He willed its existence), that individuals belonging to it should have the faculty of ruling. Among them there is one to whom that governance has been revealed by prophecy directly; he is the prophet or the one who lays down the nomos."

12. In fact, the translator provides these headings. Alfarabi's own classifica-tion is harder to discern.

over the others. Already in his opening characterization of this city, some paradoxical elements emerge:

> The democratic city is the city in which every one of its inhabitants is unrestrained and left to himself to what he likes. Its inhabitants are equal to one another, and their traditional law is that no human being is superior to another in anything at all. Its inhabitants are free to do what they like. . . . Thus there arise among them many moral habits, many endeavors, many desires, and taking pleasure in countless things . . . The public, which does not have what the rulers have, has authority over those who are said to be their rulers. The one who rules them does so only by the will of the ruled, and their rulers are subject to the passions of the ruled. If their situation is examined closely, it turns out that in truth there is no ruler among them and no ruled. (SB 51)

And this is followed shortly by what is almost a direct quotation of Plato's *poikilon* or *poikilia*, with some original detail about why such a city might in fact grow and prosper:

> Of [all] their cities, this is the admirable and happy city. On the surface, it is like an embroidered garment replete with colored figures and dyes. Everyone loves it and loves to dwell in it, because every human being who has a passion or desire for anything is able to gain it in this city. The nations repair to it and dwell in it, so it becomes great beyond measure. People of every tribe are procreated in it by every sort of pairing off and sexual intercourse. The children generated in it are of very different innate characters and of very different education and upbringing.

And so in Alfarabi, and not—explicitly at least—in Plato, the very attraction and openness of democracy to others is a reason for an ongoing further internal diversification driven by the attractive nature of its already diverse and plural nature:

> Thus this city comes to be many cities, not distinguished from one another but interwoven with one another, the parts of one interspersed among the parts of another. Nor is the foreigner distinguished from the native resident. All of the passions and ways of life come together in it.

All of which has the paradoxical upshot that the democratic city has, among contradictory qualities, the best and the worst, is in a sense as good as it is bad, not necessarily (as in Plato) fated to become a tyranny, possibly coming close to the virtuous city it also most emphatically is not, becoming simultaneously better and worse as it grows:

> Therefore, it is not impossible as time draws on that virtuous people emerge in it. There may chance to exist in it wise men, rhetoricians, and poets concerned with every type of object. It is possible to glean from it parts of the virtuous city, and this is the best that emerges in this city. Thus, of the ignorant cities this city has the most good and the most evil. The bigger, more prosperous, more populous, more fertile, and more perfect it becomes for people, the more prevalent and greater are these two [i.e., good and evil]. (SB 52)

This logic whereby democracy is as good as it is bad (and for the same reasons) obviously troubles any straightforward teleological argument in its favor: for it would follow that we do not really know, with democracy, which way things are going, whether for better or for worse, and that means we do not know exactly what it means to claim that one organization is more democratic than another.[13] As we shall see, this logic will return with devastating effect in Aristotle.

Aristotle might indeed be expected to give us some access to a more elaborated and less moralistic thinking of democracy, just because his primary objection to Plato's political theory turns around this value of unity. For Aristotle insists that the State simply cannot be thought under the sign of unity, just because by definition it is a plural entity. In the *Republic*, Socrates says: "Do we know of any greater evil for a state than the thing that distracts it and makes it many instead of one, or a greater good than that which binds it together and makes it one?" (*Republic* 462a–b), and, a little later, in an analogy which is no doubt defining for the metaphysical concept of politics: "The best city [is the one] whose state is most like that of an individual man" (*kai hētis dē engytata henos anthrōpou echei* [462c]. See too *Laws*, 829a).[14]

---

13. Cf. *Rogues*, V 60–61/36.

14. This persistent analogy of the state and the individual will of course have a long and complex history, up to Hobbes's "artificial individual" and beyond. It is still operative in Hardt and Negri, who in spite of everything want their multitude to cohere into a body analogous to some conception of a human body: "the formation of the new body of the multitude, a fundamentally new kind of body, a common body, a democratic body. Spinoza gives us an initial idea of what the anatomy of such a body might be. 'The human body,' he writes, 'is

Already in Plato, this analogy is in fact far from simple.[15] Arguably it is quite incoherent, with consequences that will reverberate through the tradition.[16] For if the analogy with the individual is designed to help unify the concept of the city, its reversibility means at the very least that it will always also tend to politicize and divide the presupposed unity of that individual insofar as politics entails multiplicity.

The whole post-Thrasymachus discussion of justice in the *Republic* is undertaken under the sign of this analogy between individual and city, mediated by a figure of writing and reading: justice is, as it were, hard to read, says Socrates near the beginning, in a passage we already had occasion to cite:

> The inquiry we are undertaking is not a simple matter. If you ask me, it requires sharp eyesight. And since we are not clever people, I think we should conduct our search in the same sort of way as we would if our eyesight were not very good, and we were told to read some small writing from a bit of a distance away, and then one of us realized that a larger copy of the same writing, apparently, was to be found somewhere else, on some larger surface. We would regard it as a stroke of luck, I think, to be able to read the large letters first, and then turn our attention to the small ones, to see if they really did say the same thing. . . . We say that there is justice in an individual; but also, I take it, justice in a whole city? . . . In that case, maybe justice will be on a larger scale in what is larger, and easier to find out about. So if you approve, why don't we start by finding out what sort of thing it is in cities? After that we can make a similar inquiry into the individual,

composed of many individuals of different natures, each of which is highly composite'—and yet this multitude of multitudes is able to act in common as one body" (*Multitude*, 189–190). *Scatter* is the refusal of "one body," under which the multitude, however monstrous (ibid., 190–196), is still unified as humanity, and in the end as One.

15. Often referred to as Plato's *makros anthropos* or "big man," e.g., by Carl Schmitt in his book *The Leviathan in the State Theory of Thomas Hobbes*, trans. George Schwab and Erna Hilfstein (Chicago: University of Chicago Press, 2008), at 19, but the phrase does not in fact appear in the *Republic*, nor, so far as I can tell, in the rest of Plato.

16. According to Jacob Taubes in *Occidental Eschatology*, trans. David Ratmoko (Stanford: Stanford University Press, 2009), 62, this is also the root of the Pauline conception of the one body of the Church in, e.g., 1 Corinthians 12:12, and so we might expect incoherencies in the analogy to surface in the Christian tradition too.

trying to find the likeness of the larger version in the form the smaller takes. (368d–369a)

But the analogy is immediately complicated by the fact that "The origin of a city lies, I think, in the fact that we are not, any of us, self-sufficient; we have all sorts of needs" (369b), and that that non-self-sufficiency of the individual (the less-than-oneness of the individual) goes along with a *diversity* of individuals: "one individual is by nature quite unlike another individual, and they differ in their natural aptitudes, and that different people are equipped to perform different tasks." (370b), even though that diversity is supposedly limited by the thought that it makes each individual good for *only one* thing or function (this will be part of the critique of democracy, where everybody wants to do everything).

The motif of self-sufficiency, supposedly to be provided by the City as a supplement to the non-self-sufficiency of the individual, will slowly open onto a certain primacy, as a mark of the political as such, of relations *between* cities or states, over any supposed self-sufficiency of the city or state. Most explicitly from Kant through Hegel to Schmitt, politics will turn out to entail a kind of primary exteriority of a plurality of states,[17] an outside that precedes all insides. As we shall see also in Aristotle's *Politics*, where the supposed autonomy of the city is troubled by a "more or less," a "so to speak," there is already a trace of this failure of *autarkeia* in the *Republic*, where the "hypothetical city" or "city of words," the imagination of which is begun at 369c (*tō logō ex archēs poiōmen polin*) is quite early on marked as needing relations to its outside. A little later Socrates says: "It will be more or less impossible to locate the city itself in a place where it won't need imports" (370e). This opening is then explicitly exaggerated in the development that follows, which identifies the origin of war in the expansion of the original city (what Glaucon calls the "city of pigs" [372d]) beyond satisfaction of its necessities: "Do we need, then, to carve ourselves a slice of our neighbors' territory . . . and do they in turn need a slice of our land . . . and will the next step be war? . . . We have discovered, in its turn, the origin of war" (373e).

Whatever the fate of this opening to the outside, the management of diversity within the *polis* by the one-person-one-function principle turns out just to be justice itself:

17. See my analysis of this moment in Kant in *Kant on the Frontier: Philosophy, Politics, and the Ends of the Earth* (New York: Fordham University Press, 2017), 60–61.

The principle we laid down right at the start, when we first founded our city, as something we must stick to throughout—this, I think, or some form of it, is justice. What we laid down—and often repeated, if you remember—was that each individual should follow, out of the occupations available in the city, the one for which his natural character best fitted him. . . . And we have often heard others say, and have often said ourselves, that doing one's own job, and not trying to do other people's jobs for them, is justice. . . . Well, it looks, my friend, as if in some way or other *justice* is this business of everyone performing his own task. . . . It is the interference of our three classes with one another, then, and interchange between them, which does the greatest harm to the city, and rightly be called the worst crime against it. . . . That, then, is what injustice is. Conversely, its opposite—the ability of the commercial, auxiliary and guardian classes to mind their own business, with each of them performing its own function in the city—this will be justice, and will make the city just. (433a–434c)

This then has to be put to the test of the broader analogy. The City is *ex hypothesi* like the individual writ large: we now think we have found what justice is in the City (everyone fulfilling one proper task); now let's see if that's what justice is at the level of the individual: "The just man in his turn, simply in terms of his justice, will be no different from a just city. He will be like the just city" (435b).

This endless reversibility or abyssal quality of the analogy, such that the City is like an individual who is like a City-like-an-individual (like a City [like an individual]), and its availability for use in terms of both body and soul, will produce slightly dizzying complications as Plato proceeds. For example, the tripartite division of the soul into rational, desiring, and "spirited" parts is established in part on the basis of the analogy of the City, and more especially of the City as subject to civil war (*stasis*) (440b and e, leading to confirmation that the soul is like the city with its three classes at 441a), and then the confirmation of the analogy at the level of justice as announced at 368d: "A just man is just . . . in the same way a city was just" (441d) . . . "each one of us will be just, and perform his own proper task, when each of the elements within him is performing *its* proper task" (441e).

Once the individual is like the city, then it is a multiplicity that must be managed and ruled, so that the individual must be "himself his own ruler" (443d), avoiding *stasis* or civil war among the elements of the soul.[18] And

18. This is the position (Socrates's "every man is his own ruler . . . one who is temperate and self-mastering [*egkrates autos heautou*]") that is quite vigorously

this is what provides for the further analogy between types of soul and types of regime: one "correct" form (monarchy or aristocracy, corresponding to the individual in which the rational part of the soul governs the others), and four bad or faulty forms (445c). But this development of the analogy generates further complications, in that a given regime will be *like* an individual of the corresponding type, but also tend to *contain* individuals of that type. Regimes that need to have individuals of *different* types (i.e., all regimes except democracy) then become difficult to figure in these terms. This complication of the analogy returns at the beginning of book 8, after the whole "digression" constituted by the construction of the ideal regime, the discussion of philosophy itself and the allegory of the cave. The four faulty regimes are now named (544c), and the analogy is invoked now as a necessary one: "for individuals also there must necessarily be as many kinds of character as there are kinds of regime" (544d). The four types of faulty regime follow cyclically from the correct type, and the principle of that change is the *stasis*, the civil war we already noted as characteristic of the unbalanced state or soul, itself a product of imbalances generated by inevitable errors in the calculation of breeding (546a–547a: it is perhaps no accident that Socrates presents this account as a prosopopoeia of the Muses, who in part lament their own progressive disappearance from the story they are telling). This cycle is one in which unity is progressively lost to the forces of dispersion, scatter and *to poikilon*. But the complexity of the analogy between state and individual increases with increasing scatter too, so that the democratic individual is so dispersed (so "postmodern," as Rancière observes) as scarcely to be an individual at all (561a–562a). By the time we reach the supposed analogy of Tyranny and the Tyrant, that complexity threatens the very coherence of the ongoing analogy on which the

---

attacked by the "Nietzschean" Callicles in *Gorgias* 491d: "he who would live rightly should let his desires be as strong as possible and not chasten them, and should be able to minister to them when they are at their height by reason of his manliness and intelligence, and satisfy each appetite in turn with what it desires. But this, I suppose, is not possible for the many; whence it comes that they decry such persons out of shame, to disguise their own impotence, and are so good as to tell us that licentiousness is disgraceful, thus enslaving—as I remarked before— the better type of mankind; and being unable themselves to procure achievement of their pleasures they praise temperance and justice by reason of their own unmanliness." See too Foucault's commentary on the formula *egkrates autos heautou* as it appears in Plato's seventh letter in *Le gouvernement de soi et les autres*, 249–250.

whole discussion of justice (and, by extension, the whole of the *Republic*) is based. The tyrant is born of the democrat and is a tyrant (in a regime of tyranny) because his soul is organized as a tyranny: the tyrant's soul is originally a democracy of desire, in which all desires are treated equally as equally desirable. But the tyrant becomes a tyrant in proportion as Lust becomes a tyrant among desires: in the tyrant "Lust dwells as an internal tyrant" (573d); "Lust itself . . . stands at the head of [the other desires] like a tyrant at the head of his bodyguard" (573e); "Lust will dwell within him as a tyrant, in total anarchy and lawlessness" (575a). The tyrannical man, it turns out, is less a tyrant than a man tyrannized by an internal tyrant. Insofar as he is like a tyrannical state, the tyrant is not so much like the tyrant within that state, as he is subject to, or enslaved by, the tyranny of Eros. This is why the tyrannical man is not always in fact a tyrant, but is more suited to becoming the bodyguard of a (foreign) tyrant, for example (575b). The tyrant corresponds to the tyrannical regime more insofar as he is tyrannized than in that he is tyrannical—whence the supplementary complication that the tyrannical man who actually *becomes* a tyrant is the most unhappy man. At any rate, the tyrannical man is his own slave and so not really even a tyrant at all (580e).[19]

The abyssal consequence of the foundational analogy between individual and city, whereby the tyrant is not a tyrant but a slave ends up ruining the analogy itself. At the other end of the cycle, the King, the most kingly man, is kingly insofar as he is king over himself. The King is his own King: the Tyrant is his own Slave. The analogy plays itself out between the extreme of self-inclusion (the King is King of himself) and the extreme of self-exclusion (the Tyrant is not even his own Tyrant but his own slave). Like tautology and contradiction bounding logical space for the Wittgenstein of the *Tractatus*, these two extremes bound political space in Plato. But as neither is strictly speaking intelligible *as* an analogy, we are inclined to say that politics happens in between, in the relative scatter of the intervening analogies in the cases of timocracy, oligarchy and democracy. It is not hard to see that insofar as these analogies depend on a differentiation that resolves neither into absolute unity (the tautology of monarchy) nor absolute contradiction (the tyranny that is slavery), then democracy will necessarily have a certain priority, as will be repeatedly confirmed, if only in the mode of denial, in all the great texts of the tradi-

19. Compare *Gorgias* 466d–e, where Socrates aligns tyrants and orators on the grounds that they have no real power, "for they do just about nothing they want to, though they certainly do whatever they see most fit to do."

tion, starting with Aristotle's *Politics*. In the case of Plato, we might want to say that the analogy between individual and State, on which the whole of the *Republic* is based, is in fact intelligible *only* in the case of democracy (all individuals in a democracy are in principle democratic individuals, and this correspondence between individual and state is not true of any other regime), but that intelligibility is immediately compromised by the fact that it engages with the rationally difficult (*pace* Hegel) thought that the *different* is the *same*. If, as Derrida suggests most forcefully in *Voyous*, there cannot really be a *concept* of democracy, then it is at least arguable that Plato's analogy here leaves us in a kind of pure *milieu* of analogy, an *ana-logos* that never quite resolves into a *logos*.[20]

20. Part of Socrates's argument leading from democracy to tyranny invokes something of a logic of unconscious desire. At the beginning of book 9, Socrates, unhappy with the earlier discussion (at 558d–559d) introduces a supplementary distinction, within the "unnecessary pleasures and desires," separating out a sub-class of "violent and lawless" desires. These desires ("Everyone is born with them, in all probability" [571b]), "are aroused in sleep . . . when the rest of the soul—the rational, gentle and ruling element in it—slumbers, and the bestial, savage part, [*to de thēriōdes te kai agrion*] filled with food or drink, suddenly comes alive, casts off sleep [in sleep the savage part does not sleep], and tries to go out and satisfy its own nature. In this state, as you know, since it is released and set free from all shame or rational judgment [*aischynēs kai phronēseōs*], it can bring itself to do absolutely anything. In its imaginings it has no hesitation in attempting sexual intercourse with a mother—nor with anyone or anything else, man or god or animal. There is no murder it will not commit, no meat it will not eat. In short, it will go to any length of folly and shamelessness. . . . There is in everyone a terrible, untamed and lawless class of desires—even in those of us who appear to be completely normal. This becomes quite clear in our sleep" (571c–d, 572b). It is tempting to think that this is already something like the unconscious, and that this might take us further in understanding the aporias in the account of the tyrant. But psychoanalysis, however illuminating here, does not simply resolve the aporias in the analogy of state and individual. Freud himself appeals to the analogy between individual and state that we are worrying about here: see, for example, in *The Ego and the Id*, where the position of the ego is likened to that of a "constitutional monarch, without whose sanction no law can be passed but who hesitates long before imposing his veto on any measure put forward by Parliament." *The Standard Edition of the Complete Psychological Works of Sigmund Freud*, 24 vols. (London: Hogarth Press, 1953–74), 19:55. Only one page later it is described as "too often yield[ing] to the temptation to become sycophantic, opportunist and lying, like a politician who sees the truth but wants to keep his place in popular favor" (ibid., 56).

In his alignment of Plato and Aristotle in their "political salute to the One God," Derrida uses the proximity of the French titles of the works to which he is referring to reinforce the parallelism between them, and gives a quite precise reference to each: "This political salute to the One God signs turn by turn *Le politique* and *La politique* (*Politikos* and *Politikon*), *Le politique* [i.e., *The Statesman*] by Plato (303ab) and *La politique* [i.e., *The Politics*] by Aristotle (III, 1283b 8, 13–15)" (V, 110–111/75–6). In the Plato passage, The Stranger proposes that the three forms of government are each split according as they do or do not obey laws, so that the rule of one can take the form either of monarchy or tyranny, the rule of a few either aristocracy or oligarchy, and the rule of the many, called by the single name democracy (though it too takes a law-following and a lawless form). Of the law-abiding forms, monarchy is the best and democracy the worst, but if the laws are not followed, the order inverts and democracy is the best, and tyranny the worst. But there is yet a seventh type of government, in which the statesman rules according to the "kingly science" famously elaborated in the *Statesman*: this "right" [*orthos*] form—of which the others are merely more or less successful imitations—being unavailable in practice, must be set apart from the others *oion theon ex anthropon*, "as God is set apart from men," as Fowler translates it, "like a god among men," as Derrida has it. It is this expression, or its near-equivalent *hosper gar theon en anthropois*, that encourages the parallelism Derrida is trying to establish between Plato and Aristotle and their "political salute to the One God."

This expression occurs in a complicated passage of Aristotle's *Politics*. Before attempting to read that passage, let me first situate a few points from the famous opening of that text (probably among the most famous and influential pages in all of Western philosophy). Derrida does not analyze these passages in detail anywhere in his published work, but he does spend some time reading them (or at least reading them out) in the final, improvised, session of volume I of the *Beast and Sovereign* seminars at the very end of his life. This opening of the *Politics* is very germane to Derrida's pair of eponymous terms in that seminar, to the point that it is a little surprising that he does not devote more time to it, especially as Aristotle already brings out the association of god and beast as a way of stressing the "naturally" political status of man. Here is Derrida quoting Aristotle and interpolating some comments in session 13 of year 1:

> From these considerations it is clear that the City is a natural reality and that man is naturally a being destined to live in a City [political animal, *tōn phusei e polis esti, kai oti anthrōpos phusei politikon zōon*: is a

political animal]; he who is cityless is, by nature and not by chance,[21] a
being either degraded or else superior to man [the one who is without
a City, who is *apolis*, who is apolitical, is either below or else above
man, either an animal or else god: the political is properly human,
what in life is properly human: "he who is cityless (*kai o apolis dia
phusin kai ou dia tukhēn*, etc.), is, by nature and not by chance, either
below or else above man"]: he is like the man Homer reproaches with
having "no clan, no law, no hearth"; a man this way by nature is by the
same token warlike; he is like an isolated pawn in chess. (BS I,
460–461/347)

To which we might want to add a slightly later passage Derrida does not
get to in this improvised session, in which Aristotle says:

> It is clear therefore that the state is also prior by nature to the indi-
> vidual; for if each individual when separate is not self-sufficient, he
> must be related to the whole state as other parts are to their whole,
> while a man who is incapable of entering into partnership, or who is so
> self-sufficing that he has no need to do so, is no part of a state, so that
> he must be either a lower animal or a god [*ei thērion ei theōs*]. (1253a28)

The man who is *not* naturally political, not by nature a *politikon zōon*, either
falls out below or rises up above the *polis* which is the primary natural real-
ity for humans, on Aristotle's account—just because the *polis* is the end of
the story about associations that Aristotle tells at the beginning of the
Politics, it is the true nature of what is being described, for "the nature of
a thing is its end" (1252b33), or else, as Aristotle presents it a little later, it
is the whole of which the individual is merely a part, and teleologically
speaking the whole precedes the parts of which it is made. In the case of
the "falling below," the falling is a radical one, in the sense that the man
who is not naturally part of the *polis* is not just like *any* kind of non-human
animal: in the translation I have just used, Rackham is reaching a little to
get "lower animal" from the Greek word *thērion*, which might just be
"wild animal" (as opposed to a domesticated one: Jowett translates it as
"beast"), but in any case just a little further on—again, beyond what Derrida gets to in that final session—Aristotle is more explicit:

---

21. Following Derrida's French translation—but it seems inaccurate, and the
sense should rather be "he who is, by nature and not by chance, cityless, is
either . . ."

> For man, when perfected, is the best of animals, but, when separated
> from law and justice, he is the worst of all; since armed injustice is the
> more dangerous, and he is equipped at birth with arms, meant to be
> used by intelligence and excellence, which he may use for the worst
> ends. That is why, if he has not excellence, he is the most unholy and
> the most savage of animals, and the most full of lust and gluttony.
> (1253a31–37)

The man who falls downward, out of his natural place in the *polis*, does
not just slip below the supposed dividing line between man and beast, but
immediately falls radically and catastrophically into the depths, to the very
bottom, as "most unholy" (*anosiōtaton*) and "most savage" (*agriōtaton*) of animals. In the apparently symmetrical "rising above" figure, Aristotle does
not explicitly relate the "god" in question directly to the figure of what
comes to be called the sovereign, but we do not need to look very far in
the *Politics* to find at least the beginnings of a link between this beast-god
parallelism on the one hand, and the figure we might indeed be inclined
to call the sovereign on the other.

Back in *Rogues*, as we have seen, Derrida explicitly and precisely references a passage from book 3 of the *Politics* in support of the association of
Plato and Aristotle in their attachment to God as the One. Although Derrida's precise reference here remains a little mysterious, in part just because
it is so precise (he gives 1283b8, 13–15, but these lines do not seem immediately or unambiguously to answer to the point he is making),[22] the logic
of Aristotle's general drift in this part of book 3 of the *Politics* is indeed
germane to the question. Aristotle is wondering and worrying about the
tension between *on the one hand* a view of justice as equality: "all men think

---

22. 1283b10–16 in the Jowett translation: "But, what if the good, the rich,
the noble, and the other classes who make up a state, are all living together in the
same city, will there, or will there not, be any doubt who shall rule? No doubt at
all in determining who ought to rule in each of the above-mentioned forms of
government. For states are characterized by differences in their governing
bodies—one of them has a government of the rich, another of the virtuous, and so
on. But a difficulty arises when all these elements co-exist. How are we to decide?
Suppose the virtuous to be very few in number: may we consider their numbers in
relation to their duties, and ask whether they are enough to administer the state,
or so many as will make up a state? Objections may be urged against all the aspirants to political power. For those who found their claims on wealth or family
might be thought to have no basis of justice; on this principle, if any one person
were richer than all the rest, it is clear that he ought to be ruler of them."

justice to be a sort of equality," he says at 1282b17. This is already a reflex-
ive and potentially abyssal formulation, in that it implies that all men *equally*
think that justice is equality, which sits in a tense relationship with
the opening claim of this section of the *Politics* which positions justice
as the end, and therefore the good, of political science, that good being the
"greatest," the "highest," and the "most authoritative" (*megiston, malista,
kyriōtatē*), the biggest, the most and, we might be tempted to say, the most
sovereign, something outstanding that is perhaps not so easily reconciled
with the concept of equality. The tension Aristotle is exploring is between
that view of justice as equality on the one hand, then, and *on the other hand*
the view that some criterion of excellence or eminence (and thereby necessarily of *inequality*) might nonetheless reasonably be invoked to influence
the distribution of political offices. Clearly not just any criterion of excellence (of inequality, then, in relation to the thought of justice as essentially
to do with equality) can be invoked (superior gymnasts or flute players, for
example, are not better qualified by virtue of their athletic or musical excellence to hold political office), but only "possession of elements that enter into the composition of the state" (1283a15). These elements might
include freedom, wealth, and lineage, but also mere numerical superiority
of the many over the few, as well as excellence in a more ethical sense. It
may seem as though the question can be settled easily enough in a given
state, but what—asks Aristotle in the first part of the passage Derrida seems
to be referring to in his very precise reference—what of the state in which
all of these diverse elements coexist? In a state in which there are rich
people *and* good people *and* well-born people (and they are not the same
people), how are we to decide who is to be in charge? "Objections," he says
in the second part of the passage Derrida points to in his reference, "may
be urged against all the aspirants to political power." These objections "appear to show that none of the principles on which men claim to rule and
to hold all other men in subjection to them are right."

Derrida's implication is that faced with this difficulty arising from the
coexistence of "diverse elements" in the state (and the state would not in
fact be a state on Aristotle's construal if there were *not* a multiplicity and
diversity of elements, this being the very principle of his consistent criticisms of Plato's *Republic*, and notably of Socrates's claim that the best state
is the one most like a single individual (*Republic* 462c answered at *Politics*
1263b30–35; we shall return to this at length)—Derrida's implication is that
Aristotle will nonetheless urge the superiority of the One, in the image of
the supreme ipseity of God that, in the *Metaphysics*, called up the quote
from Homer about the preference for one ruler that guided our discussion

in Part I of this book. And indeed Aristotle does go on immediately to consider the case of the Absolute King or *pambasileus*, the case of the "One Best Man" as Newman also glosses it in his classic commentary on the *Politics*.[23] And it must be said that at first sight this does seem to be Aristotle at his most Platonic: here is Derrida's presentation of the case, which follows Aristotle's text very closely:

> When Aristotle's *Politikon*, his *Politics*, takes up the formulation of Plato's *Politikōs*, namely, "like a god among men [*hosper gar theon en anthropois*]" (1284a11), it is again with regard to number. If there is one or more than one, but not enough to constitute an entire city of incomparable, incommensurable virtue and political ability, unequal to that of other cities, then this one or this "just more than one" will not be a mere part (*meros*, and this is the word for *turn*, *by turns*, *each in turn* [*en merei*], *alternation*), this *one* or *just more* will not belong, like the part of a whole, to what it governs. This one would not be a fraction of a whole, or an arithmetic unit in a calculable series. We would thus do such a man wrong, we would do him an injustice (*adikesontai*), were we simply to grant him rights. Equal rights, calculable right or law, and proportional isonomy would thus betray justice (*dike*) in this case. For or against such beings who are like a god among men, there is no law, no *nomos*. There is no law for them or against them, but there is the law, and they are themselves, in their very ipseity, the law (*autoi gar eisi nomos*). And that's where the fable of sovereignty returns, along with the reason of the strongest to which this text alludes. "They are themselves a law," says Aristotle, who adds: "Indeed a man would be ridiculous if he tried to legislate for them, for probably they would say what in the story of Antisthenes the lions said when the hares made speeches in the assembly and demanded that all should have equality" (1284a14–17: Rackham has a note explaining that in the fable the lions said to the hares "where are your claws and teeth?"). (V 112–113/77)

Derrida, presumably considering that he has made his case for the common "salut politique au Dieu Un" in Plato and Aristotle, breaks off his discussion and quotation at this point, with a series of unanswered questions: "The democracy to come, will it be a god to come? Or more than one? Will it be the name to come of a god or of democracy? Utopia? Prayer?

---

23. W. L. Newman, *The Politics of Aristotle*, 4 vols. (Oxford: Clarendon Press, 1887), 1:273–281.

Pious wish? Oath? Or something else altogether?" (V 113/77). He might indeed have strengthened his case by quoting from a little farther along in Book III of the *Politics*, where Aristotle, concluding his discussion of the One Best Man hypothesis, makes an apparently even more straightforward link to a theological figure, the "god among men" being likened to the god among gods, namely Zeus:

> No doubt men would not think that they ought to rule over such a man, for that would be the same as if they claimed to rule over Zeus [the Greek text has simply *tou Dios*], dividing up his spheres of government. It remains therefore, and this seems to be the natural course, for all to obey such a man gladly, so that men of this sort may be kings in the cities for all time. (1284b30–35)

And yet, complicating Derrida's claim about the reduction of diversity into the sovereign figure of the One, it seems plausible to read this discussion not simply or directly as *recommending* this solution to the problems raised by multiplicity, diversity and difference, but as pushing to a certain limit already the paradoxical—"autoimmune"—logic of sovereignty that Derrida is himself concerned to develop in both the *Beast and Sovereign* seminars and in *Rogues*. Whether or not we choose to detect a note of irony in Aristotle's "it remains therefore . . ." conclusion (where the "it remains," the "gladly" or "joyfully" [*asmenos*] and the "natural course," translating *pethukenai*,[24] might all be read as ironic, whether or not Aristotle intended them ironically), consideration of the pages between the introduction of the One Best Man hypothesis and its conclusion suggests that this preeminent or hyperbolically excellent individual (or group, but the logic of preeminence itself cannot fail to produce the image of the individual, whence many of the problems in theories of sovereignty) is less Aristotle's *solution* to his question than a further *problem* for it, a kind of limit case of the

---

24. The Liddell-Scott dictionary gives "it is natural" for this impersonal usage, and refers to an earlier instance in the *Politics*: at 1261b7, in a context germane not only to the "turn by turn" thematic Derrida discusses at length in *Rogues* but more especially to the argument with Plato as to the desirability of "unifying" the State: "it is not an outcome of nature for the state to be a unity in the manner in which certain persons say that it is, and that what has been said to be the greatest good in states really destroys states." This is the crux of Aristotle's disagreement with Plato about politics in general, which I am suggesting is more important than the apparent convergence Derrida is concerned to bring out.

political as such.[25] Whence a degree of sympathy in his discussion of how even the "imperfect" or deviant forms of state deal with such cases, through exile or ostracism of such pre-eminent individuals, in which Aristotle recognizes that "there is a kind of political justice." Indeed, this "problem" (Aristotle indeed uses the term *problema*) even *precedes* the distinction between normal and deviant forms of state, and therefore engages with the most basic definitions of the state, and therefore also of the *zōon politikon* and *zōon logon echon*, that provide the framework for the *Politics* as a whole. "The problem is a universal one, and equally concerns all forms of government, true as well as false" (1284b4–5), says Aristotle. And the nature of this problem is such that he generalizes it still further in a striking and strange series of parallels, anecdotes, comparisons or analogies, as he draws out at some, indeed gruesome, length the political problem posed by the One Best Man. This immediately follows the reference to Antisthenes's fable of the lions and the hares:

> This is why democratically governed states institute the system of ostracism, because of a reason of this nature; for these are the states considered to pursue equality most of all things, so that they used to ostracize men thought to be outstandingly powerful on account of wealth or popularity or some other form of political strength, and used to banish them out of the city for fixed periods of time. And there is a mythical story that the Argonauts left Heracles behind for a similar reason; for the Argo refused to carry him with the other

25. This difficulty in understanding the relation between Aristotle's relating politics as such to the law, and yet apparently promoting the *pambasileus*, is something that exercised medieval political thinkers: in Peter of Auvergne's continuation of Aquinas's unfinished *Commentary* to the *Politics*, for example, Peter carefully lays out the apparent contradiction in Aristotle's position, and recognizes that the *pambasileus* solution is "what is left" after ostracism and other possibilities have been considered, and that it constitutes an exception to Aristotle's usual sense of politics in that the One Best Man is not strictly a citizen in the state he rules. See Parens and Macfarland, *Medieval Political Philosophy*, 302–304, and helpful remarks by them at 244–246. See also Marsilius of Padua, *The Defender of the Peace*, 57, 62, 93, 100, 107. William of Ockham weighs arguments on both sides in his *Dialogus*. See *A Letter to the Friars Minor and Other Writings*, ed. Arthur Stephen McGrade and John Kilcullen, trans. John Kilcullen (Cambridge: Cambridge University Press, 1995), 127, 130, 150, 159ff, and 167–168: "sometimes it is beneficial for matters to be concluded by many rather than one, and sometimes it is more beneficial that they be dealt with by one."

voyagers because he was so much heavier. Hence also those who blame tyranny and Periander's advice to Thrasybulus must not be thought to be absolutely right in their censure (the story is that Periander made no reply to the herald sent to ask his advice, but levelled the corn-field by plucking off the ears that stood out above the rest; and consequently, although the herald did not know the reason for what was going on. when he carried back news of what had occurred, Thrasybulus understood that he was to destroy the outstanding citizens); for this policy is advantageous not only for tyrants; nor is it only tyrants that use it, but the same is the case with oligarchies and democracies as well; for ostracism has in a way the same effect as docking off the outstanding men by exile. (1284a15–38)

This general political problem or problem for politics as such in fact exceeds politics as such:

And this is also clear in the field of the other arts and sciences; a painter would not let his animal have its foot of disproportionately large size, even though it was an exceptionally beautiful foot, nor would a shipbuilder make the stern or some other part of a ship disproportionately big, nor yet will a trainer of choruses allow a man who sings louder and more beautifully than the whole band to be a member of it. (1284b10–17)

Aristotle says not only that in imperfect or deviant forms of state (ones where the state is not governed with a view to the common good) the use of exile and ostracism is therefore "advantageous and just," but in a correct form of state the use of exile and ostracism would give rise to doubt when used not merely against someone preeminently wealthy, strong or popular, but precisely when that pre-eminence is one of ethical or political excellence, that is, a preeminence in justice itself, which Aristotle has just said "implies all other [excellences: i.e., in wealth, strength, birth and so on]"; in other words, where the internal tension we noted a moment ago in the characterization of justice as equality emerges in this highly troublesome figure of eminent inequality that Newman calls the One Best Man. Only here, in this exceptional case, and not in general, does Aristotle's "solution" involve—making the best of a bad job, as it were—a kind of last-ditch attempt to adopt that One Best Man into the state of which however, as we saw, he cannot really be a part:

People will not say that such a man is to be expelled and exiled; on the other hand, he ought not to be a subject—that would be as if mankind should claim to rule over Zeus, dividing his offices among them. The

only alternative is that all should happily obey such a ruler, according
to what seems to be the order of nature, and then men like him should
be kings in their state for life. (1284b29–34)

The One Best Man or *pambasileus* hypothesis, then, the sovereign hypothesis, we might be tempted to call it, represents a limit case for politics as such, and for the very definition of the *polis*. Not only is this case
exceptional in that, as Aristotle seems to recognize, it is unlikely to happen, but also in that such a man (a godly or beastly man according to the
terms of the opening of the *Politics*) would be outside the law exactly in
as much as he *was* the law.[26] And this gives rise to an apparent complication in the distribution of the terms here, in that, says Aristotle a little
later, summarizing an antimonarchical argument and including a famous definition:

> Therefore he who bids the law rule may be deemed to bid God and
> Reason [*ton theon kai ton noūn*] alone rule, but he who bids man rule
> adds an element of the beast [*thērion*, again]; for desire is a wild beast,
> and passion perverts the hearts of rulers, even when they are the best
> of men [*tous aristous andras*]. The law is reason unaffected by desire.
> (1287a28–31)

The *pambasileus*, then, the One Best Man earlier tendentially identified
with God, goes catastrophically from best to beast, the end of politics not
as its realization but as its collapse, and now it is the law which is associated with god.[27]

26. Michel Foucault has a brief but suggestive discussion of these questions
in his last lecture course, *Le courage de la vérité: Le gouvernement de soi et des autres
II* (Paris: Gallimard/Seuil, 2009), 50–51, trans. Graham Burchell as *The Courage
of Truth: The Government of Self and Others II* (London: Palgrave Macmillan,
2011), 51–52, culminating in the following remark that (in spite of Foucault's persistent explicit anti-Derrideanism in these late courses) we might be tempted to
read less as a critique of democracy and more in terms of a Derridean notion of
autoimmunity: "The kingship of virtue, the monarchy of virtue, that's what finds
its place and asserts itself as soon as democracy tries to raise the question of moral
excellence. In short, when, with Aristotle, an attempt is made to give the best possible justification for the laws and rules of democracy, we see that democracy can
give only one place to moral excellence, a place which embodies the very refusal
of democracy" (51/52; translation slightly modified).

27. Even Newman, who does seem to think that for Aristotle absolute monarchy is the highest form of the State, has to concede "In the Absolute Kingship,

This bewildering structure of sovereignty in its affinity with the (counter)naturally apolitical man as rising above and/or falling out of the *polis*, like god or beast or both, recalls Heidegger's repeated engagements with a striking line from a Choral Ode in Sophocles's *Antigone* that uses the appositive expression *hupsipolis apolis* (*nomous gerairōn chthonos theōn t'enorkon dikan / hupsipolis apolis hotō to mē kalon: apolis* is also the term Aristotle uses, and that Derrida stresses, in the opening of the *Politics*.) Heidegger first comments on this in the *Introduction to Metaphysics* in 1935 and returns to it at greater length in the 1942 course on Hölderlin's poem *Der Ister*.[28] There are some interesting differences between these two treatments, notably perhaps in that the second radicalizes the interpretation of the concept of the *polis* beyond anything recognizably political toward the place of the question of Being itself, so that Heidegger can state "*The* polis *cannot be determined 'politically.'* The polis, and precisely it, is therefore not a 'political' concept" (80), and suggest that the original sense of the *polis* has thus already been mistaken in Plato and Aristotle (81). This allows for a highly ambiguous gesture whereby Heidegger can simultaneously refuse a National Socialist reading while explicitly endorsing National Socialism:

---

the highest but also the least realizable of [the] forms [of the State], many of its usual features seem to disappear. . . . Aristotle's admission of the Absolute Kingship as a possible form of the State seems altogether to conflict with his general account of the State" (1:288–289).

28. Martin Heidegger, *Introduction to Metaphysics*, trans. Gregory Fried and Richard Polt (New Haven: Yale University Press, 2000), 156ff; Martin Heidegger, *Hölderlin's Hymn "The Ister,"* trans. William McNeill and Julia Davis (Bloomington: Indiana University Press, 1996), where commentary on the Ode takes up the whole of part II (51–122). Heidegger also returns very briefly to the *hupsipolis apolis* in the *Parmenides* lecture course (1942), trans. André Schuwer and Richard Rojcewicz, (Bloomington: Indiana University Press, 1992), 90. The *Introduction to Metaphysics* interpretation is the object of detailed commentary by Gregory Fried in *Heidegger's Polemos: From Being to Politics* (New Haven, CT: Yale University Press, 2000), 140–141 and 144–145, which provides the basis for Slavoj Žižek's understanding of this motif in, for example, "Why Heidegger Made the Right Step in 1933," *International Journal of Žižek Studies* 1, no. 4 (2007): 1–43. The explicit reference to Fried disappears in the reworked version of some of this material in Žižek's *Violence: Six Sideways Reflections* (London: Picador, 2008), 68–72. I take issue with Fried's and Žižek's interpretations of this moment in Heidegger in *Scatter 1* (New York: Fordham University Press, 2016). Although Fried duly also refers to the brief discussion in the *Parmenides* course, he does not analyze the much longer treatment (also from 1942) in the Hölderlin course.

Today—if one still reads such books at all—one can scarcely read a treatise or book on the Greeks without everywhere being assured that here, with the Greeks, "everything" is "politically" determined. In the majority of "research results," the Greeks appear as the pure National Socialists. This overenthusiasm on the part of academics seems not even to notice that with such "results" it does National Socialism and its historical uniqueness no service at all, not that it needs this anyhow. . . . One does no service whatsoever to our knowledge and evaluation of the historical singularity of National Socialism if one now interprets the Greek world in such a way as to say that the Greeks were already "National Socialists." (80, 86)[29]

The context of the line from Sophocles is the Choral Ode sometimes known as the "Ode to Man," in which the Chorus begins by proclaiming that man is *deinon* and even *deinotaton*, the most wonderful, the most formidable, the most terrible, the strangest or, as Heidegger prefers to translate it, the most *unheimlich*, the most uncanny. Man, the Chorus goes on, masters the natural world, sails the oceans even in the teeth of gales, tills the earth, traps or tames the beasts, has taught himself speech and thought with which to order the *polis*, has, in short, resources for and against every eventuality except death. The subtlety of these resources, these *tekhnai*, allows man to move "now to evil, now to good": and now, in Jebb's translation: "When he honors the laws of the land and the justice of the gods to which he is bound by oath, his city prospers [*hupsipolis*]; But banned from his city [*apolis*] is he who, thanks to his rashness, couples with disgrace." (The word *hupsipolis* is, I think, a *hapax legomenon*. Different dictionaries, referring it variously to the polis or to the citizen, suggest it be translated as either "high or honored in one's city" or "citizen of a proud city.") Translators and editors of Sophocles usually supply punctuation between the two words, most typically a colon or semicolon to mark a juxtaposition of two possibilities—if man obeys the laws, then *hupsipolis*; if he does not, then *apolis*. Sophocles scholars certainly recognize an extreme tension in this formulation, and the difficulty of parsing out how to attribute the two adjectives (the standard critical question is: Which, of Creon or Antigone, is to be considered *hupsipolis*, and which *apolis*?).[30] Heidegger

---

29. For a detailed discussion of the differences between the 1935 and 1942 readings, see Miguel de Beistegui, *Heidegger and the Political* (London: Routledge, 1997), 120–145.

30. George Steiner, who sees here "a gnomic concision available only to supreme poetry," also claims, without providing evidence (or indeed clarity), that

ignores any such implied punctuation and distribution and takes the two words rigorously together, more as synonyms than antonyms, and comments as follows in *Introduction to Metaphysics*:

Not all routes into the domains of beings are named, but the ground and place of human Dasein itself, the spot where all these routes cross, the *polis*. One translates *polis* as state <*Staat*> and city-state <*Stadtstaat*>; this does not capture the entire sense. Rather, *polis* is the name for the site <*Stätte*>, the Here, within which and as which Being-here [*Da*-sein] is historically. The *polis* is the site of history, the Here, *in* which, *out of* which and *for* which history happens. To this site of history belong the gods, the temples, the priests, the celebrations, the games, the poets, the thinkers, the ruler [in the singular, *der Herrscher*], the council of elders, the assembly of the people, the armed forces, and the ships. All this does not first belong to the *polis*, is not first political, because it enters into a relation with a statesman and a general and with the affairs of state. Instead, what we have named is political—that is, at the site of history—insofar as, for example, the poets are *only* poets, but then are actually poets, the thinkers are *only* thinkers, but then are actually thinkers, the priests are *only* priests, but then are actually priests, the rulers [plural this time, *die Herrscher*] are *only* rulers, but then are actually rulers. *Are*—but this says: use violence as

---

"few words outside of scripture have drawn more intense commentary or had a more diverse legacy of theoretical and existential enactment." *Antigones: The Antigone Myth in Western Literature, Art and Thought* (Oxford: Oxford University Press, 1984), 254. As a useful general corrective to Steiner's unfailingly hyperbolic and melodramatic prose, see Jonathan Strauss, *Private Lives, Public Deaths: Antigone and the Invention of Individuality* (New York: Fordham University Press, 2013). Strauss, however, does not explicitly discuss Heidegger's interpretation of the Choral Ode. For discussions of the Ode by Sophocles scholars who are sensitive to the difficulty of interpreting the *hupsipolis apolis* univocally, see Charles Segal, *Tragedy and Civilization: An Interpretation of Sophocles* (Norman: University of Oklahoma Press, 1999), esp. 167 and further references in note 49, and Margaret Rachel Kitzinger, *The Choruses of Sophokles' Antigone and Philoktetes* (Leiden: Brill, 2008), esp. 27–28, who credits Heidegger with an "interesting" discussion. (I am grateful to Louise Pratt for indicating these sources to me.) In his discussion of Antigone, Jacques Lacan mentions the *hupsipolis apolis* very briefly, but is more interested in a slightly earlier juxtaposition (*pantoporos aporos*, also commented on at some length by Heidegger). See Jacques Lacan, *Le séminaire VII: L'éthique de la psychanalyse* (Paris: Seuil, 1986), 440; trans. Dennis Porter (New York: Norton, 1992), 275.

violence-doers [*als Gewalt-tätige Gewalt brauchen*] and become those
who rise high in historical Being as creators, as doers. Rising high in
the site of history [*hupsipolis*, then], they also become *apolis*, without
city and site, lonesome, un-canny, with no way out amidst beings as a
whole, and at the same time without ordinance and limit, without
structure and fittingness <*Fug*>, because they as creators must first
ground all this in each case. (IM 162–163)[31]

It would seem that the figure of the *hupsopolis apolis*, with the associated
inaugural violence as its condition (prior to the distinction that more traditional readings of Sophocles would bring out between the law-abiding
hupsopolis and the law-breaking *apolis*), and which Heidegger wants to associate with a kind of creative risk-taking whereby man is in essence both,
and by the same token, *hupsipolis* and *apolis*, this being an essential part of
the definition of man's superlative uncanniness—it would seem that this
figure not only captures something both of the paradoxical situation of
the counter-naturally non-political man as Aristotle describes him (who is
indeed, as we saw, qualified as *apolis*), but also that of the preeminent and
intrinsically troublesome One Best Man who *in extremis* Aristotle tries to
reconnect to the *polis* of which he does not however really form a part.

It is, then, more than curious (perhaps even a little uncanny) that Derrida, who reads this very same passage from *Introduction to Metaphysics* in
both years of the *Beast and Sovereign* seminars (indeed he already touches
on it in the recently published 1964–65 seminar on Heidegger, HQE 288–
289/198), the first year concentrating on the *deinon* as uncanny (BS I,
265ff/356ff) the second at length on the *Gewalt* and the *Gewalt-tätige* (BS II,
285ff/391ff) and its apparent limit in death, which are indeed major
themes of these pages of *Introduction to Metaphysics*—and who certainly
knew the 1942 Hölderlin course, which he refers to at least in passing in as
yet unpublished seminars[32]—Derrida nowhere, to my knowledge, so much

---

31. Although not explicitly referring to this motif in Sophocles, it seems
clear that we can link Heidegger's interpretation of it to remarks in other work
from the 1930s—for example, "The Origin of the Work of Art" and the *Beiträge
zur Philosophie*, often enough linked to the motif of sacrifice. I discuss these resonances, and the sometimes evasive scholarship to which they have given rise, in
Scatter 1.

32. Derrida very occasionally mentions this course, notably in his as yet unpublished 1989–90 seminar *Manger l'autre*, but nowhere I think refers to the discussion of the *hupsipolis apolis*. See Derrida's allusion in "Reste—le maître, ou le
supplement d'infini," in *Le disciple et ses maîtres: Pour Charles Malamoud*, ed. Lyne

as mentions this striking sovereign figure of the *hupsopolis apolis* as read by Heidegger, hiding here in plain sight, this figure which seems intrinsic to the understanding both of the uncanniness of man and of the violence that uncanniness entails, this figure of the *hupsipolis apolis*, which might well be taken to describe quite precisely the uncanny convergence of sovereign as beast and beast as sovereign, the very hesitation between "the beast *and* the sovereign" and "the beast *is* the sovereign" from which he began (BS I, 18/39), the undecidable position of the *pambasileus*.

This collapse of the political in its very emergence (what Derrida is inclined in his late work to call a structure of "autoimmunity") immediately compromises the figure of the sovereign, the One as One Lord or One God. As we have begun to suspect via the excessive quality of Plato's treatment of democracy, democracy is the concept (if it is even a concept) that will increasingly bear witness to the originary failings of the sovereign, and tell us something about the originary sense of politics as such.

Bansat-Boudon and John Scheid (Paris: Seuil, 2002), 25–63, at 61n10, where his interest seems to be on the very end of the ode and the reference to the hearth. See, too, brief references in *Of Spirit*, 4, 75, 80–81 (17, 120, 127–129).

CHAPTER 7

Democracy (Arendt, Aristotle)

Against the Platonic insistence on the need for the polis to be One, Aristotle, who we have been keen here, somewhat in spite of Derrida, to separate from Plato, has a crushing commonsense argument:

> Yet it is clear that if the process of unification advances beyond a certain point, the city will not be a city at all for a state essentially consists of a multitude of persons [*plethos*], and if its unification is carried beyond a certain point, city will be reduced to family and family to individual, for we should pronounce the family to be a more complete unity than the city, and the single person than the family; so that even if any lawgiver were able to unify the state, he must not do so, for he will destroy it in the process. And not only does a city consist of a multitude of human beings [*pleionon anthropon*], it consists of human beings differing in kind. A collection of persons all alike does not constitute a state. . . . For even among the free and equal this principle must necessarily obtain, since all cannot govern at once. (1261a17–33)

In some ways, this is *the* leitmotif of Aristotle's political thinking. Note especially the motif of "too much" or "too far," which already contains the seed of the internal ruin of the teleological principle: and this point returns a little later, when Aristotle is criticizing Plato's recommendations for the community of possessions:

> The cause of Socrates' error must be deemed to be that his fundamental assumption was incorrect. It is certain that in a way both the household and the state should be a unit, but they should not be so in every way. For in one way the state as its unification proceeds will cease to be a state, and in another way, though it continues a state, yet by coming near to ceasing to be one it will be a worse state, just as if one turned a harmony into unison or a rhythm into a single foot. (1263b30–35)

A number of consequences flow from this critique, and they all relate to this irreducible element of plurality, which, we might be tempted to say, just is the specifically political feature of politics (no politics without plurality, that is, more than two—or maybe more than three, because where there's a third party there are already many third parties).[1] *Scatter* suggests that it is just this element of (dispersive and variegated) plurality that will give the concept of democracy its curious position in political thought and mean that it will concentrate all the issues with sovereignty that we have been pursuing.

It would seem that one salient reason why the drive to unity must stop "at a certain point" is the fact of sexual difference. Aristotle's famous account of man as *zoōn politikon* at the beginning of the *Politics* already in principle troubles the possibility of the analogy between State and individual that Plato uses so insistently (and that Aristotle himself also uses on occasion):[2] in Aristotle, the individual, with which the State is supposedly analogous, is already *in* a State from the start (the state precedes the individual, as is famously stated at 1253a19). Aristotle tracks the formation of the various associations [*koinonia*] that are associated together to form the polis as the unit achieving, or all but achieving,[3] autonomy (*autarkeia*): but

---

1. See Derrida's "Le mot d'accueil," in *Adieu à Emmanuel Lévinas* (Paris: Galilée, 1997), for an extended discussion of the "political" place of the third party in Lévinas.

2. For example, at 1254b1–10, 1260a4–5, 1277a5 (where the stress, however, is still on internal differentiation), 1323b30–36, and 1334a11.

3. That "all but" is important; in fact, no state can achieve complete *autarkeia*, if only because of the need to prepare itself for protection from attack from outside. See also 1275b20.

the root necessity for the formation of associations at all is the lack of autonomy of the individual, who requires, in order to avoid extinction of the species, the asymmetrical association specifically and explicitly marked by sexual difference. Subsequent associations are all associations of two or more entities of the same type (families associate with families to form "villages"; villages associate with villages to form the state); but the asymmetry of the sexual relation at the origin (usually forgotten or repressed in the tradition) returns to trouble political philosophy sooner or later—and we might even think that Aristotle's interesting conversion of what looked like a genetic account of the state into one in which the state at the end of the story is the real nature or origin is already a quite refined version of this repression. Women are traditionally thought of as belonging on the side of nature, as it were (as opposed to politics); but as politics is the always failing attempt to eliminate nature, nature's persistence as definitive of politics is also always a mark of sexual difference, as Hegel saw. In this respect, the *most* irreducibly political issue is the issue of sexual difference, and the fact that that difference is not *resolvable* (no horizon of equality, for example, can hope to do justice to sexual difference, however politically necessary such a horizon may be) makes it a reasonable figure for the perpetual *à-venir* of democracy as Derrida presents it, already questioning thereby the fraternalist conceptualization of democracy he is deconstructing in *Politiques de l'amitié*.

This location of the importance of sexual difference might look to Hannah Arendt for support, at least in a striking assertion she makes at the end of the essay slightly misleadingly entitled "Socrates":

> Philosophy, political philosophy like all its other branches, will never be able to deny its origin in *thaumadzein*, in the wonder at that which is as it is. If philosophers, despite their necessary estrangement from the everyday life of human affairs, were ever to arrive at a true political philosophy, they would have to make the plurality of man, out of which arises the whole realm of human affairs—in its grandeur and misery—the object of their *thaumadzein*. Biblically speaking, they would have to accept—as they accept in speechless wonder the miracle of the universe, of man, and of being—the miracle that God did not create Man, but "male and female created He them." They would have to accept in something more than the resignation of human weakness the fact that "it is not good for man to be alone.[4]

4. *The Promise of Politics* (New York: Schocken Books, 2005), 39. A slightly different version of the essay was published under the title "Philosophy and Politics," *Social Research* 57, no. 1 (1990). The thought is further unpacked at the end

But this claim sits a little uneasily with remarks she makes elsewhere in her unfinished attempt to answer the question, *"Was ist Politik"*? This begins with some trenchant statements that seem to me to be more Aristotelian than Arendt here (or elsewhere) would wish to acknowledge:[5]

1. Politics is based on the fact of human plurality. God created *man*, but *men* are a human, earthly product, the product of human nature. Because philosophy and theology are always concerned with *man*, because all their pronouncements would be correct if there were only one or two or only identical men, they have found no valid philosophical answer to the question: What is politics? Worse still, for all scientific thinking there is only *man*—in biology, or psychology, as in philosophy and theology, just as in zoology there is only *the* lion. Lions [in the plural, then] would be of concern only to lions [*ein Angelegenheit, die nur die Löwen etwas anginge*].[6]

But now, rather than linking this fact or *Factum* of human plurality to sexual difference, Arendt immediately, and presumably with Aristotle in mind, launches into a diatribe about the concept of the family as reducing the politics out of politics by reducing the plurality out of humanity, as follows, in a typically tortuous sequence worth quoting at length:

2. Politics deals with the coexistence and association of *different* men [here "men" is introduced by the translator: Arendt's German has simply *"der Verschiedenen,"* but she regularly uses "Menschen" in the immediate context, beginning with the next sentence]. Men organize themselves politically according to certain essential commonalities found within or abstracted from an absolute chaos of differences [*in einem absoluten Chaos oder aus einem absoluten Chaos der Differenzen*]. As long as political bodies are based on the family

---

of the essay "The Tradition of Political Thought," in *The Promise of Politics*, 61–62.

5. In the quotations that follow I have reinstated the numbering of paragraphs as it appears in the posthumously assembled German text of *Was ist Politik?*, ed. Ursula Ludz (Munich: Piper Verlag, 1993 [2007]), 9 ff.

6. Arendt adds a paragraph here that we discussed earlier: "What is remarkable among all great thinkers is the difference in rank between their political philosophies and the rest of their works—even in Plato. The politics never reaches the same depth. The lack of depth [*der fehlende Tiefsinn*] is nothing other than the lack of sense for the depths [*der fehlende Sinn für die Tiefe*] at which politics is anchored."

and conceived in the image of the family, kinship [*Verwandschaft*]
in all its degrees is credited on the one hand as being able to unite
extreme individual differences, *and*, on the other hand, as a means
by which groups resembling individuals can be isolated and
contrasted.

In this form of organization, the original differentiation is
effectively eradicated, as the essential equality of all men, insofar as
we are dealing with *man*, is destroyed. The ruin of politics on both
sides results from the development of political bodies out of the
family. Here we have a hint of what becomes symbolic in the image
of the Holy Family—that people are of the opinion that God did
not so much create man as he created the family.

3. To the extent that we regard the family as more than participation,
    that is, the active participation of a plurality, we begin to play God,
    by acting as if we could naturally escape from the principle of
    human differentiation. Instead of engendering a human being
    [*einen Menschen zu zeugen*] we try to create *man* in our own image.
    But practically-politically speaking, the family acquires its deep-
    rooted importance from the fact that the world is organized in such
    a way that there is no place in it for the individual, and that means
    for anyone who is different [*für den Einzelen, und das heißt für
    den Verschiedensten*]. Families are founded as shelters and mighty
    fortresses in an inhospitable, alien world, into which people want to
    bring kinship. This desire leads to the fundamental perversion
    [*Perversion*] of politics, because it abolishes [*aufhebt*] the fundamen-
    tal quality of plurality, or rather forfeits it by introducing the
    concept of kinship. (*Promise*, 94–95)

But in taking the family out of the political story, if only in the interests
of plurality or multiplicity, Arendt also takes out the issue of sexual difference, which Aristotle at least registers if only to repress it, and ends up
simply with "men." And Arendt's apparently anti-Aristotelian stance here
is confirmed just a little later (though somewhat occluded in the English
translation), when she suggests two good reasons philosophy has never
found so much as the place [*niemals auch nur den Ort zu finden*, not just
"never found a place"] where politics can emerge. The first of these reasons, in the original, is given in Greek (and simply omitted in the translation) as "1) zoon politikon," unpacked as "as if there were something
political *in* man that belongs to his essence." Arendt continues:

This is simply not so; *man* [der *Mensch*] is apolitical. Politics arises
between men [*in dem* Zwischen-den-*Menschen*], and so quite *outside* of

man [*also durchaus* außerhalb des *Menschen*]. There is therefore no real political substance. Politics arises in the between [*im Zwischen*] and is established as relation [*der Bezug*]. Hobbes understood this.[7]

The end of this note (after a brief diatribe against the Western tradition's attempted escape from the impossibility of politics into history, where "the multiplicity of men is melted [*zusammengeschmolzen*] into *one* human individual, which is then also called humanity [ein *Menschenindividuum . . . das man dann auch noch Menscheit nennt*]") finds Arendt at an impasse: the insistence on multiplicity as "the absolute difference [*absoluten Verschiedenheit*] of all men from one another, which is greater than the relative difference among peoples, nations, or races [*Volkern, Nationen oder Rassen*] leads to a situation where politics has precisely no role [*hat Politik gerade nichts zu schaffen*]."

This aporia, which began (for us at least) with Arendt's tantalizing references to sexual difference as a crucial element in the "absolute difference" that here seems to make politics both necessary and impossible, might yet be more negotiable on Arendt's own terms here than she herself appears to think, for what she advances as a primacy of the "between" and the "relation" seems as though it might open onto the kind of thinking we associate with the nonabsolute thinking of difference that Derrida calls *différance*. That thinking would encourage Arendt to stay with her insight about the "between" and hold onto that insight against her own manifest tendency to fall back away from it into a picture of multiplicity ("men") as supposedly contesting the One ("man") only by being a multiplicity of ones, which are then as same as they are different. I am inclined to think that the different thinking of multiplicity and singularity associated with *différance* (and more especially, here, with scatter) can help us think in and through Arendt's aporia, and that there are resources in Aristotle that can in fact help us to do just that.

In Aristotle, this principle of multiplicity that is definitive of the polis and that Aristotle persistently opposes to Plato's attempt to think the polis under the sign of the One, gives rise not only to "the" polis, but to *poleis* in the plural, and to the potentially very different organizations of

7. A symptom that Arendt is "thinking aloud" in these notebook entries is that in the second of her two good reasons, Hobbes, whose understanding of the "betweenness of politics" presumably is not easy to detach from other salient features of his philosophy, is criticized for his "war of all against all" as depending on the idea of man as created in the image of God, and therefore as essentially solitary.

those *poleis* in terms of the possible plurality of types of regime or constitution. Aristotle says straightforwardly, "The reason why there are several sorts of constitution is that every *polis* includes a plurality of elements" (1289b27). Just because of the irreducible fact of plurality (Arendt's *Tatsache*), there are different possible ways of organizing that plurality. But among the spread of possibilities this opens up, democracy has a privilege, in that in a sense it names *just this plurality itself*, in a way that other regime names do not. The conceptual privilege of the traditional concept of democracy would in this case derive from the fact that other regime names tend toward a convergent or pyramidal representation of the polis, whereas democracy is explicitly, or at least potentially, dispersive, scattering.

This principle of plurality as named by democracy, then, opens the plurality of different types of constitution. But it also immediately compromises the purity of each of these types, so that the plurality is not ever quite going to be a plurality of atomic *elements*. Not only can there be monarchy, oligarchy and democracy because of this plurality at the root of the polis, but each of these classifications is in turn affected by plurality, so that there are many forms of monarchy, many forms of oligarchy, and many forms of democracy, and indeed the "many forms" that flow directly from the originary plurality exceed the capacity of these names to name them properly at all—and, as if by chance, this excess surfaces exemplarily in Aristotle's text on the side of democracy:

> We have in this way explained why constitutions take on many forms, and why there are some apart from those which have a name (for democracy is not numerically one, and one can say as much of the other constitutions). (1297b28–31)[8]

Now, as is well known, Aristotle is not concerned to defend democracy as a form of constitution to be preferred to others (though he talks about it at great length, and it provides him with his basic definition of a citizen as one participating in public office [1275b6]), and indeed he places it among the *perversions* or *deviations* (*parekbaseis*) of the different constitutions rather than as a pure or "correct" form. But again, the logic of this perversion turns out to be complex and quite disconcerting, and especially so in the case of democracy. The discriminating factor in Aristotle for deciding whether a form is correct or deviant is that the correct forms all govern in view of the common interest, whereas the deviant forms all govern in

---

8. See also 1316b36 on the "varieties" (*diaphorai*) of power.

view of a particular interest. Royalty, aristocracy, and "constitution" (*politeia*: though this is also the generic name for any sort of constitution) are the correct forms; tyranny, oligarchy, and democracy the corresponding deviations. Again, democracy here occupies an eccentric position with respect to the others, and there seem to be two reasons for this: (1) there is no real proper name for its corresponding "correct" form (which Aristotle just calls *politeia*)[9] and (2) it is difficult in the case of democracy to understand exactly what the distinction between the common and the particular interest would be. In the two other cases, the distinction between the one (or the few) and the many automatically opens the possibility of a particular interest coming into opposition with a common interest; but in the case of democracy, where the "particular" interest defining the perversion is itself that of the mass (1279a31), the distinction between the particular and the general or the common is harder to grasp, insofar as the mass tends to become identified with the totality, and its particular interest would then be identical with the common. Just as, in Plato's description of democracy, the bazaar that democracy is includes all forms of regime including itself, so the concept of *demos* as defining the locus of power in democracy is paradoxically both inclusive and exclusive: inclusively, the *demos* names all the people; but exclusively it names the people as opposed to something else—the rich, the elite, the nobility, and so on. As will regularly be the case in the ensuing tradition, Aristotle plays on this difficulty (or is plagued by this difficulty) by associating "the many" implied in democracy with the poor, or the indigent, or the rabble.

These difficulties around democracy and its corresponding "correct" form are difficult to overcome. One of their perverse effects takes place at the level of perversion or deviation itself. There are three correct forms of

9. "But when the citizens at large administer the state for the common interest, the government is called by the generic name—a constitution. And there is a reason for this use of language. One man or a few may excel in virtue; but as the number increases it becomes more difficult for them to attain perfection in every kind of virtue, though they may in military virtue, for this is found in the masses. Hence in a constitutional government the fighting-men have the supreme power, and those who possess arms are the citizens." (1279a37–1279b4) This is an obscure passage which has exercised the commentators for centuries, and the problem is compounded by the fact that Aristotle does in fact regularly use the word "democracy" to refer to this supposedly nondeviant form, often assimilated by translators and commentators to the "republican" form. See Derrida's discussion in PA 223–224.

constitution and three deviant forms. The three correct forms have an order: royalty is, according to what Aristotle *declares*, if not, as we have seen always according to what he *describes*, the highest and "most divine" form; then aristocracy; then the unnamed or generically named "correct" form of the deviant democracy. But the deviant forms invert this order, on the vertiginous grounds that the worst perversion is the perversion of what is best,[10] so the worst form of all is tyranny, which is the deviant form of the best form of all, namely royalty. Tyranny is in a sense as far as can be from the royalty of which it is the perversion, but we must assume that in another sense it is very close to it, that royalty or monarchy always might catastrophically flip into its deviant form, "catastrophe" here trying to grasp a sense in which that deviant form is *both* as close *and* as far as can be from that of which it is the deviant form—perhaps thereby suggesting a general logic of the "deviant" or the "perverse." According to this logic, the next worst deviant form is oligarchy (corresponding to the place of aristocracy as the next best correct form), and democracy is the *least bad* deviant form, just as the nameless or generic form is the *least good* correct form. This difficult logic of proximity and distance again picks out democracy as the most indeterminate case, as becomes clear if we schematize the logic we have just been following.

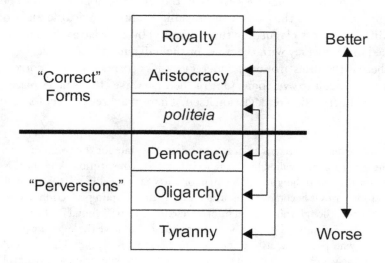

It is not difficult to imagine on the basis of this analysis that democracy, as the least bad of the deviant forms, always might be going to turn out to be the best case of all. And indeed it has been argued on philological grounds that the remarks about democracy in the *Nichomachean Ethics* really do amount to saying that it is the best form of all, and not just the least bad of the deviant forms.[11] This depends on an attempt to challenge the accepted reading of 1160b19–20: "Democracy is the least bad of the deviations; for in its case the form of constitution is but a slight deviation," where the words "of the deviations [*de mochtheron*]" are an interpolation, as is reflected, for example, in the translation by Roger Crisp, which omits these words.[12] Although it looks implausible to argue that Aristotle "really meant" that democracy is best, the drift of our argument is that, as least bad deviant form, democracy really is the best form according to a logic Aristotle does not entirely control or sign, if for example it turned out that the "correct" forms were in some sense unattainable, perhaps in the sense of being idealizations which could never be instantiated in pure form, Ideas in the Kantian sense, perhaps, or because of a general logic of deviation or perversion affecting all cases from the start (and this second case is indeed what we are suggesting, under the general heading of the politics of politics).[13] So if all regimes were *in fact* deviant with respect to the supposedly "correct" forms, democracy would turn out to be the best form *in fact*, and if all regimes were in some sense *transcendentally* deviant or perverted, and just this were the effect of the insistence of politics in philosophy, then democracy would turn out to be "transcendentally" speaking the best form. But *this* transcendental, which would have to allow for the logic of generalized deviance or perversion we are interested in, could not of course strictly be a transcendental in the traditional sense at all.

11. See Clifford A. Bates Jr., *Aristotle's "Best Regime"* (Baton Rouge: Louisiana State University Press, 2002)).

12. Aristotle, *Nichomachean Ethics*, trans. and ed. Roger Crisp (Cambridge: Cambridge University Press, 2000), 156, which reads simply, "Democracy is the least bad, because it oversteps the form of a polity only by a little." For a general argument to the effect that Aristotle really was some sort of democrat, see Malcolm Schofield, "Aristotle and the Democratization of Politics," in *Episteme, etc.: Essays in Honour of Jonathan Barnes*, ed. Ben Morrison and Katerina Ierodiakonou (Oxford: Oxford University Press, 2011), 285–301.

13. Compare Derrida's discussion of the relation of his "democracy to come" to the Kantian Idea in V 122–125/83–85. See too my discussion in *Scatter 1* (New York: Fordham University Press, 2016), 246–249.

This logic of the best as least bad, vilified by Alain Badiou,[14] is already at work in Plato. In the *Statesman*, again dividing possible constitutions into monarchy, aristocracy, and democracy and their deviations (reserving a seventh form for "the true constitution" as we saw), Plato distinguishes each of these according as they rule according to law or not; and he calls the lawless form of monarchy, tyranny; the lawless form of aristocracy, oligarchy; but the lawless form of democracy (confirming again its eccentric position) is *also* called democracy.

> STRANGER: The rule of one man, if it has been kept within the traces, so to speak, by the written rules we call laws, is the best of all six. But when it is lawless it is hard, and the most grievous to have to endure.
> YOUNG SOCRATES: So it would seem.
> STRANGER: As for the rule of a few, just as the few constitute a middle term between the one and the many, so we must regard the rule of the few as of middle potency for good or ill. The rule of the many is weakest in every way; it is not capable of any real good or of any serious evil as compared with the other two. This is because in a democracy sovereignty has been divided out in small portions among a large number of rulers. If therefore all three constitutions are law-abiding, democracy is the worst of the three, but if all three flout the laws, democracy is the best of them. *Thus if all constitutions are unprincipled the best thing to do is to live in a democracy.* (302e–303b; my emphasis)

Aristotle's explicit disagreement with this is somewhat obscure:

> A writer who preceded me has already made these distinctions, but his point of view is not the same as mine. For he lays down the principle that when all the constitutions are good (the oligarchy and the rest being virtuous), democracy is the worst, but the best when all are bad. Whereas we maintain that they are in any case defective, and that one oligarchy is not to be accounted better than another, but only less bad. (1289b5–12)

But the nuance here is probably important: what is the difference between the better and the less bad? As we are beginning to suggest, democracy might have an intrinsic link to the thought that politics is the domain of the less bad in general. Jacques Rancière has an incisive analysis of the convergence and the difference between Plato and Aristotle here, imme-

---

14. See *Abrégé de métapolitique* (Paris: Seuil, 1998), 30.

diately after his characterization of Plato's democratic man in the "post-modern" terms we saw earlier:

> This idea of the regime that each can see differently is also found in Aristotle. But Aristotle thinks this potential for multiple focus not a sign of inferiority but as a political virtue. No doubt this virtue is not, for him, the virtue of democracy. As for Plato, democracy for him is merely the least bad of the bad regimes; it is a deviant regime that must be compared with the correct regime, the *politeia* or—if you must—the republic. But, from another angle, the good regime is characterized precisely by the fact that it is always a mixture of constitutions, a bazaar of constitutions. A regime without mixture, Aristotle tells us, a regime that wants to make all its laws, all its institutions the same as its principle, is condemned to civil war and ruin, because of the very unilaterality of this principle. To approach its perfection, each regime must therefore correct itself, work on welcoming the contrary principle, make itself dissimilar from itself. There is never a good regime, only deviant regimes caught up in a perpetual labor of autocorrection, one might almost say of autodissimulation. To Plato's ridiculing of the regime-market, one might in this way oppose the text from Book IV of the *Politics* in which Aristotle explains: you have to able to see both regimes at once—democracy and oligarchy—and neither of them. The good politician is the one who simultaneously shows oligarchy to the oligarch and democracy to the democrat.[15]

Let us unpack this thought and this reference a little. Remember that the explicit ground for Aristotle's disagreement with Plato was that the defining characteristic of the polis was *autonomy* (or all but autonomy), rather than *unity*. The polis is in essence plural, and, in our reading, this means that it is from the start contaminated, like a virus, by something of the order of democracy, insofar as democracy names something of this essential plurality at the root of the political. We have also seen that this leads Aristotle to a sense, not only of a plurality of possible regimes or constitutions, but also to the thought that that plurality exceeds the available named forms, and maybe even naming itself. This principle of contamination gives rise to the thought that the polis is in principle always a *mixture* of some sort. We have already seen Plato, in *The Laws*, talking about the two strands or matrices of all constitutions, which all turn out to be woven of the warp

---

15. Jacques Rancière, *Aux bords du politique* (Paris: Gallimard, 2004), 80, my translation.

and woof of monarchy and democracy (or a principle of unification and a principle of diversification). Aristotle is scathing about this proposition: "In the *Laws* it is maintained that the best constitution is made up of democracy and tyranny, which are either not constitutions at all, or are the worst of all. But they are nearer the truth who combine many forms; for the constitution is better which is made up of more numerous elements" (1266a1–5), and tends to move further toward the thought of a scatter as the natural outcome of the original thought of plurality, and as definitive of the unnamed or only generically named "correct" form of which democracy is the deviant. For it turns out that Aristotle's unnamed or generic constitution (which, as we have seen, is called simply *politeia* in the absence of another name) is also thought of as a mix of democracy and oligarchy (that is, two deviant forms). The principles of this mix are *themselves* already plural (mixed), and this is what Rancière was pursuing:

> Next we have to consider how by the side of oligarchy and democracy the so-called polity or constitutional government springs up, and how it should be organized. The nature of it will be at once understood from a comparison of oligarchy and democracy; we must ascertain their different characteristics, and taking a portion from each, put the two together, like the parts of an indenture. Now there are three modes in which fusions of government may be affected. In the first mode we must combine the laws made by both governments, say concerning the administration of justice. In oligarchies they impose a fine on the rich if they do not serve as judges, and to the poor they give no pay; but in democracies they give pay to the poor and do not fine the rich. Now (1) the union of these two modes is a common or middle term between them, and is therefore characteristic of a constitutional government, for it is a combination of both. This is one mode of uniting the two elements. Or (2) a mean may be taken between the enactments of the two: thus democracies require no property qualification, or only a small one, from members of the assembly, oligarchies a high one; here neither of these is the common term, but a mean between them. (3) There is a third mode, in which something is borrowed from the oligarchical and something from the democratical principle. For example, the appointment of magistrates by lot is thought to be democratical, and the election of them oligarchical; democratical again when there is no property qualification, oligarchical when there is. In the aristocratical or constitutional state, one element will be taken from each—from oligarchy the principle of electing to offices, from democracy the disregard of qualification. Such are the various modes of combination.

There is a true union of oligarchy and democracy when the same state may be termed either a democracy or an oligarchy; those who use both names evidently feel that the fusion is complete. Such a fusion there is also in the mean; for both extremes appear in it. (1294a30–1294b19)

Where Plato tends to resolve the issue of plurality by the dialectical *symploke* of opposites (creating, or so we imagine, a cloth that would have to be more sober in its design than the shimmering *poikilon* fabric of democracy), Aristotle, who appears to go much farther toward a thought of multiplicity as definitive of the *polis*, resolves that multiplicity by appealing to the familiar operator of the mean or medium (*meson*), famously the fundamental operator of the *Nichomachean Ethics*.

But this thought of the medium or the mean is itself intrinsically unstable, and cannot be taken to master or dominate the basic thought of plurality or scatter that we have seen to have at the very least an affinity with the concept of democracy. The reason for this is, perversely enough, logical: Aristotle's central ethical principle prescribes the avoidance of excess in the name of the mean. It follows quite naturally that the pursuit of the mean should *itself* not fall into excess (so that there should not be an excessive avoidance of excess)—but this measured (nonexcessive) pursuit of the mean will, just because of its measured nature, never quite reach the mean or median point at which scatter could be said to be mastered.

This is a quite complex point. In the *Nichomachean Ethics* (2.6), Aristotle, having defined virtue in terms of the mean, points out that not all actions admit of a virtuous mean at all. For example, adultery, theft and homicide "directly imply evil" and not just in their moments of excess and default. This is because such actions are *already* in the domain of excess or default, and there can be no mean, excess or default *of* excess itself. And, by a difficult extension of this argument, there can be no reapplication of the logic of the mean to the mean itself:

> Not every action or emotion however admits of the observance of a
> due mean. Indeed the very names of some directly imply evil, for
> instance malice, shamelessness, envy, and, of actions, adultery, theft,
> murder. All these and similar actions and feelings are blamed as being
> bad in themselves; it is not the excess or deficiency of them that we
> blame. It is impossible therefore ever to go right in regard to them—
> one must always be wrong; nor does right or wrong in their case
> depend on the circumstances, for instance, whether one commits
> adultery with the right woman, at the right time, and in the right
> manner; the mere commission of any of them is wrong. One might as

well suppose there could be a due mean and excess and deficiency in acts of injustice or cowardice or profligacy, which would imply that one could have a medium amount of excess and of deficiency, an excessive amount of excess and a deficient amount of deficiency. But just as there can be no excess or deficiency in temperance and courage,[16] *because the mean is in a sense an extreme* [my emphasis], so there can be no observance of the mean nor excess nor deficiency in the corresponding vicious acts mentioned above, but however they are committed, they are wrong; since, to put it in general terms, there is no such thing as observing a mean in excess or deficiency, nor as exceeding or falling short in the observance of a mean.

This is taken to disallow the type of second-level argument I have just proposed: Aristotle is essentially saying that default, mean, and excess cannot be reapplied to themselves—so just as we cannot rehabilitate murder or adultery as virtues by applying the mean to them, we cannot reapply default or excess (nor therefore the mean) to the mean itself. Virtue may be defined in terms of a mean used to measure actions, but is not *itself* to be measured in terms of the mean.[17] This is why in this paragraph Aristotle says, in a more than curious parallel with the straightforwardly bad or evil cases he starts out from, that "there can be no excess or deficiency in temperance and courage, because the mean is in a sense an extreme." But he goes on immediately, with reference to a chart not actually included in *The Nichomachean Ethics* but assumed by most editors to be at least similar to one provided in the *Eudemian Ethics* (1120b38), to show that indeed there *are* excesses and deficiencies in temperance and courage, which indeed are the first two cases considered: "In fear and confidence, courage [*andreia*] is the mean . . . with respect to pleasures and pains . . . the mean is temperance, the excess intemperance." So it is difficult to see why "moderation" or "temperance" can be lost in default or excess, but not virtue itself, especially as what is translated here as moderation or temperance is *sophrosyne*, and just that quality is an essential component of moral virtue in general as Aristotle defines it.[18] But if we *do* allow the reapplication of the logic of

16. In the Loeb edition, Rackham has "justice," but the Greek is *andreias*, manliness.

17. See for example, J. O. Urmson, *Aristotle's Ethics* (Oxford: Blackwell, 1988). A useful summary of the difficulties encountered by the doctrine of the mean is provided by C. C. W. Taylor in *Aristotle: Nicomachean Ethics Books II–IV* (Oxford: Clarendon Press, 2006), notes to 1107a110–113.

18. "Actions, then, are called just and temperate [*sophrona*] when they are such as the just or the temperate [*sophron*] man would do; but it is not the man who

the mean to the thought of the mean, so that virtue would consist in a sort of moderate moderation, then the paradoxes we are looking at cannot be repressed: a virtue of *moderate* moderation or a mean, middling, application of the mean always might, on occasion, need to act excessively or immoderately.

Heidegger suggests something of this complication in his commentary on these passages in his 1924 lecture course *Basic Concepts of Aristotelian Philosophy*:

> There is no *meson* for the being of human beings because everything human is *meson pros hemas. For our being, characterized by particularity, no unique and absolute norm can be given.* It depends on cultivating the being of human beings, so that it is transposed into the *aptitude for maintaining the mean.* But that means nothing other than *seizing the moment.* . . . Aristotle emphasizes, again and again, that the *meson* is hard to find and easy to miss. To fly off the handle is easy, but to be angry at the right moment is difficult. This requires the possibility of being able to seize the moment as a whole. Therefore, acting seldom occurs on the basis of the *mesotes* and in the *mesotes.*[19]

This paradoxical logic of the mean entails that we stop short of the universal application of the mean (which thereby *itself* becomes excessive "because the mean is in a sense an extreme," as we just saw), and therefore always remains (in fact, but transcendentally in fact, if I can put it that way) in plurality or scatter, in which the singularity of the case and the concern for the moment, the *kairos*, interrupts our otherwise potentially excessive pursuit of the mean at all costs.

Indeed, this logic can help us make sense of what happens in Aristotle when the tagline from Homer, that Derrida used as a transition to the *Politics* from the *Metaphysics*, partially returns in the *Politics* itself (apparently unnoticed by Derrida), in a section a little further on than the "god among men" remark that allowed Derrida, as we saw, to assimilate Aristotle and Plato under the sign of a "salut politique au Dieu Un." Here Aristotle is talking about the different kinds of democracy (in this section at least he

---

does these that is just and temperate, but the man who also does them as just and temperate men do them. It is well said, then, that it is by doing just acts that the just man is produced, and by doing temperate acts the temperate man; without doing these no one would have even a prospect of becoming good" (1105b1–12).

19. Martin Heidegger, *Basic Concepts of Aristotelian Philosophy* [GA 18], trans. Robert D. Metcalf and Mark B. Tanzer (Bloomington: Indiana University Press, 2009), 126 and 128.

seems to think that there are five), and is led to something that looks as if precisely the tendency to the One, far from being the *antidote* to democracy and its dispersions, is in fact the internal ruin of the (always relatively gathered) dispersion that democracy more "properly" would "be" (but democracy cannot really ever be quite proper in the light of all we have seen about deviancy). The fifth type of democracy, which leads Aristotle again to quote in part the line from Homer, is described as follows:

> Another kind of democracy is where all the other regulations are the same, but the multitude is sovereign and not the law; and this comes about when the decrees of the assembly over-ride the law. This state of things is brought about by the demagogues; for in the states under democratic government guided by law a demagogue does not arise, but the best classes of citizens are in the most prominent position; but where the laws are not sovereign, then demagogues arise; for *the common people become a single composite monarch, since the many are sovereign not as individuals but collectively.* Yet what kind of democracy Homer means by the words "no blessing is the lordship of the many"—whether he means this kind or when those who rule as individuals are more numerous, is not clear. However, *a people of this sort, as being monarch, seeks to exercise monarchic rule* through not being ruled by the law, and becomes despotic, so that flatterers are held in honor. And a democracy of this nature is comparable to the tyrannical form of monarchy, because their spirit is the same, and both exercise despotic control over the better classes, and the decrees voted by the assembly are like the commands issued in a tyranny, and the demagogues and the flatterers are the same people or a corresponding class, and either set has the very strongest influence with the respective ruling power, the flatterers with the tyrants and the demagogues with democracies of this kind. And these men cause the resolutions of the assembly to be supreme and not the laws, by referring all things to the people; for they owe their rise to greatness to the fact that the people is sovereign over all things while they are sovereign over the opinion of the people, for the multitude believes them. Moreover, those who bring charges against the magistrates say that the people ought to judge the suits, and the people receive the invitation gladly, so that all the magistracies are put down. And *it would seem to be a reasonable criticism to say that such a democracy is not a constitution at all*; for where the laws do not govern there is no constitution, as the law ought to govern all things while the magistrates control particulars, and we ought to judge this to be constitutional government; if then democracy really is one of the forms of constitution, it is manifest that an organization of this kind, in which all things are administered by

resolutions of the assembly, is *not even a democracy in the proper sense*,
for it is impossible for a voted resolution to be a universal rule.
(1292a3–37; my emphasis)

In the now undecidable "deviancy" or "perversion" that democracy is, what
is really being criticized is a movement (that is of course part of democracy, part of its intrinsically deviant or perverse character, for better *and*
for worse) whereby democracy pushed to a certain limit, to the point at
which one might, in a teleological spirit, precisely, be inclined to think it
would become most *itself*, *most* democratic, closest to conformity with its
Idea, in fact flips catastrophically into monarchical and thereby tyrannical form; a kind of sovereignty that, far from being a salvation of the
multiple in and by the One, is precisely the end and ruin of democracy
itself, and indeed thereby of politics *as such*.[20]

The logic of Aristotle's discussion here is a little vertiginous. Everything
looks as though in describing these forms he is moving in a more and more
democratic direction: each form is more democratic than the previous one,
but then suddenly the last form is not only not more democratic than the
previous one, but quite the opposite of democratic: monarchical, tyrannical, perhaps not even political any more, but the dissolution of the *polis* as
such. Any apparent teleology in the progress toward "more democracy,"
with its implied *telos* of some finally achieved "true" or "real" democracy,
seems compromised by this catastrophic reversal. The implication is that
in order to be democratic, we have to be less than absolutely democratic,
that democracy involves a kind of holding back or reserve, a preservation of
itself by not attempting to realize itself absolutely—*mutatis mutandis* we
might look to Derrida's reading of Freud and the conception of "life as an
economy of death" or "life death" for the formal schema by which we might
try to think of this situation. It appears that this logic, of a kind of self-
restraining or self-interrupting teleology, is specific to democracy among
political concepts, and perhaps explains the eccentric position of that concept as always more and other than the name of a regime. Democracy is

20. See Derrida's comment in *Rogues*, "there is no absolute paradigm,
whether constitutive or constitutional, no absolutely intelligible idea, no *eidos*, no
idea of democracy. And so, in the final analysis, no democratic ideal" (V 62/37);
see V 60/35–36 on the impossibility of proving that one electoral law is "more
democratic than another," and V 58/34: "Who, then, can take it upon him- or
herself, and with what means, to speak . . . of this front, of democracy itself, of
authentic democracy properly speaking, when it is precisely the concept of democracy itself, in its univocal and proper meaning, that is presently and forever
lacking?"

internally deviant, we might say, always already deviating from any linear or circular path, and, as we will confirm in Hobbes, Spinoza, and Rousseau, it does so from the very origin, and even before the origin, of politics.

Just this paradoxical tendency of democracy to collapse away from itself as it gets closer to itself means, to use a formula I have often used in the context of the deconstruction of the Kantian Idea, that the end of democracy is the end of democracy, and perhaps explains some of the suspicions with which it has traditionally been viewed. Kant, for example, famously says that democracy is always despotic because it fails to respect the separation between sovereign and executive, which is pretty much Aristotle's point in his description of the fifth type,[21] and the phobic object called "the mass" or "the rabble" of course surfaces in Hegel and Marx and far beyond.[22] Democracy as always tending to become demagogy and thereby the opposite of itself just is what democracy "is."

Democracy can therefore only be "itself" by holding itself short of its apparent *telos*, can only *succeed by failing*. "Representative democracy" is the most familiar way of attempting this, inserting relays (or delays) into the system: democracy would then be "truly" (?) democratic (as opposed to tendentially demagogic and thereby tyrannical) only by holding up or holding back its apparent drive toward absolute, immediate, or "direct" democracy, the kind of collective acclamation that Schmitt suggests that democracy would need to be if it were to be in fact truly democratic.[23] All of which might, perversely enough, seem to bring us close to a famous quip

21. See Kant, *Political Writings*, ed. Hans Reiss, 2nd ed. (Cambridge: Cambridge University Press, 1991), 101.

22. See Marx's famous, almost Flaubertian, list characterizing the *Lumpenproletariat:* "Alongside decayed *roués* with dubious means of subsistence and of dubious origin, alongside ruined and adventurous offshoots of the bourgeoisie, were vagabonds, discharged soldiers, discharged jailbirds, escaped galley slaves, swindlers, mountebanks, *lazzaroni*, pickpockets, tricksters, gamblers, *maquereaus* [*sic*], brothel keepers, porters, *literati*, organ-grinders, ragpickers, knife grinders, tinkers, beggars—in short, the whole indefinite, disintegrated mass, thrown hither and thither [*die ganze unbestimmte, aufgelöste, hin-und hergeworfene Masse*], which the French term *la bohème* [embraces]." Karl Marx, *The Eighteenth Brumaire of Louis Bonaparte* (New York: International Publishers, 2017), 75. Hegel also mentions the *lazzaroni* in a remark to §244 of the *Philosophy of Right* in which the rabble (*Pöbel*) is defined.

23. Carl Schmitt, *Constitutional Theory*, trans. Jeffrey Seitzer (Durham, NC: Duke University Press), 302–306.

of Churchill's from 1947, after he had "won the war" and promptly been voted out of power: "Democracy is the worst form of government, except all those other forms that have been tried from time to time."[24]

This Aristotelian logic should help us to think about democracy in a number of ways. For example, it ought to make us wary of the language of "falling short" of some ideal in the (of course necessary!) criticism of actual "democratic" institutions, so that Robert Dahl, for example, can open his book *Democracy and its Critics* with the remark, "At the outset we confront the fact that in both ordinary and philosophical language democracy may properly be used to refer both to an ideal and to actual regimes that *fall considerably short* of that ideal."[25] And related to this type of criticism is one (sometimes associated with the French-language concept of *démocrature*)[26]

---

24. From a House of Commons speech on November 11, 1947. With more context: "We accept in the fullest sense of the word the settled and persistent will of the people. All this idea of a group of supermen and super-planners, such as we see before us, 'playing the angel,' as the French call it, and making the masses of the people do what they think is good for them, without any check or correction, is a violation of democracy. Many forms of Government have been tried, and will be tried in this world of sin and woe. No one pretends that democracy is perfect or all-wise. Indeed, it has been said that democracy is the worst form of Government except all those other forms that have been tried from time to time; but there is the broad feeling in our country that the people should rule, continuously rule, and that public opinion, expressed by all constitutional means, should shape, guide, and control the actions of Ministers who are their servants and not their masters." For a historical survey of Churchill's changing opinions about democracy, see Roland Quinault, "Churchill and Democracy," *Transactions of the Royal Historical Society* 11 (2002): 201–220.

25. Robert Dahl, *Democracy and Its Critics* (New Haven: Yale University Press, 1989), 6, my emphasis. The "falling short" idiom recurs throughout: see 90, 117, 131, 149, 174, 177, 223, and 271.

26. The term was coined in 1987 by the French sociologist Gérard Mermet in his book *Démocrature: Comment les médias transforment la démocratie* (Paris: Aubier, 1987), and subsequently developed especially in discussions of African politics. Some sample usages: "Les régimes dits démocratiques n'ont de démocratique que le nom et certaines formes de surface. C'est pourquoi nous préférons employer le mot démocrature (mixage de démocratie et dictature), quoiqu'il faudrait plutôt parler de démocratie totalitaire, ou de totalitarisme à visage démocratique. N'en déplaise aux prétendus humanistes, les prétendues démocraties actuelles ne sont pas les meilleurs régimes existants, on pourrait même dire que ce sont les pires." https://bit.ly/39FBGvA (last accessed April 11, 2019). Or, from a "religious communism" organization called "Mutations radicales," the following definition:

that finds that so-called democracies are in fact fake or sham, merely apparent, mere *representations* of what a true democracy would be. However important and justified critiques of apparent democracy may often be within the terms in which they are put, they all remain within the teleologics that we are trying to delimit or deconstruct here, and have no conceptual mechanism for understanding the irreducible internal "crisis" of sovereignty that we are trying to bring out (including the crisis of democratic sovereignty), and that "the politics of politics" tries to allow for.

"La démocrature est un régime qui n'est ni une démocratie ni une franche dictature. Démocrature peut désigner toutes les pseudo-démocraties qui veulent se faire passer pour des démocraties réelles (comme la France, les USA . . .). La critique des démocratures débouche sur l'abstention et la définition d'une utopie révolutionnaire." But the term can also be taken up by a discourse from what is traditionally perceived as the other end of the political spectrum: see for example, still from Belgium, from the Front Nouveau Belge, the remarks under the title "Démocrature" at https://bit.ly/2SAM6XF (last accessed April 14, 2019). More recently it has been used in discussions of French domestic politics, including the "yellow vest" protests of 2019.

CHAPTER 8

Protodemocracy and the Fall of Sovereignty (Hobbes, Aristotle)

Democracy is—sovereignty failing. Whether tendentially beast or god or criminal, the sovereign One is, as it were, always already overrun by multiplicity, diversity, *to poikilon*, democracy, the politics of politics.

We might try to grasp how this is possible by appealing to an "earlier" structure that must affect ipseity as such. It is tempting to see in this one of Derrida's most telling insights, which in his late work is often couched in the language of "autoimmunity." But the insight is already part of his earlier thinking.[1] That this is directly germane to our earlier discussion of the One can be judged from some remarkable and untranslatably gnomic formulas that Derrida comes up with to capture the issue here: "L'Un se garde de l'autre" (with the—at least—double valence "The One guards itself against the other," and "The One keeps some(thing of the) other in (or for) itself"), and "L'Un se fait violence" ("The One turns itself into

---

1. See my short essay "Auto-," in *Not Half No End: Not Half No End: Militantly Melancholic Essays in Memory of Jacques Derrida* (Edinburgh: Edinburgh University Press, 2010).

violence" (or perhaps just: "turns violent") and "The One does violence to itself").[2]

The thought here is perhaps most easily grasped in terms of what Derrida in his earlier work had called "supplementarity," and more especially the thought of a "supplement at the origin."[3] It is not a difficult task to get from origin, *archē*, to *archon* as sovereign, and indeed Derrida often stresses the relation between the two, sometimes formulated as the relation between commencement and commandment.[4] His thought is trying to grasp an extremely general structure; in one of his earliest uses of the notion of autoimmunity, Derrida indeed refers rather breezily in passing to "a sort of auto-immunity from which no region of being, *physis* or history would be exempt" (PA 94/76). At the very least, this structure would imply that no One could ever simply be itself, (at) one with itself, prior to some potentially corrosive relation to some other in general. As this other in general cannot be thought to have been *produced* by the One itself—as if it were it would not be other—it must on Derrida's view be co-originary, and the Plotinian-Dionysian "solution" of an overflowing of the One into the many (the others) is not available, and indeed is in principle refuted. Although Derrida does not work this out in close reference to political thought as such, I believe it is eminently applicable to the issue of sovereignty in general. This is not surprising given Derrida's gesture, in *Rogues*, of defining sovereignty in terms of a more general notion of ipseity. My (I think entirely Derridean) hypothesis is that the essentially failing structure of sovereignty goes along, in the political sphere, with a disavowed primacy (in a sense to be determined) of democracy, or perhaps of something we might call "protodemocracy." Whence the fact, often noted by Derrida among others, that the inherited concept of "democracy" was never simply a regime name among other regime names. This is in part because a protodemocratic dispersion, a scatter, is at the origin of politics as such: all the classical doctrines of sovereignty (even of the so-called sovereignty of the people) are erected against the real or imagined dangers of this primary dispersion and its possible return. This implies that political phi-

2. These two formulas appear together in MA 124–125/78–79.

3. G 379–445.

4. For example, MA 11; DP II, 159, 162/114, 117; the interview with Eva Meyer, "Labyrinthe et archi/texture," in Ginette Michaud and Joana Masó, *Jacques Derrida, Les arts de l'espace: Écrits et interventions sur l'architecture* (Paris: Editions de la Différence, 2015), 25–46.

losophy has always dreamed of putting an end to politics, insofar as it has dreamed of the possibility of One sovereign, or the sovereign as One.

It is not always the democrats who perceive this situation most clearly or draw its consequences as far as they can be drawn. Let's take a look at Hobbes in this regard—Hobbes widely perceived to be, with Bodin, at the origin of the "modern" conception of sovereignty, and whose texts, especially of course *Leviathan*, are certainly robust enough to invite stringent deconstructive reading, not only in their strictly political doctrine, but also in their reflections on language and reading, not to mention the density and quality of Hobbes's own rather fine prose.

In his earlier work *The Elements of Law* (1640), and indeed also in the Latin treatise *De Cive* (1642), Hobbes recognizes much more clearly than in *Leviathan* itself (1651) a certain irreducible (if ephemeral) primacy of democracy. Here is the *Elements of Law* version:

> Having spoken in general concerning instituted policy in the former chapter, I come in this, to speak of the sorts thereof in special, how every of them is instituted. The first in order of time of these three sorts, is democracy; and it must be so of necessity, because an aristocracy and a monarchy, require nomination of persons agreed upon, which agreement in a great multitude of men must consist in the consent of the major part; and where the votes of the major part involve the votes of the rest, there is actually a democracy.[5]

And in *De Cive*, chapter 7: "When men have met to erect a commonwealth, they are, almost by the very fact that they have met, a *Democracy* [*Qui coïerunt ad ciuitatem erigendam, pene eo ipso quo coïerunt*, Democratia *sunt*]."[6] As with all "social contract" theories of politics (from Hobbes at least up to Kant), it is extremely unclear how to construe this moment of passing from nature to politics: people scattered in the state of nature are brought together by the intolerable (or perhaps, as in Rousseau, merely unsustainable) nature of that state: this coming together is not yet a political union,

---

5. Thomas Hobbes, *The Elements of Law*, ed. J. C. A. Gaskin (Oxford: Oxford University Press, 1994), 118–119. On the degree of difference with the *Leviathan* on this point, see the editor's introduction to Thomas Hobbes, *Leviathan*, ed. Richard Tuck (Cambridge: Cambridge University Press, 1991), xxxv–xxxvi.

6. Thomas Hobbes, *On the Citizen*, ed. and trans. Richard Tuck and Michael Silverthorne (Cambridge: Cambridge University Press, 1998), 94; Latin text from *De Cive: The Latin Version*, ed. Howard Wallender (Oxford: Clarendon Press, 1983), 152.

and to that extent it is still a manifestation of the state of nature, but, apparently (and perhaps inexplicably) some prepolitical discussion or negotiation has to be presumed to take place that will give rise to the pact, or contract, or covenant itself. "Democracy" has the important function of naming this state between nature and convention, on the (still natural) threshold of the (in contract theory only ever conventional) space of politics. This apparent connivance of nature and (proto)democracy allows us to step over the boundary from nature into politics, which otherwise might seem an impossible crossing to make, or one that has to be presumed to have happened by some kind of magic, as we shall see in Rousseau. The difficulty is very clear in *De Cive*, where Hobbes has a lot of trouble keeping this democratic moment from collapsing back into anarchy, that is, the state of nature, and where the precarious nature of the transition is, perhaps, signaled by an "almost" (*pene*):

> . . . almost by the very fact that they have met, a *Democracy*. From the fact that they have gathered voluntarily, they are understood to be bound by the decisions made by agreement of the majority. And that is a *Democracy*, as long as the convention lasts, or is set to reconvene at certain times and places. For a convention whose will is the will of all the citizens has *sovereign power*. And because it is assumed that each man in this convention has the right to vote, it follows that it is a *Democracy*. . . . But if they split up [*si discedant*], and the convention is dissolved [*soluaturque conuentus*] without deciding on a time and place for meeting again, the situation returns to *Anarchy* and to the condition in which they were before they convened, i.e., to the condition of the war of all against all. (*On the Citizen*, 94/152)

But this primacy of democracy is vanishingly short-lived, as though the very multiplicity that marks politics as originally democratic must fatally lead to its self-destruction, or at least its immediate transition into something other than itself, namely aristocracy or monarchy. This fatal transition depends on the fact that politics entails discourse, a certain use of discourse: this relation between politics and language (and thereby politics and rhetoric) is something of which Hobbes has an acute and uncomfortable awareness, which will pursue him to the edification and ruin of the Leviathan itself.[7] This language issue will also open onto what will

---

7. For an account of Hobbes that makes his account of language central to his thought (without, in my view, fully registering the ruinous effects of that account), see Philip Pettit, *Made With Words: Hobbes on Language, Mind, and Politics* (Princeton, NJ: Princeton University Press, 2008).

become later a distinction that haunts and troubles all classical notions of sovereignty, namely the distinction between the sovereign and the executive. Here is Hobbes's memorable description (reminiscent, as so often, of the Aristotle he cannot in general criticize harshly enough) of the almost immediate self-destruction of democracy through language. This is presented most explicitly in the *Elements of Law*:

> In all democracies, though the right of sovereignty be in the assembly, which is virtually the whole Body, yet the use thereof is always in one, or a few particular men. For in such great assemblies, as those must be, whereinto every man may enter at his pleasure, there is no means any ways to deliberate and give counsel what to do, but by long and set orations; whereby to every man there is more or less hope given to incline and sway the Assembly to their own ends. In a multitude of speakers therefore, where always, either one is eminent alone, or a few being equal amongst themselves, are eminent above the rest, that one or few must of necessity sway the whole; insomuch, that a Democracy, in effect, is no more than an aristocracy of orators, interrupted sometimes with the temporary monarchy of one orator. (74–75)

Originary protodemocracy, then, by virtue of the *zōon politikon*'s being a *zōon logon echon* and to that extent able, as Aristotle has it at the opening of the *Politics*, to deliberate about the expedient and the inexpedient and thereby the just and the unjust—that deliberation just being the essential component the "good life" that is the *telos* of the *polis*—originary protodemocracy turns immediately into something else, aristocracy or monarchy. Which will motivate in Hobbes—a little paradoxically, in fact, given his preference (because of the indivisibility of sovereignty) for monarchy, which here emerges from mere rhetorical prowess (of which Hobbes will always be more than wary)—a constant suspicion of the rhetorical possibilities of language.

That suspicion is at the very basis of Hobbes's theory of language, as it is presented most notably in chapter 4 of *Leviathan*, "Of Speech." There are in fact signs of what to expect here already in the immediately preceding chapter, which deals with what Hobbes calls our "trayne of thoughts." Language already appears here as a complicating factor in that (as we shall have occasion to see more than once in Hobbes's thinking) it has what we might call a feedback effect on that train of thoughts, and in so doing both elevates man above the other animals and *by the same token* opens onto terrible possibilities of error and deception:

> There is no other act of mans mind, that I can remember, naturally planted in him, so, as to need no other thing, to the exercise of it, but

to be born a man, and live with the use of his five Senses. Those other
Faculties, of which I shall speak by and by, and which seem proper to
man onely, are acquired, and increased by study and industry; and of
most men learned by instruction, and discipline; and proceed all from
the invention of Words, and Speech. For besides Sense, and Thoughts,
and the Trayne of thoughts, the mind of man has no other motion;
though by the help of Speech, and Method, the same Facultyes may be
improved to such a height, as to distinguish men from all other living
Creatures. (23)

And already presaging trouble to come, Hobbes ends the chapter with the
claim that there can be no idea of the in-finite (all the word signifies is
that we cannot conceive of the bounds of the thing so described): so the
name "God," for example, is not a means to *conceive* of God ("for he is *Incomprehensible*; and his greatnesse, and power are unconceivable"), so any
other talk of the infinite "are absurd speeches, taken upon credit (without
any signification at all,) from deceived Philosophers, and deceived, or de-
ceiving Schoolemen" (24).

In the following chapter, Hobbes's argument, which is as usual both
rigorous and tortuous, begins with a kind of technological regression:
the invention of printing is important, certainly, but less important than the
invention of writing. But the invention of writing is itself much less important than the invention of speech:

> But the most noble and profitable invention of all other, was that of
> SPEECH, consisting of *Names* or *Appellations*, and their Connexion;
> whereby men register their Thoughts; recall them when they are past;
> and also declare them one to another for mutuall utility and conversa-
> tion; without which, there had been amongst men, neither Common-
> wealth, nor Society, nor Contract, nor Peace, no more than amongst
> Lyons, Bears, and Wolves. (24)

This speech, authored by God, gave Adam a start with language, but perhaps no more than a start, no more, at any rate, than he needed, and certainly not what for Hobbes will always be the excessive *copia* of the language
of philosophy or oratory:

> The first author of Speech was *God* himself, that instructed *Adam* how
> to name such creatures as he presented to this sight; for the Scripture
> goeth no further in this matter. But this was sufficient to direct him to
> adde more names, as the experience and use of the creatures should
> give him occasion; and to joyn them in such manner as by degrees, as
> to make himself understood; and so by succession of time, so much

language night be gotten, as he had found use for; though not so
copious, as an Orator or Philosopher has need of. For I do not find any
thing in the Scripture, out of which, directly or by consequence can
be gathered, that *Adam* was taught the names of all Figures, Numbers,
Measures, Colours, Sounds, Fancies, Relations; much less the names
of Words and Speech, as *Generall*, *Speciall*, *Affirmative*, *Negative*,
Interrogative, *Optative*, *Infinitive*, all which are usefull; and least of all,
of *Entity*, *Intentionality*, *Quiddity*, and other insignificant words of the
School. (24–25)

This relatively happy situation of man with respect to language is interrupted by the scattering event of Babel, which at the very least introduces
a nonlinear complication into the account of language based on need:

> But all this language gotten, and augmented by *Adam* and his poster-
> ity, was again lost at the tower of *Babel*, when by the hand of God,
> every man was stricken for his rebellion, with an oblivion of his
> former language. And being hereby forced to disperse themselves
> into several parts of the world, it must needs be, that the diversity
> of Tongues that now is, proceeded by degrees from them, in such
> manner, as need (the mother of all inventions) taught them; and in
> tract of time grew every where more copious. (25)

In this post-Babelian state, language has one *general* use, namely "to transferre our Mentall Discourse, into Verbal; or the Trayne of our Thoughts,
into a Trayne of Words." This general use has two sides to it, two "commodities." Names (Hobbes assumes that names are the building-blocks of
language, perhaps on the basis of the originary and happy moment of language being Adam's naming of the animals) can serve either as *marks* or as
signs. As *marks* (their "first use"[8]) they function essentially as *aide-mémoires*,

---

8. In the *Elements of Law* version, this is already supposed to separate humans
from other animals: the succession of "conceptions" in our mind is random and
depends on sense-impressions, and so "the experience we have hereof, is in such
brute beasts, which, having the providence to hide the remains and superfluity of
their meat [Hobbes does not explain this supposed 'providence'], do nevertheless
want the remembrance of the place where they hid it, and thereby make no benefit thereof in their hunger. But man, who in this point beginneth to advance
himself above the nature of beasts, hath observed and remembered the cause of
this defect [Hobbes does not say how this is possible], and to amend the same,
hath imagined and devised to set up a visible or other sensible mark, the which
when he seeth again, may bring to his mind the thought he had when he set it up"

in "the Registring of the Consequences of our Thoughts, which being apt to slip out of our memory, and put us to a new labour, may again be recalled, by such words as they were marked by." As *signs*, language (still essentially in the form of names) serves in our dealings with others, "when many use the same words, to signifie (by their connexion and order,) one to another, what they conceive, or think of each matter; and also what they desire, feare, or have any other passion for."

After this one general use with its two sides or aspects (marks and signs), Hobbes lists four "Speciall" uses of speech, which will be immediately followed by four corresponding abuses. The first special use appears to specify the general use of marks ("First, to Register, what by cogitation, wee find to be the cause of any thing, present or past; and what we find things present or past may produce, or effect: which in summe, is acquiring of Arts"); and the remaining three special uses seem to specify the general use of signs:

> Secondly, to shew to others that knowledge which we have attained; which is, to Counsell, and teach one another. Thirdly, to make known to others our wills, and purposes, that we may have the mutuall help of one another. Fourthly, to please and delight ourselves, and others, by playing with our words, for pleasure or ornament, innocently.

As soon as these uses have been thus specified, the corresponding abuses immediately follow, and they bring a lot of trouble right away:

> To these Uses, there are also foure correspondent Abuses. First, when men register their thoughts wrong, by the inconstancy of the signification of their words; by which they register for their conceptions, that which they never conceived; and so deceive themselves. Secondly, when they use words metaphorically; that is, in other sense than that they are ordained for; and thereby deceive others. Thirdly, when by words they declare that to be their will, which is not. Fourthly, when they use them to grieve one another: for seeing nature hath armed living creatures, some with teeth, some with horns, and some with

---

(34–35). See too a little later: "By the advantage of names it is that we are capable of science, which beasts, for want of them, are not; nor man, without the use of them: for as a beast misseth not one or two of her many young ones, for want of those names of order, one, two, three, &c., which we call numbers, so neither would a man, without repeating orally, or mentally, the words of number, know how many pieces of money or other things lie before him" (35–36).

hands, to grieve an enemy, it is but an abuse of Speech, to grieve him with the tongue, unless it be one whom wee are obliged to govern; and then it is not to grieve, but to correct and amend. (25–26; for a parallel passage in Aquinas, see also Chapter 4)

Of these uses and abuses, let us note first the second and the fourth: the second use, that of teaching and counsel, is especially threatened by the abuse of metaphor, and as we shall see, this will correspond in the political domain to the usurpation of true counsel by orators and their rhetoric. The fourth abuse, corresponding to an innocent and playful use of language (but, apparently, not including the use of metaphor), is more surprising: perhaps following the thought that "grieving" someone with the tongue is the opposite of "delighting" them with it—it's difficult to ignore some erotic connotations here—Hobbes gets into quite murky territory: is his point that humans are armed with some other specific organ for "grieving" (presumably hands, in the list Hobbes gives, though it is unclear why we would exclude teeth, rather close to the tongue), and that the tongue (in the sense of language) should not therefore be used for that purpose, or is he rather claiming, according to a venerable tradition, that precisely because nature did *not* provide humans, unlike the other animals, with specific means of attack and defense, that tongue (as a kind of technological prosthesis, in which case the analogy is Promethean) is supposed to stand in for that lack as an organ of debate and deliberation, but not in so direct a way that it is *itself* used as a weapon? In any case, the patently metaphorical use of "grieving" here (verbal grieving with the tongue a metaphor of physical grieving with horns, teeth, and hands) seems perilously close to being an example of the second abuse, in which case the expression "grieving with the tongue" in a sense *itself grieves the tongue*, that is, the appropriate use of language, by using a metaphor and therefore potentially misleading the reader. Unless of course "grieving with the tongue" be taken to be an instance of the fourth *use* of speech, an innocent play that might induce delight—but then Hobbes's explicit point would seem to be short-circuited: unless this simply illustrates the extreme difficulty that Hobbes will subsequently have, in both his doctrine and his own linguistic practice, of keeping use and abuse separate from each other.

We are still at the level of language conceived of as made up essentially of *names*. Hobbes's "nominalism" in fact means—though this is not at all obvious from his list of uses and abuses—that he thinks issues of truth and falsity only arise when names are somehow put together into assertions.

By a strange aftereffect, it seems that it is only after the names have been linked together that the names as such become, retroactively as it were, susceptible to falsity:

> For *True* and *False* are attributes of Speech, not of Things. And where Speech is not, there is neither *Truth* nor *Falshood*. *Errour* there may be, as when wee expect that which shall not be; or suspect what has not been: but in neither case can a man be charged with Untruth.
>
> Seeing then that *truth* consisteth in the right ordering of names in our affirmations, a man that seeketh precise *truth*, had need to remember what every name he uses stands for; and to place it accordingly; or else he will find himselfe entangled in words, as a bird in lime-twiggs; the more he struggles, the more belimed. And therefore in Geometry (which is the onely Science that it hath pleased God hitherto to bestow on mankind,) men begin at settling the significations of their words; which settling of significations, they call *Definitions*; and place them in the beginning of their reckoning. (28)

This is where the trouble really starts. Not simply (though not trivially) in that Hobbes himself begins to be, and will be increasingly, inclined to use figural, rhetorical or metaphorical language to describe the predicaments we get into with language—here the striking image of the bird caught in lime[9]—but in that the possibility of this type of "abuse" comes to seem more and more inseparable from any use at all. The suspicion of the deliberate or inadvertent abuses of language will also extend, almost immediately—reminding us of the opening sequence of the chapter, leading from printing through writing to speech—to the question of books and of reading, where the curious, now to be extended, bird analogy returns in Hobbes's increasingly bravura and even flashy prose. And as we shall see shortly, this difficulty in separating use from abuse in language, which can seem to be a marginal question to be dealt with prior to the properly political concerns of *Leviathan*, is intractable enough to generate both the

---

9. Does Hegel get this image from Hobbes? Cf. The "Introduction" to *Phenomenology of Spirit*: "If the Absolute were only to be brought on the whole nearer to us by this agency, without any change being wrought in it, like a bird caught by a limestick, it would certainly scorn a trick of that sort, if it were not in its very nature, and did it not wish to be, beside us from the start," and picked up rather discreetly by Derrida in the Genet column of *Glas* (Galilée, 1975), 148b: "Le métalangage est la vie du langage: il bat toujours de l'aile comme un oiseau pris dans une glu subtile [Metalanguage is the life of language: it always flutters like a bird caught in a subtle lime-trap]."

phantasm of sovereignty for which Hobbes is famous, and the more or less lucid perception that sovereignty is from the start doomed to failure and destruction, and that the State will always inevitably dissolve or scatter into what Hobbes so often calls "Civill Warre."[10] Here the possibility of truth will depend on the foundation of definitions, but if we avoid the birdlime of forgotten or inconsistent definition, we might yet find ourselves trapped in a different kind of space if we rely, through reading, on anyone's definitions but our own.

Here is what already starts to happen if, entering into the realm of truth and falsity, we fail to keep a grip on the meaning of our words or rely on others to provide them:

> By this it appears how necessary it is for any man that aspire to true Knowledge, to examine the Definitions of former Authors; and either to correct them, where they are negligently set down, or to make them himself. For the errours of Definitions multiply themselves, according as the reckoning proceeds; and lead men into absurdities, which at last they seem but cannot avoid, without reckoning anew from the beginning; in which lies the foundation of their errours. (28)

And now a move that will be constant in Hobbes, as though the very fact of books and the necessity of reading were of a piece with the abuses of language we are being so sternly warned against (in due course we will see that this affects Hobbes's view of the place of his *own* book and the appropriate way for it to be read):

> From whence it happens, that they which trust to books, do as they that cast up many little sums into a greater, without considering whether those little summes were rightly cast up or not; and at last finding the errour visible, and not mistrusting their first grounds, know not which way to cleere themselves; but spend time in fluttering over their books; as birds that entring by the chimney, and finding themselves enclosed in a chamber, flutter at the false light of a glasse window, for want of wit to consider which way they came in. So that in the right Definition of Names, lyes the first use of Speech; which is the Acquisition of Science: and in wrong, or no Definitions, lyes the first abuse; from which proceed all false and senslesse Tenets. (28)

10. Hobbes came from Malmesbury in Wiltshire in the west of England, so I imagine him pronouncing these words, which return as a kind of nightmare outcome to end many memorable sentences in the *Leviathan*, with a West Country burr to the double "r" in "Warre," and a definite, if slightly horrified, relish.

In a way that is not at all uncommon in Hobbes, what I am tempted to call this *flight* of memorable prose gets somewhat carried away, as though it is Hobbes's own writing that is provoking his irascibility. For there is here a general structure (which I imagine Derrida might call "autoimmune") whereby language, supposed to raise man above the other animals, always might, by *necessary possibility*, and according to the "beast and sovereign" scenario we stressed in the opening of Aristotle's *Politics*, pitch man down lower than the animals he was supposed to rise above: language provides simultaneously for the best and *thereby also* for the worst, which confirms our earlier sense that when it comes to language, use and abuse are as close as can be, reason and madness hard to tell apart:

> . . . all false and senselesse Tenets; which make those men that take
> their instruction from the authority of books, and not from their own
> meditation, to be as much below the condition of ignorant men, as
> men endued with true Science are above it. For between true Science,
> and erroneous Doctrine, Ignorance is in the middle. Naturall sense
> and imagination, are not subject to absurdity. Nature it selfe cannot
> erre: and as men abound in copiousness of language; so they become
> more wise, or more mad than ordinary. Nor is it possible without
> Letters for any man to become ether excellently wise, or (unless his
> memory be hurt by disease, or ill constitution of organs) excellently
> foolish. For words are wise men's counters, they do but reckon by
> them: but they are the mony of fooles, that value them by the author-
> ity of an *Aristotle*, a *Cicero*, or a *Thomas*, or any other doctor whatso-
> ever, if but a man. (28–29)[11]

11. See, too, the equivalently vigorous sequence in *Elements of Law*, chap. 5: "As the invention of names hath been necessary for the drawing of men out of ignorance, but calling to their remembrance the necessary coherence of one conception to another; so also hath it on the other side precipitated men into error: insomuch, that whereas by the benefit of words and ratiocination they exceed brute beasts in knowledge; by the incommodities that accompany the same they exceed them also in errors. For true and false are things not incident to beasts, because they adhere to propositions and language; nor have they ratiocination, whereby to multiply one untruth by another: as men have. . . . And men desiring to shew others the knowledge, opinions, conceptions, and passions which are within themselves, and to that end having invented language, have by that means transferred all that discursion of their mind . . . by the motion of their tongues, into discourse of words; and *ratio*, now, is but *oratio*, for the most part, wherein custom hath so great a power, that the mind suggesteth only the first word, the rest follow habitually, and are not followed by the mind. As it is with beggars,

This vein of indignation (often, as we said, accompanied by denigration of Aristotle), continues into the following chapter of *Leviathan*, "Of Reason, and Science," where Hobbes again recognizes without recognizing this autoimmune structure of *logos*, or *ratio* and *oratio*:

> I have said before, (in the second chapter,) that a Man did excel all other Animals in this faculty, that when he conceived anything whatsoever, he was apt to enquire the consequences of it, and what effects he could do with it. And now I adde this other degree of the same excellence, that he can by words reduce the consequences he finds to generall Rules, called *Theoremes*, or *Aphorismes*; that is, he can Reason, or reckon, not onely in number; but in all other things, whereof one may be added unto, or subtracted from another.
>
> But this priviledge, is allayed by another; and that is, by the priviledge of Absurdity; to which no living creature is subject, but man onely. And of men, those are of all most subject to it, that professe Philosophy. For it is most true that *Cicero* sayth of them somewhere [Cicero, whose authority was mocked in the previous chapter], that there can be nothing so absurd, but may be found in the books of Philosophers. (34)

This view of language and "letters" has a profound impact on Hobbes's strictly political thinking. I want to look in some detail at just two moments among many that seem to be peculiarly telling in this respect. The first we might call (though Hobbes presumably would not) another "reading" of the very opening pages of Aristotle's *Politics*, in the opening chapter of Part II ("Of Commonwealth") of *Leviathan*. The second is his discussion in "Of Counsell," which will see a return to some difficult questions about language.[12]

As we have seen, Hobbes is more than suspicious of philosophical authorities, and especially of Aristotle and Aristotelianism, and presents himself (in his mature work at least) as being about as anti-Aristotelian as possible—not

---

when they say their *paternoster*, putting together such words, and in such manner, as in their education they have learned from their nurses, from their companions, or from their teachers, having no images or conceptions in their mind answering to the words they speak. And as they learned themselves, so they teach posterity" (38–39).

12. See the outstanding forthcoming work by Matías Bascuñán on Hobbes's chap. 26, devoted to Civil Laws.

only in that the Aristotelians are among the main culprits of bringing what Hobbes calls "Darknesse from Vain Philosophy," and not only because they have transformed the university into a place where philosophy is no more than a "handmaid to the Romane Religion,[13]" thus turning the study of philosophy into a study that is "not properly Philosophy (the nature whereof dependeth not on Authors), but Aristotelity" (*Leviathan* 462)—but because Aristotle himself is so very wrong about so many things that Hobbes can write "I beleeve scarce any thing can be more absurdly said in naturall Philosophy, that that which now is called *Aristotles Metaphysiques*; nor more repugnant to Government, than much of that hee hath said in his *Politiques*; nor more ignorantly, than a great part of his *Ethiques*" (*Leviathan* 461–462).[14]

"Much of that hee hath said," but perhaps not all, and indeed one of the chapters of *Leviathan* that one might be excused for thinking quite central to the book, namely the opening chapter of Part II ("Of Common-Wealth"), entitled "Of the Causes, Generation, and Definition of a Common-Wealth," begins with what I suggest is a kind of rereading (or perhaps rewriting) of this opening of Aristotle's *Politics*.[15] We can set up the problem quite rapidly, helped by Hobbes's marginal annotations, which provide a kind of telegraphic version of the argument. So: "The End of Common-wealth, particular Security . . . Which is not to be had from the Law of Nature . . . Nor from the conjunction of a few men or families . . . Nor from great Multitude, unlesse directed by one judgement . . . And that continually" (117–119). This first half of the chapter is a kind of counterderi-

13. This a reference to Aquinas's famous definition, which we might reasonably take to be the culmination of the Christian theologizing of Aristotle we pursued earlier.

14. In spite of Hobbes's vehement remarks, it is at least arguable that he remains in places close to Aristotle's *Rhetoric*, of which he was in fact the first English translator: see the evidence for this proximity presented by Leo Strauss in *The Political Philosophy of Hobbes: Its Basis and Its Genesis*, trans. Elsa M. Sinclair (Chicago: University of Chicago Press, 1963), 35–42.

15. Derrida's first *Beast and the Sovereign* seminar presents, I believe for the first time in his published work, a quite extensive reading of Hobbes, but although he refers to what he calls the "enthralling" chapter "Of Persons, Authors, and things Personated," which immediately precedes this one, and analyzes at some length the immediately following chapter, "Of the Rights of Soveraignes by Institution," he does not refer to this chapter, nor apparently remark on the close relation it bears to the Aristotle passages he reads or reads out in the final session.

vation of the polis or commonwealth from its origin, which certainly has at least half an eye on Aristotle. Having reached this point in his argument, Hobbes, now with explicit reference to Aristotle, entertains a possible question about political animals (the marginal summary has: "Why certain creatures without reason, or speech [i.e., *logos*], do neverthelesse live in society, without any coërcive Power" [119]). Here is how Hobbes presents the question in the body of the text:

> It is true, that certain living creatures, as Bees, and Ants, live sociably one with another, (which are therefore by *Aristotle* numbred amongst Politicall creatures;) and yet have no other direction, than their particular judgements and appetites; nor speech, whereby one of them can signifie to another, what he thinks expedient for the common benefit: and therefore some man may perhaps desire to know, why Man-kind cannot do the same. To which I answer . . . (119)

So the problem is: there are nonhuman political animals that seem to do just fine, politically speaking, without the complex apparatus of commonwealth by institution, and notably without unified coercive sovereignty, and they do not even have language to help them figure things out. The lurking paradox would then be related to the suspicion that the very thing that makes man *more* political than other political animals somehow simultaneously brings with it a *less* political, or at least a less successfully political fate for the humankind that (or so one might think) ought to be better able to get these things right, because of the superiority of the *logos*, than bees or ants and other critters.

Hobbes does like a numbered list, perhaps because it gives the impression or the illusion of keeping at bay just the unruly features of language of which he is thematically so suspicious (but textually so enamored), and his reply to this imagined objection has six distinct points. Of these, I want to dwell on the fourth, which seems to have a certain privilege over the others, if only because it is precisely to do with language, which, as we have seen, is the specific difference from animals that Hobbes invokes in the general presentation of the problem. Fourth, then, says Hobbes, no longer explicitly referring to Aristotle, but more or less quoting him directly for the beginning of this response to the objection: "Fourthly, that these creatures, though they have some use of voice, in making knowne to one another their desires, and other affections; yet they want that art of words . . ." (119). That art of words, one assumes in the wake of Hobbes's general presentation of the problem, and in the flow of the Aristotle text that we thought Hobbes was more or less translating here, whereby they could signify to one another the expedient and the inexpedient, and by extension the just and the unjust and so on. But in fact not at all, and indeed rather the contrary. What follows is interesting to track in Hobbes from *Elements of Law* through *De Cive* to *Leviathan* itself: in all three cases, the same problem is addressed in six points, and in all three cases the specific language point is the fourth. Here is the version from *De Cive*:

> Fourthly, however well the animals may be able to use their voices
> to indicate their feelings to each other, they still do not have the art
> of words that is needed to arouse the passions, notably, to make the
> Good appear Better, and the Bad Worse than they really are. (71)

So far the problem seems to be essentially one of exaggeration: language gets humans into discussion of the good, but also gets them into exaggerating that good or its opposite. But now the text continues:

> But man's tongue is a trumpet to war and sedition; and it is said that
> *Pericles* once made thunder and lightning in his speeches and threw all
> *Greece* into confusion [*hominis autem lingua tuba quaedam belli est &*
> *seditionis; diciturque* Pericles *suis quondam orationibus, tonuisse, fulgurasse,*
> *& confundisse totam* Graeciam]. (71–72)

This seems bad enough: the very thing that in Aristotle distinguishes man from other animals, that is, *logos* in the sense of language, no sooner has him using it in the way that most clearly distinguishes it from the *phonē* of animals (i.e., not just to moan and groan, but to talk of good and bad and thus, naturally perhaps, to emerge from the nature of what Hobbes elsewhere calls "bruit beasts") than that use is *already* pushing him toward sedition and thereby civil war, that is, dragging him back down or back out into a nature worse than that of the animals who seem to do well enough in *their* politics without *logos* (or sovereignty) at all. In the version of this fourth point in *The Elements of Law*, Hobbes cuts straight to the chase and says "Fourthly, they [i.e., the other political animals] want speech, and are therefore unable to instigate one another to faction, which men want not" (105).

Bad enough, I was saying: but this "bad enough" that comes apparently straight from the ability to claim to distinguish good from bad, and that leads apparently straight to the worst thing of all ("Civill Warre"), gets *even worse* than this in *Leviathan*, if that is possible, in that what in *De Cive* is merely to do with a tendency toward exaggeration here becomes something rather more sinister altogether:

Fourthly, that these creatures, though they have some use of voice, in making knowne to one another their desires, and other affections; yet they want that art of words, by which some men can represent to others, that which is Good, in the likenesse of Evill, and Evill, in the likenesse of Good; and augment, or diminish the apparent greatnesse of Good and Evill; discontenting men, and troubling their Peace at their pleasure. (119–120)

Which pushes the exaggeration problem of *De Cive* to a kind of catastrophic point: man possessed of *logos* and not just *phonē* not only uses language to *exaggerate* good and evil, but also to *invert* them and present the one *as* the other. Which is why, one might then imagine, unlike the animals who do not have this problem, man needs a unifying and coercive sovereign will to decide and enforce what will *count* as good and evil, independently of always potentially oratorical, misleading, seditious, and factional deliberation among the *logos*-enabled people.[16]

One might at first be inclined to imagine that this is simply one side of the *logos* that distinguishes man from other political animals, namely the unfortunate tendency we have seen for language to get out of hand in the form of rhetoric, for *ratio* to become mere *oratio*, and that the dignity of man might be salvaged by looking to the other standard translation of *logos*, namely "reason" (as we saw, Hobbes duly points out in *Leviathan* that "the Greeks have but one word *logos*, for both *Speech* and *Reason*; not that they thought there was no Speech without Reason; but no Reasoning without Speech" [29]).[17] Remember that the answer we have been looking at is the fourth of six: the third answer Hobbes gives is in fact focused on reason,

---

16. As Hobbes famously formulates it in the Latin version of the *Leviathan*, *Auctoritas, non veritas facit legem*. See Carl Schmitt, *Dictatorship* (1921), trans. Michael Hoelzl and Graham Ward (London: Polity Press, 2014), 17: "The sovereign decides about what is mine and what is yours, what constitutes advantage and disadvantage, decency and indecency, right and wrong, good and evil."

17. This priority of speech over reason in Hobbes, which is of a piece with his "nominalism," is also widely supposed to be a mark of his "modernity." See Strauss, "On the Basis of Hobbes's Political Philosophy," in *What Is Political Philosophy?* (Glencoe, IL: Free Press, 1959), 170–196, at 174. (Strauss is commenting on Raymond Polin's *Politique et philosophie chez Thomas Hobbes* [Paris: Presses Universitaires de France, 1953].) See, too, on this aspect of Hobbes, Heidegger's brief remarks in *The Fundamental Concepts of Metaphysics*, 328–329, and the earlier, longer treatment of Hobbes's thinking about the copula in the 1927 course *The Basic Problems of Phenomenology*, 183–192.

and if anything the case for humanity is even worse here than in the case of language. In *De Cive*, this third answer is as follows:

> Thirdly, animals without reason neither see, nor believe they see, any defects in the conduct of their common affairs [*suarum rerum publicarum*]; but any group of men includes a large number who suppose themselves cleverer than the rest, and make attempts to change things, and they differ among themselves and try different things, and that is dissension and civil war [*distractio, & bellum ciuile*]. (71)

And in *Leviathan*:

> Thirdly, that these creatures, having not (as man) the use of reason, do not see, nor think they see any fault, in the administration of their common businesse: whereas amongst men, there are very many, that thinke themselves wiser, and abler to govern the Publique, better than the rest; and these strive to reforme and innovate, one this way, another that way; and thereby bring it into Distraction and Civill warre. (119)

However active and even activist this "reading" of Aristotle by Hobbes, it does seem to bring out something important and interesting. *Logos*, supposedly the specific possession of man, opens the possibility of politics, of the *polis*, but simultaneously opens the possibility of the collapse of politics into what Hobbes usually calls "Civill Warre," or back into the "state of nature" that is a nature much more violent than any other animal nature. In Hobbes, at least, this is a paradoxical structure just because it seems that Good and Evil, the possible confusion or inversion of which he relates to language in the political sphere, are in fact potentially confused or inverted from the start, so that politics *as such* is as good as it is bad, as good as it is evil, as artificial as it is natural, prone to ruin by the very same means that made it possible. This confusion of apparent opposites affects many moments in Hobbes, so that in this numbered sequence of six responses to our question about why other political animals do not appear to need the unifying and coercive sovereign that Hobbes claims human animals need, the fifth, perhaps unconsciously remembering the ambiguity of the Greek word *stasis*, has Hobbes claiming, on the basis of a distinction between *injury* and *damage*, that "Man is . . . most troublesome, when he is most at ease" (*Leviathan* 120: the concept of *stasis* will return in the discussion of Peterson and Schmitt that follows). As we saw earlier, in his different way, Aristotle too is haunted by such possibilities of a kind of infranature, or nature worse than that of the animals: and indeed this is the matrix of Derrida's interest in the paradoxical convergences in the tradition between beast and sovereign, for example when Aristotle famously writes in the immediate context of our passage from the *Politics* that "man is by nature a political animal, and a man that is by nature and not merely by fortune citiless is either low on the scale of humanity or above it . . ." (9; 1253a3–6), and just a little later "It is clear therefore that the state is also prior by nature to the individual . . . a man who is incapable of entering into partnership, or who is so self-sufficing that he has no need to do so, is no part of a state, so that he must be either a lower animal or a god" (11–12; 1253a26–30). And more generally in Hobbes, as we saw in our reading of chapter 4 of *Leviathan*, language as such is as close as can be to its "abuses," always on the point of drifting into what in a moment we shall be calling *rhetoric*. If *logos*, as supposedly definitive of the human, were to turn out to be inseparable from rhetoric, for example (and I think that that is indeed the case in Hobbes, much to his indignation and dismay), then there might be consequences for how we think about politics more generally. These problems show up much more acutely for Hobbes in the case of democracy, which in *The Elements of Law* we saw him describe as being no more than an "aristocracy of orators" (120). Democracy in Hobbes tends to lead to the ruin of politics just as does the rhetorical drift of language.

The possible inseparability of *logos* and rhetoric (notably in Aristotle), which I am suggesting can be seen at work in Hobbes, is also argued for in an article by the French scholar Jean-Louis Labarrière, which is nominally about the difference between human and animal imagination in Aristotle, but ends up all about questions of language.[18] According to Labarrière's Aristotle, what nonhuman animals lack in lacking *logos* is less reason or even articulate language as such—for animals *do* display rationality, and as their *phonē* is not entirely separable from certain values of *logos*, insofar as *logos* here is close to *dialektos*, and some animals (notably birds) according to Aristotle *do* exhibit something like a *dialektos*, then we might want to conclude that the distinction between *logos* and *phonē* is not as clear-cut as might appear. What nonhuman animals lack in lacking *logos* is less reason or even articulate language as such, then, than precisely *rhetoric qua* art of persuasion. Animals in fact do have *some* access to *logos*, but not to the dimension of *doxa*, opinion: and *doxa* is the basis of rhetoric. The aspect of *logos* to

18. Jean-Louis Labarrière, "Imagination humaine et imagination animale chez Aristote." *Phronesis* 29, no. 1 (1984): 17–49. This article is cited by Jean-François Lyotard in a short piece I discuss in "Political Animals," *Diacritics* 39, no. 2 (2011): 21–35.

which animals do not have access, says Labarrière's Aristotle, is precisely the rhetorical dimension in which opinions are put forward and deliberated in the public arena (32). This dimension, which Labarrière wants to claim gives human political life what he calls an "ethical surplus-value" compared to the merely "economic" rationality of the political life of nonhuman political animals (44), is manifested essentially in the speeches of orators made before the assembled citizens, in which, according to the initial definition from the *Politics*, humans discuss the useful and the harmful, the just and the unjust.[19] This leads to what Labarrière calls a "paradox," whereby the orator, who is exploiting that aspect of the *logos* that distinguishes him from nonhuman animals, sees that *logos* (that the tradition wanted to reclaim in terms of rationality) drifting toward the rhetorical, toward a persuasive and seductive eloquence, potentially exploiting all the possibilities of exaggeration and falsity that exercised Hobbes so much. Labarrière is certainly simplifying (and anachronizing) the situation by calling this dimension of language "aesthetic," and finding it merely "paradoxical" that the properly human ethical supplement of the political should thus show up "aesthetically." I want to say that this rhetorical drift marks a much graver problem—one that Hobbes really does identify—in *logos* and in politics as such. Man is naturally a political animal insofar as he is possessed of a *logos* that turns out in this rather essential or primordial way to be *rhetorical*. Rhetoric means that politics is always drawn into what I call the politics of politics, and the politics of politics is, as everyone knows and usually laments as though it could simply be avoided, the end of politics, the becoming-corrupt of the political as such, the death of politics living at the heart of politics, an essential part of its life.

Labarrière who is, understandably enough, concerned to preserve the preeminence of the ethical moment in all this, even when recognizing that it has to go via this "paradoxical" aesthetic or rhetorical path, is led thereby to what I take to be a rather desperate reading of *Rhetoric* 1418a40. Here,

---

19. According to Labarrière, then, the specifically political *logos* "indeed manifests the object of the political orator: the useful and the harmful, subjects of opinion and deliberation, useful and harmful of which the just and the unjust seem to be a consequence . . . the just is defined with respect to the laws which are themselves subject to constitutions [*Pol.* 4.1.1289a11–20]. What the logos manifests, it manifests then in the speeches, the discourses in the deliberative genre . . . made before the people gathered in assembly in the 'pubic space' . . . discourses bearing on everything of interest to the citizens and the city" (44).

near the end of the *Rhetoric*, Aristotle says "if you have no enthymemes, then fall back upon moral discourse: after all, it is more fitting for a good man to display himself as an honest fellow than as a subtle reasoner" (213).[20] It is not hard to imagine a rather different reading (which would then at first blush seem to lend itself to a Hobbesian "pessimism" about human animals), according to which Aristotle's text is really suggesting (whatever Aristotle's intention may have been) that moralism is a useful rhetorical fallback possibility for the orator who has been unable to construct a genuinely plausible discourse, and that to that extent moral talk is caught up *within* rhetoric as one of its possibilities, or even its *best* possibility, in that it can always present itself as not rhetorical at all. "Moral discourse" on this reading always might be just another rhetorical ploy (the "southern lawyer" ploy), whereby the (apparent) absence of rhetoric in (apparent) moral righteousness is just another, supplementary, turn of rhetoric. On this type of reading, rhetoric has no outside, there is no language it cannot adopt, and the *logos* that makes man naturally a political animal is not (*pace* Labarrière, who thus seems to be *himself* falling back on moral discourse at the end of his article)—not so much a paradoxical means of securing the "ethical surplus-value" of politics and thus saving the dignity of the human, as a more complex and perhaps even sinister possibility that rather resonates with the sense that contemporary political discourse has become swamped by just this kind of rhetorical hypermoralism and tends to confirm Hobbes's "reading" of Aristotle.

What I am suggesting is that this troublesome persistence of the rhetorical, as the specific feature of *logos* insofar as it distinguishes man among political animals, paradoxically complicates the very specificity it seemed to establish. For one thing, what rhetoric exploits in its *logos* is precisely

---

20. I am appealing here to the Rhys Roberts translation. John Henry Freese has, "In fact, it is more fitting that a virtuous man should show himself good than that his speech should be painfully exact." Theodore Buckley: "the show of goodness more befits a virtuous man, than accuracy of speech." C. D. C. Reeve, "To appear good fits a decent person more than an exact argument does." *Kai mallon tō epieikei harmottei khrēston phainesthai ē ton logon akribē:* the translation probably hangs on how the verb *phainesthai* is taken: to appear as what one is, or to appear to be what one is not—the suggestion is that this is undecidable, and just that is an effect of rhetoric. This apparently innocent example has some quite serious consequences in Heidegger's radicalization of phenomenology through his intensive reading of Aristotle in the 1920s, as I suggested in *Scatter 1* (New York: Fordham University Press, 2016), 27n16.

what we might be tempted to call a residual *phonē*, a kind of persistent animality of language (perhaps what Derrida in a rather different and much
earlier context calls an "animality of the letter," as the "primal and infinite equivocality of the signifier").[21] To put it more jokily (although all of
this is really pretty serious, which doesn't mean it can't also be *funny*),
among the upshot of our readings might be that *logos* is always somewhat
phony, that politics is always somewhat animal, that humanity has no
essential definition, and that the concept of sovereignty is always a rather
desperate and hollow expedient to pretend the contrary.

Turning now to the chapter of *Leviathan* that deals with counsel, we will
see a certain culmination of the issues we have started to bring out around
language and letters, rhetoric and oratory. In Hobbes's account of language
as we have seen it thus far, the always—necessarily—possible abuses were
as close as could be to the uses. The "abuse" that consists in using metaphor explicitly corresponds to the use of speech that for Hobbes includes
counsel: the second special use, it will be remembered, is "to shew to others
that knowledge that we have attained; which is, to Counsell, and Teach
one another," and the corresponding abuse consists in "us[ing] words meta-
phorically; that is in other sense than that they are ordained for; and
thereby deceive others." At the end of his chapter "Of Speech," Hobbes
returns to the question and seems to mitigate the seriousness of the abuse
a little. Hobbes has just been pointing out that the "names of such things
as affect us" are "inconstant," changing from person to person according
to their affective take on the object in question, and in the same person
across time, as our "affections" change. Examples are "the names of Vertues, and Vices; For one man calleth *Wisdome*, what another calleth *feare*;
and one *cruelty*, what another *justice*; one *prodigality*, what another *magna-
nimity*; and one *gravity*, what another *stupidity*, &c. And therefore such
names can never be true grounds of any ratiocination."[22] He then ends the

21. Derrida uses these expressions in the early essay "Edmond Jabès et la
question du livre" (ED 108–109/72). See my brief commentary in "Half-Life," in
Not Half No End, 116.

22. This is why Hobbes insists that there are, logically speaking, only three
"kinds of common-wealth," according as sovereignty is exercised by one, several,
or all, and that other names "are not the names of other Formes of Government,
but of the same Formes misliked. For they that are displeased with *Aristocracy*,
called it *Oligarchy*: So also, they which find themselves grieved under a *Democracy*,
call it *Anarchy* . . ." (*Leviathan* 129–130).

chapter, as though with an afterthought: "No more can Metaphors, and Tropes of speech: but these are less dangerous, because they profess their inconstancy; which the other do not" (31).[23] And yet the following chapter, on Reason and Science, sternly bans "the use of Metaphors, Tropes, and other Rhetoricall figures, in stead of words proper." Even catachreses, such as *"the way goeth, or leadeth hither, or thither, The Proverb says this or that* (whereas ways cannot go, nor Proverbs speak)" are allowable only in "common speech" but not in "reckoning, and seeking of truth."

Hobbes strikes a delicate balance between this condemnation of metaphor and his own recourse to it, and to other rhetorical figures, not at all limited to the figure of catachresis (and even that is not supposed to be allowed in what is after all a book engaged in "seeking of truth"), and including some quite extended cases that might even be described as conceits, including in passages condemning the very thing Hobbes appears to be indulging in his own book. Still in chapter 5, for example, using figurative language to characterize metaphor itself:

> To conclude, The Light of humane minds is Perspicuous Words, but
> by exact definitions first snuffed, and purged from ambiguity; *Reason*
> is the *pace*; Encrease of *Science*, the *way*, and the Benefit of man-kind,
> the *end*. And on the contrary, Metaphors, and senslesse and ambiguous
> words, are like *ignes fatui*; and reasoning upon them, is wandering
> amongst innumerable absurdities; and their end, contention, and
> sedition, or contempt.

And as always in Hobbes, this issue with metaphor seems to go along with mistrust of books and reading, so that just after this passage that mistrust is itself given expression in a striking simile:

> But they that trusting onely to the authority of books, follow the blind
> blindly, are like him that trusting to the false rules of a master of
> Fence, ventures praesumptuously upon an adversary, that either kills,
> or disgraces him. (37)

The place where these two suspicions in Hobbes converge is in what he calls "Counsell." We saw that that is the use of language affected by the abuse called metaphor, as could be further confirmed in chapter 8 of *Leviathan* ("Of the VERTUES commonly called INTELLECTUALL; and their contrary DEFECTS"), where Hobbes, who clearly cannot make the point often

---

23. In *The Elements of Law* Hobbes writes that "all metaphors are (by profession) equivocal" (37).

enough, firmly closes down again the possible implications of any apparent concession to nonliteral uses of language:

> In Demonstration, in Councell, and all rigorous search of Truth, Judgement does all; except sometimes the understanding have need to be opened by some apt similitude; and then there is so much use of Fancy. But for Metaphors, they are in this case utterly excluded. For seeing they openly professe deceipt; to admit them into Councell, or Reasoning, were manifest folly. (52)

Back in the "Speech" chapter, Hobbes closes it out with a parallel warning about reading:

> But in any businesse, whereof a man has not infallible Science to proceed by; to forsake his own natural judgement, and be guided by general sentences read in Authors, and subject to many exceptions, is a signe of folly, and generally scorned by the name of Pedantry. And of even those men themselves, that in Counsells of the Common-wealth, love to shew their reading of Politiques and History, very few do it in their domestique affaires, where their particular interest is concerned; having Prudence enough for their private affaires: but in publique they study more the reputation of their owne wit, than the successe of anothers businesse. (37)

So by the time we reach chapter 25, "Of Counsell," we are no longer surprised to find that it is in fact largely about language, its uses and abuses. Hobbes begins with what it is tempting to describe as a pragmatic analysis, and proceeds with something along the lines of a speech-act theory *avant la lettre*. According to the general logic we have observed thus far in Hobbes, we shall see again that he is very keen to establish clean distinctions, and that they constantly tend to break down. Our more general interest is how that breakdown is not a narrowly linguistic issue, but entails a collapse of the conceptual edifice of sovereignty itself, so that the Leviathan, the famous "Artificial Animal" described in the introduction to the book, is always already beginning to come crashing down. We will endeavor to show that the cause of this downfall is not, as is suggested by Carl Schmitt, that Hobbes unwarrantedly reserves a possibility for internal, private, dissent against the publicly mandated religion, thus opening a crack that, in Schmitt's account, "the first liberal jew," namely Spinoza, will almost immediately prize open further, but that the concept of sovereignty (including in its Schmittian deployment) is from the start beginning to fail, according to the general schemas suggested in the Derridean formulas mentioned earlier, whereby "L'Un se garde de l'autre" and "L'Un se fait violence." Or, to use the earlier Derridean language, sovereignty requires various "supplements" to make it whole, and those very supplements always compromise the same whole they alone make possible. And that too is the politics of politics, as it affects Hobbes's text itself.

Hobbes, then, opens his counsel chapter with a distinction between what we might be tempted, anachronistically, to call the "speech acts" of counsel and command. The potential confusion between them is apparently a paramount example, perhaps the best example, of the validity of the now familiar Hobbesian suspicion of language as such:

> How fallacious it is to judge of the nature of things, by the ordinary
> and inconstant use of words, appeareth in nothing more, than in the
> confusion of Counsels, and Commands, arising from the imperative
> manner of speaking in them both, and in many other occasions
> besides. For the words *Doe this*, are the words not onely of him that
> Commandeth; but also of him that giveth Counsell; and of him that
> Exhorteth. (176)

This potential confusion generated by grammar (the common imperative mood), can be clarified by appeal to what might be called a "pragmatic" analysis. Hobbes thinks the grammatical appearance that might lead to confusion of counsel with command or exhortation can readily and uncontroversially be clarified: "there are but few, that see not, that these are very different things; or that cannot distinguish between them, when they perceive who it is that speaketh, and to whom the Speech is directed, and upon what occasion." Not surprisingly, this type of pragmatic clarification is less obvious when it comes to writing, and this immediately reopens the door to confusion and to self-interested reading:

> But finding those phrases in mens writings, and not being able, or not
> willing to enter into a consideration of the circumstances, they mistake
> sometimes the Precepts of Counsellours, for the Precepts of them that
> Command; and sometimes the contrary; according as it best agrees
> with the conclusions they would inferre, or the actions they approve.

According to his own precepts (themselves presumably proffered to the reader as counsel, command, or exhortation) from the chapter on Speech, Hobbes undertakes to clarify things by starting from definitions, initially of counsel and command, where again the pragmatic circumstances of the prescriptive utterance (the more or less explicit "do this!") allow for a quite rich contrastive sense of the differences involved.

COMMAND is, where a man saith, *Doe this*, or *Doe not this*, without expecting other reason than the Will of him that says it. From this it followeth manifestly, that he that Commandeth, pretendeth thereby his own Benefit: For the reason of his Command is his own Will onely, and the proper object of every mans Will, is some Good to himselfe. COUNSELL, is where a man saith *Doe* or *Doe not this*, and deduceth his reasons from the benefit that arriveth by it to him to whom he saith it. And from this it is evident, that he that giveth Counsell, pretendeth onely (whatsoever he intendeth) the good of him, to whom he giveth it. (176)

Leaving aside for now the warning sign put up by the parenthesis, that suggests a possible difference between what the speaker "pretends" (not straightforwardly in the sense of feigning, and more in the sense of what is professed by the speech act itself) and what the speaker "intends"—as we shall see, I always might secretly be intending to further my own interests while professing (by the act of counsel itself) to further the sovereign's—Hobbes proceeds to draw a number of important consequences from this initial distinction: I am obliged to do what I am commanded to do (insofar as I am indeed subject to the one commanding), but I am not obliged to do what I am merely counselled to do (because counsel aims at the addressee's benefit, it is the addressee's loss if it not be followed): and, Hobbes adds, if I "covenant" to follow counsel, that simply turns counsel into command anyway. And further, it follows from the initial pragmatic analysis that I cannot claim any *right* to give counsel, because claiming such a right would come back to exercising my own will, seeking my own benefit, and consequently again turning counsel into command.

Hobbes has not finished drawing the consequences of this analysis. Just because I *ex hypothesi* ask for counsel (if it is imposed on me it is not counsel but command), then I am to be considered its "author," and this means that I cannot punish the counsellor for the counsel offered. The gravity of this point is such that Hobbes immediately takes the example of counselling the sovereign (and, interestingly enough in view of what is to come, finds a more telling argument in the case, not of monarchy, but of aristocratic or democratic sovereignty, giving a hint that the sovereign is, in a sense to be explored, intrinsically plural):

To ask Counsell of another, is to permit him to give such Counsell as he shall think best; And consequently, he that giveth counsel to his Soveraign (whether a Monarch, or an Assembly) when he asketh it,

cannot in equity be punished for it, whether the same be conformable
to the opinion of the most, or not, so it be to the Proposition in debate.
For if the sense of the Assembly can be taken notice of, before the
Debate be ended, they should neither ask, nor take any further Counsell;
For the Sense of the Assembly, is the Resolution of the Debate, and
End of all Deliberation.[24] And generally he that demandeth Counsell, is
Author of it;[25] and therefore cannot punish it; and what the Soveraign
cannot, no man else can. (177)

Having established this apparently firm and quite rich distinction between
counsel and command, Hobbes turns to the third term he introduced at
the beginning of the chapter, namely "exhortation," and its opposite,
"dehortation."[26] And this is where trouble begins, as these terms will introduce a supplement into Hobbes's initial distinction from which it will
never recover, a supplement that immediately lets in all the features of language Hobbes is most suspicious of. Exhortation and dehortation are indeed forms of counsel:

> EXHORTATION, and DEHORTATION, is Counsell, accompanied with signes
> in him that giveth it, of vehement desire to have it followed; or to say it
> more briefly, *Counsell vehemently pressed.* For he that Exhorteth, doth
> not deduce the consequences of what he adviseth to be done, and tye
> himself therein to the rigour of true reasoning; but encourages him he
> Counselleth, to Action: as he that Dehorteth, deterreth him from it.
> And therefore they have in their speeches, a regard to the common
> Passions, and opinions of men, in deducing their reasons; and make
> use of Similitudes, Metaphors, Examples, and other tooles of Oratory,

24. This moment of resolution would be the moment of sovereign decision à
la Schmitt, the moment of dictatorship (see also DP II, 334/251).

25. Hobbes's sense of authorship extends to authority and indeed to sovereignty, as is made clearer by definitions from chapter 16: "Of Persons, Authors,
and things Personated": "The word Person is Latine: instead whereof the Greeks
have *prosopon*, which signifies the *Face*, as *Persona* in latine signifies the *disguise*, or
outward appearance of a man, counterfeited on the Stage . . . Of Persons Artificiall,
some have their words and actions *Owned* by those whom they represent. And
then the Person is the *Actor*; and he that owneth his words and actions, is the AU-
THOR: in which case the Actor acteth by Authority. For that which in speaking of
goods and possessions, is called an *Owner*, and in latine *Dominus*, in Greek *kurios*,
speaking of Actions, is called an Author" (112).

26. "Now *rare*. 1. *transitive*. To use exhortation to dissuade (a person) from a
course or purpose; to advise or counsel against (an action, etc.)" (OED).

> to perswade their Hearers of the Utility, Honour, or Justice of
> following their advise. (178–179)

The first consequence of this is that there is a perversion, or inversion, of
the proper order of interests the initial pragmatic analysis of command and
counsel revealed. Command, it will be remembered, is given in the interest, or for the good, of the addressor of the corresponding prescriptive
utterance, and counsel in the interest, of for the good, of the addressee.
Once counsel turns into exhortation, that distribution is inverted, as it were
at a second level of analysis: at the first level, as a counselor I utter prescriptions that want (ought to want, are playing a language game that has
me "profess" to want, at any rate) the good of the addressee (exemplarily
in this context the sovereign, individual or collective); but at the second
level, as soon as my counsel becomes exhortative or dehortative, I let my
interest in having my counsel followed (whatever that counsel be) come to
the fore and trouble the interest of the addressee and the very definition
of counsel, whereby the counselor "ought to regard, not his own benefit,
but his whom he adviseth" (178). Hobbes thinks, or pretends to think, that
telling the difference between counsel proper and exhortation is not difficult: we already saw him associating it with vehemence and the "tooles
of Oratory," and now he adds, as though to reassure us, that

> That he directeth his Counsell to his own benefit, is manifest enough,
> by the long and vehement urging, or by the artificiall giving thereof;
> which being not required of him, and consequently proceeding from
> his own occasions, is directed principally to his own benefit, and but
> accidentarily to the good of him that is Counselled, or not at all. (178)

Before putting some pressure on this distinction, which is certainly not as
easy to make as Hobbes pretends here, let us note a further convergence
of the rhetorical abuse of language, counsel as such, and democratic (or at
least deliberative) politics. Hobbes seems to concede that in a deliberative
assembly, the recourse to the exhortative supplement is inevitable and perhaps even legitimate (though, as we shall see, the motif of the "multitude"
will return later in the chapter to spectacular and ruinous effect):

> The use of Exhortation and Dehortation lyeth onely, where a man
> is to speak to a Multitude; because when the Speech is addressed to
> one, he may interrupt him, and examine his reasons more rigorously,
> than can be done in a Multitude; which are too many to enter into
> Dispute, and Dialogue with him that speaketh indifferently to them
> all at once.

The resort to exhortation and dehortation (outside the assembly, we assume, then) brings with it a corruption that affects or infects what might otherwise (on the first level, as it were) perfectly good counsel:

> They that Exhort and Dehort, where they are required to give
> Counsell, are corrupt Counsellors, and as it were bribed by their own
> interest. For thought the Counsell they give be never so good [at the
> first level, then]; yet he that gives it, is no more a good Counsellour,
> than he that giveth a Just Sentence for a reward, is a Just Judge.

It seems that Hobbes is here pursuing a vanishing distinction in his more or less desperate effort to preserve the purity of counsel from contamination by the exhortative supplement. For example, we might suspect that the very fact of the imperative mood of counsel, its performative dimension that means it is not simply a constative truth-claim, entails a *structural* "vehemence," a "desire" that it be followed, a desire that could only ever be the object of a denegation if the canny counselor (we remember Odysseus and the semantic value of *metis* meaning both counsel and trickery or canniness), whether for his own perceived good or for that of his counselee, fearing that the wary counselee will suspect him of desire to see his counsel followed, deliberately presented himself as a parrhesiast, say, or simply used the ancient rhetorical trick of eschewing all rhetorical tricks and avoiding, perhaps by a display of diffidence or indifference, all the signs Hobbes seems so confident will easily identify or unmask the exhortator as opposed to the true counselor. Any counselor worth his salt, we might suppose, would be able to dissimulate his exhortation-revealing vehemence without undue difficulty.

If, then, it is, not merely difficult, but impossible to make a clear and reliable distinction between counsel and exhortation, it will follow that counsel, of which the sovereign has need in part to allow him to recover the sovereignty he is exposing by the simple and already less than fully sovereign need to ask for counsel in the first place, will *always* be uncertain as to its status, which will be undecidably exhortative or dehortative, caught up no longer merely in a *pragmatics* of counsel but in a *rhetoric* of counsel whereby it *necessarily always might* be corrupt. It is tempting to think that this is what drives Hobbes first to allow for the use of exhortation and dehortation, no longer in the Assembly (for that is still trouble, as we shall see in more detail shortly), but by the sovereign, the Commander, himself. Exhortation and dehortation are not only lawful but laudable when the apparent counsels being given *are in fact commands*, but commands that "when they are for Execution of soure labour; sometimes necessity, and

always humanity requireth to be sweetned in the delivery, by encourage-
ment, and in the tune and phrase of Counsell, rather than in harsher language of command." Once "the tune and phrase" can be imitated in this
way by the sovereign, we imagine that they can also be imitated by the
counselor.

Hobbes now gives some reassuringly simple examples of commands and
counsels, as though there were no trouble at all with the distinction. All
these examples are as if by chance taken from Scripture (most of the commands from God; most of the counsels from Jesus), and the last is especially touching: "these words, *Repent, and be Baptized in the Name of Jesus*,
are Counsell; because the reason why we should do so, tendeth not to any
benefit of God Almighty, who shall still be King in what manner soever
we rebell; but of ourselves, who have other means of avoiding the punishment hanging over us for our sins past" (178–179).

Remember the place of counsel in Hobbes's linguistic theory. As we saw,
in chapter 4 it entered into the second "special use" of speech, "to Counsell, and Teach one another." Here in chapter 25, and referred by figure or
analogy to the level of the body politic, the "artificial animal" called Leviathan, counsel occupies (or counselors occupy at any rate) a slightly different place. This place was, indeed, already prescribed in the famous
"Introduction" to the book, where Hobbes elaborates his figure of a sov-
ereignist politics that will end up condemned to the very rhetoric it is designed to exclude or reduce. Here is the celebrated opening of that
Introduction, with its abyssal figuration of human, animal, and machine:

> Nature (the Art whereby God hath made and governes the World) is
> by the *Art* of man, as in many other things, so in this also imitated,
> that it can make an Artificial Animal. For seeing life is but a motion of
> Limbs, the begining whereof is in some principall part within; why
> may we not say, that all *Automata* (Engines that move themselves by
> springs and wheeles as doth a watch) have a an artificiall life? For what
> is the *Heart*, but a *Spring*; and the *Nerves*, but so many *Strings*; and the
> *Joynts*, but so many *Wheeles*, giving motion to the whole Body, such as
> was intended by the Artificer? (9)

And this initial and quite complex relation of nature and (mimetic) art
(where art perhaps imitates nature, but nature is already the art of God
and is here itself rather placed in the position of the imitator of the non-
natural automata) allows for the strange and memorable transition whereby
from this natural-artificial pairing of machinery and body parts Hobbes
moves (helped perhaps by the verb "govern" in the opening line) to the imi-

tation of Man by the Leviathan, which within this strange milieu of analogies puts a new spin on the venerable Platonic parallelism of state and individual, the *makros anthropos* we discussed earlier:

> *Art* goes yet further, imitating that Rationall and most excellent worke of Nature, *Man*. For by Art is created that great LEVIATHAN called a COMMON-WEALTH, or STATE (in latine CIVITAS) which is but an Artificiall Man, though of greater stature and strength than the Naturall, for whose protection and defence it was intended. (9)

And not content with this general analogy, Hobbes goes on, in the wake of his specific rewriting of body parts into mechanical objects, to offer further specific analogies supposed to hold between what are, largely, parts (or attributes) of Man and parts of the State (some of these analogies are further complicated in that they have already figured in the initial list of artificial or mechanical counterparts to body parts at the level of the individual), and this is where we will see our Counselors return in a specific place:

> In which, the *Soveraignty* is an artificiall *Soul*, as giving life and motion to the whole body; The *Magistrates*, and other *Officers* of Judicature and Execution, artificiall *Joynts* [and so one imagines, following the earlier pairings to a further degree of figurality, wheels]; *Reward* and *Punishment* (by which fastned to the seate of the Soveraignty, every joynt and member is moved to performe his duty) are the *Nerves* [and therefore strings according to the earlier analogy]; The *Wealth* and *Riches* of all the particular members, are the *Strength*; *Salus Populi* (the *peoples safety*) its *Businesse*; **Counsellors, by whom all things needful for it to know, are suggested unto it, are the *Memory***; *Equity* and *Lawes*, an artificial *Reason* and *Will*; *Concord*, *Health*; *Sedition*, *Sicknesse*; and *Civill war*, *Death*. Lastly [and this one returns us in a complex way to the very opening of the Introduction, and is accordingly quite hard to know how to read], the *Pacts* and *Covenants*, by which the parts of this Body Politique were at first made, set together, and united, resemble that *Fiat*, or the *Let us make man*, pronounced by God in the Creation. (9–10, my emphasis in bold)[27]

At the level of Speech, it will be remembered, Counsel was part (alongside Teaching) of the second special use of words. Here, at the overall and thoroughly analogical level of politics as such, counsel, at least insofar as it is

27. See Derrida's reading of this passage in BS I, 50–53/26–28.

embodied by counselors, lines up with memory which, at the level of Speech, was not a *special* use, but one of the two "commodities" found in the *general* use of Speech (which is "to transferre our Mentall Discourse, into Verbal" [25]); the specific commodity in question being that of using names "to serve for *Markes*, or *Notes*, of rememberance" (ibid.). It is this "promotion" of counsel to the more general level of memory that is picked up again in chapter 25, in which, however, Hobbes will also discern an important difference between individual memory and the artificial memory provided to the State by counselors. Counselors are here again, as in the Introduction, the *analogon* of memory, and have essentially the same features, and therefore the same "virtues and defects":

> Experience, being but Memory of the consequences of like actions formerly observed, and Counsell but the Speech whereby that experience is made known to another; the Vertues, and Defects of Counsell, are the same with the Vertues, and defects Intellectual: and to the Person of a Common-wealth, his Counsellors serve him in the place of Memory, and Mentall Discourse. (179)

We might suspect, then, that without counselors, the sovereign would be deprived of memory and language, and so less than ever sovereign. But, as we are about to confirm again, the necessary supplement of counsel means that counsel *as such* is suspect to the sovereign by reason of the always-possibly dissimulated dimensions of exhortation and (thereby) rhetoric (including the second-level rhetoric of an absence of rhetoric). For whereas at the level of the individual, memory is essentially memory of experience, whose objects, *qua* natural objects, have no proper *interests*, the position of counselors at the political level again introduces a troubling supplementary, and indeed abyssal, relay into the structure Hobbes is describing:

> But with this resemblance of the Common-wealth, to a natural man, there is one dissimilitude joined, of great importance; which is, that a natural man receiveth his experience, from the natural objects of sense, which work upon him without passion, or interest of their own; whereas they that give Counsell to the Representative person of a Common-wealth, may have, and have often their particular ends, and passions that render their Counsells *always suspected*, and many times unfaithfull. (179; my emphasis)[28]

28. It would be fascinating to read Hobbes's analysis of counsel against the quite brief discussion in Hegel's *Phenomenology*, and especially perhaps the following: "The *being-for-itself*, the *willing* which as willing has not yet been sacri-

This complication of the analogy between counsel and memory, which means that counsel is "always suspected" (because always perhaps really only exhortation or dehortation, as we have seen), determines a further set of consequences. The first is quite simple and even obvious in principle, but really begs the question being raised here, and all Hobbes's italics cannot conceal that fact: "therefore we may set down, for the first condition of a good Counsellour, *That his Ends, and Interest, be not inconsistent with the Ends and Interest of him he Counselleth.*"

The second condition is more interesting, and circles back to the issues of language we have been discussing: this condition also returns to the thought, in the Speech chapter, that metaphor is the abuse attendant on the second use of language ("to Teach and to Counsell"). And this condition confirms our suspicion that for Hobbes reading and the appeal to authorities are always to be linked to that abuse represented by metaphor and, more generally, rhetoric and oratory:

> Secondly, Because the office of a Counsellour, when an action comes into deliberation, is to make manifest the consequences of it, in such manner, as he that is Counselled may be truly and evidently informed; he ought to propound his advise, in such forme of speech, as may make the truth most evidently appear; that is to say, with as firme ratiocination, as significant and proper language, and as briefly, as the evidence will permit. And therefore *rash, and unevident Inferences*; (such as are fetched only from Examples, or authority of Books, and are not arguments of what is good, or evill, but witnesses of fact, or of opinion;) *obscure, confused, and ambiguous Expressions, also all metaphoricall Speeches, tending to the stirring up of Passion* (because such reasoning, and such expressions, are useful onely to deceive, or to lead him we

---

ficed, is the inner isolated spirit of the estates, a spirit which, with respect to its talk about the *common* good, reserves to itself its *particular* common good and is inclined to make all this chatter about the common good into a surrogate for action. The sacrifice of existence which occurs in its service is, to be sure, complete when it has advanced as far as death, but the continual danger of death (when it is surmounted) leaves behind a determinate existence and, as a result, a *particular for-itself* which makes the counsel given about the common good into something ambiguous and suspect, something where the counselor in fact reserves for himself his own opinion and his particular individual will in the face of state-power. The counselor thus relates himself unequally to state-power and, as falling under the determination of the base consciousness, he is always within a stone's throw of rebellion" (§505, trans. Pinkard).

counsel towards other ends than his own) *are repugnant to the Office of a Counsellor.* (179–180)

After two further somewhat anodyne conditions, though perhaps still worth pointing to in light of some recent developments in contemporary democracies (a good counselor should know what he's talking about; in foreign affairs a good counselor should be acquainted with the affairs of the other country involved and the history of treaties between us and them), we are not entirely surprised to see the issue of rhetoric and eloquence return, again connected with the question of assemblies or multitudes and the difficult questions they always pose to Hobbes's model of sovereignty. Counsel may well "always be suspected," as we saw, and suspected of being nothing but exhortation or dehortation (themselves perhaps allowable only in an Assembly), but the last thing the increasingly paranoid sovereign[29] needs is for his counselors to form their own assembly. This prospect generates a memorable passage which unites, with great rhetorical verve and passion on Hobbes's part, the strands of counsel, rhetoric, reading, and variegated multitude, woven into a brilliant cloth in which it is hard not to see a memory of the Platonic *poikilia* and *poikilon* we saw translated as "motley" (a term Hobbes is about to use) and see associated with democracy—a passage that describes (and indeed enacts) what we now have to say is the becoming-seditious of language itself, and tendentially the ruin (the burning down) of the State and the death or downfall of the Sovereign. This is Hobbes's fifth condition for good counsel, and it has four enumerated subpoints, of which here are the first three:

Fifthly, supposing the number of Counsellors equall, a man is better Counselled by hearing them apart, then in an Assembly; and that for many causes. First, in hearing them apart, you have the advice of every man; but in an Assembly many of them deliver their advise with *I*, or *No*, or with their hands, or feet, not moved by their own sense, but by the eloquence of another, or for feare of displeasing some that have spoken, or the whole Assembly, by contradiction; or for feare of appearing duller in apprehension, than those that have applauded the contrary opinion. Secondly, in an Assembly of many, there cannot choose but be some whose interests are contrary to that of the

29. See the poster described in David Foster Wallace's *Infinite Jest* (1996) (New York: Back Bay Books, 2006), 1035n211: "the poster . . . has a careworn large-crowned King sitting on his throne stroking his chin and brooding, with the caption: YES, I'M PARANOID—BUT AM I PARANOID *ENOUGH?*"

Publique; and these their interests make passionate, and Passion eloquent, and Eloquence drawes others into the same advice. For the Passions of men, which asunder are moderate, as the heat of one brand; in Assembly are like many brands, that enflame one another (especially when they blow one another with Orations) to the setting of the Common-wealth on fire, under pretence of Counselling it. Thirdly, in hearing every man apart, one may examine (when there is need) the truth, or probability of his reasons, and of the grounds of the advise he gives, by frequent interruptions, and objections; which cannot be done in an Assembly, where (in every difficult question) a man is rather astonied, and dazled with the variety of discourse upon it, than informed of the course he ought to take. Besides, there cannot be an Assembly of many, called together for advice, wherein there be not some, that have the ambition to be thought eloquent, and also learned in the Politiques; and give not their advice with care of the businesse propounded, but of the applause of their motly orations, made of the divers colored threds, or shreds of Authors; which is an Impertinence at least, that takes away the time of serious Consultation, and in the secret way of counseling apart, is easily avoided. (181)

This bravura passage, which we might be tempted to see as the culmination of a tension between Hobbes's theory of language and his practice of writing, also leaves us wondering about the explicit status of Hobbes's text with respect to these arguments. The more especially as Hobbes, as we have seen more than once, regularly associates the rhetorical dimension of language with a certain practice of reading and quotation, and appeal to authority. Where, we might wonder, does Hobbes position his reader, and what kind of reading does *Leviathan* allow or tolerate?

Two passages, one from the Introduction, and one from the very end of Part II (the strictly political part) of *Leviathan* might be of assistance here. Already in the *Elements of Law*, Hobbes had ended his language chapter with a remark about reading (one that follows a passage we quoted earlier about the degradation of *ratio* into *oratio*) to the effect that given all the problems that have been raised, about being deceived by one's senses, about "how unconstantly names have been settled, and how subject they are to equivocation, and how diversified by passion," how subject people are to paralogism (Hobbes's word),

I may in a manner conclude, that it is impossible to rectify so many errors of any one man, as must needs proceed from those causes, without beginning again from the very first grounds of all our knowledge, sense; and, instead of books, reading over orderly one's own conceptions: in which meaning I take *nosce teipsum* for a precept worthy the reputation it hath gotten. (39)

Hobbes is pleased enough with this redefinition of what "reading" means, and with this interpretation of the famous Delphic inscription, to promote this sequence to a much more prominent position in *Leviathan*, where it occupies the second part of the Introduction. Hobbes now insists much more heavily on this value of reading, and it cannot but strike us in the context of his insistent denigration of the activity of reading as usually understood. The kind of self-reading mentioned in *Elements* is now merely the first level in a hierarchy of three, going from simplest to most difficult.

> There is a saying much usurped of late, That *Wisedome* is acquired, not by reading of *Books*, but of *Men* . . . There is another saying not of late understood, by which they might learn truly to read one another, if they would take the pains; and that is, *Nosce teipsum, Read thy self:* which was not meant, as it is now used, to countenance, either the barbarous state of men in power, towards their inferiors; or to encourage men of low degree, to a sawcie behavior towards their betters; but to Teach us, that for the similitude of the thoughts, and Passions of one man, to the thoughts, and Passions of another, whosoever looketh into himself . . . shall thereby read and know, what are the thoughts, and Passions of all other men, upon the like occasions . . . (10)

Thus far Hobbes thinks we can discern similitude of thoughts (he names thinking, opining, and reasoning) and passions (he names desire, hope and fear) which "are the same in all men." The *objects* of the passions, "which are the things *desired feared, hoped,* &c.," however, are another question, and require a more advanced mode of reading:

> For these the constitution individual, and particular education do so vary, and they are so easie to be kept from our knowledge, that the characters of mans heart, blotted and confounded as they are, with dissembling, lying, counterfeiting and erroneous doctrines, are legible onely to him that searcheth hearts. And though by mens actions wee do discover their designe sometimes; yet to do it without comparing them with our own, and distinguishing all circumstances, by which the case may come to be altered, is to decypher without a key, and be for the most part deceived, by too much trust, or by too much diffidence; as he that reads, is himself a good or evil man. (10)

But this reading of hearts does not go so very far: "let one man read another never so perfectly, it serves him only with his acquaintance, which are but few" (11). The most difficult form of reading is the one embodied in *Leviathan* itself, still presented as an extension of the self-reading from which we began, but an extension to all mankind: *Leviathan* is the record of Hobbes's own reading in this respect, and its validation requires, not, as the body of the text might often have led us to believe, some quasi-mathematical rigor of argument or demonstration—though this is still, as in *Elements of Law*, to be done "orderly"—but a kind of inner matching of the results of Hobbes's self-reading to those of the reader's own self-reading:

> He that is to govern a whole Nation, must read in himself, not this, or that particular man; but Man-kind: which though it be hard to do, harder than to learn any Language or Science; yet, when I have set down my own reading orderly, and perspicuously, the pains left another, will be onely to consider, if he also find not the same in himself. For this kind of Doctrine, admitteth no other Demonstration. (11)

But this implies that the *true* reader of *Leviathan*, its intended addressee, is not merely "the reader," nor the addressee of the book's "Epistle Dedicatory," but indeed the sovereign, "he that is to govern a whole Nation." Reading *Leviathan* is, it turns out, not really for the likes of you and me at all—not only in that Hobbes was presumably not predicting or projecting the kind of reading in which I have been indulging here, but in that reading in general in any normal sense is, as we have seen at some length, an activity so suspect that it too needs to come under sovereign surveillance and control. Hobbes certainly did not go to all the hard labor of producing his "own reading" only to have it questioned and undermined in the way we have attempted here: rather, Hobbes's true reader would be the sovereign himself, who would give his book a duly sovereign reading and recognize the excellence of Hobbes's nonhortative counsel. Of course, we might suspect that the tragedy for Hobbes here is that the sovereign as such, according to the very concept of sovereignty, does not read.[30]

So, in the second passage on reading announced earlier, which ends Part II of the book, Hobbes eases up and pulls back a little from what he has been doing, and allows himself not only to congratulate himself on his achievement, but to dream of the possibility that his book might actually receive the sovereign reading it deserves. In the dream (in the strict sense

---

30. In Derrida's *Beast and Sovereign* seminars, likewise, the sovereign does not speak, any more than the "bruit beasts" to whom, as we already saw in Aristotle, he bears such a resemblance.

of a wish-fulfillment), Hobbes succeeds where Plato did not, and success-fully resolves the relation between theory and practice, the *bios theōrētikos* and the *bios politikos*, by simply bypassing the work of any "interested, or envious Interpreter" (254) and going, as it were, straight to the sovereign and from there directly into political practice. Here is this wistful and rather touching passage:

> And thus farre concerning the Constitution, Nature, and Right of Soveraigns; and concerning the Duty of Subjects, derived from the Principles of Naturall Reason. And now, considering how different this Doctrine is, from the Practise of the greatest part of the world, espe-cially of these Western parts, that have received their Morall learning from *Rome*, and *Athens*; and how much depth of Morall Philosophy is required, in them that have the administration of the Soveraign Power; I am at the point of believing this my labour, as uselesse, as the Common-wealth of *Plato*; For he also is of opinion that it is impossible for the disorders of State, and change of Governments by Civill Warre, ever to be taken away, till Soveraigns be Philosophers. But when I consider again, that the Science of Naturall Justice, is the onely Science necessary for Soveraigns, and their principall Ministers, and that they need not be charged with the Sciences Mathematicall, (as by *Plato* they are,) further, than by good Lawes to encourage men to the study of them; and that neither *Plato*, nor any other Philosopher hitherto, hath put them into order, and sufficiently, or probably proved all the Theoremes of Morall doctrine, that men may learn thereby, both how to govern, and how to obey; I recover some hope, that one time or other, this writing of mine, may fall into the hands of a Soveraign, who will consider it himself, (for it is short, and I think clear,) without the help of any interested, or envious Interpreter, and by the exercise of entire Soveraignty, in protecting the Publique teaching of it, convert this truth of Speculation, into the Utility of Practice. (254)

We are not quite done reading Hobbes in our resolutely nonsovereign way. We have been able to link quite consistently Hobbes's suspicions of the abuses of language, rhetoric and oratory, the reading of books and authori-ties, and the motif of variegated multiplicity or motley, all of which threaten the "exercise of entire Sovereignty." It is not hard to link all these motifs to the question of democracy, which, as we saw at the beginning of our passage through Hobbes, has (at least in *Elements of Law* and *De Cive*) a definite—if vanishing—priority in thinking about how the State can pos-sibly emerge from the putative state of nature preceding it. The immedi-ate collapse of democracy into the "aristocracy of orators" or "monarchy of one orator" sets up a tense situation, to the extent that this becoming-aristocratic or monarchic of democracy is never quite achieved, and the very survival of rhetoric and oratory is the best proof of that. So even in what we assume to be a primarily monarchical view of sovereignty (which is almost inevitably Hobbes's preference, given the weight of the Christianizing tradition we have described), the "assembly" of counselors, with its associated dizzying, fiery, and motley oratorical performances, carries with it as it were a memory of all the disadvantages (or even the impossibility) of truly democratic sovereignty. In the chapter on counsel, which we have been reading, this memory shows up in another extended, and exasperated, metaphor or analogy, nominally still to do with the disadvantage of a multitude of counselors. In this passage, where Hobbes's writing is again arguably on the brink of itself getting out of control in its somewhat incongruous and extended analogy, we begin playfully enough with tennis[31] and end up with something apparently more violent altogether:

> A man that doth his businesse by the help of many and prudent Counsellours, with every one consulting apart in his proper element, does it best, as he that useth able Seconds at Tennis play, placed in their proper stations. He does next best, that useth his own Judgement only; as he that has no Second at all. But he that is carried up and down to his businesse in a framed Counsell, which cannot move but by the plurality of consenting opinions, the execution whereof is commonly (out of envy, or interest) retarded by the part dissenting, does it worst of all, and is like one that is carried to the ball, though by good Players, yet in a Wheele-barrough, or other frame . . . (182)

The players may be good, but the wheelbarrow is heavy; not all the players agree as to the appropriate course of action; the more of them the worse this gets; especially if one or more of them actually wants the main player to lose.

Shifting analogies to archery, perhaps: you might think that many eyes see better than one, but this is not true in this case, unless the final decision be that of one (thereby sovereign) man: the general logic of the monarchic tradition of understanding sovereignty entails monocularity:

> Otherwise, because many eyes see the same thing in divers lines, and are apt to look asquint towards their private benefit; they that desire

---

31. Hobbes is referring to so-called real or more properly royal tennis, known fittingly enough as "the sport of kings," a favorite of Henry VIII, already somewhat in decline in Hobbes's day.

not to misse their marke, though they look about with two eyes, yet
they never ayme but with one. (182)

And now Hobbes makes an unannounced transition from his argument
about many counselors to an argument about democracy itself, and its intrinsic instability, to the point that, here no longer at the prepolitical or
protopolitical moment described in the *Elements of Law*, it cannot sustain
itself as itself:

> And therefore no great Popular Common-wealth [i.e., a democracy]
> was ever kept up; but either by a forraign Enemy that united them; or
> by the reputation of some one eminent Man amongst them; of by the
> secret Counsell of a few; or by the mutual feare of equall factions; and
> not by the open Consultations of the Assembly. (182)

Our diagnosis, which traces the conceptual root of Hobbes's problem back
to Aristotle at least, is apparently quite different from the conclusion
reached by Carl Schmitt. In *The Leviathan in the State Theory of Thomas
Hobbes*, written in 1938,[32] Schmitt also tries to locate a "crack" or "rup-
ture" in Hobbes's theory, and also wants to find it just where sovereignty
is at its height. For Schmitt, the "zenith" of sovereign power is the point at
which it is supposed to "bring about the unity of religion and politics" (55)
by taking power over the question of miracles:

> Critical readers of Chapter 37 of his *Leviathan* must conclude that a
> belief in miracles is invariably a superstition, at best a remnant of
> radical agnosticism which, in this respect, holds certain things as
> possible but none as true. Yet Hobbes, the great decisionist, here
> too accomplished a typically decisive turn: *Auctoritas, non Veritas.*
> Nothing here is true: everything here is command. A miracle is what
> the sovereign state authority commands its subjects to believe is a
> miracle; but also—and here the irony is especially acute—the reverse:
> Miracles cease when the state forbids them. [. . .] In essence, whether
> something is to be considered a miracle is decided by the state in its
> capacity as exemplar of the public reason in contrast to the private
> reason of subjects. Sovereign power has thus achieved its zenith. It is
> God's highest representative on earth. The power of the sovereign as
> the lieutenant of God is not confined to miracles, which are addressed

---

32. Carl Schmitt, *The Leviathan in the State Theory of Thomas Hobbes: Meaning
and Failure of a Political Symbol*, trans. George Schwab and Erna Hilfstein (Chicago: University of Chicago Press, 2008).

at the very end of Chapter 37. The mortal god has power also over miracles as well as confession. (54–55)

This claim of Hobbes's notion of sovereignty to unite the political and the religious is also the focus of Derrida's only reading of Hobbes, in session 2 of the first year of his *Beast and Sovereign* seminar. Drawing on chapters 16 and 18 of *Leviathan*, Derrida (who invokes Schmitt in this immediate context but does not seem to know Schmitt's *Leviathan* book, the French translation of which appeared only in October 2002, after the seminar in question) is interested in the symmetry of Hobbes's exclusion of any Covenant with God on the one hand, and with beasts on the other. In passing, however, he suggests that the apparently "secularized" character of Hobbes's sovereign is compromised on the one hand by the *mimetic* relation the creation of the "artificial man" retains to God's creation, and on the other by the logic of *lieutenance*, whereby the Leviathan is still a mortal *God*, in the place of God:

> The (human) sovereign takes place as place-taking [*lieu-tenant*], he takes place, the place standing in for the absolute sovereign: God. The absoluteness of the human sovereign, his required and declared immortality, remains essentially divine, whatever the substitution, representation or *lieutenance* which institutes it statutorily in this place. (BS I, 86/54)

But just at that "zenith," sovereignty on Schmitt's reading begins to crack and crumble, in that Hobbes makes a distinction between public and private that will lead to the collapse of the Leviathan itself. In Hobbes's state I must obey the sovereign as regards *confession*, but my inner faith remains intact, as part of a private freedom of thought: this enclave of privacy, according to Schmitt, will bring the Leviathan down.

> For scriptural verisimilitude Hobbes invokes a passage from the Bible (Kings II: [5:]17–19), but, above all, he focuses attention on the distinction between inner and outer. ["But what (may some object) if a King, or a Senate, or other Soveraign person forbid us to beleeve in Christ? To this I answer, that such forbidding is of no effect: because Beleef, and Unbeleef never follow mens Commands. Faith is a gift of God, which Man can neither give, nor take away by promise of rewards, or menaces of torture. And if it be further asked, What if wee bee commanded by our lawfull Prince, to say with our tongue, what wee beleeve not; must we obey such command? Profession with the tongue is but an external thing, and no more then any other gesture whereby we signifie our obedience; and wherein a Christian, holding

firmly in his heart the Faith of Christ, hath the same liberty which the Prophet Elisha allowed to Naaman the Syrian. Naaman was converted in his heart to the God of Israel; For he saith (2 Kings 5:17) *Thy servant will henceforth offer neither burnt offering, nor sacrifice unto other Gods but unto the Lord. In this thing the Lord pardon they servant, that when my Master goeth into the house of Rimmon to worship there, and he leaneth on my hand, and I bow my selfe, in the house of Rimmon; when I bow my selfe in the house of Rimmon, the Lord pardon thy servant in this thing. . . .* This we may say, that whatsoever a subject, as Naaman was, is compelled to in obedience to his Soveraign, and doth it not in order to his own mind, but in order to the laws of his country, that action is not his, but his Soveraigns" (pp. 343–4). Later in the same chapter Hobbes reaffirms "it is manifest, that the Scriptures were never made Laws, but by the Soveraign Civill Power." (p. 359)]. Also, his answer to Bishop Bramhall (1682) confirms that he has dealt with this sensitive point by underscoring the importance of absorbing the right of private freedom of thought into the political system. This contained the seed of death that destroyed the mighty leviathan from within and brought about the end of the mortal god. (Schmitt, *The Leviathan . . . 56–57*)

But, Schmitt immediately goes on to claim, this "seed of death" in Hobbes's conceptuality is brought to fruition less by Hobbes himself than by Spinoza, "a liberal Jew" (57)[33]: where Hobbes had "laid the groundwork for separating the internal from the external," "the Jewish philosopher pushed this incipient form to the limit of its development until the opposite was reached and the leviathan's vitality was sapped from within and the life began to drain out of him." (57). The argument is that whereas for Hobbes sovereign power was primary and individual freedom of thought a mere proviso, in Spinoza this order is reversed, and freedom of thought, and essentially *libertas philosophandi* became the primary term: with Spinoza, "Individual freedom of thought is the form-giving principle, the necessities of public peace as well as the right of the sovereign power having been transformed into mere provisos. A small intellectual switch emanating from the nature of Jewish life accomplished, with the most simple logic and in the span of a few years, the decisive turn in the fate of the leviathan." (58) A little later:

---

33. The German text has Spinoza as the *first* liberal Jew. See Tracy B. Strong's foreword to the 2008 translation (xi).

many often opposing movements promoted the importance of this inner freedom: "secret societies and secret orders, Rosicrucians, freemasons, illuminates, mystics and pietists, all kinds of sectarians . . . and, above all, the restless spirit of the Jew," namely Moses Mendelssohn, "endowed with the unerring instinct for the undermining of state power that served to paralyze the alien and to emancipate his own Jewish folk." (60)

Despite Schmitt's underscoring of the Jewish input into what he rapidly presents as a history, his conceptual point is that the very making of a distinction between inner and outer leads to the valorization of the inner, with respect to which the state becomes *merely* external, "already dead from within. Such an earthly god has only the appearance and the *simulacra* of divinity on his side. Nothing divine lets itself be externally enforced" (61). As Schmitt's history progresses, the now merely external, police force of the state loses life and progressively becomes perceived as a bureaucratic and legislative machine (65), again in part because of a Jewish trend: Friedrich Julius Stahl-Jolson "did his work as a Jewish thinker—that is, he did his part in castrating a leviathan that had been full of vitality" (70).

Schmitt's book is very far from the conceptual acuity of his earlier *Political Theology*, and is in many ways a shabby document of blatant antisemitism. It also suffers from a serious logical flaw: Hobbes is implicitly blamed for adopting the mythological figure of the Leviathan, which supposedly brings with it material that Hobbes cannot then control. But as we can now confirm on the basis of our readings, the decisive "crack" that appears at the "zenith" of sovereignty has nothing whatsoever to do with that specifically mythological baggage, and is purely a result of the logic of sovereignty itself as we are teasing it out.

Back in *Leviathan*, the drift from the thematic of multiplicity (motley) in general to the question of democratic sovereignty is constant in Hobbes. In chapter 19, entitled "Of the severall Kinds of COMMON-WEALTH by Institution, and of Succession to the Soveraigne Power," Hobbes considers democracy as one of the only three logically possible forms of commonwealth (in every case the sovereign is the "representative of all and every one of the Multitude" [129]). Here Hobbes enumerates six points of comparison between Monarchy on the one hand, Aristocracy and Democracy—lumped together as involving more than one in the "Person" of the sovereign—on the other, and in spite of some initial appearances, all six comparisons end up in favor of monarchy. The first is a strange argument to the effect that in monarchy there is a coincidence of public and private interests such that corruption through self-interest is highly unlikely, but the second immediately anticipates, often almost verbatim, some of the motifs we picked out from the later chapter on Counsel:

> Secondly, that a Monarch receiveth counsel of whom, when, and where he pleaseth; and consequently may heare the opinion of men versed in the matter about which he deliberates, of what ranks and quality soever, and as long before the time of action and with as much secrecy, as he will. But when a Soveraigne Assembly has need of Counsell, none are admitted but such as have a Right thereto from the beginning; which for the most part are of those who have beene versed more in the acquisition of Wealth than of Knowledge; and are to give their advice in long discourses, which may, and do commonly excite men to action, but not governe them in it. For the *Understanding* is by the flame of the Passions, never enlightened, but dazled: Nor is there any place, or time, wherein an Assemblie can receive Counsell with secrecie, because of their owne Multitude. (131)

Similarly (point 3), assemblies are subject to "Inconstancy from the Number" and more likely than an individual to change their mind from day to day, and (point 4) "a Monarch cannot disagree with himself, out of envy, or interest; but an Assembly may; and that to such a height, as may produce a Civill Warre" (132).

For the final two points of comparison, Hobbes's argumentative strategy changes to a more "playground" variety: in both points 5 and 6 he begins by apparently conceding a disadvantage of Monarchy, but then counters that concession with the claim that in fact things are as bad if not worse in Democracy. So a Monarch, under the sway of flatterers, may dispossess some subject to enrich the flatterer, "which I confesse is a great and inevitable inconvenience,"

> But the same may as well happen, where the Soveraigne Power is in an Assembly: For their power is the same; and they are as subject to evill Counsell, and to be seduced by Orators, as a Monarch by Flatterers . . . (132)

What is more, says Hobbes, whose arguments become less plausible and more arbitrary as he continues, there are many more favorites (and their "Kindred") in an Assembly than flatterers (and their kindred) of a Monarch; and flatterers at least do some good (to their friends) as well as harm (to their enemies):

> But Orators, that is to say, Favourites of Soveraigne Assemblies, though they have great power to hurt, have little to save. For to accuse, requires lesse Eloquence (such is man's Nature) [so the problem is not, apparently, with the expert Orators after all] than to excuse; and condemnation, than absolution more resembles Justice. (132)

So far, then, monarchy is winning out on every count. But it is on the sixth and final point of comparison that Hobbes will encounter the greatest difficulties. Here the underlying problem (to which Hobbes devotes the second part of his chapter), is the general question of succession, and specifically the possibility that in a Monarchy "the Soveraigntie may descend upon an Infant, or one that cannot discerne between Good and Evil." In which case, provision must be made to place the *use* of sovereign power (but not that power itself) in the hands of one or more people—but this is no more inconvenient than the fact of government in general being carried out by one or more people, and so any apparent inconvenience comes not at all from the monarchic form of sovereignty, but from the mere fact of there being any form of sovereign power at all, monarchical or not, subject in general to misdeeds on the part of the subjects. And what is more, says Hobbes, now on the (rather childish) counterattack ("childish yourself"), the democratic form of sovereignty is intrinsically childish or childlike anyway, and (upping the ante) *even more childish* than the child:

> On the other side, there is no great Common-wealth, the Soveraignty whereof is in a great Assembly, which is not, as to consultations of Peace, and Warre, and making of Lawes, in the same condition, as if the Government were in a Child. For as a Child wants the judgement to dissent from counsel given him, and is thereby necessitated to take the advice of them, or him, to whom he is committed: So an Assembly wanteth the liberty, to dissent from the counsell of the major part, be it good, or bad.

And now an almost literally Schmittian argument based on the state of exception:

> And as a Child has need of a Tutor, or Protector, to preserve his person, and Authority: So also (in great Common-wealths,) the Soveraign Assembly, in all great dangers and troubles, have need of *Custodes libertatis*; that is of Dictators, or Protectors of their Authoritie; which are as much as temporary Monarchs; to whom for a time, they may commit the entire exercise of their Power; and have (at the

end of that time) been oftner deprived thereof, than Infant Kings, by
their Protectors, Regents, or any other Tutors. (133)

Despite this outcome (Monarchy 6, Democracy 0, as it were), when Hobbes,
having first clarified with admirable consistency (that he might in this case
have learned from Bodin) some issues about "Elective or Limited Monar-
chies" and the like by specifying in each case where sovereignty actually
lies (the general principle being "he that is not superior, is not supreme;
that is to say not Soveraign" [134]) comes on to the more general issue of
succession, he very grudgingly has to admit what it is hard not to think of
as an advantage to democracy. It seems as first as though Hobbes is trying, with a bold notion of "Artificial Eternity," to assimilate all forms of
government in dealing with the question:

> Of all these Formes of Government, the matter being mortall, so that
> not onely Monarchs, but also whole Assemblies dy, it is necessary for
> the conservation of the peace of men, that as there was order taken
> for an Artifiall Man, so there be order also taken, for an Artificiall
> Eternity of life, without which, men that are governed by an Assembly,
> should return into the condition of Warre in every age; and they that
> are governed by One man, assoon as their Governour dyeth. This
> Artificiall Eternity, is that which men call the Right of *Succession.* (135)

But just a few lines later in the discussion of this issue (complicated enough
in the case of monarchy to have spawned over the preceding centuries the
whole complex doctrine of "The King's Two Bodies"), Hobbes has to recognize that this is not an issue in the case of democracy, where "the whole
Assembly cannot faile, unlesse the Multitude that are to be governed faile
[i.e., unless the state in question simply dissolves back into the state of na-
ture]. And therefore questions of the right of Succession, have in that
forme of Government no place at all" (135).

In Hobbes, then, the memory of that initial protodemocratic moment
from which we began, foregrounded in *Elements of Law* and *De Cive* and
somewhat repressed in *Leviathan*, returns in more or less direct ways in all
of his negotiations of the relation of sovereignty (as we have said, always
tendentially monarchical) to the multitude over which it is to be sovereign
by "representing" that multitude. The systematic convergence in Hobbes
of the motifs of language as co-originary with its own abuses, of the dangers and pitfalls of rhetoric and oratory, of reading and the quotation of
authorities, and of the natural home of those dangers and pitfalls in the
motley democratic assembly, give us the splendid spectacle of a firm (tendentially sovereign) denunciation of those elements in the interests of a true

sovereignty, written in an often spectacular prose that regularly exploits all the elements it thematically denounces. In the tension between those two levels (as Derrida might put it, between what Hobbes *declares* and what he *describes* (more or less in spite of himself), or between what he says he means and what he actually does in his writing, there emerges for us the possibility of what I would tentatively claim to be a democratic *reading* of Hobbes, one that runs counter to his own dream of a sovereign, noninterpretative reading (which would have to be performed by the tendentially monarchical sovereign himself) and in so doing tries to bring out the ways in which sovereignty is, as always, already failing from the start.

CHAPTER 9

Nature, Sovereignty, Government
(Spinoza, Rousseau)

We might further illustrate the complex position of the concept of (proto) democracy, and its tendency to invade the whole conceptual space of political thinking, by looking to Spinoza and Rousseau, as thinkers who certainly registered the force of Hobbes's *Leviathan*.

Spinoza is an especially interesting case here, not at all for the reasons Schmitt suggested and that we mentioned earlier, nor even for the questions of politics and religion for which the *Tractatus Theologico-Politicus* is famous. Indeed it is striking that in the history of the general difficulties philosophy has always had with politics, from which we started out, Spinoza is calmer and more lucid than most, especially in remarks he makes at the beginning of the unfinished *Tractatus Politicus*, which opens on a balanced pair of paragraphs that assess the relation of philosophy and politics, first thinking about politics from the *bios theōrētikos* side of our opening distinction, and then from the *bios politikos* side. First, he is quite caustic about philosophers' attempts at political philosophy, and he identifies a strain of "piety" in political philosophy that we might think survives today in the endemic moralism of political thinking (and that my "politics of politics" doublet attempts to short-circuit or displace):

Philosophers conceive of the passions which harass us as vices into which men fall by their own fault, and, therefore, generally deride, bewail, or blame them, or execrate them, if they wish to seem unusually pious [*qui sanctiores videri volunt*]. And so they think they are doing something wonderful, and reaching the pinnacle of learning, when they are clever enough to bestow manifold praise on such human nature, as is nowhere to be found, and to make verbal attacks on that which, in fact, exists. For they conceive of men, not as they are, but as they themselves would like them to be. Whence it has come to pass that, instead of ethics, they have generally written satire, and that they have never conceived a theory of politics, which could be turned to use, but such as might be taken for a chimera, or might have been formed in Utopia, or in that golden age of the poets when, to be sure, there was least need of it.[1] Accordingly, as in all sciences, which have a useful application, so especially in that of politics, theory is supposed to be at variance with practice [*maxime Politices Theoria ab ipsius Praxi discrepare creditur*]; and no men are esteemed less fit to direct public affairs than theorists or philosophers [*regendae Reipublicae nulli minus idonei aestimantur, quam Theoretici, seu Philosophi*].[2]

And although Spinoza recognizes that politicians are the object of suspicion, he thinks that that suspicion derives from essentially the same source as the piety of the philosophers, now explicitly qualified as theological:

But statesmen [*Politici*], on the other hand, are suspected of plotting against mankind, rather than consulting their interests, and are esteemed more crafty than learned [*potius callidi, quam sapientes*]. No doubt nature has taught them, that vices will exist, while men do. And so, while they study to anticipate human wickedness, and that by arts, which experience and long practice have taught, and which men generally use under the guidance more of fear than of reason, they are thought to be enemies of religion, especially by divines [*Theologis*], who believe that supreme authorities should handle public affairs in accordance with the same rules of piety, as bind a private individual. Yet there can be no doubt, that statesmen have written about politics far more happily [*Politicos multo felicius de rebus Politicis scripsisse*] than

---

1. Although apparently merely polemical here, this motif will communicate with a major theme of Rousseau's political theory, which we might describe with the line "if it could work, we wouldn't need it."

2. Spinoza, *A Theologico-Political Treatise and A Political Treatise*, trans. R. H. M Elwes (Mineola, NY: Dover Publications, 1951), 287.

philosophers. For, as they had experience for their mistress, they
taught nothing that was inconsistent with practice. (287–288)

Spinoza will himself follow neither of these paths but will simply "deduce
from the very condition of human nature, not what is new and unheard of,
but only such things as agree best with practice," because, given the very
canniness or craftiness (*metis*, or *to poikilon*, we are tempted to say) of politicians ("men of the utmost acuteness, or, if you like, of great cunning or
craft" [*viris acutissimis, sive astutis, sive callidis*]). This "very condition of
human nature" will reckon with the passions, not as an object of moralistic or theological disapproval, but (Spinoza refers to his own *Ethics*) as necessary features of humans: religion and reason can restrain the passions,
but

> we showed too, that reason can, indeed, do much to restrain and
> moderate the passions, but we saw at the same time, that the road,
> which reason herself points out, is very steep; so that such as persuade
> themselves, that the multitude or men distracted by politics can ever
> be induced to live according to the bare dictate of reason, must be
> dreaming of the poetic golden age, or of a fable [*saeculum Poëtarum
> aureum, seu fabulam somnient*]. (289)

Let us turn to the more famous *Tractatus Theologico-Politicus*, in chapter 16
of which Spinoza begins by defining natural right as coextensive with the
power of nature, which is the same as the power of God, and by claiming
that "it is the sovereign law of nature that each thing strives to persist in
its own state so far as it can, taking no account of another's circumstances
but only of its own, it follows that each individual thing has a sovereign
right to do this, i.e. (as I said) to exist and behave as it is naturally determined to behave."[3]

Sovereignty in this sense is importantly the same for humans and animals, for the rational and the irrational, the sane and the insane:

> Here we recognize no difference between human beings and other
> individual things of nature, nor between those human beings who are
> endowed with reason and others who do not know true reason, nor
> between fools or lunatics and the sane. For whatever each thing does

3. Spinoza, *Theological-Political Treatise*, ed. Jonathan Israel, trans. Michael Silverthorne and Jonathan Israel (Cambridge: Cambridge University Press, 2007),
195–196 (translation slightly modified to maintain consistency: *summum ius* and *lex
summa* are given here as "sovereign right" and "sovereign law," respectively).

by the laws of its nature, that it does with sovereign right, since it is
acting as it was determined to by nature and can not do otherwise.
Hence as long as people are deemed to live under the government of
nature alone, the person who does not yet know reason or does not yet
have a habit of virtue, lives by the laws of appetite alone with the same
sovereign right as he who directs his life by the laws of reason. That is,
just as a wise man has a sovereign right to do all things that reason
dictates, i.e., [he has] the right of living by the laws of reason, so also
the ignorant or intemperate person possesses the sovereign right to
[do] everything that desire suggests, i.e., he has the right of living by
the laws of appetite. This is precisely what Paul is saying when he
acknowledges that there is no sin before law is established, i.e., as long
as men are considered as living under the government of nature. (196)

The natural law of desire and force is, then, as sovereign as the law of
reason. And there is even reason to think that it is in some important
sense *more sovereign*, more originally sovereign, than the laws of reason,
for as Spinoza goes on to say, reason appears only very late in the story
he is telling, and nothing like so naturally as the nature that gives desire
and force:

> Each person's natural right therefore is determined not by sound
> reason but by desire and power. For it is not the case that all men are
> naturally determined to behave according to the rules and laws of
> reason. On the contrary, all men are born completely ignorant of
> everything and before they can learn the true rationale of living and
> acquire the habit of virtue, a good part of life has elapsed even if they
> have been well brought up, while, in the meantime, they must live and
> conserve themselves so far as they can, by the sole impulse of appetite.
> For nature has given them nothing else, and has denied them the
> power of living on the basis of sound reason, and consequently they
> are no more obliged to live by the laws of a sound mind than a cat is by
> the laws of a lion's nature.[4]

This nonrational natural situation will nonetheless give rise, still naturally,
to a political organization. The argument goes as follows: nature, wherein
man "is only a small part" (*particula*: Elwes translates the same word as

---

4. A page earlier, Spinoza's first example was of fish: "For example, fish are
determined by nature to swim and big fish to eat little ones, and therefore it is by
sovereign natural right that fish have possession of the water and that big fish eat
small fish." The cat-lion example seems less clear, if only because a lion *is* a cat.

"atom" in the corresponding passage of the *Tractatus Politicus*) may well be beyond the grasp of the laws of reason, and therefore our perception of certain elements of nature as "ridiculous, absurd or evil" is merely to do with the narrow limits of our rationality; *nevertheless*, it is better for us to live according to the laws of reason (however limited they may be in the general context of nature). This is so first because reason has the good for its object, but also (rather more convincingly in this context, perhaps) because otherwise men (asserting their natural sovereign right to whatever they desire and can obtain by force) will necessarily, in Hobbesian fashion, live in fear of each other, and so the best way of securing something of their sovereign right is to collaborate and form a collective sovereign. Whence a "compact," motivated, still entirely naturally, by fear: only fear will really, and naturally, maintain the good faith of those who form a society:

> Now we have already shown that natural right is determined solely by each person's power. If, therefore, willingly or unwillingly someone surrenders to another a portion of the power they possess, they necessarily transfer the same amount of their own right to the other person. Likewise, it follows that the person possessing the sovereign power to compel all men by force and restrain them by fear of the supreme penalty [*summi supplicii*] which all men universally fear, has sovereign right over all men. This person will retain this right, though, for only so long as he retains this power of doing whatever he wishes; otherwise his command will be precarious, and no stronger person will be obliged to obey him unless he wishes to do so.
>
> Human society can thus be formed without any alienation of natural right, and the contract can be preserved in its entirety with complete fidelity, only if every person transfers all the power they possess to society, and society alone retains the sovereign natural right over all things, i.e., sovereign power, which all must obey, either of their own free will or through fear of the ultimate punishment. (199–200)

"Without any violation of natural right," and indeed apparently without the kind of break with nature that is needed in Hobbes and other contract theorists, in whom the state (of politics) is instituted by a cut from the "state of nature," to which it constantly threatens to return (Hobbes's "Civill Warre"). When asked by a correspondent about his difference from Hobbes, Spinoza replies tersely, "As regards political theories, the difference which you inquire about between Hobbes and myself, consists in this, that I always preserve natural right intact, and only allot to the chief magistrates in every state a right over their subjects commensurate with the excess of their power over the power of the subjects. This is what always takes place in the state of nature" (Letter L).

This continuity with nature in Spinoza has definite conceptual advantages over the standard social contract thinking that requires, but cannot really think, a clean break with nature at the moment of the contract.[5]

The difficulty of thinking the passage from a state of nature to a political state affects, as we said above, all contract theories. It is perhaps Kant who is most thorough in striving to face those complications. In *Kant on the Frontier*, I laid out the basic difficulty of understanding what Kant presents as an obligation to leave the state of nature behind: if man in the state of nature can hear that obligation, then he must already have left the state of nature behind as a condition of leaving it behind. Let me extend that account a little here before returning to Spinoza.

In the *Rechtslehre*, Kant implicitly recognizes the existence of a right before right, in the state of nature: in §44, having rehearsed the argument whereby "the first decision an individual will be obliged to make, if he does not wish to renounce all concepts of right, will be to adopt the principle that one must abandon the state of nature," Kant goes on to refine the "injustice" of that state as follows:

> The state of nature need not necessarily be a *state of injustice (iniustus)* merely because those who live in it treat one another solely in terms of the amount of power they possess. But it is a *state devoid of justice (status*

5. See Derrida's comments on this structure in Hobbes: "Sovereignty, laws, law and therefore the state are nothing natural and are posited by contract and convention. They are prostheses. If there is a prosthetic structure to the Leviathan as political animal or monster, this is because of its conventional, thetic, contractual structure. The opposition between *physis* and *nomos* (nature and law), as opposition between *physis* and *thesis* (nature and convention, or nature and positing), is here fully and decisively functional. It follows that law, sovereignty, the institution of the state are historical and always provisional, let's say deconstructible, essentially fragile or finite or mortal, even if sovereignty is *posited as immortal*. It is posited as immortal and indivisible precisely because it is mortal and divisible, contract or convention being destined to ensure for it what it does not have, or is not, naturally. So that if sovereignty is, as Hobbes says, the 'Soule of the Common-wealth,' 7, this soul is an artificial, institutional, prosthetic and mortal soul: it lasts only as long as law, sovereignty, and the state are able to *protect* fearful subjects against what is causing them fear" (BS I 71–72/42).

iustitia vacuus), for if a *dispute* over rights (*ius controversum*) occurs in it, there is no competent judge to pronounce legally valid decisions. Anyone may thus use force to impel the others to abandon this state for a state of right. . . . If no-one were willing to recognize any acquisition as rightful, not even provisionally so, before a civil state had been established, the civil state would itself be impossible. For in relation to their form, the laws relating to property contain exactly the same things in a state of nature as they would prescribe in a civil state, in so far as we conceive of this state only in terms of concepts of pure reason. The only difference is that in the second case, the conditions under which the laws are applied (in accordance with distributive justice) are given. Thus if there were not even a *provisional* system of external property in the state of nature, there would not be any rightful duties in it either, so that there could not be any command-ment to abandon it.[6]

Earlier in the same text, in §41, there is a supplementary precision about the relation of the state of nature and the civil state: between the two we now find something Kant calls society or a *status artificialis*, which is still on the side of the state of nature:

Even in a state of nature, there can be legitimate societies (for example conjugal, paternal, domestic groups in general, and many others) concerning which there is no a priori law saying "Thou shalt enter into this condition." On the other hand, it can indeed be said of the juridical state of affairs that all persons ought to enter it if they ever could (even involuntarily) come into a relationship with one another that involves mutual rights.

Kant would say that this difficulty about the founding contract breaking with the state of nature does not make that moment false or even fictional, but rather the object of an Idea of Reason:

This, then, is an *original contract* by means of which a civil and thus completely lawful constitution and commonwealth can alone be established. But we need by no means to assume that this contract (*contractus originarius* or *pactum sociale*), based on a coalition of the wills of all private individuals in a nation to form a common, public will for the purposes of rightful legislation, actually exists as a *fact*, for it

6. *Kant's Political Writings*, ed. Hans Reiss, trans. H. B. Nisbet, 2nd ed. (Cambridge: Cambridge University Press, 1991), 137–138; hereinafter KPW.

cannot possibly be so. Such an assumption would mean that we would first have to prove from history that some nation, whose rights and obligations have been passed down to us, did in fact perform such an act, and handed down some authentic record or legal instrument, orally or in writing, before we could regard ourselves as bound by a pre-existing civil constitution. It is in fact merely an *idea* of reason. . . . ("Theory and Practice," KPW 79)

Kant's rigorous radicalization of contract theory thus both sharpens up and renders hopelessly complex the very oppositions of *physis* and *nomos* or *physis* and *thesis* from which it departs, and can make the Spinozan alternative appear attractive for that reason.

This becoming-confused (or even unintelligible) of the distinction between a state of nature and a state of politics (or right) is also in part what is at stake in Leo Strauss's objections to Carl Schmitt's *Concept of the Political*, whereby Schmitt's insistence on the real possibility of war (the decision as to friend and enemy) as the mark of the political, means that the true political state is in fact the state of nature itself:

> Hobbes understood the *status civilis* in the sense of the specifically modern concept of culture—here let it remain an open question whether, strictly speaking, there is any concept of culture other than the *modern* one—as the *opposite* of the *status naturalis*; the *status civilis* is the presupposition of every culture in the narrow sense (i.e. every nurture of the arts and sciences) and is itself already based on a particular culture, namely, on a disciplining of the human will. We will here disregard Hobbes's view of the relationship between *status naturalis* and culture (in the broadest sense) as an opposition; here we only emphasize the fact that Hobbes describes the *status naturalis* as the *status belli*, simply, although it must be borne in mind that "the nature of war, consisteth *not in actual fighting*; but in the known *disposition* thereto" (*Leviathan* XIII). In Schmitt's terminology this statement means that the *status naturalis* is the genuinely *political* status; for, also according to Schmitt, "the political" is found "*not in fighting itself* . . . but in a behavior that is determined by this real *possibility*" (37). It follows that the political that Schmitt brings to bear as fundamental is the "state of nature" that underlies every culture; Schmitt restores the Hobbesian concept of the state of nature to a place of honor (see 59). Therewith the question about the genus within which the specific difference of the political is to be stipulated has also been answered: the political is a *status* of man;

indeed, the political is *the* status as the "natural," the fundamental and extreme, status of man.[7]

In Spinoza, as in Rousseau (and indeed Hobbes), but without the troublesome discontinuity, as it were, this initial situation is explicitly described as one of *democracy*, just because it "wields all its power as a whole," as Spinoza puts it, and sovereignty is here already both *exceptional* and *absolute*: "the sovereign power is bound by no law and everyone is obliged to obey it in all things" (200). Some strange consequences flow from this: for example, just by ceding all rights to the whole (which they must on pain of "dividing and therefore destroying" sovereign authority), again engaging the "least bad" logic we described earlier,

> compelled as they were by necessity and guided by reason. It follows that unless we wish to be enemies of government and to act against reason, which urges us to defend the government with all our strength, we are obliged to carry out absolutely all the commands of the sovereign power, however absurd they may be. Reason too bids us do so: it is a choice of the lesser of two evils. (200)

So, once the sovereign is constituted politically, it inherits, as it were, the intrinsic potential irrationality or absurdity that we have seen to characterize sovereignty as naturally given; but at this level of the description, it would be irrational to oppose that sovereignty (however absurd or irrational it in fact be itself). The always potential irrationality of the State rationally trumps the possible rationality of the individual: but in any case, Spinoza claims, because sovereignty lasts only so long as the sovereign

---

7. Leo Strauss, "Notes on *The Concept of the Political*," in Heinrich Meier, *Carl Schmitt and Leo Strauss: The Hidden Dialogue*, trans. J. Harvey Lomax (Chicago: University of Chicago Press, 1995), 98–99. On Strauss's construal, this means that Hobbes in fact (though for reasons apparently rather different from those adduced by Schmitt in his later *Leviathan* book) is the true founder of liberalism. In *Politics of Friendship*, Derrida is intrigued by the modality of "real possibility" in Schmitt (PA 105–107), but it would seem that this is essentially a Hegelian modality: in Hegel, too, the state is essentially determined by the real possibility of fighting at its border. See my discussion in *Frontiers: Kant, Hegel, Frege, Wittgenstein* (CreateSpace, 2005), 153–163, on the political writings, and 202–203 for "real possibility" in the passage from contingency to necessity in the *Science of Logic*. See too a very active reading of Hobbes in this regard in Michel Foucault, "*Il faut défendre la société*": *Cours au Collège de France, 1976* (Paris: Gallimard/Seuil, 1997), 78–80.

power in fact *has* sovereign power "it can very rarely happen that sover-
eigns issue totally absurd commands," and this is especially the case in a
democratic state, where—one measures the difference from Hobbes—"it
is almost impossible that the majority of a large assembly would agree on
the same irrational decision" (200–201).

And just this is democracy insofar as it is still at least somewhat natural:

> With this, I think, the fundamentals of the democratic republic are
> made sufficiently clear, this being the form of state I chose to discuss
> first, because it seems to be the most natural and to be that which
> approaches most closely to the freedom nature bestows on every
> person. In a democracy no one transfers their natural right to another
> in such a way that they are not thereafter consulted but rather to the
> majority of the whole society of which they are a part. In this way all
> remain equal as they had been previously, in the state of nature. (202)

Democracy is, then, a kind of degree zero of politics, on the very edge of
the state of nature, the state-of-nature-of-politics, the nature that remains
to haunt politics even as politics is supposed to be the emergence from
nature.[8]

Unlike in Hobbes, however, Spinoza, having laid out this kind of formal account of the possibility of a state naturally grounded in a contract,
draws some less than absolutist consequences about sovereignty. For it
seems to flow from the nature of the naturality in the argument here (the
same nature that means that a cat cannot be made to live as a lion, but also
that humans are less than fully rational, necessarily subject to passions, still
somewhat animal) that the transition from natural right into politics is *essentially* limited. Spinoza says at the beginning of the following chapter
that this means that the theory "in many respects it will always remain
merely theoretical" (208). This ideality leaves an *essential* (and not merely
contingent) role to the less-than-ideal (what I earlier referred to as a kind of
'transcendental exposure'). Spinoza puts it like this: "No one will ever be
able to transfer his power and (consequently) his right to another person

---

8. See, too, the earlier summary discussion in chap. 5, 72–73. In the *Tractatus
Politicus*, 6.4–5, this primacy of democracy is confirmed, and its instability (the
traditional predicate of democracy since Plato) is recognized. Unlike the Platonic
kyklos of regimes, however, in Spinoza this leads to a situation of tension between
the "natural" claim of democracy and the apparent superiority over it of monarchy, which, however, always in fact resolves into a kind of aristocracy.

in such a way that he ceases to be a human being; and there will never be a sovereign power that can dispose of everything just as it pleases" (208).

> If people could be so thoroughly stripped of their natural right that they could undertake nothing in the future without the consent of the holders of sovereign power, then certainly sovereigns could dominate their subjects in the most violent manner. However, I believe no one would accept that. (208–209)

So it seems that, as we saw in a different way in Hobbes and will see in a different way again in Rousseau, the sovereign is never quite or entirely sovereign.

It will be remembered that in Hobbes, and more especially in the work prior to the *Leviathan* itself, democracy (or, as we called it, protodemocracy), occupied a privileged (or at least eccentric) place in the general account of how political organization emerges from the "state of nature": the protodemocratic moment, however fleeting (because of the "aristocracy of orators" argument), is irreducible in Hobbes's account. The difficulty of this transitional moment (endemic to contract theory, as we said earlier) reappears in Rousseau, even as he strives to distinguish his version of the contract from that of Hobbes. Part of the difficulty of Hobbes's position flows from its recognition that the original covenant founding a commonwealth must take place as a multiplicity of covenants between individuals. Hobbes is quite clear about this in the *Elements of Law*:

> In the making of a democracy, there passeth no covenant, between the sovereign and any subject. For while the democracy is a making, there is no sovereign with whom to contract. For it cannot be imagined, that the multitude should contract with itself, or with any one man, or number of men, parcel of itself, to make itself sovereign; nor that a multitude, considered as one aggregate, can give it self anything which before it had not. Seeing then that sovereignty democratical is not conferred by the Covenant of any multitude (which supposeth union and sovereignty already made), it resteth that the same be conferred by the particular Covenants of every several man, that is to say, every man with every man, for and in consideration of the benefit of his own peace and defence, covenanteth to stand to and obey, whatsoever the major part of their whole number, or the major part of such a number of them, as shall be pleased to assemble at a certain time and place, shall determine and command. And this is that which giveth being to a democracy, wherein the sovereign assembly was called of the Greeks by the name of *Demus*, (*id est*, the people), from whence cometh

democracy. So that where, to the supreme and independent court, every man may come that will and give his vote, there the sovereign is called the people. (119)

Rousseau makes two specific interventions in this scene: the first, concentrating on the question of language, makes the difficulty of understanding how this initial covenant is (or these initial covenants are) supposed to happen all but insuperable, by generating what is properly speaking an aporia through which it seems no passage can be made; the second is a kind of magical resolution of that aporia (as memorably pointed out by Louis Althusser) that will have effects throughout Rousseau's political thinking.

The first intervention, then, is to do with language. Given the state of nature as a state of dispersion or scatter (whether that state be determined as an intolerable state of violence, as in Hobbes, or as altogether more appealing, as in Rousseau, is immaterial here), how exactly are the individuals supposed to come to their agreements? Where Hobbes presupposed not only that individuals gathering to covenant possessed language but also a "copious" enough language to allow already for some degree of rhetorical prowess (whence the "aristocracy of orators" argument), Rousseau (perhaps already foreseeing his later, "magical," solution as it will appear in the *Social Contract*), indulges, in the *Discourse on Inequality*, in a long and quite compelling account of the aporetical question of the relative priority of language and social organization. Condillac, Rousseau's explicit reference point here, gave an account of the origin of language (qua "instituted signs") that, as Rousseau points out, presupposes some at least minimal society already established. In depriving himself of that presupposition, Rousseau is able to accumulate difficulties as follows: Given that humans in the state of nature were *ex hypothesi* in a state of scatter, why would they have needed (still less been able) to invent language?[9] If, as is often supposed, languages emerged in the relation of mother to children, that would at best suggest a scatter of languages as great as the scatter of individuals: mothers could not originally teach language to their children (because it does not yet exist); children needing perhaps to invent languages to communicate their needs would each invent their own, "which multiplies Languages by as many as there are individuals who speak them; their roving and vagabond life further

---

9. This scattered state is what allows Althusser, much later, to situate Rousseau as belonging to the tradition of the "materialism of the encounter," in *Ecrits philosophiques et politiques* (Paris: Stock/IMEC, 2004–2005), 1:570–575.

contributes to this multiplication of languages, since it allows no idiom enough time to stabilize."[10]

Let's imagine that we have overcome this difficulty and seen that the invention of language somehow became necessary. It is still inexplicable how it was even possible: "for if Men needed speech in order to learn how to think, they needed even more to know how to think in order to find the art of speech." Even assuming that we can understand the passage from the "cry of nature" to articulated speech (from *phonē* to *logos*, then), it is incomprehensible how mankind could have progressed from particular names to general ideas. And so, concludes Rousseau without concluding,

> I pause after these first steps, and beg my Judges to suspend their Reading here, to consider, in the light of the invention of Physical nouns alone, that is to say in the light of the most easily found part of Language, how far it still has to go before it can express all of men's thoughts, assume a stable form, admit of being spoken in public, and have an influence on Society. . . . As for myself, frightened by the increasing difficulties, and convinced of the almost demonstrated impossibility that Languages could have arisen and been established by purely human means, I leave to anyone who wishes to undertake it the discussion of this difficult Problem: which is the more necessary, an already united Society for the institution of languages, or already invented Languages for the establishment of Society? (151/149)

In the *Social Contract* itself, where Rousseau is not attempting the same kind of anthropological derivation of society and language, and where in fact he supposes that the "state of nature" has, through a long and complex process, reached a situation as intolerable as Hobbes imagines it always was, the issue does not emerge in quite the same way. Here Rousseau simply claims that "the social order" is not natural and must be grounded on convention. Having dismissed arguments that claim that the social order can be grounded on the right of the strongest, the right of slavery or of conquest, Rousseau approaches the "social pact" he will propose by stating that in any case, even if he hadn't refuted those other theories, they would still not have accounted for what is to be accounted for, which is the kind of

---

10. Jean-Jacques Rousseau, *Discours sur l'origine et le fondement de l'inégalité parmi les hommes*, in *Oeuvres complètes*, ed. Bernard Gagnebin and Marcel Raymond (Paris: Gallimard, 1959–1995), 3:147; trans. Victor Gourevich in Rousseau, *The Discourses and Other Early Political Writings* (Cambridge: Cambridge University Press, 1997), 145–146.

bond that resists the forces of scattering through the formation of some One thing over and above the elements of which it is composed:

> There will always be a great difference between subjugating a multitude and ruling a society. That scattered men [*des hommes épars*], of whatever number, be subjugated to a single one, I see nothing there but a master and some slaves, not a people and its chief; it is, if you will, an aggregation, but not an association; there is here neither public good nor body politic. That man, even if he had enslaved half the world, is only a private individual. If this same man happens to perish, his empire after him remains scattered [*épars*] and without a bond, like an oak tree falls apart and collapses into a heap of ashes after the fire has consumed it.[11]

Against Grotius, who thinks a people can give itself to a king, Rousseau objects that this presupposes that the people is already a people when it does so, and the question remains entire as to how that people became a people (rather than a scatter): and unless a prior convention were assumed, whereby at least the principle of majority vote were agreed to (unanimously, according to Rousseau, apparently demanding more than did Hobbes), then Grotius's scenario could not even arise.

The original pact or convention is more than the mere assent to the protodemocratic principle of majority vote, and this is where Rousseau's negotiation of the aporetic passage from the putative state of nature to the political state is quite different from that of Hobbes, and will regularly resort to figures of *instantaneity* and what we might call (following Deleuze and Guattari) "incorporeal transformation,[12]" with perhaps the proviso that in Rousseau's eyes the transformation is not exactly incorporeal, in that it gives rise, precisely, to a "body politic" that did not exist before. The words constituting the contract (which Rousseau, before Kant, admits need never have been formally pronounced, and probably never have been in fact) are these: "Each of us puts his person and his full power in common under the supreme direction of the general will; and in a body we receive

---

11. *Du contrat social*, in *Oeuvres complètes*, 3:359; trans. Victor Gourevich in Rousseau, *The Social Contract and Other Later Political Writings* (Cambridge: Cambridge University Press, 1996), 47.

12. Gilles Deleuze and Félix Guattari, *Capitalisme et schizophrénie: Mille plateaux* (Paris: Editions de Minuit, 1980), 103: "in Rousseau, the passage from the state of nature to the civil state is like a jump on the spot, an incorporeal transformation that takes place at moment Zero" (my translation).

each member as an indivisible part of the whole." And, beginning a new paragraph, *à l'instant*, at once, immediately and instantaneously, the body politic is produced. Unlike in Hobbes, where as we saw each individual has laboriously to contract with every other individual (making an intuitively unmanageably large number of covenants ($n^*(n-1)$)), here Rousseau solves his problem, much to Althusser's indignation,[13] by having each individual contract with the body as a whole (so only n contracts, one per individual: a thousand individuals would make only a thousand contracts, as opposed to the 999,000 that Hobbes's model would require), which body is only brought into existence by the contract itself. In a temporal twist which might be irreducible in any attempt to think this kind of discontinuous passage between nature and convention, and that certainly bears comparison with Derrida's analysis of the American Declaration of Independence, where the "we" making the declaration is produced only by the performance of the declaration itself, in what Derrida calls a "fabulous event,"[14] one of the parties to the contract only comes into being through the enactment of the contract to which it is supposed to be a party. In a magic flash, *à l'instant*, this impossible "act" generates a whole set of entities and relations between them:

> At once, in place of the private person of each contracting party, this act of association produces a moral and collective body made up of as many members as the assembly has voices, and which receives by this same act its unity, its common *self* [*moi*], its life and its will. The public person thus formed by the union of all the others formerly assumed the name *City* and now assumes that of *Republic* or *body politic*, which its

13. Louis Althusser, "Sur le *Contrat social*," *Cahiers pour l'Analyse* 8 (1967): 5–42.

14. Jacques Derrida, "Déclarations d'Indépendance," in *Otobiographies: L'enseignement de Nietzsche et la politique du nom propre* (Paris: Galilée, 1984), 21–23; trans. Tom Keenan and Tom Pepper in Jacques Derrida, *Negotiations: Interventions and Interviews 1971–2001*, ed. Elizabeth Rottenberg (Stanford: Stanford University Press, 2002), 46–54, at 49–50: "The 'we' of the Declaration speaks 'in the name of the people.'/But this people does not exist. It does not exist *before* this declaration, not *as such*. If it gives birth to itself, *qua* free and independent subject, *qua* possible signatory, this can depend only on the act of this signature. The signature invents the signatory. This signatory can authorize itself to sign only once it has got to the end, as it were, of its signature and in a kind of fabulous retroactivity . . . With this fabulous event, with this fable that implies some trace and is in truth possible only through the inadequation to itself of a present, a signature gives itself a name."

members call *State* when it is passive, *Sovereign* when it is active, *Power* when comparing it to similar bodies. As for the associates, they collectively assume the name *people* and individually call themselves *Citizens* as participants in the sovereign authority, and *Subjects* as subjected to the laws of the state. (361–362/50–51)

The advantages bought by this moment of magic are considerable. For example, sovereignty is constituted as inalienably collective (it can never be bestowed unilaterally on one person, as it can in Hobbes), and space is opened for a clear distinction (again not the case in Hobbes) between the sovereign and the government.

In Rousseau, the collective sovereign thus constituted is the source of all political legitimacy, and, as always general will, is necessarily perfect: "The Sovereign, by the very fact that it is, is always everything it ought to be" (363). Yet it suffers from constitutive failings that will dictate the need for a number of supplements that will end up destroying it. Politics will be the process of that inevitable (though somewhat deferrable) destruction that results from the very perfection of the body politic as constituted by the founding contract. Perhaps the principal reason for these failings is the peculiar temporality of the sovereign, which is again a temporality of the instant, but one slightly different from that of the founding contract. For the sovereign exists in a perpetual present moment, as Rousseau stresses more than once. In the chapter entitled "That Sovereignty is Inalienable," for example, he points out that it is possible that the general will of the sovereign might happen to coincide with the particular will of one, but on the one hand that coincidence could not be "durable and constant" (because particular will tends to the particular, precisely), and on the other any attempt to guarantee (or promise) such an agreement would run afoul of the logic of sovereignty—and this is also why, unlike with Hobbes, the people cannot promise to *obey* the sovereign (because the people *are* the sovereign):

The Sovereign may well say, I currently will what a given man wills or at least what he says he wills; but it cannot say: what this man is going to will tomorrow, I too shall will it; since it is absurd for the will to shackle itself for the future, and since no will can consent to anything contrary to the good of the being that wills. If, then, the people promises simply to obey, it dissolves itself by this very act, it loses its quality of being a people; as soon as [*à l'instant que*] there is a master there is no more sovereign, and the body politic is destroyed forthwith. (368–369/57)

This temporal quality, which is a general feature of sovereignty, as Derrida points out twice in *Rogues*,[15] is made even more clearly in some of Rousseau's draft materials for the *Social Contract*. So, in the corresponding chapter of the so-called "Geneva Manuscript," Rousseau writes,

> The general will that must direct the State is not that of a past time, but that of the present moment, and the true character of sovereignty is that there is always agreement of time, place, effect, between the direction of the general will and the use of public force. (3.296)

And, more succinctly still, in a fragment: "Each act of sovereignty, like each instant of its duration is absolute, independent of the preceding instant, and the sovereign never acts because it has willed, but because it wills [now]" (3.485).

This absolute quality of sovereignty in its perpetual first-person plural present makes it in a certain sense helpless, like his majesty the baby, a body politic perhaps, but a body politic—as we shall see—that is a little like what Deleuze and Guattari initially called an "egg," and subsequently, borrowing from Artaud, a "body without organs." Totally absorbed in its pure presence of self-contemplation, self-regard (*bios auto-theōrētikos*, perhaps), the sovereign, we might suspect, is fundamentally mute. This failing in a sovereignty that is in principle perfect dictates a logic that occurs often in Rousseau, and that we might nickname "if it could work we wouldn't need it," such that politics becomes a name for the necessary imperfection of its own best arrangements. In his chapter on the Law, Rousseau says that the social pact has given "existence and life" to the body politic, but only legislation can give it movement and will. Legislation is necessary just because we are no longer in nature, where "what is good and in conformity with order is so by the nature of things and independently of human conventions." But we have somehow, magically as we saw, crossed the dividing line into convention, and another way of stressing the implications of that crossing is to say that "all justice comes from God, he alone is its source; but if we knew how to receive it from so high we should need neither government nor laws" (378/66). This inaccessibility of divine law means that the sovereign must give *itself* the law, the formal perfection of which is

15. "The act of a sovereignty . . . is an event as silent as it is instantaneous, without any temporal breadth" (V 29/10), and "In a way, sovereignty is ahistorical; it is the contract contracted with a history that retracts into the instantaneous event of the deciding exception, an event that is without temporal or historical breadth" (V 144/101).

guaranteed by the fact that it has a general object (the sovereign utterance of the general will always concerns the body politic as such, and never particular individuals). But given that formal perfection, how is the sovereign to proceed? For the sovereign has neither voice to speak nor eyes to see, and this organic deficiency will give rise to the first major supplement that alone will allow the sovereign to be sovereign.

> For how is the sovereign to come up with the law?
>   Will it be by common agreement, by a sudden inspiration? Has the body politic an organ to state its wishes? Who will give it the foresight necessary to form its acts and to publish them in advance, or how will it declare them in time of need? How will a blind multitude, which often does not know what it wants because it rarely knows what is good for it, carry out an undertaking as great, as difficult, as a system of legislation? By itself the people always wills the good, but by itself is does not always see it. The general will is always right [*droite*], but the judgment that guides it is not always enlightened. It must be made to see objects as they are, sometimes as they ought to appear to it. . . .
>   This is what gives birth to the need for a Legislator. (380/68)

The legislator or lawgiver, then, is the first major supplement needed by the sovereign. As I have argued at length elsewhere,[16] the legislator is a priori a foreigner to the state, for otherwise that state would already have within itself the capacity the very lack of which is the premise for the necessity of the legislator. This foreign legislator speaks a language that the people by definition cannot understand (if they could understand the law they would have been able to give it to themselves). And by definition the people cannot be certain that the legislator is in fact the legislator and not merely a charlatan. In order to persuade the people that he really is the legislator, the legislator *always* lies to them by saying that his legislation comes from God (whereas we have seen that *ex hypothesi* we have no such access to divine justice once we are in convention rather than nature). We might add that even if the legislator *were* sent by God, he would be unable to prove the authenticity of that mission: as Rousseau shows mercilessly in a lesser-known text he wrote from exile after the *Social Contract* and *Emile* had been banned and burned, namely the *Letters Written from the Mountain*, there can by definition be no indubitable sign that someone is sent by God, just because it is an essential feature of signs that

---

16. See my *Sententiousness and the Novel* (Cambridge: Cambridge University Press, 1985), 168–171, and *Dudding: Des noms de Rousseau* (Paris: Galilée, 1991).

they can always be forged or counterfeited. (We might add to Rousseau's analysis the additional point that, according to this same logic, even the legislator himself cannot know that he is the legislator and not a charlatan.) The legislator comes in from a radical elsewhere and cannot stay. Once his legislation is done, he must leave again.

In this rather desperate situation Rousseau suggests two proofs that will separate the legislator from the charlatan. The first, the "true miracle that must prove his mission," is the legislator's "great soul." As it is unclear how the legislator can demonstrate that he has a great soul other than by actually legislating and in so doing expose the people to the risk that he is only a charlatan, this true miracle has to play itself out through (second "proof") the success and (especially) the durability of the legislation proposed. This does not of course help the people at the moment the legislator rides in over the hill talking his incomprehensible talk, but might perhaps give some retrospective legitimacy to what, at the moment of legislation itself, is radically undecidable.

> It does not belong to just any man to make the Gods speak, nor to be believed on this score when he announces himself as their interpreter. The great soul of the legislator is the true miracle that must prove his mission. Any man can carve tablets of stone, or buy an oracle, or feign a secret communication with some divinity, or train a bird to speak in his ear, or find other crude ways to impress the people. Someone who can only do that [Rousseau has already conceded that even the true legislator must *also* do that] might even by chance assemble a troop of lunatics, but he will never found an empire, and his extravagant piece of work will soon perish with him. Vain tricks form a passing bond, only wisdom makes it lasting. (384/71)[17]

And Rousseau's two examples of legislation that can retrospectively be judged to have successfully negotiated the irreducible moment of deceit involved in getting any legislation accepted are, quite strikingly, not taken from the strictly political (or at least state-political) domain at all, but are clearly (if in a quite complex way) theological-political:

> The Jewish law which still endures, that of the child of Ishmaël which has ruled half the world for ten centuries, still announce today the great men who dictated them; and while proud philosophy or blind

---

17. Rousseau gives the example of Venice (4.4), where longevity is not in fact proof of the quality of legislation.

party spirit sees in them only lucky impostors, the true politician
admires in their institutions that great and powerful genius that
presides over durable establishments. (384/71–72)

This is nonetheless quite explicitly a *political judgment* on Judaism and Islam, and not a theological one: the appeal to God is still and always part
of the necessary use of trickery to which the legislator must resort, given
the structural impossibility of his being indubitably recognized as the legislator (including his self-recognition).[18] The sovereignty of the sovereign
is in this way radically *exposed*: it cannot even get going, as it were, without
this moment of the legislator, but its chances of thriving on the basis of
that legislation are structurally open to chance, trickery, deceit, and luck—
another figure of the politics of politics.

The sovereign had no voice and no eyes, whence its need for a legislator. It turns out it is also lacking limbs, and notably arms and hands. One
imagines that even if it could survive in the disconnected absolute nows of
its existence and make its endlessly ephemeral general statements about itself that are formally speaking laws, it would be hard to think that the
sovereign was really *being* sovereign in any meaningful political sense unless
it managed to act and get something done. And this dictates the second,
quite different, supplement it will need, namely an executive, the subject
of the third book of the *Social Contract*.[19] Whereas the legislator got in

18. The legislator always might tell himself that his legislation comes from
God, but cannot make that belief available as proof to others: as Wittgenstein
points out memorably in the last of the fragments collected under the title *Zettel*,
"'Gott kanst du nicht mit einem Andern reden hören, sondern nur, wenn du der
Angeredete bist.'—Das ist eine grammatische Bemerkung. ['You cannot hear
God speaking to someone else, but only if you are the addressee.' That is a gram-
matical remark]" (*Zettel* §717). See, too, the use made of this remark by Lyotard in
Le différend, §145.

19. See, too, Giorgio Agamben's comments on the sovereign/executive distinction in Rousseau; *The Kingdom and the Glory: For a Theological Genealogy of
Economy and Government*, trans. Lorenzo Chiesa (Stanford: Stanford University
Press, 2011), 272–277. Agamben wants to denounce the effect on modern political
thought of this distinction as supposedly taken by Rousseau from theological roots
in Malebranche, and to suggest that it is necessary to recognize the primacy of
government over sovereignty (276). See, too, Carl Schmitt, *Dictatorship* (London:
Polity Press, 2013), 88–89 and n23. Agamben may be correct as to some of the explicit claims of Rousseau's texts (the analysis he offers is too rapid to be conclusive),

and out, as it were, at the origin of the State, the executive (or Prince) will stay, and will stay until the bitter end. And as we shall see, again it is Democracy that comes to have a special place in Rousseau's story, both in and of itself as a form of government, and as a new and different avatar of the "protodemocracy" we saw in Hobbes.

Curiously, Rousseau saves his account of how the government can be formed until chapter 17 of that third book, after having defined at length government in general and discussed the different forms it can take. Government is force or action to the sovereign's will; it deals with particulars whereas the sovereign deals in generalities ("the sovereign, all of whose acts can only be laws" [395–396]). If, as we saw earlier, the social contract establishes a circuit whereby the people are both part of the sovereign (and therefore participate in legislation) and part of the State (subject to that same legislation), then the government is supposed to ensure the appropriate circulation of that circuit, the "communication between the State and the Sovereign" supposed to secure the success of this self-legislation or auto-nomy. The government is, in Rousseau's less striking image, like the union of body and soul, and, in his more striking image, like a postal service, "an intermediary body established between the subjects and the Sovereign for their mutual correspondence."

Finally, Rousseau comes in chapter 17 to consider how the government can even be instituted. After firmly demonstrating that this institution cannot take the form of a contract, he describes a complex (and again somewhat magical or fabulous) moment. First, there needs to be a law stating that there is to be a government (*qua* law, this is, then, an act of the sovereign); second, the law has to be applied (executed). This application or execution cannot be a law, because it has to specify particulars and name individuals. So, two acts:

> By the first, the Sovereign enacts that a body of Government of this form or that shall be established; and it is clear that this act is a law.
>
> By the second, the People appoints the chiefs who will be entrusted with the established government. Now since this appointment is a particular act it is not a second law, but merely a consequence of the first and a function of Government.
>
> The difficulty is to understand how there can be an act of Government before the Government exists, and how the People, which is only

---

but even at the level of "declaration" Rousseau, as we shall see, is not shy in suggesting that government always usurps sovereignty.

either Sovereign or subject, can become Prince or Magistrate in certain circumstances. (433/117)

It is easy to see that this is a version of the temporal twist we already saw at the moment of the contract itself, when one of the parties to the contract came about only as a result of the contract to which it was a party. The difference is that now the State is at least minimally up and running, as it were, the basic relation of sovereign to subject that the contract produced allows for a more specific trick, and an almost explicit "incorporeal transformation":

> Here again is revealed one of those astonishing properties of the body politic by which it reconciles apparently contradictory operations. For this one is accomplished by a sudden conversion of Sovereignty into Democracy; so that *without any perceptible change*, and simply by a new relation of all to all, the Citizens having become Magistrates pass from general to particular acts, and from the law to its execution. (433–434/117–118, my emphasis)

This "sudden conversion," and the solution it offers to what otherwise appeared to be an insuperable problem, cannot fail to provoke the thought that democracy would thereby have, not only the kind of temporal or genetic priority among types of regime (as it did also in Hobbes), but also a conceptual advantage, such that it would be in a sense the most obvious or, as in Spinoza, the most natural form for government to take. That this is an awkward issue for Rousseau is shown, perhaps, by the fact that he immediately needs to claim that this astonishing conversion is not merely a "speculative subtlety," but can be observed in practice in for example the British Parliament, a very rare positive reference to the British for Rousseau,[20] and then very rapidly acknowledges that this is

---

20. "The English people thinks it is free; it is greatly mistaken, it is free only during the election of Members of Parliament; as soon as they are elected, it is enslaved, it is nothing. The use it makes of its freedom during the brief moments it has it fully warrants its losing it" (*Oeuvres complètes*, 3:430/114). See, too, in *Emile*, "It is certain that great meat-eaters are in general more cruel and ferocious than other men . . . English barbarism is well-known" (*Oeuvres complètes*, 4:411), and in the "Histoire du précédent écrit" appended to the dialogues *Rousseau juge de Jean-Jacques*, "I accused myself of madness for having confided in an Englishman, a nation personally ill-inclined towards me, of which nation no-one has ever cited any act of justice contrary to its own interest" (*Oeuvres complètes*, 1:983).

indeed an advantage of democracy while implying that most often this passage through democracy will indeed be rapid: not, as in Hobbes, because of any "aristocracy of orators" argument, but out of a positive choice in favor of a different type of government. The chapter ends as follows:

> Such is the advantage proper to Democratic Government that it can be established in fact by a simple act of the general will. After which, this provisional Government remains in office if such is the form adopted, or establishes in the name of the Sovereign the Government prescribed by law, and thus everything is in order. It is not possible to establish Government in any other legitimate manner without renouncing the principles established above. (434/118)

And in fact Rousseau had indeed entertained and dismissed this apparent advantage of Democracy in the earlier chapter dealing with that specific form of government, in which there is no mention of this *general* role of democracy in establishing any legitimate regime at all. Chapter 4 of the third book opens on exactly the "advantage" recognized at the end of chapter 17, generating a striking, almost Blanchotian characterization of democracy:

> He who makes the law knows better than anyone else how it should be executed and interpreted. It would therefore seem that there could be no better constitution than one in which the executive power is joined to the legislative. But this is precisely what makes this Government inadequate in certain respects, for things that ought to be kept distinct are not kept distinct, and the Prince and the Sovereign being but the same person, they form, so to speak, only a Government without Government. (404/90)

And if it is not immediately obvious why certain things "ought to be kept distinct," this will be explained in precisely the "if it could work we wouldn't need it" form of argument we have suggested informs Rousseau's political thinking in general. If we could stay in the state of nature we would, but the best proof that we couldn't is that we haven't; if we could come to a political organization that worked, we wouldn't need political organization in the first place; if we could be prince or legislator, we would govern and legislate rather than writing political theory.[21] Here, if democracy as a form of government could work, we wouldn't need *any* form of government

---

21. From the prologue to Book 1: "I shall be asked whether I am a prince or a legislator to be writing on Politics. I reply that I am not, and that is why I write

at all (not even democracy). The reason that things "ought to be kept distinct" is that if they are not, the properly particular focus of government will impinge on and corrupt the generality of the general will. This is a worse problem than the possibility of government abusing the law for particular ends, because in the former case, "the State being adulterated in its substance, any reform becomes impossible." So fusing the sovereign and the executive (as was the case in chapter 17 as a momentary solution to the general problem of how any government could be formed) would in fact work only if we were able to do without government altogether: "A people which would never misuse Government would not misuse independence either; a people which would always govern well would not need to be governed" (404/91).

This logic has two consequences (or perhaps a single consequence described in two different ways) in the chapter on democracy: (1) "a true Democracy has never existed" (just because, as we already suspected for the perpetual present of the sovereign general will, the people cannot in fact be constantly assembled—again, if they could, we would need no politics), and (2), the famous conclusion of the chapter, "If there were a people of Gods, it would govern itself Democratically. So perfect a Government is not suitable for humans" (406/92).

The interesting point here is perhaps less, *pace* Derrida, the introduction of the motif of plurality in the "people of God*s*," nor even perhaps the (important) point that democracy in Rousseau's description, at least insofar as it *has* had historical instantiations, has no fixed form, no *eidos*—more interesting is the implication that politics in general is rooted in a logic of necessary failure, such that any political organization is, by the very fact of its existence, proof that politics has (already) failed to bring politics to its end (for, remembering our slogan, the end of politics is the end of politics), that the sovereign has been less than sovereign, that the legislator did not produce a perfect system of legislation. Democracy is again the limit or test case for politics, just because democracy is what politics would look like if we did not need it, just as a people of gods would not need politics. This indeed bespeaks a failure of sovereignty to be truly sovereign, not directly because of the introduction of divisibility and plurality into the sovereign figure of the One God (the putatively perfect political regime in Rousseau is already managing a plurality from the moment of the original convention onwards), but because of what Rousseau

---

on Politics. If I were a prince or a legislator, I would not waste my time saying what needs doing; I would do it, or keep silent" (351/41).

describes in a narrative of decline, whereby the government (the second major supplement, then, after the legislator required by the sovereign if it is to have any chance of being sovereign) always and inevitably usurps the sovereign power and leads to the undoing of the state.

The most striking version of this narrative is given, not in the *Social Contract* itself, but in the *Letters Written from the Mountain*, where the example of Rousseau's native Geneva is taken to represent the fate of democracies more generally:

> What has happened to you, Gentlemen, is what happens to all governments similar to yours. First, the Legislative and executive powers that constitute sovereignty are not distinct from it. The Sovereign People wills by itself, and by itself it does what it wants. Soon the inconvenience of this concourse of all in everything forces the Sovereign People to charge some of its members with the execution of its wishes. After having fulfilled their charge and reported on it, these Officers return to the common equality. Soon these charges become frequent, and eventually permanent. Insensibly a body is formed that acts always. A body that acts always cannot report on every act: it only reports on the principal ones; soon it gets to the point of reporting on none. The more active the acting principle, the more it enervates the willing principle. Yesterday's will is assumed to be today's; whereas yesterday's act does not dispense one from acting today. Finally the inaction of the willing power subjects it to the executive power; the latter gradually renders its actions independent, and soon its will: instead of acting for the power that wills, it acts on it. There then remains in the State only an acting power, the executive. The executive power is mere force, and where mere force reigns the State is dissolved. That, Gentlemen, is how all democratic States perish in the end. (815)

But this narrative, exemplarily true of democracies (the form of government that would be best if we needed no government) is in fact *a fortiori* true of nondemocratic forms too. In Rousseau, government of whatever form *always* ends up usurping sovereignty, and although the narrative form he gives to that usurpation is compelling, it seems clear that this is a structural problem, that the usurpation has always already begun, from the moment that the sovereign was bound to give itself a government (even in the government-without-government form of democracy). Back in the *Social Contract*, and even before explaining how government in general can be formed, Rousseau gives a general version of the narrative that in the

Letters he nominally applied only to democracy. The chapter "Of the Abuse of Government and of Its Tendency to Degenerate" opens thus:

> As the particular will acts incessantly against the general will, so the Government makes a continual effort against Sovereignty. The more this effort increases, the more the constitution becomes adulterated, and since there is here no other corporate will to resist the will of the Prince and to balance it out, it must sooner or later happen that the Prince end up oppressing the Sovereign and breaking the Social treaty. That is the inherent and inevitable vice that from the moment the body politic is born relentlessly tends to destroy it, just as old age and death destroy the human body. (421/106)

If politics could work, we would not need it: so politics is from the start this ongoing usurpation of sovereignty. What we might call this negative teleology in Rousseau (politics always goes to wrack and ruin) gives a different reading to our "end of politics is the end of politics" slogan. Here the politics of politics is the only life politics has, and that life is determined by the inevitability of death. We do not need to push very hard at Rousseau's thinking here to say that just this structure of (exemplarily democratic) politics as the standing failure of sovereignty gives access to something we might think of as *politics as such*, in its finitude, removed from any redemptive horizon, and to that extent withdrawn from metaphysical recovery. We might take this insight from Rousseau and reapply it to our earlier puzzlement over the "precarious" place of political philosophy more generally, and to the suspicion that Machiavelli (for whom Rousseau had great admiration) is the standing reminder to philosophy that politics will remain (philosophically speaking) intractable and irredeemable.

A slightly less dramatic way of formulating this in Rousseau is that politics becomes the art of delaying the inevitability of this decline and collapse. On this view, that politics be always already the end of politics, or politics coming to an end, is no more tragic than that individuals live only insofar as they are already dying. Rousseau makes good use of this analogy, which modifies the usual way the "body politic" is understood, in the next chapter, "On the Death of the Body Politic," which opens on an eloquent statement of inevitability and then pivots on a "But . . ." which displaces slightly the analogy and will open onto some further complications:

> Such is the natural and inevitable tendency [i.e., the tendency to degenerate posited by the previous chapter] of the best constituted

Governments. If Sparta and Rome perished, what State can hope to last forever? If we want to form a lasting establishment, let us therefore not dream of making it eternal. To succeed one must not attempt the impossible, nor flatter oneself that the work of men can be endowed with a solidity human affairs do not allow for.

The body politic, just like the human body, begins to die as soon as it is born, and carries within itself the causes of its destruction. But . . . (424/109)

For Rousseau, we cannot intervene in our natural bodily constitution to prolong our life: but the fact that politics is a matter not of nature but of art means that the state can be constituted in such a way as to prolong its lifespan, although not indefinitely. The next three chapters will suggest ways this might be attempted, and Rousseau will return to the issue in the fourth book. In all cases the point is to complicate the narrative of gradual decline by introducing a variety of delaying mechanisms or loops, further supplements beyond the supplement of government itself, supplements to that supplement: and whatever we have seen Rousseau explicitly claiming as to the (perhaps exemplary) impracticability of democracy, we will see that the ghost of (proto)democracy is never far from these mechanisms.

The first mechanism is simply that of the direct assembly of the people. "The Sovereign can act only when the people are assembled" (425/110): and the fact that (or so Rousseau claims), such assemblies were possible and even common in the populous city of ancient Rome and elsewhere proves that this is at least possible. Such assemblies cannot be permanent (as we have seen), but they need to be regular (the sovereign's work is not all done at the beginning, when the laws and form of government are decided) and are themselves prescribed by law. Again, Rousseau is unimpressed by arguments of practicality (here as to the feasibility of assembling the people in states comprising several cities) and more interested in the temporal structure of such assemblies, which temporal structure, as we saw several times previously, has the *à l'instant*, interruptive or suspensive quality here supposed to resist the declining flow of narrative time: "The instant [*à l'instant que*] the People is legitimately assembled as Sovereign body, all Government jurisdiction ceases, the executive power is suspended, and the person of the last Citizen is as sacred and inviolable as that of the first Magistrate, because where the Represented is, there no longer is a Representative" (427–428/112).

This is clearly enough a repetition or commemoration of the original moment at which the government was formed in the "astonishing" moment of democracy that alone allowed legitimate government of whatever form to come about. But here, now that there is a government in place, that government will tend to resist such a repetition, these *"intervalles de suspension"* (428/112) in which the government really is "without government." Such efforts, which play on the citizens' weakness, laziness, and avarice, are part of the government's inevitable usurpatory tendencies, such that "Sovereign authority finally melts away, and most cities fall and perish before their time."

It is crucial to Rousseau that such assemblies be assemblies of the people itself, and not of its supposed deputies or "representatives," the supposed "intermediary power" (*pouvoir moyen*) that is sometimes introduced between the Sovereign and the Government. As we saw, "where the Represented is, there no longer is a Representative," and this is part of the Sovereignty of the Sovereign: "Sovereignty cannot be represented, for the same reason that it cannot be alienated; it consists essentially in the general will, and the will does not admit of being represented: either it is the same or it is different; there is no middle ground." (429/114) This is part (perhaps the core) of a more general suspicion in Rousseau of representation in general,[22] and that gives rise here to a more general diatribe: and leads to a kind of negative mirror-image of the *à l'instant* structure of suspension at the beginning of the previous chapter: "the instant a People gives itself Representatives, it ceases to be free; it ceases to be" (431/115).

But if representatives in general are never a good idea, Rousseau will in a much later chapter give an extremely positive account of the Tribunate as a mechanism whereby the inevitable collapse of sovereignty can be deferred. And here the structure becomes more complex than in the case of simple periodic suspension of government by an assembly of the people, to the point that we might begin to compare the Tribunate to the Pauline *catechon*, the restrainer that holds back the advent of the antichrist and also (thereby) the second coming of the Messiah, and that will reappear later in our discussion of Erik Peterson and Carl Schmitt. The Tribunate may not be representative in the sense Rousseau has excoriated, perhaps not a *"pouvoir moyen,"* but it is nonetheless a *"moyen terme"* (454) that can be introduced between the Sovereign and the Prince, and/or between the Prince and the people, to correct those relationships when they have become adulterated.

22. See Derrida's commentary in *De la grammatologie*, 418–419: one of relatively few passages from the *Social Contract* analyzed in Derrida's book.

This supplementary supplement has some features of the two major supplements we have identified as both making sovereignty possible and
compromising it. For example, the legislator's position "which constitutes
the republic, does not enter into its constitution" (382/69), has "no legislative right" and "an authority which is nothing" (383/70). Similarly, the Tribunate "is not a constitutive part of the City, and must have no share of
the legislative or the executive power" (454/136). This semi-external position, figured in the case of the legislator by the fact of foreignness and arrival from elsewhere, and the (as we saw, deceitful) appeal to "an authority
of another order," that is, God, finds an echo in the fact that the Tribunate's own power, being external to the system it is designed to regulate,
is thereby disproportionate:[23] "No share of the legislative or the executive
power," perhaps, "but precisely because of this its own power is all the
greater; for while it can do nothing, it can prevent everything." And just
as the legislator, deceit notwithstanding, had a quasi-divine status, so the
Tribunate "is more sacred and revered as the defender of the Laws than is
the Prince which executes them [thus far perhaps understandably, but what
follows is a surprise] and than the Sovereign which promulgates them"
(454/137). This potentially terrifying superpower, alongside or even above
the Sovereign itself, designed to delay or inhibit usurpation of sovereignty
by government, is itself tendentially usurpatory, on the way to tyranny, and
apparently necessarily so, because (almost) any power it has is already too
much power:

> A wisely tempered Tribunate is the firmest support of a good constitu
> tion; but if it has even a little too much force it overturns everything:
> As for weakness, it is not in its nature, and so long as it is something, it
> is never less than is necessary.
>
> It degenerates into tyranny when it usurps the executive power, and
> tries to administer the laws which it ought only to protect. (454/137)

And it turns out that in the cases both of Rome and of Sparta (the two examples Rousseau gave to show that even the greatest states cannot hope to
be eternal), it was this (rather than the direct usurpation of sovereignty by

---

23. Compare Derrida's commentary on the "simple movement of a finger"
that in Rousseau's *Essay on the Origin of Languages* tilts the earth on its axis and
gives rise to the differences in climate that have a determining effect on differences of language: "A force that is almost nothing is a force that is almost infinite
once it is rigorously external to the system it sets in motion" (*De la grammatologie*,
363).

government) that was the agent of their downfall—the Ephorate in Sparta was fine so long as Sparta didn't need it (another inflection of our "if it could work we wouldn't need it" logic), but not only failed to delay decline but actually accelerated it once corruption set in, because the Ephors committed crime, but also because they were punished for it; and in Rome "the excessive power the Tribunes had gradually usurped served, with the help of laws that had been made for the sake of freedom, as a safeguard to the Emperors who destroyed freedom" (454/137).

As always, the supplement is as good as it is bad; in this case the intended delaying mechanisms always might speed things up and hasten the very downfall they were designed to defer. Rousseau bravely (and a bit proudly: no one, he says, has tried this before) suggests that this fate of the Tribunate might be held off by a *further* suspensive delay-loop, whereby the Tribunate would not be a permanent body but would have hiatuses of nonexistence, making it harder for it to develop, as it were, a tradition of usurpatory practices.

Rousseau's sovereignty, then, is originarily compromised: the atomistic temporal structure of its always-all-it-ought-to-be perpetual present means that it can be sovereign in any meaningful political sense only by accepting into itself (*L'Un se garde de l'autre*) the supplements of legislator and government, and the further supplementary supplements such as the tribunate, which allow it to "be" sovereign only by compromising the sovereignty they also make possible. This perhaps explains why sovereignty "as such" is not really in fact a political concept, not even a "secularized" one, but a stubbornly theological one. Just as Aristotle's One Best Man or *pambasileus* tended to fall out of the polis into divinity or bestiality, thus marking a kind of limit case of politics, so the sovereign in general enters into politics only at the cost of its sovereignty, and that too is the politics of politics.

CHAPTER 10

Stasiology (Rothaug, Peterson, Schmitt, Gregory of Nazianzus)

During one of the post–World War II Nuremberg trials (often referred to as the "Justices Trial"), Oswald Rothaug, one of sixteen Nazi judges being tried on four counts,[1] was asked by his defense counsel Rudolf Koessl about a phrase he had been known to use:

Q: Now one last question in connection with that group of questions. To characterize your attitude as a whole in the political field as well as in other fields, Ferber quotes a phrase which you frequently used. It deals with the system of ruling according to which only one man is supposed to rule. What did you mean to express by that?

A: It is a well-known Greek quotation. "Uk agathon polykoiranie, heis kyrannos esto, heis basileus," "It is not good that many should rule, one should be ruler, one should be king." The quotation itself is so ageless that it certainly was not applied by me to the present political

---

1. The four counts were (1) conspiracy to commit war crimes and (2) crimes against humanity, (3) commission of those crimes, and (4) membership in criminal organizations.

conditions and not put in any relation with them with the meaning at the present time. It is a saying such as many others which are attributed to me, but never had a serious background nor a serious purpose; but in all cases and certainly also in this one, they were connected somehow with something humorous. But one thing is true—I do not consider this Greek saying as wrong.[2]

I do not know how unusual it might have been for a German prosecutor in the interwar period to have been in the habit of quoting Homer in Greek (perhaps a little inaccurately, though that might simply be an issue with the transcript). Rothaug does not attribute the line to either Homer or Aristotle and presents it rather in its "anthologized" light, as an "ageless" claim the truth of which might be assessed independently of any particular context in which it might be used. Rothaug seems perhaps understandably cagey about any application to the Nazi period (although one might think that "Führer" would be an eminently plausible candidate to translate "koiranos" into German) and keen to put some distance between himself and the import of the line (it is one of many such lines I might use, there was always something humorous about my use of it, I really didn't mean anything special by it). As with all the jurists on trial at Nuremberg, Rothaug is accused of a perversion of legality itself under Nazism, which perversion is diagnosed largely on the basis of Hitler's gradual assumption of ever greater powers of sovereignty—including the description of him not just as sovereign legislator, whose every word was in principle law, but also as sovereign judge, with powers to intervene in individual cases, to the

2. The transcript is retrieved from https://bit.ly/3aowQZR (last accessed March 16, 2019). This part of Rothaug's testimony is not included in the excerpts published in the 1236 page volume *Trials of War Criminals before the Nuernberg Military Tribunals Under Control Council Law No. 10, Nuernberg October 1946–April 1949, Volume III, "The Justice Case"* (Washington, DC: US Government Printing Office, 1951)—the full transcript of the proceedings runs to almost 11,000 pages—nor does it appear in the fictionalized version of the trial in the movie *Judgment at Nuremberg* in which the character Emil Jannings, played by Burt Lancaster, appears to be a composite of Rothaug and his codefendant, the more senior and more eminent jurist Franz Schlegelberger. Rothaug, described in the judgment as "a sadistic and evil man" (*Trials of War Criminals*, 1156) was found guilty under count three (with "no mitigating circumstances; no extenuation" [ibid.]) and sentenced to life imprisonment (ibid., 1201), subsequently reduced to twenty years. He was released on parole in 1956 and died a free man in 1967.

extent of overturning judgments and ordering retrials.[3] The issue of sovereignty then becomes a difficult issue in the Nuremberg Tribunals' own claims to authority to judge German nationals, and opens onto complex questions about international law (and more especially international criminal law) in general, as law that is nowhere promulgated by any sovereign authority at all,[4] whence no doubt the strategy of Chief Prosecutor Telford Taylor in his opening statement, to the effect that

3. "As Eichmann never tired of repeating, 'the words of the Führer have the force of law.'" Giorgio Agamben, *State of Exception*, trans. Kevin Attell (Chicago: University of Chicago Press, 2005), 38. Of course, Hitler also accrued spectacular elements of the "glory" aspect of sovereignty, as explored by Agamben in *The Kingdom and the Glory: For a Theological Genealogy of Economy and Government*, trans. Lorenzo Chiesa (Stanford: Stanford University Press, 2011). Interestingly enough, the narrative of this process given in prosecutor Telford Taylor's opening statement, subsequently echoed in the court's final judgment, highlights the arrogation of clemency—one of the traditional prerogatives of the sovereign—to the Reich, and in the last analysis to Hitler himself, as an initial movement in this direction. See *Trials of War Criminals*, 35–36 and 1007.

4. On all these issues, see the fascinating dissenting opinion by Judge Blair to the judgement of the court, *Trials of War Criminals*, 1178–1199, and especially the following: "these crimes [crimes against peace, war crimes, and crimes against humanity] are not crimes because of the agreement of the four governments [of the occupying Four Powers], but that the governments have scheduled them as coming under the jurisdiction of the Tribunal because they are already crimes by existing law. On any other assumption the court would not be a court of law but a manifestation of power." (1191; Justice Blair is quoting from an article by Lord Chief Justice Wright), and "It may be here again observed that international law is an un-written law. There has never been an international legislative authority. The law of nations is founded upon various international rules and customs, which gradually obtain universal recognition and thus become international law. Likewise the law of war is built upon treaties and upon the usages, customs, and practices of warfare by civilized nations, which gradually obtain universal recognition, and also become established by the general principles of justice as applied by jurists and military courts, tribunals, or commissions" (1193). The delicacy of this situation leads to some almost contradictory statements: so that "although this indictment is brought in the name of the Government of the United States, this case in substance is the people of the world against these men who have committed criminal acts against the community we know as the world. . . . Although this Tribunal is internationally constituted, it is an American court" (105–106).

This case is unusual in that the defendants are charged with crimes committed in the name of the law. These men, together with their deceased or fugitive colleagues, were the embodiment of what passed for justice in the Third Reich.

Most of the defendants have served, at various times, as judges, as state prosecutors, and as officials of the Reich Ministry of Justice. All but one are professional jurists; they are well accustomed to courts and courtrooms, though their present role may be new to them.

But a court is far more than a courtroom; it is a process and a spirit. It is the house of law. This the defendants know, or must have known in times past. I doubt that they ever forgot it. Indeed, the root of the accusation here is that those men, leaders of the German judicial system, consciously and deliberately suppressed the law, engaged in an unholy masquerade of brutish tyranny disguised as justice, and converted the German judicial system to an engine of despotism, conquest, pillage, and slaughter. (31)

And a little later:

In summary, the defendants are charged with judicial murder and other atrocities which they committed by destroying law and justice in Germany, and by then utilizing the emptied forms of legal process for persecution, enslavement, and extermination on a vast scale. It is the purpose of this proceeding to hear these charges and to render judgment according to the evidence under law. (32)

This line of argument, which amounts to asserting that these jurists were not administering anything recognizable as law, attempts to outflank the defense that they were merely applying the law as they were given it to apply:

a "National Socialist system of law" is a preposterous contradiction in terms. It never was an objective of the Third Reich to create any system of law. On the contrary, it was its fundamental purpose to tear down every vestige of law in Germany, and to replace it with a mere bureaucracy which would mete out reward and punishment in accordance with the tyrannical ideology and tactical necessities of the dictatorship. (42)

As it happens, it is Rothaug's defense counsel, Rudolf Koessl, the one who asked about the Homer line, who addresses some of these more general questions in his opening statement. His line of defense essentially relies on the argument that his client was merely applying what were properly constituted legal systems and processes, which should, as such, be *them-selves* protected by the very international law that is being invoked by the prosecution:

> This touches on the legal question, whether official functions resting on the official Reich legislation which, up to this very moment, is covered in international law by the principle of nationality and sover-eignty, functions which were carried out in public, may be conceived as actions of persecution on racial, religious, or political grounds and may be treated as being on the same level as actions which were carried out secretly and without control, and which could be recognized as wrong already by their cruelty and severity by every person concerned as offending against justice and law.
>
> Here, I wish to convince the Court that offenses of the latter kind, if they ever did happen within the legal sphere could and should only be known to the immediate participants but not to persons who held positions like the defendant Rothaug. (155)

The lead defense attorney, Dr. Kubuschok, in his opening statement on behalf of all the defendants, tries to make a more general argument that, far from constituting a radical departure threatening law as such, the Nazi reforms of the juridical system on the one hand respected the essentially codified nature of German (and more broadly continental) law, which cod-ification precluded the gradual processes of the Anglo-American "com-mon law" and meant that change could *only* be sudden:

> The written law is inflexible. New concepts of the law cannot succeed in the administration of justice as is the case in the gradual development of the "common law." The German—as well as the continental—principle of the codified law permits the incorporation of new legal concepts only through sudden changes [*sprunghafte Veraenderungen*][5] of the written law. (108)

And on the other hand, this very schema of "sudden change" of the law due to an intrinsic inflexibility of written law-as-code, was *itself* increas-ingly written into German law itself by the fact that "the weight of legisla-tion shifted in ever increasing measure toward the right of the Reich President to issue emergency decrees" (109). This shift, whereby the sud-denness of sudden change is itself codified, is of course the background to (or is in part encouraged by) Carl Schmitt's famous 1924 definition of sov-

---

5. German terms as supplied in the *Trials of War Criminals* volume.

ereignty which, we might say, both captures something inescapable about the concept of sovereignty itself, and is written into (or out of) a context in which a Hitlerian version of sovereignty can always seem not far away.[6] The inescapable issue that the prosecution is understandably trying to out-flank is one that has been haunting our discussion at least since Bodin (himself of course very favorably referenced by Schmitt in *Political Theology*), namely that the sovereign pronouncement is, as such, undecidably legal and illegal, that it makes *and* breaks the law in its vanishing instant, and that sovereign pronouncement is clearly embodied in the *Führerprinzip*, which is an extreme exacerbation of the principle that *ouk agathon polykoiranie*.

One can imagine that Oswald Rothaug might have encountered our tag-line from Homer while studying ancient Greek as a student, or perhaps when studying the law according to a once-excellent tradition of legal education that the prosecution tries to show was reduced to a travesty under Nazism. But he might also have picked it up, precisely, from an anthology, as an item of proverbial wisdom that might have circulated beyond the lecture-hall. For example, in Georg Büchmann's *Geflügelte Worte: Der Citatenschatz des deutschen Volkes gesammelt und erläutert*, first published long before, in 1864, but "a bestseller that was on hand in every good bourgeois household,"[7] often republished through the second half of the nineteenth century, and subsequently revised and enlarged through the twentieth and even into the twenty-first[8] (I have consulted the nineteenth edition from 1898), the line appears on page 321, with references both to Homer and to Aristotle's quotation at the end of *Metaphysics* Lambda, both in Greek characters, and in the canonical 1793 translation by Johann Heinrich Voss we

---

6. Schmitt also contributed quite directly to political and legal developments in Weimar Germany, notably an essay on "The Dictatorship of the President of the Reich according to Article 48 of the Weimar Constitution," included as an appendix to *Dictatorship: From the Origin of the Modern Concept of Sovereignty to Proletarian Class Struggle*, trans. Michael Hoelzl and Graham Ward (Cambridge: Polity Press, 2014). See, too, Jeffrey Seitzer and Christopher Thornhill's helpful and abundantly referenced "Introduction" to Schmitt's *Constitutional Theory*, trans. Jeffrey Seitzer (Durham, NC: Duke University Press, 2008).

7. See the German Wikipedia article "Geflügelte Worte," https://bit.ly /2PhsAgP (last accessed March 16, 2019).

8. See, for example, Georg Büchmann, *Der große Büchmann: Geflügelte Worte*, ed. Jürgen Bolz and Claudia Krader (Munich: Knaur, 2003).

saw used by Werner Jaeger: "Niemals frommt Vielherrschaft im Volk; nur einer sei Herrscher, Einer König allein."[9]

Whatever the source of Rothaug's knowledge of our Homeric tagline, he would probably have learned it at broadly the same time as his near-contemporary, the Catholic theologian Erik Peterson,[10] whose famous tractate "Monotheism as a Political Problem," originally published in Leipzig in 1935,[11] quotes (though misattributes) our line at its very opening and gives learned references to its having been quoted by several of the ancient authors we have discussed.[12] Peterson's piece is perhaps most famous (outside theological circles, at least) for its parting shot at Carl Schmitt's famous claim in *Political Theology* that "all significant concepts of the modern theory of the state are secularized theological concepts,"[13] and for having provoked at a distance of several decades Schmitt's long and complex reply published as *Political Theology II*. This exchange is also discussed at some length by Gorgio Agamben in *The Kingdom and the Glory*, who, however, somewhat forecloses the issue by quite rapidly—though certainly not entirely inaccurately—writing off to anti-Semitism Peterson's arguments about the Pauline *katechon* or restrainer, interpreted by Peterson as being constituted by the refusal of the Jews to accept Jesus as the Messiah, thus indirectly giving rise to the institution of the Church.[14]

9. Like Derrida and others, Büchmann wrongly implies that Aristotle includes the *heis basileus* in his quotation.

10. Peterson was born in 1890, Rothaug in 1897.

11. In Erik Peterson, *Theological Tractates*, ed. and trans. Michael J. Hollerich (Stanford: Stanford University Press, 2011), 68–105. I have consulted the German text in Peterson's *Ausgewählte Schriften* (Würzburg: Echter Verlag, 1994), 1:23–81.

12. Peterson is the source for some of Zeegers-Vander Vorst's references. Given Peterson's quite extravagant erudition and depth of scholarly reference (the editor and translator of the *Theological Tractates* refers to "the near-legendary collection of citation cards that in [Peterson's] biographer's estimate had swollen to the hundreds of thousands by the time he died" (*Theological Tractates*, xiv), and the notes to "Monotheism As a Political Problem" rival and even exceed the body of the text in length), it is striking that he misattributes our tagline to Agamemnon (who really is the one king designated as such by "the son of crooked-minded Cronos"), rather than to Odysseus.

13. Carl Schmitt, *Political Theology: Four Chapters on the Concept of Sovereignty*, trans. George Schwab (Chicago: University of Chicago Press, 1985), 36.

14. Peterson's argument is definitely anti-Judaic. Unlike Schmitt, however, Peterson was never a Nazi and, to my knowledge, not more anti-Semitic than is implied in general by his view of the existence of the Catholic Church: see the

One thing that is striking in Peterson's essay, beyond or before the confidence with which in the preamble he can assert that "for Christians, political involvement [*politisches Handeln*] can never take place except under the presumption of faith in the triune God" (68/24), is that politics *always* precedes and determines metaphysics: "the ultimate formulation of the unity of a metaphysical construction of the world [*Weltbildes*, world-picture] is always co- and pre-determined by a decision [*Entscheidung*] for a particular political conception of unity [*für eine der politischen Einheits-Möglichkeiten immer mit- und vor-bestimmt ist—* literally, by one of the political unity-possibilities]" (71/27): a little later he will specify that in the case of Jewish monotheism, "the decision even in the metaphysical world seems to have been arrived at from a political perspective" (74/30). In the case he is pursuing, Peterson finds, especially in Philo Judaeus, a logic that we might almost see foreshadowing the "onto-theology of national-humanism" diagnosed by Derrida at the beginning of a seminar on philosophical nationality and nationalism,[15] whereby the correlation of the One God with the One (chosen) people

---

remark by Jacob Taubes in *To Carl Schmitt: Letters and Reflections*, trans. Keith Tribe (New York: Columbia University Press, 2013), 37–38: "Erik Peterson . . . formulated it as follows: 'The Church exists only on the assumption that the Jews, as God's chosen people, do not believe in the Lord.' Only then and for that reason does the Church exist. . . . The Church is anti-Judaic, anti-Semitic." For a quite detailed discussion of the exchange between Peterson and Schmitt (and indeed Taubes), including their respective readings of Gregory of Nazianzus, to which we turn shortly (and indeed interesting discussions of a number of other texts and authors discussed in this book), see Roberto Esposito, *Two: The Machine of Political Theology and the Place of Thought*, trans. Zakiya Hanafi (New York: Fordham University Press, 2015), which pursues a quite different (Spinoza-Schelling-Bergson-Deleuze) line through the history of political theology. Esposito never mentions or cites Derrida in his book, but he finds a more subtle way of acknowledging Derrida's importance for his project by appealing repeatedly to the concept of deconstruction, notably ascribing a "powerful deconstructive charge" to Deleuze (14), but using the term liberally to describe the work of any number of other thinkers too: see 8 (Hegel), 13 (Nietzsche), 25 (Heidegger), 33 (Weber), 70 (Assmann), 82 (Esposito himself), 109 (Hobbes), 128 (Hegel), 152, 153, 157 (Giordano Bruno), 158, 161, 166 (Averroes), 178 (Nietzsche), 184, 186, 187 (Bergson), and 195 and 197 (Deleuze).

15. Jacques Derrida, "Onto-Theology of National-Humanism (Prolegomena to a Hypothesis)," trans. Geoffrey Bennington, *Oxford Literary Review* 14 (1992): 3–23.

then extends to the entirety of humanity and of the universe: "the political-theological results of this transformation of Jewish monotheism into a cosmic 'monarchy' are obvious: they perforce make the Jewish people priests for 'the whole human race [*das gesamte Menschengeschlecht*]'" (73/29).[16] But the reader already gets a sense that Peterson is himself driven in his interpretations here by a "decision" that we must assume is itself, by his own lights, "political": for it turns out that Philo, whose work at this point is being used to provide the basic evidence for the metaphysical construal of monotheism as divine monarchy, should really support some rather different metaphysical model, given that he is, as we saw earlier and as Peterson concedes, "a passionate friend of democratic ideals" (75/31), and given Peterson's general claim that it is a political decision that determines metaphysical commitments. In flat contradiction of his initial claims, Peterson says simply that "it is clear that Jewish religious faith kept [Philo] [*verbot*: forbade him] in this context from speaking of a metaphysical, divine democracy" (75/31).[17] And just a little later this inconsistency is repeated when we learn that "it thus becomes clear that, while it was indeed possible on the basis of paganism to speak of a divine monarchy . . . this could not be done from the presuppositions of the Jewish concept of God and of creation" (75/31). And it is in the wake of this inconsistency that Peterson comes to Philo's quotation of the line from Homer as quoted by Aristotle, that we read on its own terms earlier. Again in a strange and tortuous sequence, Peterson wants to say that Philo—who we have just learned could not have found the model for divine monarchy

16. Peterson inserts a footnote here (already number 28 out of the 168 that punctuate his text) and quite mildly suggests that this point of view "appears to me to be contested by Saint Paul in Romans 2:19." In that verse, Paul is commenting sarcastically to a Jewish addressee "[Thou] art confident that thou thyself art a guide of the blind, a light of them that are in darkness," as part of a sequence (vv. 28–29) that leads up to the famous "For he is not a Jew, which is one outwardly; neither is that circumcision which is outward in the flesh: But he is a Jew, which is one inwardly; and circumcision is that of the heart, in the spirit, and not in the letter; whose praise is not of men, but of God."

17. In support of the claim about Philo's position on democracy, Peterson inserts an unhelpful footnote that reads simply "Recall the meaning of the doctrine of *isotēs* (equality) for Philo." But in fact it is not hard to find explicitly prodemocratic passages in Philo, as we saw earlier. Schmitt invokes this passage in *Political Theology II* less to point out the "flat contradiction" we just identified and more to point out that Peterson's more generally avoiding consideration of democracy in this context is dogmatic and unargued (72).

directly in Jewish theology, but who was nonetheless driven by his Jewish faith into conceiving of the world as a divine monarchy (rather than as a democracy, as Philo's politics should by Peterson's own lights have dictated)—must thereby have derived his conception of the divine monarchy from other, Greek and probably Peripatetic sources, as evidenced precisely by his quoting of the Homer line exactly as it appears in Aristotle: but his quoting of this line does *not* imply his taking a Homeric view of kingship at all. That Philo is working "with a Peripatetic model [*mit peripatetischen Ideal*]"

> is shown by the fact that Philo, in *De confusione linguarum* . . . cites the Iliad verse, *ouk agathon polykoiraniē, heis koiranos estō*, exactly as at the end of the twelfth book of Aristotle's *Metaphysics*. Philo says that the verse can be used of God and the world with at least as much right as of the state and human beings, for there is "One ruler and leader and king, for whom alone it is permitted to control and to administer the universe" (*heis archon kai hēgemōn kai basileus, hōipryntaneuein kai dioikein monoi themis ta sympanta*). The formulation shows that the concept of Homeric kingship has no longer found linguistic expression here [*nicht eigentlich mehr einen sprachlichen Ausdrück gefunden hat*]; rather, the title of king stands somewhat artificially alongside that of the official titulature of the Greek polis, which has been transferred to God. (76/32)

But just how "awkward" the juxtaposition of the terms *archon*, *hēgemōn*, and *basileus* is supposed to be is not at all clear: Peterson seems simply to forget that the term "*basileus*" appears in the Homeric quotation immediately after the words quoted by Aristotle, and, as we saw, *hēgemōn* appears regularly in the *Iliad*, so it hardly seems justified to claim that the title of king stands awkwardly here at all, unless a prior interpretative decision has again led Peterson to emphasize the paramount importance of the non-Homeric term *archon* (indeed a political title in Athens, but not at all limited to that reference).[18] Peterson then uses this claimed importance of the "titular" *archon* to assimilate Philo's view to the Stoic picture of the world as a *polis*, leading to the all but arbitrary claim (assuming it is even entirely comprehensible) that "the Peripatetic material has determined the choice of the Iliad verse and the elaboration of the image—while by contrast the transfer of

18. See, for example, Aeschylus, *Seven Against Thebes*, l. 674, where the term has a quite generic sense of "leader" or "commander." Homer does use the form *archos* at *Iliad* 1.144.

the official titulature of the polis to God has the affective flavor more of
'respect' (*time*) than of a conceptual statement [*einer begrifflichen Aussage*]"
(76/32–33).

Peterson's claim that metaphysical positions emerge from political
choices seems on firmer ground in his discussion of a perceived convergence between the expansion of the Roman Empire at the expense of
nation-states starting under Caesar Augustus, and the spread of Christianity made easier by the peace and unification of that Empire, such that
"monotheism is the metaphysical corollary of the Roman Empire which
dissolves nationalities [*Zum Imperium Romanum, das die Nationalitäten au-
flöst, gehört metaphysisch der Monotheismus*]" (94/50). Eusebius of Caesarea
(writing a little later under the Emperor Constantine) is Peterson's best
example here:

> The cessation of national sovereignty is documented with historical
> dates, but in this historical demonstration, which appears as a fulfil-
> ment of Old Testament prophecies, a choice is at the same time made
> politically for the Roman Empire. National sovereignty is allied
> intimately with polytheism, with the effect that the Roman Empire is
> then pressed into service in the struggle against polytheism. . . . The
> three concepts: Roman Empire, peace, and monotheism, are thus
> inextricably linked with one another. But now a fourth impetus
> intrudes: the monarchy of the Roman Emperor. The *one* monarch on
> earth—and for Eusebius that can only be Constantine—corresponds
> to the *one* divine monarch in heaven. Despite the influence of ancient
> philosophy and rhetoric on Eusebius, there should be no mistake that
> the whole conception [*Gesamtkonzeption*] linking empire, peace,
> monotheism, and monarchy consists of a unity fashioned by Chris-
> tians. (96/51)

It is this unity (tendentially heretical in its proximity to Arianism) that then
enters into conflict with what Peterson affirms to be the true Trinitarian
doctrine of Christianity. The whole history as he has told it, whereby political choices dictate metaphysical positions, leads to the salutary dissolution of that very link between the political and the metaphysical-theological;
that in turn frees Christianity from its bondage to the Empire and releases
it into a higher truth that is, supposedly, no longer politically "chosen" at
all. Only Judaic monotheism and pagan monarchism are in fact possible
objects of a "political theology." In this way, Christianity is divided into a
true form quite different from the politically motivated forms Peterson has
spent his immense erudition tracking ("a fundamental break was made with

every 'political theology' that misuses the Christian proclamation for the justification of a political situation" [104/59]), and also, by the same token, Christianity is elevated to a plane quite beyond the reach of Judaism and paganism, which for their part line up together with any political theology at all. On which basis Peterson can exit his text on a reference to "the mystery of the Trinity" (which it is not the task of his essay to expound as such), and a final famous footnote (168), which, decades later, will provoke Carl Schmitt's long reply: "To my knowledge, the concept of 'political theology' was introduced into the literature by Carl Schmitt, *Politische Theologie* (Munich 1922). His brief arguments at the time were not systematic. Here we have tried to show by a concrete example the theological impossibility of a 'political theology'" (233–234/81).

The detail of Schmitt's complex and quite crabby reply need not detain us at length, though it might be hard to disagree fundamentally with his diagnosis of "the real weakness of Peterson's treatise, its feeble structure, the inconsistency between the evidence presented and the conclusion" (56). Schmitt's real objection is that for Peterson the supposedly true theology of trinitarian Christianity allows him to position politics as such, and political theology more specifically, entirely on the side of the Jews and the Gentiles, and to withdraw Christianity thus understood from any historical or political specificity:

> Peterson's argument revolves around a distinction between the purely theological and the impurely political, in an abstract and absolute disjunction which enables him to circumvent the mixed nature of the spiritual-secular combination of any specifically historical event. (93)

It is this very gesture that then allows Schmitt to suggest that Peterson's concluding announcement that political theology is *theologically* undone is inconsistent:

> How should a theology, which explicitly separates itself from politics, be able *to put an end*, theologically, [to][19] either political authority or a political claim? If *the theological* and *the political* are two substantially

---

19. The text as given in the translation seems to require this insertion. The German sentence reads "Wie will eine Theologie, die sich von der Politik entschieden absetzt, eine politische Größe oder einen politischen Anspruch theologisch *erledigen*." Carl Schmitt, *Politische Theologie II: Die Legende von der Erledigung jeder Politischen Theologie*, 6th ed. (Berlin: Duncker und Humblot, 2017), 82. The verb translated as "put an end [to]," corresponds to the noun *Erledigung* in the book's subtitle, which the English translators discuss in their Introduction: "'Erledigung,'

separate spheres—*toto caelo* [completely] different, then a *political*
question can only be dealt with *politically*. The theologian can
reasonably declare the closure of issues of political significance only
by establishing himself as a political voice which makes political
claims. Whenever he gives a theological answer to a political
question, either he simply ignores the world and the sphere of the
political or he attempts to reserve the right to impact directly or
indirectly on the sphere of the political. . . . The statement "political
monotheism is theologically brought to an end" implies the theologian's claim to the right of making decisions in the political sphere
too, and his demand for authority over the political power. This claim
becomes politically more intense along with the degree to which
theological authority claims to supersede political power [*je höher die
theologische Autorität über der politischen Macht zu stehen beansprucht*;
more literally, "the higher the theological authority claims to be
above political power"]. (113)

In the wake of this reproach, Schmitt is able to make what amounts to a
counterstrike in the other direction, as it were, no longer simply pointing
out that there is an inconsistency in Peterson's claim to be above politics
and yet to be able to resolve a political issue theologically, but looking for
a political motif right in theology, and more especially in the very theology (the Christian theology of the trinity) that Peterson thought allowed
him his resounding conclusion. This happens in a "Postscript" to *Political
Theology II*, in which Schmitt is primarily focused no longer on Peterson
at all, but on Hans Blumenberg's celebrated and influential 1966 volume
Die Legitimität der Neuzeit, which, according to Schmitt at least, attempts
"to negate *scientifically* any political theology" (117).[20] But after discussion
of Blumenberg and the interesting claim that Blumenberg has confused
legitimacy with mere legality,[21] Schmitt returns to Peterson and makes a

---

in this context, means both the elimination of a person and the bringing to an
end of a discussion by a conclusive argument" (28).

   20. Hans Blumenberg, *The Legitimacy of the Modern Age*, trans. Robert M.
Wallace (Cambridge, MA: MIT Press, 1983). The translation is of the second,
revised, edition of Blumenberg, from 1973–76, which includes a much expanded
discussion of Schmitt and, saliently, a response to the criticisms advanced in *Political Theology II* (89–102).

   21. As previously explored by Schmitt in *Legality and Legitimacy*, trans. Jeffrey Seitzer (Durham, NC: Duke University Press, 2004).

startling claim on the basis of a quotation from Gregory of Nazianzus, as referred to by Peterson himself in conclusion to his argument.

Here first is Peterson, summarizing Gregory in the body of his text:

> Even after the Arian controversies, people did not stop talking about the divine Monarchy [as usual, Peterson gives some learned references in a note], but the phrase loses its political-theological character alongside the orthodox dogma. Gregory of Nazianzus gave it its ultimate theological depth when he declared, in his *Third Theological Oration* [here Peterson inserts a note with a lengthy quotation in Greek, untranslated in the German edition, to which we shall return in a moment], that there were three opinions about God: anarchy, polyarchy, and monarchy. The first two assumptions unleashed disorder and revolt in God, and ultimately dissolution. Christians, on the other hand, confessed the Monarchy of God. To be sure, not the Monarchy of a single person in the godhead, for this bore the seed of schism within itself, but the Monarchy of the triune God. This conception of unity had no correspondence in the created order. With such arguments, monotheism is laid to rest as a political problem. (103)

The crucial difference that Peterson is claiming brings all Christian political theology to an end is the sentence he here summarized as, "To be sure, not the Monarchy of a single person in the godhead, for this bore the seed of schism within itself, but the Monarchy of the triune God [*Freilich nicht zur Monarchie einer einzigen Person in der Gottheit, denn diese trage den Keim des Zwiespaltes in sich, sondern zu einer solche des dreieinigen Gottes*]." This notion that the One bears the seed of splitting into two, or of dichotomy, obviously cannot fail to be of interest to us. In Gregory's text itself, this moment is given a more complex presentation: here is the complete passage Peterson gives only in Greek in his note, as translated for the English reader of the *Theological Tractates*:

> There are three predominant opinions about God: anarchy, polyarchy, and monarchy. The first two were the playthings of the Greeks, and let them play their games with them. The anarchic principle is disordered and the polyarchic principle is subversive, hence both anarchic and disordered. Both of them tend to the same end, disorder, which is dissolution, for disorder is preparation for dissolution. But with us it is monarchy that is honored. A monarchy, however, that is not limited to one person, for a single person can produce [divisive] plurality if he rebels against himself. We honor a monarchy that is constituted by a natural equality of honor, a harmony of mind, an identity of movement, and a

convergence of its elements toward unity, something that is impossible
for created nature. (231n164)

Let us take the time to compare this with a different translation:

> The three most ancient opinions concerning God are Anarchia,
> Polyarchia, and Monarchia. The first two are the sport of the children
> of Hellas, and may they continue to be so. For Anarchy is a thing
> without order; and the Rule of Many is factious, and thus anarchical,
> and thus disorderly. For both these tend to the same thing, namely
> disorder; and this to dissolution, for disorder is the first step to
> dissolution.
>
> But Monarchy is that which we hold in honour. It is, however, a
> Monarchy that is not limited to one Person, for it is possible for Unity
> if at variance with itself to come into a condition of plurality; but one
> which is made of an equality of Nature and a Union of mind, and an
> identity of motion, and a convergence of its elements to unity—a thing
> which is impossible to the created nature—so that though numerically
> distinct there is no severance of Essence.[22]

Note first the quite rich and rigorous vocabulary used in the dismissal of
Anarchy and Polyarchy: Gregory is not quoting Homer for authority and
is not content just to say "not good" when it comes to polyarchy. The Greek

---

22. Trans. Charles Gordon Brown and James Edward Swallow in *Select Orations of Saint Gregory Nazianzen*, in *A Select Library of Nicene and Post-Nicene
Fathers of the Christian Church*, ed. Henry Wace and Philip Schaff (Oxford: James
Parker and Company, 1894), 7:301. Given the manifest difficulties here, it is perhaps worth adding a third version, this one by Stephen Reynolds: "The three
most ancient opinions concerning God are Anarchy, Polyarchy, and Monarchy.
The first two are the sport of the children of the Greeks, and may they continue
to be so. For Anarchy is, in effect, pure disorder. Polyarchy is a state of discord,
and thus anarchy, and thus disorder. For both these tend to the same thing,
namely disorder—and disorder leads to disintegration, for disorder is the prelude
to disintegration./It is Monarchy that we hold in honour—but not a Monarchy
that is contained in one single person. For it is possible for this one person, if at
variance with itself, to become a plurality of persons. But it is a plurality which
consists of an equality of nature, a unanimity of will, and an identity of action,
and which converges back into the One from which they come—a thing unheard
of among created natures." See https://bit.ly/3bZQcAs (last accessed April 25,
2019). Reynolds has a helpful note pointing out that this is the first time that
Gregory uses the term *prosopon*, person, originally in the sense of a theatrical
mask, to talk of God.

text here makes careful use of repetition and gradation to reduce polyarchy to anarchy and its "disorder" (*atakton*), which leads to dissolution (*lusis*). Polyarchy *is* anarchy in that it is, using a word the root of which that will become important in the exchange between Peterson and Schmitt, *stasiōdes*, "factious" or "subversive": "*to te gar anarchon atakton. to te polyarchon stasiōdes, kai outos anarchon, kais outōs atakton. eis tauton gar amphotera pherei, tēn ataxian, e de eis lusin. Ataxia gar melete luseōs*": "For Anarchy is a thing without order; and the Rule of Many is factious, and thus anarchical, and thus disorderly. For both these tend to the same thing, namely disorder; and this to dissolution, for disorder is the first step to dissolution." A little like a Hobbesian graded descent into "Civill Warre," polyarchy *qua* factious is anarchic; anarchy is disorder; disorder leads to dissolution, and therefore polyarchy is always already (on the way to) dissolution.

The crux of the passage, however, seems to come in the characterization of Monarchy, once anarchy and polyarchy have been successfully dismissed in this way. "A monarchy, however, that is not limited to one person, for a single person can produce [divisive] plurality if he rebels against himself," "It is, however, a Monarchy that is not limited to one Person, for it is possible for Unity if at variance with itself to come into a condition of plurality," "but not a Monarchy that is contained in one single person. For it is possible for this one person, if at variance with itself, to become a plurality of persons." The Greek text reads "*monarchia de ouk hēn hen perigraphei prosōpon esti gar kai to hen stasiazon pros heauto polla kathistasthai*," with the crux of the translation issues concentrated on the phrase "*to hen stasiazon pros heauto polla kathistasthai*," literally perhaps "the one by being at odds with itself can come to many."[23] As Schmitt quite correctly points out, the verb *stasiazo*, to be at variance, to be in a state of discord, to be in disagreement, seems to carry the weight of the interpretation here, although he does not seem to notice the echo of the earlier *stasiōdes*, applied, as we saw, to polyarchy. Peterson's gloss, "bore the seed of schism within itself [*trage den Keim des Zwiespaltes in sich*]" seems unnecessarily to introduce the "seed," as well as the "two," and the English translation of *Zwiespalt* as "schism" seems a little overdetermined in the context of Church history.

Schmitt's interpretation of this text is itself typically robust and tendentious. First, he claims that Peterson "refers decisively [*entscheidend*]" to

23. Compare Esposito's discussion of this passage in *Two*, 61–62, where Esposito's focus on the "two," precisely, seems to me to limit his reading of the motif of "plurality" here.

this passage, which does not "revolve around," as the translation has it, but "at the kernel of which stands the following formulation [*in deren Kern folgende Formulierung steht*]," namely, *to hen stasiazon pros heauton*, which Schmitt translates as "The One is always in uproar against itself [*Das Eine ist immer im Aufruhr gegen sich selbst*]" (PT2 122/90), whereas nothing in the Greek text really justifies the "always" (compare the translations we just read). Then he claims that "Right in the middle of the most precise formulation of this difficult dogma [i.e., that of the Trinity] [*Mitten in der einwandfreiesten* (the most perfect, the most impeccable, the most indisputable—the inner dispute is found at the heart of the indisputable) *Formulierung des schwerigen Dogmas*], we find the word *stasis* in the sense of 'uproar' [*begegnet uns* (we are met with) *das Wort* stasis, *im Sinne von* Aufruhr]."

Although strictly speaking it is the verb *stasiazo* rather than the noun *stasis* that we are met with in the quotation from Gregory, it seems undeniable that the noun *stasis* is at the root of that verb. Famously, as Schmitt is about to detail, *stasis* as a noun can mean both station or standing, placement or position, *and* discord, dispute or, as Schmitt has it here, "uproar."[24] Here is Schmitt's gloss:

> The etymology and history of the word *stasis* deserves to be mentioned in this context. It extends from Plato (the *Sophist*, 249–254, and the *Republic*, Book V, 470),[25] through the Neoplatonists, Plotinus in particular, to the Greek church fathers and teachers. With this concept an intriguing contradiction of a dialectical nature [*ein Widerspruch mit spannender Dialektik*, a contradiction with a striking dialectic] emerges. *Stasis* means in the first place quiescence [Ruhe, emphasized by Schmitt], tranquility, standpoint, status; its antonym is *kinesis*, movement. But *stasis* also means, in the second place, (political) *unrest* [*Unruhe*],

24. Giorgio Agamben's short and rather diffident treatment of *stasis* in *Stasis: Civil War as a Political Paradigm*, trans. Nicholas Heron (Stanford: Stanford University Press, 2015), concentrates, in the wake of Nicole Loraux, whose work he is largely content to summarize, on the relation between the family and the polis and does not address Schmitt on this point.

25. In the long sequence from the *Sophist* referenced here, the Stranger does indeed repeatedly, as Schmitt goes on to say, oppose *stasis* and *kinesis* but does not exploit the antonymic sense of *stasis* as unrest. In the passage from the *Republic*, Socrates proposes (again without exploiting the antonymic sense) a terminological distinction between "war," *polemos*, as waged between Greeks and barbarians, and "civil war," *stasis*, as waged by Greeks against other Greeks.

movement, uproar and civil war. Most Greek dictionaries put those
two diametrically opposed meanings together, without any attempt to
explain them—which, to be fair, cannot be expected from them.[26]
Even the sheer listing of numerous examples of such opposition
provides a rich resource for the observation of political and politico-
theological phenomena.

And this allows him to claim immediately that "At the heart [*im Kern* again,
at the kernel] of the doctrine of Trinity we encounter a genuine politico-
theological *stasiology*. Thus the problem of enmity and of the enemy cannot be ignored" (92/123).

It is not difficult to see that Schmitt has quite egregiously misrepre-
sented Gregory's point (and thereby also Peterson's): far from finding the
stasis and its inner dialectical contradiction (its inner *stasis* in the sense of
division or variance from itself) "at the heart of the dogma of the Trinity," Gregory is *contrasting* that possibility or inevitability of *stasis*, which
would (or always might) be found in a "simple" (perhaps heretical) monotheism, with the doctrine of the Trinity that is supposed, precisely and
explicitly, to *avoid* the stasiology Schmitt is so keen to attribute to it. This
is abundantly clear if we read a little further in Gregory's *Oration*, immediately following on from the quotation as given by Peterson:

> It is, however, a Monarchy that is not limited to one Person, for it is
> possible for Unity if at variance with itself to come into a condition of
> plurality; but one which is made of an equality of Nature and a Union
> of mind, and an identity of motion, and a convergence of its elements

26. Schmitt inserts a long footnote which begins with a partial exception to
this claim, and indeed an exception that, if correct, would mitigate the "gripping"
nature of the dialectic Schmitt is keen to find: "A remarkable exception can be
found in the *Thesaurus Linguae Graecae* 7.1848–54, cols. 656–665. The *Thesaurus*
seeks to explain the surprising transition from stillness to movement in the following way: at the bottom of col. 660, it interprets the emergence and formation
of a *faction* or *party* as being related to a standpoint, a point of view, which seems
to point to a bridge from stillness to movement without complex dialectical evo-
lutions" (149n3). It might also be worth pointing out (1) that the entry for *stasis* in
Liddell and Scott presents a less stark sense of the "contradiction" than does
Schmitt, never in fact directly associating *stasis* with rest as opposed to movement, and (2) that the verb form, which is after all the one that appears in Gregory, does *not* in fact, alongside the sense of "being at variance," have the sense of
"being at rest." For a different nondialectical exploration of the term *stasis*, see
Nicole Loraux, *La cité divisée* (Paris: Payot, 1997), 102–106.

to unity—a thing which is impossible to the created nature—so that though numerically distinct there is no severance of Essence [*all hēn physeōs homotimia synistēsi kai gnōmēs sympnoia kai tautotēs kinēseōs kai pros to hen tōn ex autou synneusis hosper amēchanon epi tēs gennētēs physeōs hōste kan arithmō diapherē tē ge ousia mē temnesthai*]. Therefore Unity having from all eternity arrived by motion at Duality, found its rest in Trinity. This is what we mean by Father and Son and Holy Ghost [*dia touto monas ap archēs eis dyada kinētheisa mechri triados estē kai touto estin hēmin ho Patēr kai ho Huios kai to hagion Pneuma*].

So Gregory's claim is that the dogma of the Trinity overcomes (or at least avoids) any "stasiology" that would be, perhaps dialectically, implicit in a "monarchian" view of God, and that it does so via a "convergence of its elements to unity [*pros to hen tōn ex autou synneusis*]." This may be a "difficult dogma," as Schmitt says, and it may even be unintelligible, philosophically speaking,[27] but it certainly does not, in these canonical formulations by Gregory of Nazianzus at least, immediately or explicitly

27. See Kant's famous remark "if this faith (in a divine Trinity) were to be regarded not just as the representation of a practical idea [as Kant is urging], but as a faith that ought to represent what God is in himself, it would be a mystery surpassing all human concepts, hence unsuited to a revelation humanly comprehensible, and could only be declared in this respect as mystery. Faith in it as an extension of theoretical cognition of the divine nature would only be the profession of a creed of ecclesiastical faith totally unintelligible to human beings or, if they think that they understand it, the profession of an anthropomorphic creed, and not the least would thereby be accomplished for moral improvement.—Only what we can indeed thoroughly understand and penetrate in a practical context, but which surpasses all our concepts for theoretical purposes (for the determination of the nature of the object in itself), is mystery (in one context) and can yet (in another) be revealed." Immanuel Kant, *Religion within the Boundaries of Mere Reason and Other Writings*, trans. and ed. Allen Wood and George di Giovanni (Cambridge: Cambridge University Press, 1998), 143. See, too, some interesting, and interestingly complex, philosophical attempts in a more "analytic" mode to produce a comprehensible account of the Trinity as it is understood in Catholic doctrine, in Thomas McCall and Michael C. Rea, eds., *Philosophical and Theological Essays on the Trinity* (Oxford: Oxford University Press, 2009), and Daniel Molto, "The Logical Problem of the Trinity and the Strong Theory of Relative Identity," *Sophia* 56 (2017): 227–245. It is hard for the nonbeliever not to think that the doctrine must be in some trouble when its best illustrative example is—as often in these discussions—drawn from classical mythology, in the form of the three-headed dog Cerberus, hardly a reassuring figure for the Godhead.

install the kind of stasiology at its heart that Schmitt is claiming. Even if we want to say that there is something of the order of an "uproar" between the doctrine of the Trinity on the one hand and various heretical versions of Christian monotheism on the other, so that there is indeed a "political" history of the Church (as Peterson would certainly not deny), it seems that Schmitt's attempt to install that stasiology at the heart of the Trinitarian doctrine itself rests on a demonstrable misreading of Gregory's text. This does not of course mean that Peterson is correct in his reading either, in that he presents as what is essentially a magical solution a doctrine that is still fundamentally mysterious.

In a long note to *Politics of Friendship*, Derrida quotes at some length and takes these claims of Schmitt's at face value, and goes on to make a more general claim:

> As for the stasiology evoked therein (which is supposedly at work
> either at the heart of the One, or at the heart of a Trinity or a Holy
> Family), this is a motif which—in different words, in another style and
> with a view to different consequences—could quite well describe one
> of the subterranean but most continuous themes of the present essay:
> how the One divides and opposes itself, opposes itself in positing itself,
> represses and violates the difference it carries within itself, wages war,
> *wages war on itself* [itself becomes war: *se fait la guerre*], *scares itself* [itself
> becomes fear: *se fait peur*], and *does violence to itself* [itself becomes
> violence: *se fait violence*], transforms itself into frightened violence in
> guarding itself from the other, for *it always guards itself from the other*
> [keeps some other for or in itself: *se garde de l'autre*], always, It, the
> One, the One "differing from itself." (PA 110/108–109n13)

The question would be that of the suggested equivalence (*soit . . . soit . . .*) here between the stasiology of the One (as posited by Gregory) and the (supposed or invented) stasiology within the Trinity (as tendentiously claimed by Schmitt), the more especially given that the Trinity is being presented (by Gregory) as the (very precisely nonstasiological) *solution* to the former stasiology. To make good on Derrida's subsequent claims, we would have to show (as Schmitt certainly does not show) that the trinitarian "solution" to the problem of the One remains subject to the logic it is explicitly claiming to overcome. It seems as though this would involve not merely a restatement of the reasons why Derridean *différance* is not susceptible to dialectical resolution (and therefore cannot really be aligned with Schmitt's claims as to the "dialectical" nature of *stasis*, nor with Esposito's reading of the relationship between the One and the Two), but a further exploration of why the argument about "convergence," the movement *pros to hen*, always reopens, fractally, the issue about the One, *to hen*, toward which that convergence is supposedly directed. This would involve another turn to Aristotle and an attempt to clarify the Derridean distinction between polysemia and dissemination, another figure of the (nondialectical) difference (or *différance*) between *différance* and (dialectical) difference.[28]

28. This problem is the object of work in progress. See an initial approach in my paper "*Geschlecht pollachos legetai:* Translation, Polysemia, Dissemination," *Philosophy Today*, 64:2 (Spring 2020), 423–440.

"Scatter" rhymes with "matter," and this conceptually groundless "poetic" effect has certainly influenced my choice of "scatter" as the generic title for the project of which this is the second volume. If poetry and politics are resistant to metaphysical comprehension and reduction, this might indeed seem to be because they both, in their different ways, have an irreducible *material* dimension. This "materialism" of poetry and politics, like all the other concepts to which we have had recourse, both inherits from and resists its metaphysical characterization. For example, the thought of scatter, here and elsewhere, takes up and tries to exploit the metaphysical understanding of matter as essentially dispersed or dispersive, as tendentially always *dust*.[1] More generally, Derrida's thinking of the trace (his fundamental thought) both inherits from a traditional determination of writing (in the "vulgar" sense) as to do with material marks or imprints, and radicalizes the notion of writing well beyond the grasp of the conceptual pair of ideality and materiality, or indeed any related metaphysical op-

[1]. See my forthcoming volume of essays *Down to Dust: Essays in the Deconstruction of Politics.*

position, up to and including the opposition of presence and absence. One of the difficulties (or delicacies) of that thought and its radicalization is that it is itself subject to the structures of restraint and interruption we have followed in Aristotle and elsewhere, such that detailed concern with the specifics of different writing systems, for example, and their different relationships with different surfaces of inscription, are never "left behind" in some triumphant arrival of deconstruction at some telos it might be imagined to have. There is no such telos.[2]

In his as yet unpublished seminar on the "Theory of Philosophical Discourse" from 1970–71, Derrida wonders in his introductory remarks why philosophy considers its own text, its own inscription, to be "secondary, accessory, even accidental," "a mere means, a technical tool," and rapidly suggests that asking this question already opens onto the question of philosophy's endemic idealism, here seen as characterized by a structural failure to take account of its own textual status: the text of philosophy is "either not considered, or else is considered as an expressive medium that should be granted the greatest transparency or the greatest possible univocity, or else as an accidental signifier which must each time be gone beyond in the direction of its signified that precedes and commands it, that is anterior and superior to it." The apparently "materialist" implication of pointing this out, however, is complicated by the fact that many supposedly materialist philosophies in fact share this generally idealist presumption about the status of the text in which they are expounded. And so, if the study of philosophical textuality is to take a critical view of the idealist failure to take its own text into account, that study "could situate itself in a materialist field only on condition of reconstructing the concept of matter, of deconstructing in it all the features that make it the opposite of ideality, especially with regard to its textual inscription."

But such an attempt to deconstruct and reconstruct a concept of matter other than the metaphysical concept of matter provokes Derrida to ask two questions: (1) Why even call the new nonmetaphysical concept "matter" at all? (2) Why not deconstruct and reconstruct the concept of *ideality*, given that, in spite of everything, the idealist tradition has at least paid signifi-

---

2. This is why the figure of the catechon is only ambiguously helpful in thinking about deconstructive issues, in that in its traditional Pauline guise it is always restraining or holding back the predicted *advent* of some further or future state. The reticence or modesty of deconstruction appeals to no such state (whence Derrida's attempt to think through a "messianicity without messianism" in *Specters of Marx*).

cant attention to the structure of language and of its own ideality, and given that, in the wake of Mallarmé, one might "propose a theory of the Idea, or even an idealism that would make a decisive break with the philosophical idea and idealism"? Derrida's slightly elusive response is that there is a "dissymmetry" here, and (or so I take him to be saying), that dissymmetry, leaning in favor of the "materialist" option, concerns the whole of philosophy and so cannot itself be decided in philosophical terms (by appealing to the value of truth, for example), cannot be given a "discursive and decidable" answer, such that "it must be subjected to a practical and strategic elaboration, to a textual operation no longer subjected to a philosophical authority."

Such an elaboration might perhaps be called "political," on condition that the concept of the political itself be subjected to deconstructive attention. This is what we have attempted here: we have seen that the endless trouble that philosophy has had with politics (a trouble equal, we suggested, to the trouble it has had with poetry) involves the deconstruction of the oppositions between theory and practice, *bios theōrētikos* and *bios politikos*, that have habitually been used for orientation in this domain. Our attention to scatter takes us into a zone that is not exactly that of politics nor that of philosophy (nor of course that of poetry), but that might reasonably claim in its reading and writing to exceed the jurisdiction of those terms and promote an understanding (an "elaboration," as Derrida says) of a generalized "politics"—and therefore of a politics of politics—irreducibly at work and at play in and between all such domains. Such an elaboration, which must in principle resist any simple disciplinary identification, is not infinite (scatter is always somewhat gathered, always finite), but, like democracy, it has no end.

GEOFFREY BENNINGTON is Asa G. Candler Professor of Modern French Thought at Emory University.

CPSIA information can be obtained
at www.ICGtesting.com
Printed in the USA
LVHW112337071220
673606LV00005B/467

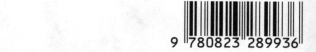